# THE WELSH WARS OF
# EDWARD I

WALES & the MARCH in the Time of Edward I.

# THE WELSH WARS
## OF
# EDWARD I
*A Contribution to Medieval Military History*
*Based on Original Documents*

# John E. Morris

**DA CAPO PRESS**

Originally published by Oxford at the Clarendon Press in 1901.

Published by Da Capo Press
A Member of the Perseus Books Group
http://www.dacapopress.com

*Library of Congress Cataloging-in-Publication Data*

Morris, John Edward, 1859-1933.
    The Welsh wars of Edward I / John E. Morris.
        p.   cm.
    Includes index.
    Previously published: New York, Haskell House Publishers. 1969.
    ISBN 0-938289-67-5. -- ISBN 0-938289-68-3
    1. Wales--History--1063-1536.  2. Edward I, King of England.
    1239-1307.  3. Great Britain--History--Edward I, 1272-1307.
    4. Great Britain--History, Military--1066-1485.  I. Title.
    DA715.M67   1996                                        96-7110
    942.9--dc20                                                CIP

*Printed in the United States of America.*
10  9  8

# PREFACE

If it be true that the English learnt on the battle-
fields of Scotland the experience which was destined
to make them the victors at Crecy and Poitiers, it is
equally true that the preliminary experience had been
learnt in Wales. It was precisely because I wanted
to trace back the evolution of the typically English
combination of knights with archers beyond the battle
of Falkirk, which is usually considered to have been
the first great victory of the longbow, that I began to
study the documents of the Welsh wars. The period,
rather more than eighteen years, is of peculiar interest.
The rolls are tolerably exhaustive; we have minute
details concerning the men in the king's pay in most
of his armies, besides evidence which enables us to
conjecture the strength of others. Feudal and paid
troops are found fighting side by side. We can form
a good picture of Edward as he steadily fought
Llewelyn and David for fifteen months without pause,
grimly determined to succeed, though he had to keep
the field through the winter and to bring up mercenaries
from Gascony after a serious defeat. We see him able
to devote his whole attention to the task, for there was
no agitation of earls and barons hampering him in his
military needs by insisting that he should confirm the
charters, whereas the first and foremost of the reasons
of his failure in Scotland, in spite of the victory at
Falkirk, was the baronial agitation in England. We
have an insight into the various subsidiary tasks of

the war, details of the woodmen who cut the paths
through which the soldiers marched, of the expenses
of castle-building, and so forth. But especially important is the knowledge, which documents alone can
give, of the earliest efforts in four wars of that infantry,
a raw and untried infantry, which, under Edward's
organization, learnt the art of war so that their grandsons under his grandson were able to startle Europe
by their good shooting on the terraces of Crecy. It is
clear that the earliest foot, partly spearmen, partly bow-
armed, were drawn alike from the Welsh 'friendlies'
of marcher lordships and from the border counties between Lancashire and Gloucestershire, while the men
of nearly all the other English counties had yet to be
trained in the Scottish wars. Edward's employment of
his late enemies in Wales to fight for him in Flanders
and Scotland is suggestive.·

The documents are chiefly the pay-rolls among the
Exchequer Accounts preserved in the Record Office.
Very often the pipe rolls give us facts which are not
to be found elsewhere, and the patent and close rolls
are helpful; it is more than likely that I have missed
some material among the mass of writs, for the great
length of these rolls is bewildering when there is no
printed calendar at hand. The marshal's rolls for
1277 and 1282 are printed in the *Parliamentary
Writs*. The most useful of the chroniclers I have
found to be Hemingburgh and Trivet (English Historical Society), and Wykes of Osney (*Annales Monastici* in the Rolls Series), while Mr. Martin's Preface to
the *Letters of Archbishop Peckham* (Rolls Series) has
led me to work out several points.

Although my chief object has been to depict an
English army in the field at the most critical point in

mediaeval military history, namely at the very beginning
of a systematic organization of infantry, I have thought
it best to treat the story of the Welsh struggles con-
secutively, sketching roughly the course of the Anglo-
Norman aggressions, the creation of the marcher lordships, the Welsh reaction in the days of civil war in
England, and Edward's reasons, indeed his justifica-
tion, in attacking Llewelyn. It is clear that there was
no bond of union between the Welsh of the north and
the centre and south, and independence was represented by the princely house of Gwynedd alone. The
strength of the one strong section of the Welsh race
was the mountain fortress of the range of Snowdon,
where guerilla tactics were possible. The two centuries
of the successful resistance of Gwynedd up to Edward's
reign are quite intelligible, and we have an object-lesson
in Wales of the geographical problem in military undertakings. It is easy to sneer at the powerful tyrant
who crushes a brave little race struggling for liberty,
but military students must admit that resources and
good organization alone can prevail where geography
helps the numerically weak defenders. The larger
and stronger race often has to incur the accusation
of tyranny, even if provocation is undoubted and the
need of union is great.

I submit that the Welsh wars have an influence on
English constitutional history. I have tried to show
the weakness of the feudal system and the genesis of
the paid soldier, who was a native Englishman or
a Welsh friendly, and no longer a foreign mercenary
as under the Angevin kings, an occasional importation
of Gascons notwithstanding. The custom of the march
explains much of the obstinacy of some of the barons
in their defiance of the crown, and grievances which

seem to have originated in Wales come to the front when the new enemy is Wallace. The money question is also important, because Edward could afford to fight to the end in Wales, but the expense incurred in Scotland was very considerable.

I have nowhere found a satisfactory detailed account of these campaigns, for the chroniclers write so vaguely that they are most misleading unless compared with each other and with the documents. It is only after close research that I venture to offer this contribution to mediaeval military history.

Lastly, I have to apologize, if one ought to apologize for anything done deliberately, for repeating in many cases the exact words which have been used in a previous chapter, for I have often, in reading some book, felt annoyed at having to turn back for information.

J. E. M.

# CONTENTS

## CHAPTER III

## CHAPTER IV

# CHAPTER V

# CHAPTER VI

# CHAPTER VII

# CONTENTS

## CHAPTER VIII

# THE WELSH WARS OF
# EDWARD I

# THE WELSH WARS OF EDWARD I

## CHAPTER I

### ENGLAND AND WALES BEFORE 1277

THE conquest of Wales was first taken in hand by the restless adventure-loving Normans who had come over with William the Conqueror. It is quite true that Saxon Harold had already made an impression, and the final annexation by Edward may very fairly be regarded as the assertion of English supremacy. But, during the two centuries which separated Harold and Edward, the prominent figure on the march of Wales was the Norman adventurer. He had fought at Hastings as an adventurer looking forward to a grant of English land as his reward, and he had been disappointed ; for William conferred manors, but took good care that the baron should not become independent of the crown of England. On the borders of Wales, however, things were different. There was a hardy and active race to be conquered, and regular methods of war were out of place. The men of the mountains fought in the guerilla fashion. They had natural fortresses to which to retreat, and it could never be expected that, being beaten in one battle, they would submit at once and for ever. Therefore William and his sons could authorize, or else tacitly allow, what in England they were determined to prevent. If their Norman lords loved adventure and fighting, they might settle on the march, conquer as much of Wales as they could, and hold as their own what they had conquered ; so that their high spirit might be thus diverted into a country where they had plenty to do, and little opportunity to make themselves dangerous to their king. To the native Welsh chroniclers the invaders of their country were ' Frenchmen,' who fought in the ' Gallic ' style. The mailed horseman and the stone castle were always in evidence, the grim Norman fighting-man and the grim Norman fortress.   Like their ancestors who conquered Normandy, like their kinsfolk who pushed on to Italy and Sicily, the Norman lords who settled on the borders of Wales—lords marchers they came to be called—domineered and grasped. They conquered for their own profit, and they satisfied the ambition which was characteristic of their race.   They had their fill of the fighting which they loved, they had excitement, and they were their own masters.   They were much more free than the barons of England.   Or it might be that some lord had both fiefs in England and lands on the borders of Wales: in the one case he was fettered in various ways, might not build castles at his will, and had to perform the duties imposed on him by the conditions of feudal service: in the other he was free to fight his way into Wales, and to build castles so as to hold what he had won.   In this way the work of 'Normanisation' was more complete on the march than elsewhere in our island [1].

One can hardly say, however, that the early Norman kings deliberately devised this method as the cheapest way of conquering Wales and also of giving to their barons plenty of that hard fighting which would keep them too busy to rebel.   The 'custom of the march,' namely, that the lords marchers could wage private war at will, grew up rather as a natural consequence of the state of affairs which prevailed after the Conquest.   None of the kings could spare the time which was necessary for a permanent conquest of Wales.   They had to organize and govern in England, look after their possessions in Normandy or Aquitaine, gratify their ambition by the more highly attractive task of crusading, or crush baronial risings.   Thus for more than two centuries no king put himself resolutely to subdue Wales until Edward did.   Royal expeditions were, indeed, frequent, but spasmodic and rarely successful.   Meanwhile, the resistance of the Welsh was being gradually worn down by the lords marchers, who had a direct

---

[1] Morgan, *England under the Norman Occupation*, p. 87 ; *Eng. Hist. Review*, Jan. 1900, p. 74.

profit in the work, the kings rather allowing than actually authorizing them to do so. The lords who were originally planted by the Williams on the flanks of the Welsh, their direct descendants, or the new men who by marriage with heiresses came in to carry on their work, must have the sole credit for the successful wearing down.

But in saying this we have to make a strong distinction between the fortunes of the Norman invaders on the northern and middle marches and those of their more lucky comrades of the south. There are two separate chapters in the history of Wales up to the reign of Edward. North Wales and South Wales were quite distinct both politically and geographically, the great block of central mountains forming a barrier to keep them apart. The Princes of Gwynedd, a district roughly equivalent to Snowdonia and outlying valleys, claimed at times overlordship over the Princes of South Wales, Cardigan, and the Vale of Towy. But rarely did they actually penetrate to the south with an armed force. Similarly, the Earls of Chester and their neighbours had little in common with the lords marchers of Glamorgan and Gwent. And as war was waged independently in either direction, so the results varied. In the two centuries the Norman conquest from Monmouth to Pembroke and Cardigan was steadily successful, following the line of the coast and striking up the valleys of the Usk and Wye, and this region was studded over with Norman castles. On the other side very little advance was made beyond the present boundary lines of Cheshire and Shropshire, the efforts to conquer along the north coast were unsuccessful, and a belt of fortresses rather protected the western parts of England than threatened the north-east borders of Wales. When Edward came upon the scene he found South Wales more or less securely held by the marchers, but he had to start from the very confines of Chester itself to carry out his great invasion of Gwynedd.

William I began by creating two counties palatine—counties whose earls were practically independent administrators,— namely, Chester over against the Princes of Gwynedd, whose power stretched out from Snowdon to Flint; and Shrewsbury against the Princes of Powys, who were settled on the upper Severn and upper Dee. There was also an outwork at the mouth of the river Clwyd, where rose the castle of Rhuddlan, some three miles from the sea on the right bank. The earls palatine had to hold the border, and to conquer across the border as they could. William was, in fact, making a dangerous precedent. He, whose great aim in England was to avoid the creation of powerful feudal baronies which might be too strong for the crown, was on the Welsh border founding two such possible sources of danger. So he had to choose his men carefully. The first Earl of Chester was his own nephew, Hugh of Avranches. Hugh held Rhuddlan of the king, and kept half of the borough in his own hands *in dominio*, while a certain Robert was his man and held the other half. The Earl of Shrewsbury was Roger of Montgomery, who in 1066 had been left behind in Normandy as one of the regents. Personal loyalty was the tie which was expected to bind them to the crown; for, if to lands in Normandy and England they should add by conquest large possessions in Wales, and then aspire to be altogether independent, they would be accomplishing the very thing which it was the Conqueror's life-work to prevent. Roger was especially powerful; he held fiefs in Normandy and Picardy through his father and his wife, was Earl of Arundel and Chichester in England, and now founded a new Montgomery in Wales in remembrance of his Norman home. On his death, the hereditary possessions passed to his eldest son Robert, the acquired possessions to his second son Hugh.

A quantity of valuable evidence has been collected by Miss Bateson[1], which shows that a group of lords marchers co-operated in the work of Normanisation on the Welsh borders. Certain burgess rights were introduced from Breteuil in Normandy to Hereford, Shrewsbury, Ludlow, and other places in the west of England; hence they were passed on to Rhuddlan and Montgomery, to Cardiff and Haverfordwest. Some of the evidence is direct and undoubted, coming from Domesday Book; some is indirect, and the existence of the rights

---

[1] *Eng. Hist. Review*, 1900, especially pp. 76, 302, 306, 307, 520.

at the end of the eleventh century is inferred from their existence later. The various lords marchers who introduced them
were connected with each other, most of them also being
kinsmen of the Conqueror, and it would follow that there
was a conscious co-operation under the sanction of the king
himself. Near a castle was formed a bourg, a *Frankville*,
where *Francigenae burgenses* lived in enjoyment of certain
privileges as tenants of some great lord: these would be
Norman adventurers attracted to settle on favourable terms
alongside an existing English borough, or to form an entirely
Norman nucleus in a new foundation. William FitzOsbern,
cousin of the Conqueror, and already seneschal for him of
Breteuil, then created Earl of Hereford, must have first introduced the 'laws and customs': the phrase in Domesday Book
is expressive, '*leges et consuetudines quae sunt in Hereford
et in Bretuill,*' and FitzOsbern's connexion with both places
points to him as the originator. Under Hugh of Avranches
and Robert of Rhuddlan the laws were extended to Rhuddlan; under FitzOsbern or, more likely, under Roger of Montgomery, to Shrewsbury and to Montgomery, where they are
undoubtedly found in the thirteenth century; under Roger de
Lacy, 'son of Walter de Lacy, who was FitzOsbern's man,'
to Ludlow; under Arnulf, son of Roger of Montgomery, to
Haverfordwest; and under Robert FitzHamon, a son-in-law,
to Cardiff. The cumulative evidence thus adduced by Miss
Bateson is very strong, even if the connexion in each case
cannot be proved directly. A Norman colony with its own
rights was planted at many of the most important posts on
the border. So valuable was this Norman element, or so
welcome were the rights conferred by the 'laws of Breteuil,'
that they spread to many new places later on in Wales and in
Ireland as fast as the Normans conquered in each country.
Though it is true that the laws were introduced to other
places than the march, still these other places were in the
west of England and under the influence of members of the
same group of families; for instance, Roger le Poitevin, another
son of Roger of Montgomery, gave them to Preston, and a
kinsman of FitzHamon gave them to Bideford.

Hugh of Chester, Roger and Hugh of Montgomery, and Robert of Rhuddlan all contributed towards the work of conquering Wales which had been assigned to them. Success seemed to be certain, and even the island of Anglesey was for a time occupied. But then the Welsh roused themselves, and with the aid of Norse Vikings regained the island. Hugh of Montgomery was shot by an arrow in the eye, 'as though paying the wergeld for England's fallen king[1].' His death was of great importance. Not only did the Welsh roll back the tide of Norman advance, but also the county palatine of Shrewsbury, becoming vacant, reverted to the elder brother Robert. An apology is necessary for the introduction of so well known a figure, yet it is not out of place to discuss his position. He now succeeding to Hugh's inheritance could control the resources of the county palatine, the Sussex fief and earldom of Arundel, both his father's and his mother's lands across the Channel, with his wife's possessions in Ponthieu; in history he is generally known as Robert of Bellême, the county which was his earliest inheritance through his mother[2]. He acted as his wealth and influence tempted him to act. On the chance of finding Henry I weak on his accession, he aspired to play the part of an independent baron, was unexpectedly crushed, and driven out of England. It was a critical moment in the history of the Welsh march. Henry acted with vigour. Not content with crushing Robert he also crushed another brother, Arnulf of Montgomery, who was settled in Cardigan, for it was imperative to extirpate the family which had dared to dictate to the King of England. Montgomery became a royal castle: Shrewsbury ceased to be a county palatine, and was joined to Staffordshire as a county of the ordinary type under the same sheriff. Thus, on the one hand, was overthrown a power which would have been a bulwark against the Welsh of Powys and a base for the gradual conquest of Central Wales; but, on the other hand, a serious attempt to utilize the peculiar position of a palatine earl towards overawing the crown of England was

[1] *Norman Conquest*, vol. v. p. 113.
[2] *Dict. Nat. Biog.*, vol. iv. p. 183.

thwarted. No family rose to take the vacant place. The Fitzalans obtained the lands of Clun in the south-west of Shropshire and Oswestry in the north-west, and succeeded in course of time to the earldom of Arundel; but they held by knight-service, and were hampered by the ordinary feudal restrictions. The Mortimers became an important family on the middle march: Ralph, their founder, was both a sub-tenant of Robert of Bellême and a tenant-in-chief of the crown. But, as a rule, they were either loyal or prudent, and did not yet aspire to independence.

The Earls of Chester, the other county palatine, were loyal; at least, they did not set themselves in opposition to the crown. They must have been engaged in constantly fight-ing the Welsh. But the lords of Gwynedd, when once they had recovered Anglesey, more than held their own against the Normans of the march. Frequently we find Rhuddlan occupied by the invaders, but as frequently it was conquered or destroyed by the Welsh. Diganwy, on the right shore of the estuary of the Conway, changed hands in the same way. Neither Rhuddlan nor Diganwy was a centre for gradual conquest and Normanisation. The 'Four Cantreds,' the dis-trict lying between the Conway and the Dee, that is to say between Gwynedd and Chester, were often the battle-ground of Welshman and Norman; but, when at last they were thoroughly reduced by Edward I, they were still quite Welsh at heart.

There was a line of Norman castles built westwards, and therefore forming a sort of advanced screen ahead of Chester and Shrewsbury. Such were Mold, Hawarden, Oswestry, Caurs, Bishop's Castle, Ludlow, and of course Montgomery. But, as was suggested above, they rather formed a belt of fortifications to protect the western borders of England than were bases for the gradual absorption, under Norman influ-ence, of the Four Cantreds or Powys. The result was that the western parts of the present counties of Cheshire and Shropshire were securely held, and were acclimatized to the Anglo-Norman system of government, the inhabitants being very largely Welsh, until a line of demarcation was at last drawn between England and Wales. But hardly any impression was made further westwards beyond this belt. The reason is probably to be found in the suppression of Robert of Bellême by Henry I. The crown had had a lesson, and could not afford to let any other family rise to a similar position of independence. Where there was no incentive to private adventure, there was no powerful irruption of Norman adventurers into the heart of Wales. But an exception may be made in the case of the Mortimers, who conquered along the upper Severn.

The failure to conquer along the coast, and thence up the Clwyd and Conway, is also explained by geography. There is a very narrow strip between the sea and the mountains, and the mountains were then covered with dense forest. The Welsh had cover close upon the flanks of an invading force. Not being able to maintain themselves on this narrow strip, the Normans had no base from which to advance inland up stream. To venture with inadequate transport to cross the watersheds, so as to conquer down stream, was out of the question. Lastly, Chester was not a good naval base. When we come to consider what difficulties were surmounted by Edward, how with a genius for organization and great resources at his back, he could only by great effort cut his way into Wales, hewing paths through the forests and maintaining his lines of communication by sea with ships brought up from Kent and Sussex, we can then understand how, before his time, natural obstacles defied invasion.

Kings such as Henry II and John often invaded in force right up to Snowdon. But these royal expeditions utterly failed. The armies were either composed of the feudal vassals of the crown or of mercenaries. In any case, they were clumsy and unfitted for an invasion of mountainous districts in the face of an active race of patriots. Time after time they penetrated far west. The Welsh retreated upon their natural fortress of Snowdon, restricted themselves to guerilla warfare, and relied upon the rains and the difficulties presented by the geography of their country. They were easily able to reoccupy whatever land they had temporarily abandoned, for sooner or later the heavy columns of the invaders, wearied out by the bad weather and profitless tramping through path-less forests, had to fall back. Had these kings been able to devote several years to the work, without being hampered by their possessions in France or by civil war, they might have slowly conquered Wales by a steady advance, building castles at each step as solid bases for the next move. To plunge into the mountains was to court disaster. Thus we come back to our previous argument. The royal expeditions into North Wales failed because the path of conquest had not been prepared beforehand. Resistance had not been suffi-ciently worn down by a chronic warfare of self-reliant lords marchers, encouraged to conquer and hold as their own what they had conquered. There was no carefully prepared 'jump-ing-off ground' from which the royal armies could complete the work of thorough conquest, and the natural obstacles continued to defy invasion.

Hence it came about that to the Welsh of Gwynedd the enemy was the King of England or the Earl of Chester, who may fairly be called the king's representative. They had not to fear a race of lords marchers always pushing ahead, always fighting to grasp more lands, building new castles, partly foes to them, and partly defiant of the king himself. Princes of Wales and Kings of England were directly face to face. And the princes more than held their own, for the royal expeditions were only spasmodic. Homage might be claimed and occasionally paid, but it was a deception which deceived nobody: practically, Gwynedd was free. More than that, Gwynedd was the only possible centre of Welsh unity. The great mountain fortress of Snowdon seemed to be impregnable, and therefore where there was strength there was a sense of unity. The Princes of Gwynedd came to be called Princes of Wales. Really, there was no more union among the Welsh than among the clans of the Highlands of Scotland : they fought against each other and against the English. But in the north there was less disunion than in South Wales, simply because the princes were powerful men with a powerful country behind them. There was no national cause of Wales, but the cause of Gwynedd came nearly to be national.   Llewelyn the Great and his grandson, Llewelyn, Edward's enemy, were national champions at the expense of coercing other Welshmen, and even members of their own family.   Yet with all their power they had not the tenacity of the Bruce : let us add that, like Bruce, they were successful in proportion to the extent of the baronial opposition in England against the King of England.   The Llewelyns and Bruce were strongest just when there was civil war in England, or bitter civil dissension on the verge of war.

We turn to South Wales as to an almost distinct country. The block of mountains of which Cader Idris is the centre, and Plinlimmon lying just below, form a considerable barrier at the waist of Wales, and the county of Merioneth we judge from the facts of various wars to have been thinly populated. Next, the land of Powys, the valley of the upper Severn, is marked off from the Wye by a watershed continuing the barrier eastwards.   In the distinct district to the south of the mountains the advance of the Norman invaders of the regions was guided by geographical conditions.   From the estuary of the Severn an old Roman road led along the coast, and four river valleys in turn attracted them into the interior—those of the Wye, Usk, Taff, and Towy.   On these lines rose the Norman castles, which, commanding coast or mountain-pass or river, were the solid centres of dominion against which the wild attacks of Welsh insurrection were broken.   The lords marchers, therefore, won their way under conditions such as were not enjoyed by their comrades of the north : they had a good route by the sea and coast-road, a good base in Gloucestershire and Herefordshire, and the great advantage of being able to work up stream.

A Norman colony was founded at Hereford in the days of Edward the Confessor, and the Conqueror settled there William FitzOsbern, who first introduced 'the laws of Breteuil.'   Fighting was chronic.   The march indeed began at Hereford, and a century later, in the pipe rolls of Henry II, we find that the official title of the county was ' Herefordshire in Wales.'   But it was under Rufus that the first invasion of South Wales on a large scale was systematically carried out. Legend had it that he made a definite offer to his favourite, Robert FitzHamon, and twelve comrades that they should conquer the land of Morgan ; they might hold by the sword what they could win by the sword. But the story presents great difficulties. Legend has a knack of growing up to manufacture a reason to explain existing circumstances. It would be better to suppose that the war of Rufus 'was not the mere enterprise of individual chieftains, but was a regular warfare carried on in the name of the kingdom[1].' But if the expedition into Glamorgan was directed by Rufus, at least he left behind him a new group of lords marchers who finished the work of occupation, continuing the war in their own name and to their own profit. Thus was naturally formulated the 'custom of the march,' which was so prominent down to Edward's days, and which was much stronger in the southern march, for indeed it may be said to have only existed there —the custom to fight and annex without restriction from the crown of England, and to allow no appeal from the sub-tenants of the march to the King of England as overlord. Rejecting the idea that Rufus created the custom *ab initio* by making a bargain with FitzHamon, we can see how it grew up naturally as FitzHamon and his comrades and their descendants were the men in possession. One right was always enjoyed by the crown. If a lord marcher lost his lands by a successful Welsh rising, and if the aid of royal forces was called in to reconquer them, the lands thus reconquered reverted to the crown.

The most important of this earliest group of Normans in South Wales were these. Robert FitzHamon settled on the lower Usk and westwards in Glamorgan ; he was lord of the honour of Gloucester, his daughter and sole heiress married Robert, the natural son of Henry I, by whom he was created Earl of Gloucester, and the unbroken connexion between the earldom and the great marcher lordship seems to explain why

---

[1] *Norman Conquest*, vol. v. p. 111, and App. S. Also G. T. Clark, *Land of Morgan*, p. 18.

Glamorgan was never called a county palatine[1]. Bernard de Neufmarché, or of Newmarch, struck up the Usk into Brecknock, where he killed the last ' King' of South Wales, Rhys ap Tudor. William de Londres occupied the coast of Carmarthen at the mouth of the Towy, where Kidwelly became an important fortress. Arnulf of Montgomery settled in Pembroke. The first change in this settlement was made by Henry I, who, when he crushed Robert de Bellême, involved the younger brother, Arnulf, in his fall. But while extirpating a dangerous family he did not destroy the custom. To take the vacant place he called in the representative of a notable family, namely Gilbert FitzRichard de Clare, 'a friend of the king and an honourable man in all his actions[2].' ' The king said to him, " Thou wert continually seeking for a portion of the land of the Britons from me, I will now give thee the land of Cadwgan son of Bleddyn; go and possess it."' Whereupon the Clare entered into Cardigan and Pembroke, and built castles. The story goes to show that a baron could not commence to conquer in the march without the king's leave, but being once allowed to go he had a free hand. Thus planting in Wales a strong man, who was also personally attached to him, Henry did not foresee to what strength the family would attain. He also brought into Pembroke the Flemish colonists who formed the celebrated ' little England beyond Wales.' They might be trusted to be both loyal to the crown and hostile to the Welsh. Pembroke became in reality, and indeed it was even styled, a county palatine[3]; its lords, whether of the houses of Clare or Valence or Hastings, were recognized as earls.

The Clare family descended from Richard, a kinsman of the Conqueror, who fought at Hastings and received the honours of Clare in Suffolk and Tunbridge in Kent. His son was the Gilbert whom Henry I brought into Cardigan. A younger son, Walter, was settled on the Wye in Monmouth, and his chief title to fame is the foundation of Tintern Abbey. Gilbert had two sons, from whom descended two branches of great

---

[1] Clark, p. 23; Tout, *Y Cymmrodor*, vol. ix. p. 208.
[2] *Brut y Tywysogion*, p. 106.　　　[3] Tout, as above, p. 207.

warriors. The elder line received a new title, the earldom of Hertford, retaining the honours of Clare and Tunbridge; and for about a century they held their own as at least titular lords of Cardigan. They lost Cardigan, and Pembroke went to the younger branch; yet they gained at once much more than they lost, when a marriage with the heiress of Fitz-Hamon's family brought to them the much more valuable march of Glamorgan, together with the earldom of Gloucester. The power of this line may be estimated by the fact that the service of over 400 knights was due for the honours of Gloucester and Clare, besides that they were practically independent princes in Glamorgan. They were thus in a position to insist on and strengthen the custom of the march more than FitzHamon had ever done. In the thirteenth century it would not be too much to say that the two Clares, Richard and Gilbert, each in turn Earl of Gloucester, held the balance of power between the king and the faction of Simon de Montfort. The conduct of this last Gilbert requires our attention at nearly every step in Edward's wars, and it is *qua* lord of Morgan much more than *qua* Earl of Gloucester and Hertford that he gave trouble to both Simon and Edward. Thus by sketching the history of the Clares down to the period when they were not only powerful but also a serious weight upon the action of the crown, we get some idea of the growth of the custom. As we look back to the first Gilbert and his introduction into Cardigan, we cannot conceive that the custom was so strong as likely to be dangerous to the crown, for otherwise Henry I, in crushing Arnulf of Montgomery, would have crushed other marchers. Not created *ab initio* by Rufus, therefore not suspected by Henry, it grew strongly because it grew slowly. Now, it was precisely in Glamorgan that it took deepest root from the seed planted by FitzHamon, and the fostering care of the Clares strengthened it. Glamorgan, 'a county palatine without the name,' became a principality; the earls had their own sheriffs, chancery, great seal, courts, *iura regalia*, and so forth; their vassals owed to them the service of nearly forty knights; but they owed no knights to the crown except for their English fiefs,

though this probably means that Glamorgan was absorbed in
the honour of Gloucester as regards feudal service ; and their
tenants could not appeal against them to the King of England[1]. Neighbouring marches claimed similar peculiar rights,
and thus, when Edward I set himself to uproot the custom
in Glamorgan, the whole body of lords marchers resented such
interference. What had grown to such strength during two
centuries was regarded as an inherent privilege.

The younger branch of the Clares started with another
Gilbert who was heir to his uncle Walter. On the one hand
he was Earl of Pembroke, on the other Earl of Strigul, his
lands lying along the Wye where was the castle of Chepstow
or Strigul[2], including the district of Netherwent or lower
Gwent, and stretching westwards towards the Usk, while he
held the greater part of the present Pembrokeshire. His son
Richard was the celebrated conqueror in Ireland. The two
branches of the Clares thus possessed between them the most
important part of the march along the coast. Netherwent
and Strigul, the earldom of Pembroke, and the new fiefs in
Ireland passed by marriage with Strongbow's daughter to
the celebrated William the Marshal. It is hardly out of
place to notice here that Mr. Round has established that
neither Gilbert nor Richard de Clare ever held the office of
marshal[3].

Another family came to have great power in the south-east
march, succeeding by marriage to the lands of one of Fitz-
Hamon's comrades. The Braose ancestral home was in Normandy, the chief English fief was Bramber in Sussex. William
de Braose married the granddaughter and heiress of Bernard
de Neufmarché, thus obtaining Brecknock on the upper Usk,
and, lower down that river, Overwent or upper Gwent. Abergavenny castle was the centre of his power. His was the
preponderating influence in the northern part of Monmouth,
while the Clares held the coast. The family had a great

---

[1] Clark, *Land of Morgan, passim*, especially p. 24.

[2] Ormerod, *Strigulensia* ; the castle and honour usually were spoken
of as Strigul, the town as Chepstow.

[3] *Commune of London*, p. 302.

deal of hard fighting to subdue the Welsh of Gwent; fierce fighting indeed there was, and marked by a peculiarly unscrupulous ruthlessness. All the Welsh were breezy and tempestuous in character, hating restraint, devoted to an irregular warfare of surprises and even treachery which patriotism disguised and sanctioned, and always breaking out in a new place. But the men of Gwent are especially noticed by our great authority, Giraldus Cambrensis. They were proficient in the use of the longbow, and thus have their place in military history, for it is clear that from them and their neighbours the English learnt its use, and finally made it the chief English weapon. The Braose lords in course of time wore down and pacified the men of Gwent, and also they conquered up to Builth on the upper Wye, thus reaching towards the Mortimers on the middle march, and forming a link between south and north.

A great chronicler, worthy to be called an historian, has described the state of affairs in the last half of the twelfth century. Giraldus Cambrensis, otherwise Gerald de Barri, was grandson of Gerald, Constable of Pembroke, and the Princess Nesta [1]. He was an ardent cleric, and Archdeacon of Brecknock: he passed his life in vain hopes of preferment, his dream being to become Bishop of St. David's and to see the Welsh Church independent of the see of Canterbury. But while his mixed blood put him in an anomalous position in the Church, he was able to see much of both sides of the question in political matters, the power and adventurous spirit of the Anglo-Normans, and the love of liberty of the South Welsh. The Norman strain in his blood made him admire the ideas of chivalry and conquest, his Welsh strain no less led him to sympathize with independence. His own kinsfolk took part in the great invasion of Ireland from Wales; and if he is not a good authority to follow literally on the facts of the battles, he had on the other hand a clear insight into the military needs of the time. He has graphically described the Welsh manner of fighting, the advantage of an active infantry in loose formation, able also to ride if need were, their skill

[1] Barnard, *Strongbow's Conquest of Ireland*, p. 202.

in irregular warfare, their skirmishes and surprise attacks, their light equipment of spears and bows, helmets and targets. In the field their ardour loved a wild impetuous charge, which exhausted itself when resolutely faced, but their rapid retreats to the mountains and the extreme rapidity of their movements rendered a thorough conquest most difficult. Especially we get from Gerald a valuable picture of the archers of Gwent, with their 'bows made of wild elm, unpolished, rude and uncouth, not only calculated to shoot an arrow to a great distance, but also to inflict very severe wounds in close fight[1].' They could pierce an oak gate a palm thick: they could drive an arrow through the skirt of a knight's mail shirt, his mail breeches, his saddle, and so into the horse's flank: and when he swerved round, a second arrow pinned his other leg to the horse's other flank. These wonderful feats were performed at or near Abergavenny castle in war against the lords of Braose. To meet such enemies the Anglo-Normans held their castles and brought out constant reinforcements of mercenaries. It was a mere question of money, one side fighting for lucre and land, the other for liberty. But while the relays of mercenaries were always forthcoming, the death of every Welshman meant a thinning out of the population. The mailed horsemen fighting in the typical Norman style, 'the Gallic style' Gerald calls it, were really too heavily equipped[2]. They could offer a solid resistance to the typical Welsh rush. But to conquer Wales thoroughly there was only one sure method. The Welsh 'friendlies,' to put that modern term into Gerald's mouth, must be utilized; as one district was conquered with difficulty, time helping the invaders, the conquered Welsh should be turned against those still independent.

Anticipating the facts, we may say that the advice given by Gerald was actually followed. There was such a complete lack of unity among the South Welsh that each district was conquered in turn without much outside help. Not only were friendlies enlisted in the Anglo-Norman cause, but they proved

---

[1] Giraldus, vol. vi. p. 54, in his *Itinerarium* (Rolls Series).

[2] Idem, *Descriptio Cambriae*, pp. 209, 219, &c.

to be most valuable allies. By the middle of the thirteenth century certain marches had been thoroughly reduced. The whole of Monmouth, both Overwent and Netherwent, Glamorgan, Gower, Kidwelly, Llanstephan, and Pembroke, will be found sending men to Edward's armies, fighting as a matter of course, and fighting well, under the banners of their lords. As might be expected, the men of Gwent, who had been the fiercest enemies of the house of Braose, were among the best of Edward's allies. There are various indications that they were regarded as the pick of the South Welsh infantry. The case of the Sikhs is parallel, for they gave us most trouble in India, and have since been our best soldiers. On the other hand, the Welsh of the upper Wye and upper Usk, Builth and Brecknock, being further inland and in a more mountainous country, were not so thoroughly reduced, but broke out against Edward and their lords marchers on every occasion. The Vale of Towy, the inland parts of the present Carmarthenshire, and Cardiganshire across the western watershed, were not conquered. These districts at times acknowledged the over-lordship of the crown, but they were never converted into march-lands.

One more hint we get from Gerald. In praising the archery of the south generally, and of Gwent and Morgan in particular, he contrasts strongly the spear-armed Welsh of Snowdon and Merioneth [1]. In the Evesham campaign of the civil war, as well as in Edward's regular wars against Wales, these bowmen of the south were mostly Edward's allies, and Llewelyn's men were the spearmen. An exception has to be made, indeed, in connexion with the campaign of 1294, but even then it will be found that the men of Morgan, and probably those of Gwent also, revolted against their march lords and not against the king.

Returning to the twelfth century, we find that the invasion of Ireland gives a fine object-lesson as to the military resources of the march. Gerald's enthusiasm was evoked by the exploits of just those two classes to which he was allied by blood, the Norman adventurers and the South Welsh foot. The princess Nesta was daughter of the Rhys slain by Bernard of New-

[1] Giraldus, *Descriptio Cambriae*, p. 177.

march, sister of Gruffudd, and aunt of another Rhys, who were princes in turn[1]. The legitimate descendants of Nesta and Gerald of Pembroke were the historian's immediate kin, and her illegitimate descendants shared together in the invasion. The first body, which sailed for Ireland in three ships under Robert FitzStephen, one of the latter class, was composed of 90 mailed men-at-arms and 300 foot-archers 'of the flower of the young men of Wales[2].' Other detachments included 'many' archers, a hundred, seventy. Finally, Richard de Clare, Strongbow, took over 200 horsemen and 1,000 foot, recruiting these as he marched along the coast-road from Chepstow[3]. The combination of heavy Anglo-Norman horse with picked Welsh archers was irresistible. 'If Ireland,' says Gerald, 'was to be further conquered, the same policy should be pursued as in Wales; castles should be built as centres of permanent occupation, and in the field lances and bows should always be combined.' *Semper arcarii militaribus turmis mixtim adiiciantur.* This was the secret not only of momentary triumphs in Ireland : the Edwards perfected such tactics in the Welsh wars—for twice the men of Snowdon went down in pitched battle, at Orewin bridge and near Conway, before archers interlaced with horse—in the Scottish campaigns at Falkirk and Halidon Hill, and finally in France. Gerald's pride in his countrymen was justified by the successes of the English, who from them learnt archery and the tactics suited to archers.

The successes in Ireland taught Henry II to make sure that the rights of the crown were not endangered. He was keenly intent upon forcing the conquerors to acknowledge his overlordship, and this was a true instinct. Strongbow and his allies had come from a country where march custom contested the right of the crown to interfere inside the march boundaries, and the same men could not be allowed to be semi-independent both in Wales and in Ireland. Henry, as we saw, effected no lasting conquest in North Wales itself,

---

[1] Barnard, *Strongbow's Invasion*, Appendix.
[2] Giraldus, *Expugnatio Hibernica*, vol. v. p. 230 (R. S.).
[3] Ibid., p. 254.

was twice beaten back in the north, and was content to receive a nominal homage, which merely spared him the disgrace of having to admit defeat [1]. But in the south he received the homage of Rhys, whom he appointed to be a royal justiciar, and that Rhys was at least outwardly loyal is seen in his sending troops into England to assist the king. Perhaps in this reign we feel more strongly what vaguely we cannot avoid thinking on other occasions, namely, that the royal power is not so hostile to the South Welsh as to the Princes of Snowdon. Where the lords marchers are strong, there the crown is a sort of controlling authority, being jealous lest the marcher should be too independent, but not severe on the Welsh who accept the overlordship ; but where there is no power on the border capable of conquering the North Welsh in its own name, the crown is the direct enemy.

The civil wars of John and Henry III quite altered the position of affairs in Wales [2]. Llewelyn the Great seized his opportunity when England was weakened and divided, and his marriage with King John's daughter did not stand in his way. His power was felt right down to Pembroke and Glamorgan. He appeared as a new enemy to the Braoses, accustomed as they were to fight their immediate neighbours, and it was something new to find a Prince of Snowdon actually taking prisoner William de Braose, the lord of Brecknock and Abergavenny. Yet there is something illogical in Llewelyn's career ; he was an ally of the baronage in the days of Magna Carta against the crown, and yet attacked a family which was bitterly opposed to John. In fact, though it was convenient for him to support an English faction, he was really a national champion against all Englishmen. A patriot is none the worse for being, and in fact must be, illogical. Llewelyn seriously damaged the English cause in Wales, and stemmed the tide of conquest. He created a sense of national unity which had been previously wanting, and if some of his raids into South Wales were mere raids with no lasting result, at

[1] Norgate, *England under the Angevin Kings*, vol. i. p. 437 ; vol. ii. p. 181.

[2] *Annales Cambriae* and *Brut, passim* (R. S.).

C 2

least he created a tradition of Welsh unity which his grandson took up later. A national hero frequently does more for the future than for the present. Scotland of the seventeenth and eighteenth centuries furnishes a sort of parallel, for succeeding generations have made national heroes of Claverhouse and Prince Charlie, who in their day could command the devotion of but a fraction of the clans, and never effected a union of Highlands and Lowlands. Llewelyn did more for Wales than they for Scotland, and really created a national cause by helping the South Welsh. At various periods he· destroyed, wholly or in part, the castles of Caerleon, Abergavenny, Carmarthen, and Kidwelly, and fought the Flemings and burnt Haverford. In the north he destroyed Diganwy and Rhuddlan, and drove King John out; when Ranulph, the last of the great Earls of Chester, rebuilt these castles, he once more destroyed them in 1213, when the troubles in England were coming to a crisis, and naturally the Welsh reaction was more pronounced. Further, he later on entered even Shrewsbury, and burnt Oswestry. And as a champion of nationality must war even on those of his own speech whose opposition threatens to destroy the union, he was frequently fighting against Gwenwynwyn, the lord of Powys, thus driving one section of Welsh into the arms of England. He died in 1240.

At this point it is not amiss to take a new survey of the march. The senior branch of the Clares were still powerful in Glamorgan, in spite of Llewelyn's raids, and were very keen to stand upon their rights. The lands of the younger branch had passed to William the Marshal by his marriage with Strongbow's daughter, and then, after the tragic series of events which destroyed in turn each of his sons, to his several heiresses. The eldest daughter, Matilda, had married Hugh le Bigod, Earl of Norfolk, and so passed on to her son the lands of Netherwent, the castle of Strigul, that is Chepstow, and the office of hereditary Marshal of England, in 1246. Isabella had married her own cousin, Gilbert de Clare, the first Earl of Gloucester of this family; her son received very large lands in Ireland, and the march of Usk between Glamorgan and Strigul. Eva, wife of the William de Braose whom Llewelyn executed, transmitted to her daughters the Marshal lands which formed a triangle between Cardigan, Haverford, and Carmarthen. Lastly, William de Valence, half-brother of King Henry III, obtained through his wife Joan, granddaughter of the Marshal, the greater part of the lands of Pembroke, and ultimately the earldom. Thus we find in the pipe rolls that the debts claimed by the crown from the family, some £1,096, were apportioned out in equal shares[1]. Norfolk was supposed to be responsible for one-fifth, Gloucester for one-fifth, the three heirs of Braose for one-fifteenth each, Valence for one-fifth, and various barons, whose connexion with the property it would be too lengthy to discuss, other fractions. Also the crown claimed some part of the old Marshal lands, for Llewelyn the Great, in his continual wars, had occupied certain districts, and the crown later on put in a claim on the theory of reconquest.

The division of the Marshal lands was connected with the division of those of Braose, and not only Brecknock and Builth and Overwent, but Haverford and St. Clears and Cilgeran, had to be apportioned out among heiresses after the death of William de Braose, Llewelyn's victim, whose three daughters inherited, except that the march of Gower went to their cousin William[2]. Eva brought Overwent, the honour of Abergavenny, and the march of Cilgeran and Emlyn near Cardigan to the Cantilupes; her daughter in turn to Henry de Hastings. Matilda married Roger de Mortimer of Wigmore, who thus added Builth on the upper Wye and St. Clears to the west of Carmarthen to his considerable possessions in England and to his march on the upper Severn, and became not only powerful beyond the average power of a lord marcher in central but also in South-west Wales. Eleanor married Humphrey de Bohun, who died before his father, and therefore never enjoyed the earldom of Hereford, but her son received all the march of central Brecknock and Haverfordwest, thus with the earldom and office of constable holding a position not quite as powerful as that which the Earls of

---

[1] e. g. 11 Edward I under 'Herefordshire.'
[2] See pedigrees Nos. III and VI at end of Appendix.

Gloucester held in Glamorgan.  The three families of Hastings, Mortimer, and Bohun owed to the crown a total service of 78½ knights for their shares of the Braose lands.

The Lacy family, on the confines of Brecknock and Herefordshire, where the border line was extremely vague, held the march of Ewyas.  The grand-daughters of Walter de Lacy divided this land in the middle of the thirteenth century, the one marrying Geoffrey de Geneville, the other Theobald de Verdun ; Geoffrey also obtained the lordship of Ludlow.

Along the coast, the projecting piece of the present county of Glamorgan between Swansea and Carmarthen, then constituting the march of Gower, was held by the other branch of the Braose family in the male line.  Westwards Kidwelly and the lands up to the Towy came to Patrick de Chaworth, who married a descendant of William de Londres, one of the original conquerors with FitzHamon[1].  Across the Towy the march of Llanstephan belonged to the Camville family, who came from and still held land in chief in Devonshire, and Laugharne to Guy de Brian.

To the north the new inheritance of Roger de Mortimer, the march of Builth, became a connecting link towards Radnor and Montgomery.  On the borders of Shropshire the Fitzalans, Earls of Arundel, held the forest of Clun and Oswestry by feudal tenure.  The Bishop of Hereford had lands round a great stronghold at Bishop's Castle.  The Corbets owned Caurs, and the l'Estranges Ellesmere and Knockin.  An outpost towards the unconquered Welsh west of the Dee was Hawarden, belonging to the family of Monthaut or Mold.  So the connexion is carried into the county palatine, which by the extinction of the line of earls in 1237 reverted to the custody of the crown.

On the death of Llewelyn the Great the English cause regained ground for a few years, as was but natural on the removal of so great a warrior ; ' a second great Achilles ' he is styled[2].   Henry III at once tried to reoccupy the coast of the Dee, and rebuilt Diganwy.  He insisted on the restoration of Powys to Gruffudd ap Gwenwynwyn, whose jealousy of the

---

[1] *Brut*, 365.                    [2] *Annales Cambriae*, p. 82.

Princes of Gwynedd was an advantage to England.  In the south there was a new advance on Cardigan, and the Earl of Gloucester reasserted himself in Glamorgan.  Everywhere the lords marchers rebuilt the castles destroyed by Llewelyn. Even when the grandson, Llewelyn ap Gruffudd, succeeded to the principality the national cause seemed to be lost. Yet the circumstances were favourable to the Welsh as soon as a strong prince appeared, for Henry was feeble, and the extermination of the Marshal family was incalculably fatal.

The arrival upon the scene of the destined conqueror of Wales first brought out the strength of the new Llewelyn, his destined victim.  The earldom of Chester had lapsed, and in 1254 Prince Edward became earl.  First he compelled Llewelyn to cede all the Four Cantreds, the district lying between Chester and the Conway, which the Welsh had hitherto successfully defended except so far as a few settlements were at times made on the coast.  Then he pushed his influence southwards, and his design was to create two counties under royal auspices in Cardiganshire and Carmarthenshire.  For this purpose he partly strained the rights of the crown to overlordship over the South Welsh, and partly he seems to have claimed the right of reconquest. We find both Cardigan and Carmarthen held in the name of the crown, evidently on this theory, and Patrick de Chaworth, lord of Kidwelly and a powerful marcher, was royal steward of Carmarthen.  Also at Carmarthen Edward instituted a county court, or *comitatus*, to which the neighbouring lords marchers were constrained to do suit and service. This can only mean that the elder Llewelyn had conquered their lands, and that after his death Edward, in reconquering them, claimed the right of the crown to break down march privilege[1].  But Llewelyn the grandson soon asserted his power.  In 1256 and subsequent years he attacked Gruffudd ap Gwenwynwyn in Powysland, wrested Builth from Mortimer, gave back to the Welsh of Cardiganshire and Carmarthenshire

---

[1] Tyssen and Alcwyn Evans, *Carmarthen Charters*, p. 48; Tout, *Y Cymmrodor*, vol. ix. p. 212.

their independence, slaying Patrick de Chaworth and others, and even penetrated to Pembroke and Glamorgan. The Welsh chroniclers show how universally he was accepted by the southerners, and it was acknowledged that 'those of North Wales were indissolubly confederated with those of South Wales, a thing which had not been seen before[1].' The Four Cantreds were also freed, and though Edward brought up mercenaries from Gascony, he was unable to check Llewelyn's career. A Welsh bard commemorates how his hero reoccupied Diganwy and advanced as far as Chester, fought a pitched battle in Snowdonia, and was generally triumphant 'from Pulford (near Chester) to Kidwelly,' and 'from Rhos to Pembroke,' two ways of expressing the Dan and Beersheba of Wales[2]. An interesting point in this struggle is the alliance made against England between the Scottish and Welsh nobles[3].

The troubles in England, culminating in 1264 in the baronial war, made Llewelyn all the stronger, for he carried hostilities into the enemy's country. As it was the crown of England which had been the enemy of his house, as well as of himself, he made alliance with Simon de Montfort and sent troops to Lewes. Now his very successes served to betray him. It was brought home very convincingly to the minds of the lords marchers, that by assisting the barons Llewelyn was getting all the profit for himself; if at one time they were glad to have Welsh aid to win their rights from the crown, they soon saw that they would have to join the crown to save themselves from the Welsh. In fact they held the balance of power. Such a state of affairs explains the otherwise meaningless vacillations of the Clares and Bohuns in particular. It was as lords of Glamorgan and Brecknock, not as English barons, that they played their part, and their chief object was to maintain their position as semi-independent magnates privileged by march custom to raise their own armies and make war at will. Holding thus the balance of power, we find that

[1] Matthew Paris, vol. v. p. 645 (R. S.).
[2] Stephens, *Literature of the Cymry*, p. 346.
[3] Rymer, March 15, 1258.

Richard de Clare, Earl of Gloucester, was a leader of the barons even more important than Simon himself, until his death in 1262. His son Gilbert fought side by side with Simon at Lewes, swung round and served on Prince Edward's side through the campaign which ended at Evesham, and lastly threw his influence once more against the crown to prevent the proscription of the baronial remnant after Evesham, even allying himself with Llewelyn and marching to London in arms; neither Edward nor Llewelyn should become too powerful if he could help it. One Humphrey de Bohun, Earl of Hereford, fought for the king at Lewes; his son, the Humphrey who married Eleanor de Braose, was with Simon. One thinks of the Highland clan which was represented by father and son in the Hanoverian and Jacobite camps. Henry de Hastings, who through his wife was lord of Abergavenny and Overwent, was with Simon. On the other hand the Fitzalan and the Bigod of the period were loyalists, and, more important than they, Roger de Mortimer was not only loyal but a source of great strength, owing to his territorial power, to Edward. It is true that Roger had been acting a somewhat suspicious part at first, for he was one of the baronial party in 1258, and, more than that, he was accused of treachery at the time of Llewelyn's seizure of Builth. His mother, Gladys, was a daughter of Llewelyn the Great, and therefore the present prince's aunt. But, in spite of the relationship, 'it was extremely difficult for Mortimer to remain long on the side of the barons' and their Welsh ally[1]. In 1260 the question of his treachery, which Prince Edward had at first believed, was investigated, and he was formally acquitted[2]; in 1261 he was pardoned by the king, and henceforward he was a tower of strength to the royalist cause. In 1265 it was to his lands that Edward fled on his escape from captivity. And the reason is not far to seek. Llewelyn's power was remote from Glamorgan and Brecknock, and therefore Clare or Bohun might be justified in wavering; but Gwynedd was much too close to the Mortimer march, and Builth had yet to be recovered.

[1] *Dict. Nat. Biog.*, vol. xxxix. p. 132.   [2] Rymer, July 30, 1260.

The campaigns of Lewes and Evesham are not only important because we find Llewelyn on the barons' side, Mortimer on the king's, and Clare and Bohun wavering, but also as being landmarks in military history. They are the last two battles in England in which the mailed horseman is quite supreme, for with Edward's Welsh wars the age of the foot-archer is dawning. When we study such a book as Mr. Oman's *Art of War*, or Mr. Hereford George's *Battles*, we see that the one need in the Middle Ages was combination, horse with foot, missiles with hand weapons. But up to our period combination was not systematically studied, was in fact neglected except at long intervals and under special, almost accidental, circumstances.

At Hastings the Normans triumphed by virtue of their superior mobility, and by an alternation of volleys of arrows with rushes of horse, over an enemy as brave as themselves but motionless. The bow was the weak short bow, which was then held of no account ; the string was pulled only to the chest, and the arrow, except at close quarters, was shot high into the air, a high trajectory being in itself a confession of weakness. The lance was also short, and for the most part was wielded overhand. The moral of Hastings is that even these immature weapons must prevail, when skilfully combined, over the simple and antiquated formation of a dense phalanx of shields and battle-axes or spears, but will prevail only after a hard struggle. The powerful longbow and the heavy couched tilting-lance of Poitiers would have annihilated Harold's men in an hour. Now there is one factor in war which the progress of time and science, carefully elaborated tactics and improved weapons, will never eliminate, and that is the high courage of cool-headed and well-trained men fighting hand to hand. But granted on the one side such high courage, coolness, training, but the men condemned to stand still, while on the other side there is skill in combining the various modes of attack, the army on the offensive must win. It wins quickly if the weapons are powerful of their kind, slowly if they are comparatively weak and immature, but win it must. Mere steadiness in defence is useless without ability to make a counter-attack, unless panic, bad generalship, or disaffection spoil the army which is attacking. Thus combination and skill triumphed at Hastings.

At Northallerton an infantry of short bows and spears again won. But among the most warlike powers of Europe the mailed and mounted man-at-arms was the conspicuous figure, and he disdained to be combined with a rabble of foot. In Europe he maintained his proud position. But in the East the first crusade taught that the heavy horseman must change his tactics against the light swarming Turks. So in the third crusade we find a new type of soldier, the foot crossbowmen, drawn up to form a screen in front of the cavalry, and trained to let the cavalry pass through them when the counter-attack was sounded [1]. Richard I was not indeed the sole, but the greatest exponent of these tactics ; Genoa and Pisa supplied the best crossbowmen. Other bows were used and horse-archers were created on the Turkish model, but the Italian arblast was the champion weapon of its kind. Arsuf was the typical victory during Richard's march south from Acre. The combination of foot with mailed horse did not however spread from Palestine, where necessity was the mother of adaptation, to Western Europe. At Bouvines there was a useless mass of infantry in the centre of each army screening the important reserve of horse, but it was exposed only to be slaughtered. When we come to look at the British Isles, it was only in the invasion of Ireland that the combination was properly and systematically used. Except that the Norman lances and South Welsh archers fought in an unknown corner of Europe, it is wonderful that the methods of their successes were not imitated elsewhere.

The history of the crossbow after the age of the crusades is interesting. It became in Europe the chief weapon of two classes, the citizen militia of chartered towns, and mercenaries. With the first class it was found useful for the defence of walls ; but citizen levies did not fight except in cases where they were specially interested, and they certainly did not influence military history. The mercenaries were different

---

[1] Oman, pp. 309, &c.

and were ubiquitous.   The Genoese and Pisans clung to the
crossbow, which originally brought reputation to them in
Palestine, but they chiefly served on shipboard as marines.
The levies of the Low Countries and the Gascons also used
it, on foot and on horseback.   In England it was banned, not
for the sentimental reason which led the Popes to condemn
it as a weapon unfit for Christian use, but because the
mercenary system was hateful, so that Magna Carta brought
the matter to a decision, and condemned crossbows and
mercenaries alike.   The crossbow never was popular as an
English weapon, yet it was considered to be much superior
to the bow until the beginning of the fourteenth century.
The bow appears in Henry III's assize of arms as a fit
weapon for county levies.   At present weak, it was capable
of great development.   But the process of development was
slow, and meanwhile it had no repute, and Mr. George has
shown on the clearest negative evidence that it played no
part in the crisis of Lewes and Evesham.

As a typical battle of the early thirteenth century, where
cavalry alone were regarded, I venture to take that of
Muret[1].   M. Dieulafoy has written an interesting monograph
on the subject after close examination into the topography,
and certainly makes out a strong case for upsetting the views
of M. Delpech on this battle, views which Mr. Oman has
adopted.   He insists that there were no elaborate manœuvres.
Simon de Montfort drew up his cavalry, from 800 to 1,000 of
all ranks, out of sight of the enemy, personally arrayed and
dressed his lines in three bodies, brought them round the
town still out of sight, and thence across a bridge over the
river Louge just where it falls into the Garonne—it is by
establishing the existence of this bridge and the road leading
down to it that M. Dieulafoy upsets the previous account of
the fight—reformed and launched his men straight at the
enemy.   His one warning was that they should charge
steadily and level; 'boot to boot' we say nowadays.   The
Frenchmen were outnumbered as one to three in cavalry

---

[1] *Mémoires de l'Académie des Inscriptions*, tome xxxvi.

only, but they were war-hardened fanatics ; more than that, they were adventurers to whom victory brought profit, and therefore had a sense of discipline. Their opponents were hardly at all organized and were soon cut to pieces, first the cavalry who rode each man for himself, next an innumerable and useless infantry. The battle was won not by elaborate combinations and flank attacks, but by a simple level charge ahead. Two points are to be observed. The horses were slow and clumsy, the rider in his coat of mail and leggings was heavy, and the massive lance was awkward ; rapid movements were out of the question. Secondly, there was no system of subordination of commands. The commander-in-chief had to be literally ubiquitous.

Now, referring back to the battle of Hastings, we see that cavalry action had undergone changes. William's Normans and other adventurers could and did manœuvre, they did not carry a great weight of mail and had much slighter lances, and their horses were not encumbered by body-armour ; thus they could not break the Saxons by one ponderous charge, but could wheel. A century and a half later, at Muret, the equipment was altogether heavier. It was still the period of mail, but much more of it was worn on both man and horse, and the development of the massive tilting-lance made a great difference. Simon's Frenchmen had to be slowly dressed in line, and probably could not have wheeled, but their steady charge in line was ponderous, and carried all before it. One thing there was in common. Each army submitted to discipline and carried out the leader's orders, because to adventurers obedience is profitable. Lands and plunder were before their eyes.

These remarks gain much more force when we turn to a feudal levy. Each feudal lord brings up his contingent of heavy horse ; but there is no cohesion between the units, no sense of discipline because no overpowering zeal, and no hierarchy of command. There is a commander-in-chief, perhaps. Below him each leader has his own unit. Therefore, if we find the elder Simon de Montfort obliged to array personally his experienced veterans, what are we to expect of Simon the son when he leads an incoherent force of barons to Lewes?

The English of Henry III were quite raw fighters. Every fact of the career of Edward, whether as prince or as king, shows that he was teaching the art of war to poor material. But at Lewes he was yet young and himself in the learning stage. Simon de Montfort, the rebel, was the most experienced leader of the day, and had been brought up in his father's ideas of cavalry action[1]. He did exactly the same work which his father did at Muret; as there was not a single English baron who had the requisite experience, he had to array personally his whole force upon the downs which rise above Lewes. The array was performed out of sight of the enemy, whose bad scouting was typical. It was the same simple array as at Muret, consisting of three bodies of horse, but there was also a reserve. The foot were quite worthless, including the Welsh sent by Llewelyn as ally of the barons and the Londoners. I cannot find any ground for supposing, with Mr. Oman, that a body of foot was brigaded with each body of horse; such an arrangement would not have suited the ideas of the day when combination was despised, especially as cavalry never dismounted to fight; yet the Londoners were on foot on Simon's left wing. Thus arrayed the baronial army moved down on Lewes. The fortune of the day was governed entirely by the lie of the ground. Two spurs of down descend towards Lewes, and there is a hollow between, so that the army was divided, the right and centre followed by the reserve moving fairly straight on, while the left was separated as it took the eastern spur. Now the royalists had been taken quite by surprise; yet they had some little time to fall into order, for the advance of the barons must have been slow. Prince Edward was on the right, and got into position the most quickly, probably being warned the soonest; and he and his men held the castle of Lewes, while his father and uncle were on the lower ground to the south by the priory. It so fell out by accident, or else he had an eye ready to seize the advantage of the

[1] Oman, p. 420, &c.

position, that he formed up his wing below the castle and opposite to the hollow which split the barons' left wing from their centre. Without hesitation, and before the main bodies on either side could meet, he delivered his counter-attack ; charging to his own immediate front he caught his foe obliquely, rolled them up across the foot of the spur, not up the spur, and so pursued them into the flat ground beyond out of sight of the main battle. He pursued and killed until his horses were blown. Climbing back afterwards to the point where Simon's force had passed to deliver their main attack, he found his uncle a prisoner, and his father blockaded. The obvious criticism is that the first conception of his charge was brilliant and worthy of Rupert ; it may have been due to accident and the nature of the ground, or he may have intended it ; he had the enemy at a disadvantage, struck in so as to drive their left away from their centre, and allowed them no chance of rallying. Meanwhile, the royalist centre and left were entangled and cooped up on the low ground, could not take up a position to fight, and were broken.

I have given my own idea of this battle in spite of the high authority of Mr. George, for he seems to me to make the field too wide by assigning to Simon's right a third spur to the south ; the fighting is more intelligible if we consider that his whole army, except the beaten left, advanced down one broad spur in compact order, and Mr. Oman seems to me to be correct in this respect. As the direction of Edward's charge depends on an accurate understanding of the ground, I have worked out my account *in situ.*

Mr. George and Mr. Oman have both noticed that the only mention of archery in this campaign is in connexion with the Welsh. Some Welsh archers are said to have harassed the royalists as they traversed the Weald of Sussex. They were not necessarily Llewelyn's men. The Earl of Gloucester and other marchers were fighting on Simon's side, and therefore this body may have been from the bow-using districts of South-east Wales.

When Prince Edward escaped from captivity he threw

himself on the loyalty of Roger de Mortimer, and the most powerful marcher, the Earl of Gloucester, joined him. The theory that certain marchers, such as Gloucester, deserted Simon's cause to join the king when Simon's ally, Llewelyn, seemed likely to become too powerful, has the merit of explaining the change of sides. In the campaign there was much marching and counter-marching in the basins of the Usk and Wye, as well as of the Severn, so that Edward was able to learn much of the geography of the country. Welsh archers were probably in his army under Gloucester's banner. In Earl Simon's army were Llewelyn's spearmen, and probably some of the archers as well, for Henry de Hastings and Humphrey de Bohun were with him. Yet at the final scene of Evesham all the serious fighting fell upon the cavalry, though each side was numerically weak in that arm. Our interest is not attracted by the battle, but by the skilful out-witting of the Montfortians by the prince's strategy. It is to be noticed that good work was done on the king's side by John Giffard, who at Lewes had been a Montfortian.

Many years were yet to elapse before it was generally recognized that foot were not to be despised. So far we have seen Edward only as a learner, able to bring off a brilliant charge and to pen in his enemy by brilliant marching, yet still a learner. He would prove in his Welsh wars, when he had become king, that he had profited by his experience. His knowledge of Welsh methods came from the days when he had fought Llewelyn for the possession of the Four Cantreds, and later from the Evesham campaign. He probably knew by tradition and by experience the excellence of the South Welsh archers. Then when he took the cross he must have seen archers in the East, even if the story of his being himself wounded by an arrow be mythical. But it is not enough to know that he had seen the effects of archery. The question is, had he begun systematically to introduce the bow and arrow as the weapons of English infantry before the Welsh wars, or did he do so only during the Welsh wars? It is well known that the bow has a place in the assize of arms of Henry III. I believe that Edward was making some effort to create an efficient bow-armed English infantry, at least from 1265 onwards, if not earlier. The facts are meagre, but are suggestive.

A quite unique document[1] shows that in 1266 and 1267 Reginald de Grey commanded at Nottingham Castle a mixed force of two knights with their attendant troopers, twenty mounted crossbowmen and a captain, ten foot crossbowmen and twenty archers ; the knights served for 263 days, the others for 436 days, *ad debelland inimicos domini regis*. The enemy could be no other than outlawed Montfortians, who were being hunted down in the forests. There were two considerable engagements, one in the heart of Sherwood Forest itself, and the royalists lost several horses. Now one of the sober accounts of Robin Hood makes him a Montfortian, and it is therefore interesting to trace the presence of a force which was serving for a very long time and included some royal archers, in the very neighbourhood of his legendary home, and moreover suffering some loss at the hands of the outlaws. No one who has studied the development of military archery could dream of a Robin Hood of the thirteenth century drawing a six-foot longbow, a weapon which was only at its beginnings, yet one naturally expects to find the early good shots among the outlaws and poachers of Sherwood. In this connexion it is to be noticed that Notts and Derbyshire sent foot to all the Welsh wars of Edward, and were the only counties not bordering on Wales which did so, while Warwickshire and Worcestershire never did. It is a far cry to 1333, the date of Halidon Hill, but it is striking to find poachers from Sherwood pardoned on condition of entering the king's army and helping to gain that notable victory of the longbow. Archery began to flourish just in the counties where we should expect to find it.

As Edward returned home from his crusade, he fought in France the 'little war' of Chalons[2]. He had with him a numerous infantry, and some proportion of them had bows and slings.

In the first war against Llewelyn, in 1277, we find relays

---

[1] *Exch. Acc.* $\frac{3}{10}$.    [2] Hemingburgh, vol. i. p. 338 (Eng. Hist. Soc.).

of infantry brought from the border counties and Derbyshire, and friendly marchers, composed of both *sagittarii* and *lanceati*[1]. The proportion of bowmen to foot spearmen or knifemen is never stated. The important point is that bows were already the recognized weapons of some of the county levies, as the assize of Henry III ordained. The language of some of our military historians is often misleading; they speak of archery as if it had its beginnings during these wars. The truth is that it had already been introduced before, but was much improved during the wars. One corps must be specially noticed. A hundred picked men of Macclesfield were purely archers unmixed with foot spearmen, they served from the first to nearly the last day of the war, whereas the other infantry came up in relays for short periods, they earned an extraordinary wage of 3*d*. a day, and they came from the king's own lands. It is not too much to see here the personal interest of Edward towards the improvement of archery. The only other purely bow-armed corps in 1277, a corps which also served for a fairly long period, came from Gwent and Crickhowell. The rise of English infantry to be a real power in Europe depended upon this bow being a true long-bow drawn to the ear, and, the attitude once learnt, it could be developed both in length and in strength. That the weapon patronized by Edward before his Welsh wars, and improved during them in the hands of his own English and his Welsh friendlies, was the real thing is proved by its rapid development. It only remained for him and for his grandson to get the English to become expert in its use by practice, to improve their range, and to learn discipline. Once more be it said, there is no question of archery being learnt from the Welsh enemy; the bow-armed Welsh were Edward's allies.

[1] *Exch. Acc.* $\frac{3}{11}$.

# CHAPTER II

## AN EDWARDIAN ARMY

IN examining a typical thirteenth-century army we must begin with the cavalry. To raise cavalry Edward had at first no choice but to call on his feudal tenants. Magna Carta had so decidedly condemned the employment of mercenaries that the feudal was the only system remaining. In 1277 and 1282, again in 1298 and onwards, the crown tenants were summoned in the most formal manner. Yet military needs compelled the king to supplement the quite inadequate feudal array by paid troops. Magna Carta could not be disregarded, so the only alternative was to enlist Englishmen for pay, the funds being provided by legal votes. Gascons were at intervals brought over, a large corps of 1,500 in the winter of 1282-3, and a smaller number in 1298, but as they were subjects of Edward as Duke of Aquitaine, and as they were paid by money voted by Parliament, no protests were made.

What was the nominal maximum strength of the feudal host of England? If every tenant-in-chief brought the exact number of knights which the conditions of his tenure demanded, what would be the total of mailed cavalry forthcoming? The question has more than an antiquarian interest. It is only by knowing the details that we can appreciate the inherent weakness of the feudal system, a weakness so pronounced that Edward I took a very important step towards substituting a paid national army for the feudal. Without knowledge of his preliminary innovations we cannot understand the constitution of the army of Crecy and Calais, which was paid from Black Prince and bishop and earl down to the humblest knife-armed Welshman. Edward III did not suddenly introduce such a system of payments. The

tendency to substitute paid for feudal service begins with
Edward I, just because the formal feudal service was unsatis-
factory.

Mr. Round's answer is well known. 'The whole *servitium
debitum*, clerical and lay, of England can hardly have
exceeded, if indeed it reached, 5,000 knights[1].' I venture
to think that the nominal strength in the thirteenth century
was somewhat higher. The evidence of the pipe rolls is
fairly exhaustive. The sheriffs were ordered to collect a
scutage two years after the first Welsh war at a rate of
40s. per fee. They drew up their lists in a purely formal
manner, and made no allowance for military service actually
performed, or for fines paid at the time. Very few tenants
took any notice, fortunately for us, for the renewed entries
of sums claimed year after year enable us to check doubtful
or illegible entries in the roll of 1279. The figures which
I offer may be slightly inaccurate, for it would be a sheer
waste of time to add up carefully all the fractions, but the
margin of error is not likely to be large. I make out a total
of just about 6,000 knights. Allowance being made for
certain palpable omissions would raise it towards 7,000.

The following are the totals arranged by counties. They
are taken from the pipe roll of 7 Edward I, except in the
case of four counties for which the returns were sent in next
year. Fractions have been omitted.

| | *Number of knights.* | | *Number of knights.* |
|---|---|---|---|
| Northumberland . . . . | 93 | Worcestershire. . . . . | 78 |
| Cumberland . . . . . | 3 | Lincoln . . . . . . . | 384 |
| Devonshire . . . . . . | 419 | Norfolk and Suffolk . . . | 649 |
| Herefordshire . . . . . | 256 | Cambs and Hunts . . . | 154 |
| Hampshire . . . . . . | 141 | Yorkshire . . . . . . | 422 |
| Essex and Herts . . . . | 678 | Gloucestershire . . . . | 409 |
| Oxfordshire . . . . . . | 82 | Leicester and Warwick. . | 287 |
| Berkshire . . . . . . | 37 | Wiltshire. . . . . . . | 180 |
| Surrey . . . . . . . | 10 | Northants . . . . . . | 133 |
| Sussex (8 Edward I) . . | 284 | Beds and Bucks . . . . | 273 |
| Somerset and Dorset . . | 320 | Shropshire (8 Edward I) . | 63 |
| Notts and Derby . . . . | 293 | Staffordshire    „ | 128 |
| Kent . . . . . . . . | 155 | Chester    „ | 70 |

[1] *Feudal England*, p. 292.

Two questions at once present themselves. Is there, so to speak, any overlapping? What allowance must be made for the counties omitted, and for a few honours entered in blank?

First one would say that the officials might be expected to draw up accurate lists of the number of knights due from each fief. They had consulted a *liber feodorum* and previous lists. Only in a very few cases did the crown claim service which the tenant did not 'recognize.' Experience after many years of tax-gathering would show how the money of some very large fief could be best collected. Here the *Testa de Nevill* is helpful, or more strictly one should say the various miscellaneous lists of fees which have been printed together with the real *Testa*. It was customary to collect such money in one county only, though the manors might be scattered over several. This explains why so few fees are returned from Surrey and Worcestershire, and none from Rutland and Middlesex, the lands forming part of honours which were assessed elsewhere; for instance, in Surrey were many manors of the honours of Wallingford, Clare, Gloucester, and Warenne [1]. Of the seventy-eight Worcestershire fees, no less than seventy-one were held by churchmen, the remaining seven by William de Beauchamp, and other manors were assessed on the Staffordshire and Warwickshire lists. The careful arrangement of the scutage lists seems to prove that there was no overlapping, that is to say that a tenant was not charged for the same manor twice over by different sheriffs.

The figures of the pipe roll of Edward I frequently correspond exactly to those of the various documents of the printed *Testa de Nevill*. Internal evidence shows that many of the lists of fees in the latter belong to the first twenty or thirty years of Henry III; for instance, there is a partial list of the fees of the honour of Warenne when held in wardship by Peter of Savoy, i. e. before the Earl of Surrey reached his majority in 1240. In 1235 was taken from the laity an aid *ad maritandam sororem regis* on the occasion of the marriage of Isabella to the emperor. Let us take the case of Shropshire to make a comparison. In 1277–9 the sheriff was Bogo

[1] *Testa*, pp. 39 onwards, and 219 onwards.

de Knoville, who was in the thick of Edward's first Welsh war, and must have known perfectly well the exact amount of military service performed by the Shropshire tenants—service indeed which we shall see that they gave ungrudgingly, as the war was very near to them. He made his list of scutage money in 1279 entirely from old lists of Henry III. He named the tenants who held the fiefs under Henry III as if they owed the money to Edward I, and made no allowance for the actual service of several present tenants. Thus he entered £10 as due from five fees of Thomas Corbet; now Thomas Corbet paid in 1235 on a fraction under ten fees at half the usual rate because *de veteri feoffamento*, but the inquisition of John's reign assessed Robert Corbet at five fees[1]. Peter Corbet, who was a very active soldier under Edward I, and had a personal animosity against Llewelyn, served in 1277 with two knights and six servientes, i. e. the exact equivalent of five knights, and moreover served beyond the legal forty days of feudal service. If, therefore, Bogo de Knoville drew up his scutage list in such a manner, it only proves how entirely formal the lists were; he entered a dead Corbet as owing scutage in spite of the fact that the living Corbet had performed more than the duty of the fief.

We can even go back beyond Henry III, and compare the scutage lists of 1279 with the figures which Mr. Round gives of the feudal obligations under Henry II[2]. Several fiefs are now assessed at exactly the same number of fees, and named after the tenant who had held more than 100 years earlier. Thus 'the fees of Henry of Essex,' who had been dispossessed in 1163, are entered as owing £113 4s. 0d., and £15 14s. 0d. are paid. The descendants of Walter de Wahulle and Hugh de Bayeux are assessed at thirty and twenty fees respectively, the same as when these men were living. Hubert de Rye used to owe thirty-five, and his heirs are charged for two portions of 17½ each; the ten fees of Nigel de Lovetot have become three of 3⅓ each, and the ten of Richard de Cormeilles four of 2½ each. It is interesting to find these similarities, for they prove that various inquisitions into the extent of feudal

[1] *Testa*, pp. 44, 55.        [2] *Feudal England*, p. 254.

obligations had not altered or added anything.  The formal demand for money was in these cases the same as under Henry II.

Taking the large fiefs, as they existed under Edward, we are struck to find the Earl of Gloucester owing the service of as many as $455\frac{2}{3}$ knights.  Is this a case of overlapping? He was assessed at $261\frac{1}{2}$ on the Gloucestershire list, $141\frac{9}{10}$ in Norfolk, 43 in Beds and Bucks, and 9 in Kent.  Now in 1235 the custos of the honours of Gloucester and Clare acknowledged an obligation of £534 16s. 8d. [1], which at two marcs per fee gives $402\frac{1}{4}$ fees, corresponding closely to the $261\frac{1}{2}$ + $141\frac{9}{10}$ as above.  The two honours, it is proved by this coincidence, were taxed in different counties.  The forty-three are half of the fees of the honour of Giffard.  The nine entered in Kent for some special reason are some extra ones of the honour of Gloucester.  Similarly, the fees of the Earl of Norfolk are entered in three counties, $168\frac{11}{12}$ in Norfolk being his Bigod inheritance, $67\frac{1}{2}$ in Gloucestershire coming from the Marshals for the honour of Strigul, and 43 the second half of the honour of Giffard; total $279\frac{5}{12}$.  The Earl of Hereford is entered on the Essex list for $98\frac{1}{3}$, apparently made up of 60 Mandeville and 30 Bohun fees, and $8\frac{1}{3}$ as one-third of some other inheritance; he owed $26\frac{1}{6}$ in Herefordshire as his share of the Braose inheritance, and with a few minor additions his total comes to $151\frac{1}{2}$.  To speak generally, one sees from the close correspondence of the figures of 1235 with those of 1279 that the obligations of the great feudatories were apportioned out under various counties, according as the lands came into the possession of their families; if the honour of Clare had been always in the past taxed in Norfolk, and that of Gloucester in Gloucestershire—or occasionally in Herefordshire, but this does not spoil the argument—then when they were united in the same hands they were still taxed separately.  The greater figures do not include the less.

On the other hand, there are certain obvious omissions.  Of the 6,000 only 640 are clerical fees.  Mr. Round has calculated that 784 were due from churchmen, and as his figures

[1] *Testa*, p. 413.

correspond so far to those of the pipe rolls of Edward I, it is safe to add on the extra 144; Canterbury, Bath and Wells, Glastonbury, and a few smaller houses are those whose fees are omitted. Then the Earl of Lancaster was assessed for 210 fees in Derbyshire and Leicestershire, where he held the confiscated lands of Robert de Ferrars and Simon de Montfort, but not for his honour of Lancaster; his obligation would thus come to a large total, for recent investigation tends to show that he owed a service of 263[1], and he himself professed not to know its full extent. The Earl of Surrey was assessed only for his sixty fees of the honour of Warenne, and more must be allowed for at least his Yorkshire lands, on which it is notorious that he would not allow the royal officials to hold an inquisition[2]. John of Brittany was assessed at $27\frac{1}{2}$ fees in Cambridgeshire, and he also held the honour of Richmond, from which Mr. Round says that fifty fees were due in Yorkshire alone. The service of $121\frac{8}{15}$ knights is the official total in the reign of Henry III as due from the honour of Boulogne[3]. The honour of Wallingford, held by the Earl of Cornwall, was entered in blank by the Sheriff of Berkshire; according to the *Testa* the enfeoffed sub-tenants owed a service of $95\frac{1}{4}$ knights[4]. The earl was assessed at $20\frac{1}{4}$ fees in Devonshire, $90\frac{1}{2}$ in Norfolk, and a few elsewhere, so that he would be liable for a total of 220. But he recognized, as will be seen later, a larger *servitium debitum* than any other baron. The pipe rolls do not include a list of fees from Cornwall; the collectors of the aid *ad maritandam* in 1235 account for 236 fees, Mortain fees or *minuta feoda*, at a special rate of 16s. 4d. per fee[5], and although some of these in 1279 are accounted for by the Sheriff of Devonshire, the earl's 220 must be considerably increased, and allowance also made for other tenants in Cornwall.

The counties of Rutland and Middlesex need not be

[1] *Eng. Hist. Review*, Jan. 1895, p. 40.

[2] *Kirby's Inquest*, pp. 3, 227 (Surtees Society). See *Dict. Nat. Biog.*, vol. lix. p. 366.

[3] *Testa*, pp. 265, 274, 275, 285. I take vi. xx[li] as a misprint for vi. xx[ti] on p. 275.

[4] Ibid., pp. 115, 116.         [5] Ibid., p. 201.

considered, as the lands formed part of honours assessed elsewhere; also the Archbishop of Canterbury held much land in Middlesex. Westmorland is omitted; but there were only seven fees, of which four were held by the heiresses of Robert de Vipont for the barony of Westmorland, and three by the baron of Kendal [1].

A doubtful point arises in connexion with Shropshire. We saw how Bogo de Knoville assessed the Corbet fief at five knights, although Peter Corbet served in the war. But he entirely omitted to assess Roger de Mortimer. The *Testa* shows $18\frac{11}{12}$ Mortimer fees due from enfeoffed sub-tenants, irrespective of the $26\frac{1}{8}$ which, being a share of the Braose inheritance, came on the Herefordshire list. Roger himself acknowledged a service of six knights as his quota for both Braose and Shropshire lands, and his normal retinue apparently consisted of twenty lances.

Owing to the fact that the county palatine had come into the king's hands, the pipe roll of 1280 contains a list from the Justiciar of Chester. He accounted for £140 paid up for seventy fees for which no military service was done, chiefly from lands held in wardship, and added a note that all the other tenants—*homines regis*, he termed them—had served in the army, and were therefore quit of scutage. It is impossible to say what figure should be calculated. Reginald de Grey acknowledged a service of two knights in respect of a quota of his full obligation.

Thus, adding the service due from certain clerics, from the Earls of Lancaster and Surrey, from the honours of Wallingford and Richmond, from Westmorland and Cornwall, and from Roger de Mortimer, adding also those due from the Cestrians and the tenants of the honour of Boulogne—we have to raise the 6,000 to some figure short of 7,000.

Comparing the details of the aid *ad maritandam* in 1235 and the demand for scutage in 1279, we see at once that the payments were made in the first case, or at least there was a promise to pay, for the aid was taken by consent. But, it must be repeated, the lists of 1279 were purely formal.

---

[1] *Testa*, p. 412.

A certain amount of money came in. A few small tenants who owed the service of one knight, or a fraction, also a few who held by serjeanty, paid small sums, in some cases by instalments of a few shillings at a time, spread over several years; they were doubtless in such a position that they were afraid to refuse. The prompt payment by the tenants of Chester, who were directly under the king's control, was exceptional. So, too, was the case of the sub-tenants of the Fitzalan lands in Shropshire, from whom was collected a sum of £44 out of a total of £64 owed; these lands were then held in wardship, and were near to the scene of war, whereas no money was forthcoming from other Fitzalan manors in Sussex and Norfolk. The only other sheriff who collected a considerable sum was the Sheriff of Devonshire, rather over £138 being raised, of which £56 came from half of the honour of Totnes. Some tenants, both lay and clerical, we shall see, had offered fines *pro servitio* during the progress of the war, but they had paid into the wardrobe. The sheriffs, being responsible to the exchequer, took no notice at first; when these payments were officially proved to them they crossed off the debts. For instance, the Abbot of Peterborough paid 250 marcs in 1277, and was formally acquitted on the pipe roll of 1280, and others later. But many tenants who paid did not take the trouble to gain quittance, nor did the great feudatories who actually fought in the war take trouble to prove their services. The sheriffs went on entering the supposed debts year after year. But, indeed, nominal debts did not distress a feudal lord. Very large sums of money were still in arrears to the crown for previous scutages of Henry III's time, the 'scutage of Poitou,' the 'scutage of Gascony,' and so on. The tenants of the Marshal fief owed £1,096; the Earls of Norfolk, Gloucester, and Pembroke were each supposed to be liable for one-fifth of this sum, three other barons for a fifteenth each, and eight others for smaller fractions[1]. Robert de Ros owed over £2,000. Probably they would argue that military services cancelled the debts. Besides, the custom of voting direct taxes on property by

[1] 9 Edward I, under 'Herefordshire.' See above, p. 21.

Parliament had come in. So a demand for scutage was disregarded, especially as the tax of a fifteenth brought in nearly ten times more than the whole nominal feudal service of England would have yielded if every tenant paid up 40s. a fee without doing any service at all in war.

When we turn to the actualities of the first Welsh war, we find a wonderful contrast. Those tenants who paid fines immediately in lieu of military service assessed themselves at an average rate of 40 marcs per fee, but they acknowledged a service of much fewer fees than appeared on the sheriffs' lists. Here are some instances gleaned from occasional entries on the marshal's register[1], a schedule attached to the patent roll of 1277, or from the pipe rolls when the sheriffs, as indeed rarely happened, quitted a tenant in consideration of the voluntary fine. Ralph Paynel and John de Stoteville paid 10 marcs each for a quarter of a fee, and Peter de Coudray 20 for a half; these were the full obligations, and yet the men taxed themselves at the higher rate. Gerard de Wakesham offered 20 marcs for one fee. Gilbert Pecche acknowledged the service of two knights, and gave £60; that is, he taxed himself at 45 marcs per fee, for which reason a special note of the sum was entered on the marshal's register. His nominal obligation, according to the sheriffs' lists for Kent and Cambridgeshire, was $18\frac{1}{12}$ fees, i. e. £36 3s. 4d. at the 40s. rate. Therefore Ralph, John, and Peter, in their honesty, paid 1,333 per cent. too much, Gerard 666 per cent., and Gilbert 66 per cent.; if they had waited until the sheriffs called upon them at the 40s. rate they would have had an advantage. It is to be hoped that, having thus brought their fines to minister to the king's immediate necessities, they received compensation when the next property tax was voted. On the other hand, let us take the Countess of Devon; she acknowledged and paid on only $2\frac{1}{2}$ fees, presumably 100 marcs at the average rate of 40 marcs; her nominal obligation was eighty-nine fees in Devonshire alone, that is, £178; she paid £111 6s. 8d. too little, and there is no record that she ever made the balance good.

[1] *Parl. Writs*, vol. i. p. 199.

The great majority of the clerical tenants paid sooner or later, or else sent soldiers. One imagines that the crown could put special pressure upon them, and thus it is easy to understand why they were impatient of taxation during the whole reign. They paid in a variety of ways. The Abbot of Tavistock did not offer a fine during the course of the war of 1277, waited for the Sheriff of Devonshire to assess him on sixteen fees at the 40s. scale, and paid £32 in 1279; in 1282 he offered at once 40 marcs on the higher scale for one fee which he 'recognized,' a gain for him of £5 6s. 8d. The Bishop of Ely recognized six fees, and paid £160; his nominal obligation was forty fees, i. e. £80 on the lower scale. The Abbot of Peterborough recognized five fees, and, at a specially high rate of 50 marcs per fee, paid £166 13s. 4d.; on his nominal obligation of sixty fees he would have paid £120. The Archbishop of York sent four knights to the army, owing a service of twenty. The Bishop of Hereford sent three knights and four servientes, the equivalent of five knights, owing a service of fifteen. Other churchmen, especially the wealthier, performed similarly a fractional part of their duty, a quarter, an eighth, a tenth, or a twelfth. In the marshal's register the formula runs, '*A* recognizes the service of *x* knights, which he performs by *y* knights and *z* servientes,' or 'for which he made a fine then'; the nominal obligation is not stated, and has to be found from the pipe rolls. The difference between the reduced and the nominal ought to be according to the proportion of the shilling to the marc, one to thirteen and a third.

On the other hand, the following 'recognized' the full nominal obligation. The Abbot of St. Albans sent one knight and ten servientes, owing a full service of six knights; the Abbot of Sherburne, owing the service of two, sent four servientes; the Abbot of Malmesbury first paid 100 marcs, then sent six servientes for three knights. From Ramsey and several small houses fines were forthcoming on the full obligation, but, as no note is appended to the register, we are driven to conclude that the forty-marc scale was used. The Abbot of Abbotsbury sent 30 marcs for one fee. All these clerical tenants had therefore an undoubted grievance, for no reduction was allowed to compensate for the scale being high. Yet in 1282 the same houses provided men or money once more in full.

The case of the Bishop of Durham is peculiar. Mr. Round shows that Henry II raised the service of that see from ten to seventy knights [1]. According to the pipe rolls of Edward I the assessment was on ten fees in Lincolnshire and one in Yorkshire; in 1277 a fine was paid precisely on ten, in 1282 four knights and twelve servientes were sent to the war. I would suggest that the service of ten—the extra one in Yorkshire being disregarded—was due from that part of the fief outside, and that Henry II had attempted to claim a full service for the knights enfeoffed within the county palatine. The incumbents of the see would argue that they were bound to send to a Welsh war only the ten knights, or the equivalent; when a war should break out against the Scots they would be ready to equip the sixty whom they had enfeoffed of their own accord within the see. Therefore full service was done both in 1277 and 1282; later on Antony Bek, being bishop, led very large contingents into Scotland.

But the important question is not, How were the fines paid? but, How large a force of cavalry was raised for a war? The marshal's register of 1277 shows an official record of 228 barons and knights, and 294 servientes [2]. This represents a total of 375 knights, as two servientes were uniformly reckoned the equivalent of one knight. In the figures is included the feudal service of those who were attached to the armies of Montgomery or of South Wales, as well as those who were at headquarters with the king. In 1282 the registered total is smaller, 123 barons and knights, and 190 servientes [3]; but this represents the army at headquarters only, and considerable numbers of feudal tenants were fighting elsewhere, but were not enrolled.

A body of 375 knights represents about an eighteenth part of the maximum nominal strength of all England. Moreover,

[1] *Feudal England*, p. 246.     [2] *Parl. Writs*, vol. i. p. 197 onwards.
[3] Ibid., p. 228 onwards.

the individual retinues were very small. The Earl of Cornwall brought fourteen knights, himself being the fifteenth, an
exceptionally large retinue. The Earl of Surrey recognized
a *servitium debitum* of eleven, Gloucester of ten, but Oxford
of only three, and, among the barons, Roger de Mortimer and
Robert de Ros of six each, Peter Corbet of five, and a few
others of four. The very great majority of feudal tenants
were represented by but one to three lances.

One explanation of the lowness of the figures is that the
barons ' were bound to produce only the service due for the
demesne lands of their baronies[1].' A tenant might owe a
service of sixty knights, and having enfeoffed, let us say, fifty,
or divided part of his lands among sub-tenants owing to him
a collective service of fifty, he was therefore only bound to
produce the remaining ten for his demesne, or *dominium*, or
non-infeudated portion of the fief. The crown had already
a claim on the fifty, for all who held land of a certain value
could be called upon. But it is difficult to maintain the theory
without exact knowledge of the proportion of infeudated land
to demesne in every fief. Moreover, the fact that Edward
issued his writ for distraint of knighthood in 1278, the year
after this war, and probably because of the needs arising from
this war, tells against it. I know of no undoubted instances
where the phrase *servitium debitum* is used of service from the
demesne only. The Corbet fief was entirely infeudated, yet
we saw that Peter Corbet did a full service[2].

The other theory is that crown tenants were expected to
bring to the army a quota instead of a full number of knights.
The king bargained that a baron should provide six or ten
knights in place of possibly a hundred, and it was clearly
arranged what the number should be, for the baron ' recognized '
the service. As we shall see later, great feudatories were
expected to bring knights up to the covenanted number, adding a proportion of at least twice as many troopers ; lesser
tenants might make up a unit of two knights and six troopers
to represent five knights. In case any tenant, lay or clerical,

---

[1] General Wrottesley, *Collections of the William Salt Archaeological
Society*, vol. viii. 23.  [2] *Testa*, p. 45.

preferred to pay a fine *pro servitio*, there were the two systems of assessment; he might pay on the full nominal obligation in shillings when the sheriff called upon him, or he might offer immediately on the reduced obligation in marcs. Therefore the proportion of the marc to the shilling ought to be the proportion of the old to the new number. But we have seen some tenants losing, some gaining, as they paid in one or the other manner, and St. Albans and other houses still did their full service. Probably the king had made allowance, in settling the size of a quota, for an increase in wealth since the reigns of William I or Henry II, so that the ratio $13\frac{1}{3} : 1$ was not constant.

The principle of a quota is a very natural and a very reasonable one, being a sort of compromise. It would be alike unfair and inexpedient to insist upon the feudatories bringing to every war the whole number of their knights, for such a course would be equivalent to calling out all the reserves at once. The Angevin kings had frequently demanded the service of a third or a tenth of the feudal host, and the understanding was that, as a proportion was summoned, more than forty days' fighting was expected [1]. As a matter of fact, the greater feudatories, earls, and barons of some prominence, such as Mortimer, gave more than forty days' service in 1277, and again in 1282, without any complaint, as far as we know. Edward never wanted to vex his barons needlessly, and if he obtained an efficient force of cavalry by accepting a proportion in place of the whole, he lost none of his legal or customary rights over the baronage. Moreover, when once the quota was settled by a bargain between crown and feudatory, there could no longer be any dispute as to the exact amount of service which the latter owed. That there was such a bargain, well understood upon both sides, is seen in the acceptance of the quota by the crown, in the continuance of much unpaid service over the forty days, and also in the use of the very words *servitium debitum* to indicate the quota: *qui servicium debent Regi offerunt et recognoscunt servicium subscriptum.* Obviously a danger might suddenly crop up in the future.

[1] Stubbs, vol. ii. p. 293; Medley, p. 416.

Some baron might argue that he had fulfilled all his feudal duties by producing his quota, and that yet he could not be compelled to serve beyond the orthodox time. Such a crisis arose in 1298, when the Earls of Norfolk and Hereford were in a very quarrelsome mood. But no danger arose in the Welsh wars, for it was to the interest of the greater barons themselves, very many of them being also lords marchers, to fight the Welsh till they were conquered.

But if the principle of a quota was advantageous to a baron, by releasing him from the necessity of bringing his full number of knights, it benefited the crown more. Barons accustomed to raise large squadrons of a hundred or hundreds of horse in the king's service would be sorely tempted to raise them against the king. Even if not actually rebellious, they could cripple him at the critical point of some campaign by withdrawing their contingents under some excuse, e.g. that the forty days were over. This is practically what Norfolk and Hereford did in 1298, and so spoilt the effect of the victory of Falkirk. The argument is, that if these two could injure Edward's plans so seriously, though they were attended each only by his quota, much more would the crown have been a slave to the baronage if every baron brought to every war his full strength. In later days, when the system of raising troops for pay by contract was customary, the lords who enlisted men for the crown had all the machinery ready for enlisting them against the crown ; hence the troubles of Richard II and Henry VI. Edward I was certainly wise in recognizing the bargain by which a quota was considered to be the full *servitium debitum*.

Several facts support the theory. In 1282 Edward complained that the Sheriff of Somerset and Dorset accepted bribes to excuse the best and strongest men, and compelled inferior men to serve[1]. The context shows that the king referred to feudal service. The obvious inference is that the sheriffs, collecting the lesser crown tenants for war, that is to say, the men who owed the service of only a few knights, were expected to apply the principle of a quota, but to get the

[1] *Welsh Roll*, Nov. 12, 1282.

best men to join the quota, using even compulsion if need were.

The obligation of the Braose march was 78½ knights, the recognized quota seems to have been five[1]. Now when Edward conquered and allotted the lands of the Four Cantreds in 1282, he disdained to fix a high obligation; he conferred the lordship of Denbigh for a service of six knights, Bromfield for four, and Ruthin for three[2]. That is to say, he preferred to fix a low figure at once. This is in strong contrast to Henry II, who bestowed Meath for fifty and Leinster for a hundred. It was useless for Edward to create large fiefs and then to allow a quota of knights to represent the whole number; so he made the new fiefs small *ab initio*.

I would suggest that the great increase in the cost of equipment had much to do with the question. The knights of Edward I were altogether more heavily armoured than those of William I, and probably rode much more expensive horses. The valuable *dextrarii* of the barons and bannerets cost from 60 up to even 120 marcs[3]; one can hardly call them chargers, for they were of the heavy shire-horse type, slow, but capable of carrying a great weight. The humbler knights-bachelors rode *equi* costing from 20 to 40 marcs. We have noticed how the art of war had progressed since the day of Hastings. The cavalry then were lighter and more nimble, more able to manœuvre, but not very effective in shock of battle against the wall of Saxon shields. Now the horses were ponderous, and much more costly. When pay was given, the normal wages of a banneret were 4s. a day, of a knight 2s. Under Henry II a knight had 8d. But let us look onwards to Henry V. Except during a period after the Black Death, when the dearth of men and the needs of the crown more than doubled all wages of war, the rates of 4s. and 2s. were constant, being found in 1415. Between Edward I and Henry V mail had given place to plate, and the plate armour of at least the richest knights was complicated and therefore expensive; yet there was no difference in wages, whereas the century between

---

[1] See below, Table B.          [2] *Welsh Roll*, 1282, Oct. 7 and 16.
[3] *Exch. Acc.*, horse-inventories, especially $\frac{6}{39}$ and $\frac{6}{40}$.

Henry II and Edward I saw wages trebled. This is precisely the century which also saw the heavy feudal obligations cut down to a comparatively light proportion, when the principle of the quota was accepted.

The 'knights' or *milites* of the Norman conquest correspond to the *servientes ad arma* of the thirteenth and the *scutiferi* or *armigeri* of the fourteenth century[1]. Such is the substance of an argument of Mr. Oman with which I agree in the main. Mr. Round[2] has sharply criticized him as being ignorant of the meaning of tenure by serjeanty, and certainly *servientes* in the two writs which he quotes has the appearance of meaning tenants by serjeanty. I venture to suggest that the confusion arises from the word being used in two senses. In a war, *serviens* means simply a soldier, *serviens ad arma* a mounted soldier. Except during that period of inflated wages after the Black Death, the horsemen next to the knights, the rank and file of the heavy cavalry, or we might call them troopers, drew their 1s. a day from the wars of Edward I to those of Henry V, in spite of the rapid development from mail to plate. These men may have been sub-tenants of feudal lords or small land-owners. Naturally the officer who enlisted them sought to find men born and bred in the country and able to ride. But there is nothing to suggest that they must be sub-tenants or landowners, or that *serviens* in the sense of a soldier came from *serviens* meaning a tenant. Therefore, to an amendment of Mr. Oman's argument I should entirely agree. The Conqueror allotted lands to his followers for the service of so many horsemen equipped according to the custom of the period, that is knight-service. As time went by, and the ideas of chivalry expanded, the word *miles* was applied to a superior horseman who had undergone the process of dubbing, *serviens ad arma* to the horseman of inferior birth or age. If the knight of Edward I had invariably a wage of 2s. and the trooper of 1s., while the knight of Henry II had only 8d. a day, it is easy to understand why the principle of a quota was introduced. It would have been unjust to expect a baron of the thirteenth century to raise a number of knights, drawing

[1] *Art of War*, p. 365.     [2] *Commune of London*, p. 61.

2*s*., each equal to the number of horsemen on the condition of whose service William originally granted the lands.

But Mr. Oman is not right in assuming that *servientes ad arma* and *scutiferi* or *armigeri* were words used in different centuries to designate the same men. A very large number of pay-rolls prove that already, in the thirteenth century, all these words and others were used as absolutely synonymous, and all referring to the horseman drawing 1*s*. a day. *Servientes* is usually found in the marshal's registers of feudal retinues. *Armigeri* sometimes designates the young esquires of good birth, sometimes troopers of any condition. In the pay-rolls *scutiferi* is the more common word, in the inventories of horses, *valetti*. *Homines ad arma* was a generic term for all the heavy cavalry, knights included. *Armati* is used in the same sense by chroniclers, but in the fourteenth century was technically confined to light cavalry. Later on, Jehan le Bel and Froissart used *armures de fer* in a generic sense. *Constabularii* must have had the same meaning, being members of a *constabularia* or unit of heavy cavalry; in the documents they are the centenars or mounted officers of the county levies of infantry, at the same pay of 1*s*., and under the same necessity to ride a fully barded horse.

Not often do we find the names of the *servientes* or *scutiferi* given, but when we do we can glean much information. The marshal's registers give nearly all names, and we can trace how a few rose to be knights. The pay-rolls give names of the royal household; the *servientes regis ad arma* were most valuable men, were engaged in doing the king's business in many ways, looked after the transport and workmen, commanded crossbowmen, and so on, but very rarely received knighthood. But Eustace de Hacche, a prominent banneret of Welsh and Scottish wars, would seem to be the same as Eustace de Hacche the *serviens* of 1276; his promotion was rapid, and the manor given to him in Dorset, to hold during the royal pleasure, must have been a reward for services in war, and to enable him to support his new rank[1]. Fuller information comes from the inventories of horses. Complete

[1] *Pipe Roll*, 11 Edw. I.

rolls are extant for the years 1297 and 1298, on which the value of every horse is entered, with the name of the rider [1]; the former show the absolute total of the cavalry taken over to Flanders by Edward, the latter only the total of the cavalry in the king's pay in the Falkirk campaign, the retinues of feudal lords who did unpaid service being excluded. A great many *valetti* were in each war, but several contingents having been in Flanders, were reorganized to proceed to Scotland, new names appearing. Many who were *valetti* in Flanders appear as knights in Scotland, such as Robert de Tony, a lord marcher who had just succeeded to his father's march of Elvael; John de Vaux the younger, a tenant-in-chief who had also just succeeded his father; and Philip Paynel, who held land in Somerset over the value of £20 a year, and was thus liable to distraint of knighthood. Young men of good birth, it is thus proved, had to pass through the ranks, being *scutiferi* or esquires in the narrower sense of the word as aspirants to knighthood, and were ranked with the plebeian *scutiferi* in the wider sense as troopers at the 1*s.* wage. In the train of Hugh le Despenser in 1298 were two valets with very celebrated names, Giles de Argentine and Reginald de Cobham [2]. These must have been young esquires, who were destined to become famous in history, the one as the hero of Bannockburn on the English side, the other as one of the most prominent commanders under Edward III. As an interesting instance in later days, I would notice how the earliest record of the famous career of Nigel de Loring shows him to have been a trooper, drawing the orthodox shilling, at the siege of Dunbar in 1337–8 [3]; he was not attached to any retinue, but came to the army independently with a *socius*.

The qualification which separated the troopers of this kind from the light horsemen or hobelars—who, it may be remarked, were not an organized corps, and were very rarely found in the armies of Edward I—was that they should ride 'covered'

---

[1] *Exch. Acc.* $\frac{6}{28}, \frac{6}{37}, \frac{6}{39}, \frac{6}{40}$.

[2] Another Reginald de Cobham this same year is found in Norfolk's retinue.

[3] *Exch. Acc.* $\frac{20}{23}$.

horses. Whenever the mount was 'uncovered,' wages immediately fell to 6*d.* or 8*d.* Now, what was the 'covering' of horse-armour, which, in the thirteenth century, differentiated the occasional hobelar from the regular 1*s.* trooper? We are well acquainted with the appearance of the barded horse of the later days of plate. We can also be sure that Edward I and his well-mounted knights placed some skirting of chain mail over their horses. In an entry of a miscellaneous roll of 1277 [1] we find that 16*s.* were paid for two linen coverings to put under the mail, to prevent it from galling the horse: *pro duabus partibus lineorum coopt ad ponend super duos dextrar regis subt coopt ferr.* But the question does not concern the *dextrarius,* whose strength and bone could easily support the weight of its own armour, as well as of the armoured rider. The horse-inventories show that the valets rode mere *runcini,* the rounseys familiar to us from Chaucer; just a few of them were as highly priced as the *equi* of the knights, far below the value of the *dextrarii,* but about £5 to £8 was the average. Could such a horse bear an iron covering and an iron-clad rider? The evidence of the pay-rolls is very strong; *cum equo coop* is the definition of a trooper entitled to his shilling. But there might be a great deal of latitude. The rider might wear less mail than the knight, a shorter hauberk, and perhaps no leggings, and both he and his horse might have boiled leather in place of mail [2]. In fact, the normal equipment of a trooper was probably the same as that prescribed by the Statute of Winchester for the second class of the national militia. We must remember that the brasses and seals of the thirteenth and early fourteenth centuries show us the figures of men of high rank only mailed from head to foot. There are no illustrations of the troopers, and their equipment must have been lighter if they did not want to crush their £5 rounseys. Yet the rounseys had to be up to a certain weight, had to carry *homines ad arma, servientes ad arma,* or *scutiferi,* that is, men who had a certain amount of mail, and to wear some sort of covering. To come back to the original point, the trooper of Edward I was probably, in general equipment

[1] *Exch. Acc.* 3/15.                    [2] Hewitt, *passim.*

of defensive armour and mount, not unlike the knight of William I. The chief point of difference would be that he used a longer and heavier spear.

Hemingburgh's description of the battle of Falkirk is a *locus classicus*. He gives the cavalry as composed of 3,000 armed men on armed horses, and 4,000 armed men on non-armed horses[1]. These figures are impossible. No one who has studied the documents can admit that England ever sent out 7,000 cavalry for a campaign. Neither do the documents allow that light-armed hobelars were raised in large numbers. But it is possible to admit that the knights and best-equipped troopers were to the troopers mounted on the cheapest rounseys in the proportion of three to four. Mostly knights and best troopers were in the front line of the charge; for the inventories show exactly how many horses of the paid portion of the cavalry were killed in the battle, and almost all of them were those of knights and superior troopers. Yet even the inferior troopers were all shilling men; there is no pay-roll extant of this campaign, but a large number of rolls of the period prove conclusively this statement.

I have made this digression in order to go over the evidence, scanty at the best, which gives some idea of the status of a trooper. To prevent confusion, I propose to use this term henceforward to designate the *servientes* of the feudal retinues and the *scutiferi* of paid corps, for under either name they were men of the same class, two being the equivalent of one knight, and I would repeat that young esquires of good birth and plebeians who could rarely aspire to knighthood were ranked together. There is this in common in both feudal and paid troops: a lord or a captain of stipendiaries might enlist sub-tenants if he chose—that was his own business—and the crown only required a certain number of horsemen.

If we return to the feudal quotas of 1277 and 1282, this question arises: Were the quotas actually of the exact registered strength? One thing is very clear. When a baron recognized a service of $x$ knights, and registered the names of precisely $x$ knights, we must allow for at least $2x$ troopers

[1] Hemingburgh, vol. ii. p. 173.

in attendance. The proportion is not a fixed one. In paid corps two or three, even as many as five, troopers appear with each knight. The baron, therefore, in producing $x$ knights to satisfy the marshal, may have had a total number of $3x$ or $4x$ horsemen. All the earls, except Lincoln, who for a *servitium debitum* of $7\frac{1}{2}$ registered six knights and three troopers, registered knights only ; so did a few other barons. Most of the lesser barons owing a service of $x$ knights registered $\frac{1}{2}x$ knights and $x$ troopers, and this satisfied the marshal. I think that it can be made out from the facts of the wars that feudal etiquette made a strong distinction between the earls and the others as regards the service of the quotas. An earl, having the number of his quota fixed, was expected to bring that number of knights plus an adequate complement of troopers, and moreover was expected to serve —and to maintain his status as a great feudatory did serve— over the forty days. The lesser barons were allowed to make up their quotas of knights and troopers equivalent to the recognized number, and when the forty days were up, were taken into pay if they chose to continue in the field. To this last statement Roger de Mortimer, Robert de Ros, and possibly some others, may be exceptions. They were as proud of their status as any earl might be, and the Mortimers and Corbets and their neighbours wanted no pay as an incentive to fight the Welsh ; but as documentary evidence is lacking, it is difficult to prove more than this, that they served in 1277 at least with their own resources. But whatever the Salopians thought of the question of wages, the Cestrians had no pride, and though equally near to Wales, they frequently did their extra-feudal service for pay.

It is not likely that any baron brought a larger number of knights to a muster than what he actually registered. It is so common to find feudal service done according to the exact letter of the obligation that to go beyond would be strange. The Earl of Hereford, Pain de Chaworth, Walter de Huntercumbe, and others, owing the service of $\frac{1}{6}$ or $\frac{1}{4}$ of a knight, carefully registered a trooper *cum equo discooperto*. The Earls of Warwick and Norfolk, in 1282, recognized a service of six and five knights respectively, did not enter the names, but are registered as serving personally with a fitting following: *facit per se ipsum cum decenti comitiva*[1]. It is not likely that they brought more than their number of knights with a suitable number of troopers. Many barons spoke as if they were not sure what their quotas ought to be. The formula used by the earls is *ita quod si plus tunc*, or *ita quod si plus tunc, et si minus tunc*. Gloucester says *ita quod si inveniatur quod plus debeat, plus faciet*. This was probably the merest formula intended to guard the baron against possible extra claims against him in the future; he knew quite well the figure of his quota and clearly he limited himself to it, for exactly the same service was recognized in 1282 as in 1277, except that Warwick declared his service to be six knights in place of 6½[2]. Lancaster, bringing a retinue in 1282 and ignorant of his exact obligation, was very anxious, king's brother though he was, that if he had brought too large a number of men it should not be counted against him in the future; *quod non cedat ei in preiudicium si maius servicium Regi faciat ista vice quam facere teneatur.* The record of letters of protection may seem to tell the other way. On the patent roll of 1277, it is recorded that 170 men had protections from the king, seventy of them being also entered on the marshal's register, and 100 not. But many of these latter may have been in the following of lords marchers, or else were those *servientes* of the feudal units who, as we have seen, must be added wherever a lord gave in the names of knights only to represent his quota. This evidence gives four more names to Norfolk's retinue beyond those that he entered, two more to Cornwall's, and two to Lincoln's.

The lists of letters of protection in many rolls, a few pay-sheets, and the horse-inventories, when extant as in 1297 and 1298, can be compared with the quotas of 1277 and 1282, to show what was the average strength of each retinue during some twenty-five years. The case of the earls had better be taken separately, for they very rarely took pay. There is the exceptional case of the Earl of Lincoln, who had a squadron of paid horse at Montgomery in the spring of

[1] *Parl. Writs*, vol. i. p. 229.      [2] Ibid., p. 236.

1277 ; himself, six knights, and twenty-three troopers formed his own troop.    In the feudal muster the following summer, he registered the names of himself, five knights, and three troopers as satisfying his *servitium debitum* of 7½ knights.    Two of the knights and one trooper occur in each retinue[1], and it seems that thirty lances formed his normal strength.    He had men in pay again in 1282, but only for a few days while the main army was being collected, and did his service throughout most wars as a feudal duty.    Edmund, Earl of Lancaster, had in 1294 and 1295 some fifty lances, fourteen of them knights, with letters of protection ;  his son, Thomas, in 1298 had forty-five lances in pay, eleven of them knights, himself and his brother Henry included.    It does not follow that when a retinue was in pay it was of the same strength as when it was doing feudal service, but these coincidences strikingly show that the Lancaster retinue averaged about fifty strong, and one may guess that the same figure would represent Cornwall's average strength.    Warwick's will be seen to vary between twenty and forty, and his son, Guy, commanded a retinue of twenty-five in pay in Flanders and on the border of Scotland, doing on the latter occasion garrison duty before the king's army moved up for the main campaign of 1298.    The young Earl of Arundel—whose lands were held in wardship in 1277 and 1282, so that money in place of men was forthcoming from his Shropshire fief—had a troop of forty lances in pay at Berwick in the winter and early spring of 1298.    On the same occasion five earls had 500 horse in pay under contract, an entirely unprecedented occurrence which was due to the exigencies of the war in winter.    Arundel and Guy alike did feudal service in the summer.    Arundel's letters of protection were no more than four, but probably ten lances of William le Latimer are to be added, and Guy similarly had fourteen.

The fact is that the earls were opposed to the principle of pay.    The regular summer campaigns saw them all, except occasionally Lincoln or Thomas of Lancaster, serving as a feudal duty both in Wales and in Scotland ; the Flanders campaign was a thing apart.    Great feudatories on becoming

[1] *Patent Roll*, 1277, and *Marshal's Register*.

stipendiaries would lose caste. They had duties but they also had privileges, and to escape the duties for pecuniary advantage would be fatal to the privileges. I infer from the circumstances of Norfolk's and Hereford's action in 1298, that they looked to the performance of strict feudal duties as a power over the crown, and they had a better chance to make the crown feel their power in the Scottish wars. In the Welsh wars they fought loyally, but they could not avoid being loyal outwardly as long as their own marches were in danger. The really loyal earls of the reign are Lancaster and Cornwall—the king's kinsmen, it is true, but the next reign was to prove that kinsmanship was not necessarily a bond of loyalty—Lincoln, Warwick, Arundel when he obtained possession of his estates, and, in spite of his 'rusty sword' melodrama, Surrey. Gloucester, and in a less degree Hereford, were assertive and almost rebellious at times. The theory which accounts for their action in the civil war accounts for all their actions. They posed as important lords marchers, hostile to Llewelyn, and at the same time resenting the king's interference with their march rights. We shall be able to trace their change of attitude towards the crown from year to year, as the crown needed their services against the Welsh or wanted to extinguish their march rights. Norfolk showed no signs of insubordination before 1297, and I believe that his conduct then and afterwards was the outcome of his resentment at Edward's treatment of him in the last Welsh war of 1294. Gloucester being dead, Norfolk joined himself to Hereford as a willing ally, and so we get the celebrated scene when he would 'neither go nor hang.' Now, whether personally loyal to Edward or not, all the earls did their feudal service in war, served for long periods over forty days, and only in the rare instances given above raised horse in the king's pay. I have not mentioned William or Aymer de Valence. Probably the others regarded them as foreign intruders and adventurers, and they had no large fief in England. Hardly ever is either of them styled in a document Earl of Pembroke, and Aymer led large contingents of paid horse as a professional captain.

The following table gives all the figures which I have been

able to collect. Surrey, it ought to be mentioned, declared eleven knights as his due service; but four he produced as a protest of his rights over Stamford, the citizens contesting and also producing men to do the service for them, and this leaves him with seven knights, nearly on a par with Lincoln and Warwick. The first column indicates that certain fees are entered on the pipe rolls as due from some honour or from some fief by the name of a deceased tenant. In the last column, where the evidence comes from letters of protection, the retinue may have been much stronger; the clerk who drew up the roll did not necessarily enter the names of all soldiers who had protections, and many would serve without them. But internal evidence seems to show that some retinues appear in full, for instance Lancaster's in 1294 and 1295.

Lastly, I would add that on reading over the marshal's register one is tempted to guess that there is some omission; five earls and their retinues are entered under one county. Have we to add men from their other fiefs? I believe that this would be an error, and that the whole number of knights is entered, as has been just argued. The clerk of the register probably entered the names of the counties carelessly, for he was concerned with the men and not the places they came from. That this statement is true is seen in Lincoln's case. His retinue of $7\frac{1}{2}$ is entered under Suffolk, and later on he is credited with a *servitium debitum* of five under Lincolnshire and Chester; but the second entry is cancelled, as clearly the five were already included in the $7\frac{1}{2}$.

Norfolk registered his own name as serving in person for his office as marshal, presumably offering no other service for his inheritance of the honour of Strigul and other lands from the Marshal family. Hereford similarly registered himself in his office as constable, three knights for his English fief, and $1\frac{2}{3}$—a knight, a trooper, and a light horseman—for his Braose march. Therefore, Norfolk's quota of five has to be compared with his 211 English fees, and Hereford's quota of three with his 125, just as Gloucester's quota of ten with his 455. The ratio of the reduced to the nominal is therefore 1 : 42 or 1 : 45. But let us add the unnamed, but assuredly present *servientes*, and we have a ratio very nearly of $1 : 13\frac{1}{3}$, the shilling to the marc, on which basis the calculation of the quotas was probably made.

TABLE A.—THE EARLS.

| Number of fees as in pipe rolls. | | Quota in 1277[1]. | Strength of retinues in lances in certain wars. |
|---|---|---|---|
| 263 in all { 131. Ferrars<br>60. Montfort<br>38. Various<br>plus Lancaster | Lancaster | | 46 to 50. Wales 1294: letters<br>21. Flanders 1297: horses: (son)<br>45. Scotland 1298: horses: (sons) |
| 220 { 125. Various<br>95. Wallingford<br>plus Cornwall | Cornwall | 15 | |
| 455 { 261. Gloucester<br>141. Clare<br>52. Various | Gloucester | 10 | (46. Scotland 1298: letters:<br>Ralph de Monthermer, who<br>married his widow.) |
| 245 { 117. Lacy and Salisbury<br>68. Earl of Chester<br>60. Winchester<br>Plus co. of Chester | Lincoln | $7\frac{1}{2}$ | 30. Montgomery 1277: pay<br>14. Scotland 1298: letters |
| 60. Warenne<br>plus Yorks. and Lincolnshire | Surrey | 7 | 26. Wales 1294: letters<br>18. Wales 1295: letters<br>46. Scotland 1298: letters |
| 135 { 103. Beauchamp<br>32. Plessetis: Oxon.<br>plus co. of Chester | Warwick | $6\frac{1}{2}$<br>(or 6<br>in<br>1282) | 21. Wales 1294: letters<br>36. Wales 1295: letters<br>27. Flanders 1297: horses: (son)<br>25. Scotland 1298: pay: (son)[2]<br>14. Scotland 1298: letters: (son)[3] |
| 279 { 211. Bigod & Giffard<br>$67\frac{1}{2}$. Marshal | Norfolk | 6 | 28. Wales 1294: letters<br>50. Scotland 1298: letters |
| 151 { 60. Mandeville<br>30. Bohun<br>35. Various<br>26. Braose | Hereford | 5 | 12. Wales 1294: letters<br>14. Scotland 1298: letters |
| 32. | Oxford | 3 | 12. Scotland 1298: letters |
| 89 { 32. Shropshire<br>57. Other counties | Arundel | | 40. Scotland 1298: pay[2]<br>14. Scotland 1298: letters[3] |

In the next table I have grouped the lords marchers, most of whom were also tenants-in-chief in England, and in some cases we know how many knights they owed for their marches and how many for their English fiefs. The case of Roger de

[1] *Parl. Writs*, vol. i. p. 197, &c.  [2] Spring campaign.
[3] Summer campaign as a feudal duty.

Mortimer is most interesting. He and Ralph de Tony both laid claim to Elvael, and each offered a service of two knights to substantiate his claim. Mortimer also brought one for the rest of his Braose inheritance, but none for Builth. His normal retinue is a doubtful quantity, but six knights would mean at least twenty or thirty lances in all. In 1282 he will be found garrisoning his own castles of the march with twenty-five horse and eighty-two foot at his own expense; he once had seventeen lances in royal pay in his *comitiva* at Montgomery, but otherwise the documents shed no light on his forces. His successor, Roger l'Estrange, had permanently a troop of twenty, and his son took also twenty to Scotland in 1298. Geoffrey de Geneville, lord of Ludlow, owed 2½ knights as having married one of the co-heiresses of Walter de Lacy, one-tenth of the nominal obligation; he acted as assistant-marshal for the Earl of Norfolk in 1282, and as marshal in Flanders in 1297 when the earl was deposed, having then a special retinue of twenty-eight lances. Hardly ever are lords marchers found to be taking the king's pay, for they evidently wanted to maintain their status as independent of the crown. Thus, Geoffrey de Camville had a troop of thirteen lances in pay in the May of 1282 for one week only, the men coming from his English fief and being paid only during the period of mobilization in England; as soon as he came into Wales he served at his own expense. The king warmly thanked him for this gratuitous service [1], implying very clearly that he might have continued to draw the pay for his English troop though fighting in the immediate neighbourhood of his march of Llanstephan. Pain de Chaworth with his own troop fought at his own expense in 1277, though he had 75 paid English lances raised by other bannerets. William de Braose once or twice had a few horse in pay in 1282 and 1287. Very rarely did these marchers go abroad or to Scotland. Robert de Tony went to Flanders, and also to Scotland with eighteen lances, where also John Tregoz had twelve. The Cliffords practically ceased to be marchers, and all their interests were in Westmorland and Yorkshire.

---

[1] *Welsh Roll*, 10 Edw. I, July 27.

## TABLE B.—THE LORDS MARCHERS.

| Number of fees. | | Recognized quotas in 1277. | |
|---|---|---|---|
| ? Salop, &c. | Roger de Mortimer | 3 | |
| ? Radnor | | 2 | For Elvael |
| 26⅛. Braose | | 1 | But Builth 'in manu regis' |
| 23. Herefordshire | Robert de Mortimer | 3 | Of Richard's Castle |
| 5. Salop | Peter Corbet | 5 | |
| 1. Staffs<br>25. Ewyas Lacy | Theobald de Verdun | 3½ | |
| 25. Ewyas Lacy | Geoffrey de Geneville | 2½ | 28 lances in 1297 : horses |
| 2. Hampshire<br>19. Ewyas Harold | John Tregoz | 3 | 12 lances in 1298 : horses |
| | Ralph de Tony | 2 | 18 lances in 1298 : horses : (son) |
| | Roger de Clifford, senior | 1½ | 'Pro Monemue' |
| ? Wiltshire<br><br>9. Herefordshire | John Giffard | 3 | One knight 'in baronia sua'<br>Four knights entered, two of which cancelled, for wife's lands[1]. |
| 10. Sussex<br>Gower | William de Braose | 2½<br>1 | One knight recognized for march |
| 14. Glouc. & Hants<br>44. Bruere<br><br>Kidwelly | Pain de Chaworth | 1 | Does not know his liability<br>Three light horse for Kidwelly |
| 56. Devon | Geoffrey de Camville[2] | 2 | This service is recognized for English fiefs only. |
| 10. Somerset | Nicholas FitzMartin | 3 | |
| 27. Various cos. | Reginald FitzPeter | 2 | |
| 26⅛. Braose | John de Hastings | | |
| 15. Herefordshire | Earl of Lancaster | | |
| 26⅛. Braose | Earl of Hereford | 1⅔ | |
| 67½. Strigul | Earl of Norfolk | 1 | Served in person as marshal |

[1] The march of Clifford, also the commot and part of the town of Llandovery, came to him through his wife.

[2] His son, William de Camville, served as the knight of Pain de Chaworth.

TABLE C.—BARONS: TENURE IN ENGLAND.

| Number of fees as in pipe rolls. | Barons. | Kn. | Tr. | Retinues in various wars, total number of lances. |
|---|---|---|---|---|
| (?) Chester, Beds, Herefordshire | Reginald de Grey | 2 | | 26. Wales 1277 : pay<br>35. Wales 1295 : pay |
| 69. Linc., Norfolk, Sussex | Robert de Tateshale | 3 | | 15. Wales 1277 : pay<br>15. Wales 1282 : pay<br>20. Wales 1294 : letters<br>12. Flanders 1297 : horses : (son) |
| 40. Norfolk, Sussex<br>2½. Chester | Roger de Monthaut (in wardship) | | | 20. Wales 1295 : pay<br>18. Scotland 1298 : horses : (son) |
| 7. Northumberland<br>(?) Mother's inheritance | Walter de Huntercumbe | 3 | 1½ | 10. Wales 1282 : pay<br>13. Wales 1295 : pay<br>16 to 32. Scotland |
| 2. Essex | Ralph Pipard | 1 | 2 | 10. Wales 1295 : pay<br>21. Scotland 1298 : horses |
| 2. Notts, Linc. | Philip de Kyme | 1 | 2 | 12. Wales 1282 : pay<br>13. Wales 1295 : pay |
| 26. Yorks., Linc., Northumb.<br>33. Leic. (wife) | Robert de Ros<br>1277<br>1282 | 4<br><br>3 | 4<br><br>6 | 10. Wales 1277 : pay |
| 18. Yorks., Linc. | Baldwin Wake | 4 | | 16. Wales 1294 : letters : (John Wake) |
| 63. Essex | Robert Fitzwalter | 3 | | 15. Wales 1282 : pay |
| 36. Yorks., Northumb. | John de Vescy | 3 | | 15. Montgomery 1277 : pay |
| 5. Essex | John de Vaux | 1 | | 10. Montgomery 1277 : pay |
| | William de Leyburn | 2 | | 10. Montgomery 1277 : pay<br>10. Wales 1282 : pay<br>23. Flanders 1297 : horses<br>16. Scotland 1298 : horses |
| Two fees each in Westmorland, and others in Yorkshire | Roger de Leyburn<br>Roger de Clifford, junior | 2 | 5<br>1 | 14. Scotland 1296 : horses : (son)<br>35. Scotland 1298 : horses : (son) |
| 69. Lincolnshire | Gilbert de Gaunt | 2 | 2 | 12. Flanders 1297 : horses : (son) |
| 34 (?) Yorkshire | William de Greystock | 2 | 4 | |
| 35. Lincolnshire | Edmund d'Eyncourt | | 4 | |
| 24. Herts and Kent | Alex. de Balliol | 3 | | 10. Wales 1277 : pay |

TABLE C.—BARONS: TENURE IN ENGLAND (*continued*).

| Number of fees as in pipe rolls. | Barons. | Kn. | Tr. | Retinues in various wars, total number of lances. |
|---|---|---|---|---|
| 35. Northumb. Essex | John de Balliol 'pro Devorgilla' | 1 | 1 | |
| 11½. Essex | Robert & Richard de Bruce, 'pro Roberto patre.' | 2 | | 11. Wales 1282: Robert<br>8. Wales 1282: Richard |
| 92. Devon | Hugh de Courtenay | | 6 | 12. South Wales 1282: pay<br>12. Scotland 1298: horses |
| 11. Somerset | Hugh Pointz | 1 | | 4. South Wales 1277: pay<br>.6. South Wales 1282: pay<br>6. Scotland 1298: horses |
| (?) | Alan Plukenet | 1 | | 10. South Wales 1277: pay<br>10 to 13. South Wales 1282: pay<br>14. Scotland 1296: horses |
| 25. Bedfordshire | Ralph Daubeny | 1 | | 10. South Wales 1277: pay<br>12 to 18. South Wales 1282: pay |
| 8. Gloucestershire | Roger de Molis | 2 | | 10. South Wales 1277: pay<br>10. North Wales 1282: pay |
| 43. Somerset ? | John de Mohun | 3 | | 10. South Wales 1277: pay<br>10. South Wales 1282: pay: (brother) |
| 5. Gloucestershire ? plus | Maurice de Berkeley | 3 | | His son has 15, and grandson 11 in retinue of Aymer de Valence |
| 10. Norfolk 1. Hants | William de Valence | | | His son Aymer has<br>50. Flanders 1297: horses<br>50. Scotland 1298: horses |
| ¼. Leicestershire ? Worcester | Hugh le Despenser | | | 15. Wales 1294: letters<br>25. Scotland 1296: horses<br>50. Scotland 1298: horses |

In Table C it will be seen that almost every baron at one time or another served the king for pay, most of them on several occasions. Interesting cases of exact service are those of Ralph Pipard and Philip de Kyme [1], who, owing only the service of two knights, came each in person with two troopers. Walter de Huntercumbe brought almost as many lances as his full obligation demanded, also Maurice de

---

[1] Philip de Kyme was also enfeoffed for the service of fourteen knights as a sub-tenant of the Earl of Lancaster; *Inq. p. mortem*, p. 142.

Berkeley. The quota of others will be seen to range from a fifth to a twenty-fifth part of the nominal. Those who brought knights and troopers are clearly not to be credited with a retinue larger than what they registered, but the three Berkeley knights, Maurice himself with his son and one other, would represent a troop of ten lances. The cases of Grey and Clifford are peculiar ; Grey was the chief warrior of Chester, and later on became justiciar, and when he recognized a service of two knights, but had squadrons of twenty-five or thirty-five lances in pay on other occasions, he is not to be supposed to have actually had a feudal retinue during the forty days some twelve or seventeen times stronger than the number registered ; Clifford's son was later on a great man on the borders of Scotland, and therefore to compare the father's small feudal retinue with the son's large one of twenty years later would be misleading. Aymer de Valence and Hugh le Despenser in the days of the Scottish wars also led large retinues out of proportion to their importance as tenants-in-chief. The normal paid troop of the Welsh wars was some ten or, more rarely, fifteen lances strong, and in the later days of the wars in Scotland the general tendency was to enlist large troops, professional soldiers serving without regard to their feudal status.

If we allow that the tenants-in-chief were not likely to have brought to the feudal muster more knights than they registered with the marshal, but that they had troopers two or three times more in number than the knights, we can calculate that the army of 1277 came to some 850 lances, of whom 650 were at headquarters with the king. The household cavalry and the mounted crossbowmen may raise the figures to 1,000 and 800 respectively. In 1282 the 123 barons and knights may represent a total of 450 to 500, with the unregistered retinue of the Earl of Lancaster added, this being the strength at headquarters only. The horse of the lords marchers is a doubtful quantity.

These are brigades of tolerable strength. Were they good fighting material ? Returning to our discussion of the battles of Muret and Lewes, we remember how the elder Simon de

Montfort personally arrayed his whole force, war-hardened
veterans and fanatics though they were, evidently because he
could not trust this work to subordinates, while the son had
to do the same with his raw and inexperienced Englishmen.
There was very little real military training in those days, and
the English barons, except the lords marchers, had had hardly
any experience.    It is to be noticed that men who had served
abroad, Otto de Grandison, Hugh de Turberville, Luke de
Tany, the two latter having held the post of Seneschal of
Gascony [1], were brought to the front in Wales.    Tany, indeed,
conspicuously failed in war, but he was given an independent
command in 1282 obviously because of his supposed experience.    The rout of his knights near Bangor in that year was
due to a panic which proves how poor was the material.    The
rout of Stirling Bridge or Bannockburn equally proves the
inability of the English to rally and restore a fight in spite
of numbers still superior to the enemy ; the defeat of part of
an army led to panic, and panic in each case led to the
evacuation of almost the whole of Scotland.    Even the first
charge at Falkirk was unsuccessful, and Falkirk might have
been a previous Bannockburn if Edward's skill had not turned
the battle.    The conclusion is that without an able commander-in-chief the cavalry of the close of the thirteenth
century were disorganized, personal bravery never compensating for lack of organized skill.    Pride was the great fault of
the period ; one might say it was the personal fault of the
feudal baron.    The more deeply lying fault was want of
discipline due to want of proper subordination of commands.

Let us picture the feudal army of 1277 at the very outset
of Edward's series of wars.    The king has a genius for war
which he has shown at Evesham, and has had experience
also in the East.    He has two hereditary officials, a constable
and marshal, who have not as yet shown capacity for war.
He has some half a dozen capable barons and bannerets,
some of them possessing a record for skill and experience,
others whose skill will be brought out in the coming wars ;
the Earl of Lincoln has done good service quite recently on

[1] Rymer, June 5, 1272.

the upper Severn against Llewelyn before the feudal army was mobilized; Reginald de Grey has served against the faction of Montfort; Robert de Tibotot, Otto de Grandison, John de Vescy, and a few others are destined to prove their worth in war, and the fact that the king puts them in the front in 1277 shows that he knows something of their worth already. Marchers like Pain de Chaworth and Roger de Mortimer, and we may add John Giffard, are able men, but are now occupied in the southern or middle marches, and thus are not available at headquarters. There are several earls at headquarters, each with a 'decent' retinue, several barons with retinues of perhaps ten lances in strength, and several lesser tenants-in-chief with two or three lances each. There is absolutely no combination. The king has himself to create an organization among them. At present he is a commander-in-chief with many captains, but no hierarchy of commands from himself down to the men and no experienced staff. It is this which he has to create. So far we have pictured the feudal cavalry. The king has also to create an organization for the transport, to educate infantry, to combine various arms, and to utilize the fleet of the Cinque Ports. He has the class of men at hand who will help him to organize and to create army traditions—Lincoln, and it is fair to add Warwick, Grey and Tibotot, the future Justiciars of Chester and South Wales, his energetic secretary, Antony Bek, and a score of bannerets—Alan Plukenet, Eustace de Hacche, Hugh de Turberville, Grandison, the future first Justiciar of North Wales, and John de Havering, his deputy and successor. But while the king and his picked bannerets are creating, it is lucky that Llewelyn was overawed in 1277; there are evil days in store in the second war, when mercenaries from Gascony will have to be fetched up to restore the fighting tone. If twenty-one years later, in spite of Edward's training, the feudal barons throw discipline to the winds, scoff at the warning of Antony Bek—*vade missam celebrare si velis*—and indulge in a senseless cavalry charge straight at the rings of Scottish pikes without waiting for the king's reserve and the infantry, of what deadly folly might they not have been guilty in the first Welsh war, when their ideas were much more raw? For twenty-one years the king has been organizing and educating, yet feudal pride nearly makes Falkirk a defeat; but the king restores, by combination of horse and foot, the battle which the feudal horsemen try to lose. After his death the lack of discipline is deplorable, and the result is Bannockburn. Some sensible men, probably men of the rank of the professional bannerets, are determined to succeed, submit to discipline, return to the tactics of Edward I and improve them, avenge Bannockburn at Halidon Hill, and prepare the way to Crecy.

Therefore the work which Edward I had to do from 1277 onwards, which he could not complete because the baronial pride was too strong even for him, which was quite abandoned under his son, and which was resumed and carried to a triumphant development under his grandson, was the work of organization. The key was the systematic use of pay. The paid squadrons under professional captains could be combined, and were more effective than the incoherent units of a feudal host. The lesson being learnt, even the earls became paid professional soldiers in the Hundred Years' War. Of course there was a new and great danger ahead. The powerful earl, being both a feudal territorial lord and a professional soldier, became the rebel, so that the development of the system of Edward I produced in a bad form the exact evil which he set himself to avoid, namely civil war. But between him and Henry VI there were great military triumphs which his military reforms first made possible.

Pay produces discipline, and naturally leads to a subordination of commands. The baron or banneret raises by contract 100 lances ; we may fairly call it a squadron. It is composed of troops of varying strength, the captain's own troop some thirty or forty strong, the remainder under less prominent bannerets, who take sub-contracts, perhaps ten or fifteen strong. The squadron is thus an organized unit. The squadrons joined together to form a brigade give the king the subordination of commands which he wants, though even yet the discipline is not perfect. The earliest instances of such troops in the king's pay, contract being reasonably inferred from the details, occur in 1277. Wages were issued for forty days at a time, clearly in imitation of the feudal forty, and as the needs of the war demanded and the men were willing to renew their contract, a second and a third period of paid service was done. The Earl of Warwick had such a squadron for 120 days at Chester from January to May, probably 125 lances strong, but the details are not extant. Lincoln had at Montgomery for exactly the same time [1], three periods of forty days, 101 men of all ranks, himself included and drawing a banneret's pay of 4s.; his own troop was thirty strong, two other troops fifteen each, three ten each, one five, and one six. Pain de Chaworth at Carmarthen had seventy-five lances [2]; himself a lord marcher and fighting near his own lands he took no pay, and one can imagine that his own troop was twenty-five strong, thus making up the full hundred; five troops were of ten lances each, and the others of irregular strength. He served for eighty days from the same January.

The next August, immediately the forty days of feudal service expired, we find that some of the retinues were taken into pay, and especially one squadron under Reginald de Grey. His own troop was of twenty-five lances, Robert de Tateshale had fifteen, and four other bannerets ten each [3]; Robert de Ros contributed ten troopers without knights, and it certainly seems that, had the latter come in person with knights, he would have raised that particular troop to twenty and the whole squadron to 100; it looks as if he took a sub-contract and did not perform it in full, and, as he never at a later period had men in pay but did feudal service again in 1282, he may have repented of lowering himself to being a stipendiary. This squadron under Grey is of particular interest, as the date coincides with the expiry of the feudal forty days, and we can picture the tenants of Chester and their comrades combining various small units of horse, which had just done feudal service, into organized and fairly strong troops. As was

---

[1] *Exch. Acc.* $\frac{3}{12}$.                   [2] Ibid. $\frac{3}{13}$.

[3] *Pipe Roll*, 8 Edw. I, under heading ' Flint.'

suggested above, the size of the retinues now in pay is not to be taken to prove that Grey, for instance, had been already serving as his feudal duty with the same number. The service of the same men in 1282 cannot be traced, but on one occasion that year Tateshale had fifteen lances, and two other bannerets ten each, at Hope castle under Grey's command[1], whose whole squadron may have again been about 100 strong. In 1295 he had out once more 108 lances, his own troop being thirty-five[2].

In the April of 1282 Alan Plukenet drew forty days' pay in advance for a squadron just short of 100 men[3] who were mobilized at Gloucester to proceed to South Wales. His troops were of rather irregular strength, himself and four other bannerets having thirteen, nine, twelve, or fifteen lances each, and seven knights four or six each.

In these cases, especially where the round numbers occur and the existence of a contract is fairly marked, the troop may be made up in many ways ; the banneret may have two knights and seven troopers with him, or three knights and six troopers, to form a unit of ten men. One would suppose that the sub-contract was for ten or fifteen men as the case might be, and then the banneret made up his unit as he chose.

With all its faults the feudal system lent itself to the new one. Tenants-in-chief in 1277 and 1282, instead of bringing their small units of horse to the general incoherent muster, are in a few cases found serving under an earl. Thus Ralph Pipard in 1277, though recognizing the service of himself and two troopers as performing his own feudal obligation, was also entered in the feudal retinue of the Earl of Lancaster, whose sub-tenant he was, in 1282 was in Cornwall's, and in 1295 was in Grey's paid squadron. Baldwin Wake was with the Earl of Gloucester in 1277, and offered the service of his own four knights for the second forty days of the campaign ; John de St. John, a notable warrior, and two other tenants-in-chief were also Gloucester's men in 1282. Walter de Huntercumbe alternately did feudal service and paid service

[1] *Misc. Chanc.* $\frac{1}{2}$.　　　　[2] *Exch. Acc.* $\frac{5}{18}$.　　　　[3] Ibid. $\frac{1}{4}$.

with ten or twelve lances, and in 1285 was in Cornwall's retinue. Finally, Huntercumbe and Pipard, and others like them, became professional soldiers, and regularly organized paid troops. The history of the Berkeleys is even more instructive. There were four members of the family, two named Maurice and two Thomas. The elder Maurice and Thomas served in 1277 as tenants-in-chief in the feudal army; Thomas and the younger Maurice were in 1294 under the banner of the Earl of Norfolk, while their neighbours, west-countrymen and tenants-in-chief like themselves, John de Columbers, Nicholas de Carew, and John de Rivers, were in the same army under the banner of William de Valence. Finally, in 1297, Thomas and Maurice made a formal contract with young Aymer de Valence to maintain knights and troopers at a fixed fee in peace, ready to serve at the usual wages when war broke out, themselves as bannerets, Thomas the younger, Columbers, Carew, Rivers, and two others as knights, each banneret to have two esquires, each knight one, besides troopers. Reinforced for active service by more troopers the squadron went over to Flanders with Aymer, and next year was in the charging line at Falkirk. The professional career was not, however, very lucrative, and Aymer fell into debt. Thus the original contract had to be modified, both it and the revised contracts being extant [1].

The captain of the paid squadron was usually a man of some status. The bannerets who led the troops were usually tenants-in-chief, but with rather small feudal obligations in many cases. Otto de Grandison is an exception. Often they were landowners living near to each other and to their captain. That 'banneret' was purely a military title is proved by the promotion of many a successful soldier from the rank of knight-bachelor, the step being clear from entries in pay-rolls. Barons were already bannerets by presumptive right, but any soldier could earn the right to fly a square banner. But there was a prejudice, one might almost say a rule, in favour of the prominent soldier being a landowner. So we

[1] Mr. Bain's *Calendar of Documents relating to Scottish History*, Nos. 905, 981, 1004 ; *Exch. Acc.* $\frac{6}{27}$ and $\frac{6}{39}$, horse-inventories.

find Edward granting a landed status to Eustace de Hacche, to Hugh de Turberville, to his favourite Gascon leader of mercenaries, William de Monte Revelli, and others. We remember how the great Chandos was not a banneret until a time as late in his career as the eve of the battle of Najara ; his story proves that such an officer must be a real fighter and must have land to support his rank[1], for he got his step after he had obtained the great estate of St. Sauveur in Normandy, on the first campaign after he had obtained it. Edward III often made grants to his bannerets to enable them to maintain their position. Huntercumbe and Tateshale, Pipard and Kyme, were not as great men as Chandos and Audley, Felton and Calverley, but were good forerunners. The willingness of these men to help Edward I to create an army tradition must have been very useful to him.

If Edward's purpose was to raise an efficient cavalry, which by the very system employed to raise it would fall into coherent units, which could be called to serve at any time and for any time, and which would in fact become professional because paid, his next object was to find a good recruiting ground. This question did not directly affect the great feudatories, who evidently accepted the principle of a quota. It was rather a question of reaching the smaller crown tenants, the freemen, and the feudal sub-tenants among whom the greater feudatories had parcelled out their fiefs. Edward was not an innovator. His measures show him to have merely extended the national system of defence as it already existed. The assize of arms of Henry II organized the militia, and defined what may be called the first class of the army ; every tenant-in-chief was to keep as many sets of armour and arms, mail and helmet, shield and lance, as he owed knights from his demesne ; on infeudated land every knight owing service was to have ready a similar set ; also every free non-tenant possessing goods or lands beyond the value of 16 marcs a year. The supplementary assize of Henry III raised the limit to £15 and specified a horse as well as the armour. Edward's writ for distraint of knighthood in 1278 went

---

[1] Hewitt, *Ancient Armour*, vol. ii. p. 10.

one step further. He did not regard himself as introducing anything new, for he claimed that 'we and our ancestors have been wont' to exact the taking up of knighthood[1]. He simply widened out that superior class of the militia to include all those qualified for knighthood, *qui habent viginti libratas terrae vel feodum unius militis integrum valens viginti libras, de quocunque teneant,* that is to say, lesser crown tenants, sub-tenants, and tenants in socage, 'the most thoroughly English part of the population.' The limit was fixed at £20, but varied during the reign, and in fact the procedure varied considerably[2]. Sometimes the sheriffs were ordered to enforce knighthood, sometimes they merely warned those who were qualified to hold themselves in readiness for active service. Edward's object was not to make a fetish of knighthood, but to create a cavalry caste, a professional caste, connected, as by the nature of things was essential, with the land, of sufficient means to bear the cost of equipment, and accustomed to horses. His next step was to pass the Statute of Winchester in 1285, by which the two assizes were brought up to date. The second class of the militia was defined to include all those whose landed property was between the limits of £15 and £20, or who had goods to 40 marcs; they were to have armour and arms of inferior quality and horses, and they would supply the troopers of a cavalry on active service. Below them came four classes of infantry. The obvious aim of the legislation is simplification. The whole of the national army was classified, arms were viewed twice a year so that it might be ready at an emergency, and in theory it was ready for any call. But here the theory stopped short. As an arm of offence the national army could not be used as it stood. From the highest class to the lowest, from the men distrained to take knighthood down to the mere knifemen of the poorest infantry, a sensible commander would enrol only the best men.

It is hardly likely that Edward was only thinking of the fines to which he would be entitled from those who refused to take knighthood. The question of distraint seems to run on

[1] *Select Charters*, p. 457.       [2] *Parl. Writs*, vol. i. *passim*.

much the same lines as the burning question of scutage in previous reigns. All military legislation comes primarily from military needs; a William allots lands for so many knights' fees as a means for raising cavalry, a Henry allows money compositions for the sake of convenience, the scutage being assessed at the rate which will just allow a substitute. Mr. Round acknowledges that scutage was not the most important element in the royal revenue of the twelfth century[1]. When we come to Edward I, we find that in his war-budget direct taxation and customs were vastly more productive than fines in lieu of service. The original purpose of distraint was not connected with money; this hardly admits of argument. Neither can it be argued that a king would try always and in every campaign to raise the maximum force of cavalry. If we are right in supposing that Edward was simplifying the previous methods of enlistment by merely extending the scope of the assizes of arms, his purpose was to create a large reserve force from which to draw men for active service. The obligation was to have the arms and horses and to be ready; then came in the principle of a quota, voluntary enlistment would be accepted, or as a last resource the sheriff would be expected to apply pressure to fill up some required number.

Let us glance at the feudal and the paid service of the second and succeeding wars. In April, 1282, immediately after David's seizure of Hawarden, Edward wrote to six earls and to many tenants-in-chief 'affectionately requesting' them to take the field 'at our wages[2].' This is not a demand upon them as feudal tenants but as soldiers, and it is important to note that the 'affectionate request' is coupled with the offer of pay, important for this reason, that from other writs it might be assumed that this formula referred to non-feudal but unpaid service. Now the words *ad vadia nostra* are quite unprecedented as addressed to earls and great feudatories, and it is reasonable to infer that Edward, having seen from the war of 1277 how useful paid troops were, now wished to raise an army entirely composed of them and not to call out the

---

[1] *Eng. Hist. Review*, July, 1898, p. 560.
[2] *Parl. Writs*, vol. i. p. 222.

feudal levy. The six earls were Lincoln, Pembroke, Surrey, Warwick, Norfolk, and Oxford; the omission of Lancaster and Cornwall, the king's kinsmen, is not strange. Gloucester and Hereford were the two who would naturally, from what we know of their character, object to the new idea of dispensing with feudal service, and precisely these two at the same place and date are found receiving each some separate acknowledgement from the king, which has quite the appearance of a bribe to induce them to consent to the raising of a paid army. Six weeks later, however, Edward summoned the full feudal levy in the most formal manner[1]. Does not this suggest that in the interval a certain amount of pressure was put on the king to make him recognize the privilege of the great feudatories to bring their unpaid quotas as an outward sign of their baronial status? In the war paid and feudal retinues alike fought. Over £17,000 in all were paid to cavalry, but unluckily details are extant only in the case of the king's headquarters army, and of the armies of South Wales and Hope. It is clear, however, from these details that large bodies of horse were in pay up to the feudal forty days, that customary service was then done, and that many troops were again taken on in pay to the end of the war. Not a single earl can be found drawing pay personally, except Lincoln once for three weeks, Oxford also for a very short time, and Hereford's son with one knight. All of them were in the war, and the frequent evidence of the rolls that they were at headquarters with the king—for they attested deeds or are otherwise known to have been present—together with the entire absence of their retinues from the cavalry pay-roll, proves that, true to their position, they served without wages. In the campaign of South Wales, of which the details are exhaustive, neither Pembroke nor Gloucester had any horse in pay, while other feudal lords sandwiched, so to speak, their forty days between two periods of wages, possibly having larger troops out during the obligatory period than either before or after. In the army whose base was at Mongomery it is a very doubtful point whether Mortimer

---

[1] *Parl. Writs*, vol. i. p. 225.

and his fellow tenants-in-chief served at all for pay, but money was drawn for cavalry at that centre.

Such facts being undoubted, we have next to consider a writ of 1285[1]. Edward wrote to the sheriffs to bid them not distrain for knighthood upon any landowners whose holdings were of less than £100 yearly, in consideration of their 'good and gratuitous service kindly given.' The words are strong :—*ob bonum et gratuitum servicium nobis a communitate eiusdem regni in expedicionibus nostris Wallie benivole impensum.* But in view of that £17,000 how can we take them literally? 'Community' could not refer to the earls' and marchers' unpaid cavalry. One is driven to conclude that the formula 'gratuitous service,' like the other formula 'affectionately requesting,' was applied to all non-feudal service, even if paid, for at any rate it was done voluntarily.

The next piece of fighting took place when the king was absent in Gascony. The regent, the Earl of Cornwall, did not call out the feudal host, but merely issued writs to certain lords individually to come to a council of war with arms and horses. No cavalry roll is extant. But large sums were paid to barons[2], even to earls such as Surrey and Warwick, and as the infantry rolls are quite complete such sums could only have been intended to maintain horse. Gloucester and Hereford, and Cornwall himself as a matter of course, did not receive a penny for their mounted retinues.

An army was collected in the summer of 1294 to proceed to Gascony[3]. Writs of summons were sent to fifty-four tenants-in-chief individually to come to Portsmouth *cum toto servicio quod nobis debetis.* Three women were also summoned to send retinues. But in the list of fifty-four there is not a single earl, though Lancaster and Lincoln were commanding the expedition. Most of the names are those of the very bannerets who were the leaders of paid squadrons and of troops in Wales, such as Reginald de Grey, Alan Plukenet, Walter de Huntercumbe, Philip de Kyme, Robert de Bruce. The writs are feudal in form, but it may be

---

[1] *Parl. Writs,* vol. i. p. 249.    [2] *Patent* and *Welsh Rolls, passim.*
[3] *Parl. Writs,* vol. i. p. 259.

supposed that the recipients understood that they were to enroll horsemen for paid service ; in fact they were commissions of array disguised in feudal language. Otherwise it would be a great hardship if the most willing fighters alone were singled out from the whole body of feudatories to do unpaid service. At the same time the sheriffs were ordered to warn the whole body of crown tenants, whether by knight-service or by serjeanty, and tenants of lands in wardship. Distraint of knighthood is not specified, but this was a general summons to the class liable to distraint.

The last Welsh revolt occurred just when one detachment had set sail for Gascony and another was soon to sail. This second detachment was countermanded. New writs of summons to proceed to Wales were issued to seven earls, some of the same bannerets who had been summoned for the expedition to Gascony, and to several more. As in 1287, they were to appear at a council of war with arms and horses, but this time they were 'affectionately requested.' There were no signs of raising a full feudal levy. Three months later, February, 1295, Edward required reinforcements of 'knights and others[1].' Distraint is not mentioned, but a limit of £40 was fixed; all above that limit were to hold themselves in readiness to mobilize for a period of three weeks, and when summoned they would be taken into the king's pay ; *ad eundem in obsequium nostrum et morandum ad vadia nostra ad voluntatem nostram quandocunque super hoc ex parte nostra per spacium trium septimanarum fuerint premuniti.* Below the £40 limit any who had horses and arms might volunteer for pay. There is no question here of the compensating fines. The men were wanted. It was just a few weeks later that Reginald de Grey had out his squadron of 108 lances in pay, the bannerets in command of the troops under him being Walter de Huntercumbe, Ralph Pipard, Philip de Kyme, Richard FitzJohn, Roger de Monthaut, and William de Mauley. Other barons may have raised similar squadrons and other bannerets similar troops, for the documentary evidence of this war is very scanty, and only a few single

[1] *Parl. Writs*, vol. i. p. 267.

sheets of accounts are extant[1]. It is lucky that the one sheet
of the payments to Grey's men is preserved.

In the October of 1295 the war in Gascony was again taken
in hand[2]. Several of the same group of bannerets received
writs of summons to accompany Edmund of Lancaster, and
this time one earl is included. Richard Fitzalan, Earl of
Arundel, now appears, in spite of his rank, as one of the royal
officials, and later on he inspects the general array of the £40
class, raises horse in the king's pay, and is much more a
professional soldier than a great feudatory. The troops
enlisted for Gascony were to be concentrated at Plymouth,
and we now find a precise statement that their horses would
be valued and a first instalment of their pay given out.
Inventories, it is clear, were only taken of the horses of
stipendiary troops, so that the value of a mount lost on the
king's service might be made good ; this was not done in the
case of the feudal quotas which served as a duty. Up to
the date now reached it was evidently regarded as an established principle that the cavalry raised from the £40 or
£20 landowners and the greater part of all the horse of
tenants-in-chief, except merely those who preferred to stand
on their dignity, should receive the wages of the period.

Thus the same bannerets and tenants-in-chief appear in
almost every war, some after service in Wales going on to
Gascony and Flanders, and most of them subsequently to
Scotland. For the Scottish campaigns the troops were raised
at greater strength than at first for Wales. New men came
forward who had not been old enough to be prominent before.
Of these, Aymer de Valence has been already noticed, and in
his case the evidence of a contract is undoubted. His body of
fifty horse both in Flanders and in Scotland was quite above
the average strength of the retinues in Wales, being a weak
squadron of three troops under the three banners of himself and
the Berkeleys. But we do not know how it was brigaded with
other squadrons. Similarly we see Hugh le Despenser commanding in turn fifteen men in Wales, twenty-five in the first,
fifty in the second invasion of Scotland. It is recorded in the

inventory that he lost some horses at Falkirk, and therefore he did his fair share of the fighting.    He cannot have been really deserving of the name of the ' cowardly knight,' which unpopularity and not military inefficiency conferred on him [1].    But also in the Scottish wars we find a number of quite independent units side by side with the large retinues.    Groups of half a dozen *socii*, even individual horsemen, came to the king's armies and had their horses valued, and these were the men below the £20 limit, who were paid, but did not join any of the organized squadrons; and some of them were probably mounted officers of infantry.    The army of Falkirk mustered probably 2,400 strong in cavalry, all told ; there were the quotas of eight earls, the Durham contingent under the bishop, paid troops both of the household and of the contracting bannerets, Gascon mercenaries, and the unattached small units of the £20 men. How Edward organized them must be left to the imagination. He had four brigades, and certainly each brigade was of horse only.    The crisis of 1297 and 1298 strained the relations between crown and baronage, and I propose to discuss later how the question of feudal obligation was at stake at this time. I would, however, notice the case of Theobald de Verdun. In 1297 [2] he was still under the king's displeasure, because he was one of the contumacious marchers of 1291, and when he tried to excuse himself from service in Flanders the king insisted that he should send a son as his deputy, but that son, compelled to serve as a punishment, nevertheless received pay.

The largest force raised by contract in this reign was for service in Scotland in 1297–8, for winter work.    The Earl of Surrey had 500 horse in pay, with power to raise another 200 ; they were divided into six squadrons, one under Surrey himself, four under other earls, and the last under Henry Percy [3]. Here we have a regular brigade.    But the reforms of Edward I stopped at this point ; he never brigaded horse with foot.    It remained for the advisers of Edward III to complete the reforms.    The earliest good documentary evidence at our dis-

[1] Geoffrey le Baker, p. 8, edit. E. M. Thompson.
[2] *Parl. Writs*, vol. i. p. 295.
[3] Bain, No. 1044.    Mr. Bain has mistaken the date by accident.

posal is the pay-roll of the army besieging Dunbar in 1337–8 ; all ranks were paid from earl to trooper, and mounted archers were added to mailed lancers in each retinue ; in pitched battle at least, whatever may have been the order of march, dismounted knights and dismounted horse-archers and foot-archers were brigaded together in each of the three normal divisions of an army.

A rough estimate may be made of the maximum force of cavalry which Edward could claim to call to his standard. Of course the feudal lords brought in their retinues and the bannerets in their paid squadrons the best men available. Compulsion applied without discrimination would produce an incompetent rabble. But the following figures are helpful towards making an estimate of the possible strength of England. Some of them have been used by General Wrottesley[1], but with some slight inaccuracies. Return A was made by eight sheriffs in 1297, giving names of those qualified at £20 a year *de quocunque teneant*[2] ; B was made by five sheriffs in 1300, the limit being £40 ; list C[3] comes from a series of writs addressed in 1301 to certain landowners only, a quota being summoned from each county and no limit of property being fixed, while earls and prominent men were summoned by a separate series of individual writs. The figures of B are much the highest. Therefore, if those of other counties not in B are raised roughly in proportion, we shall get an estimate of some degree of accuracy.

To list C must be added 28 names in Wiltshire, 77 in Devon, 53 in Essex and Herts, 32 in Beds and Bucks, 5 in Worcestershire, 4 in Middlesex, 58 in Cambs and Hunts, 103 in Norfolk and Suffolk, 12 in Rutland, 40 in Warwick and Leicester, so that the total comes to 935. No figures are given of Kent, Chester, Lancaster, Durham, and the three northern counties. Now in the B returns there is much overlapping, for many landowners are entered under each county in which they had lands, while those of C are simply returns of available soldiers,

---

[1] *Collections of the William Salt Archaeological Society*, vol. viii. p. 22.
[2] *Parl. Writs*, vol. i. p. 285 onwards, p. 331 onwards.
[3] Ibid. p. 349 onwards.

on the principle of a quota, but without overlapping as far as I read. Therefore, at first sight, one would suppose that the C figures ought to be increased in the ratio of 573 to 242. But that would be excessive, and probably even doubling would be too much. Doubling, however, we get 1,870; the seven missing counties would raise the total to 2,500, or at the most to 2,750.

| | A : £20 *limit*, 1297. | B : £40 *limit*, 1300. | C : *no limit*, 1301. |
|---|---|---|---|
| Cornwall | 50 names $= \begin{cases} 24 \text{ milites} \\ 26 \text{ others} \end{cases}$ | | 22 names, 16 the same as in A |
| Herefordshire | 33 : 1 earl included | | 37 ,, 8 ,, |
| Notts & Derby | 135 | | 35 ,, 18 ,, |
| Northants | $139 = \begin{cases} 1 \text{ earl} \\ 97 \text{ milites} \\ 41 \text{ armigeri} \end{cases}$ | | 75 ,, 51 ,, |
| Berks. & Oxon. | 106 | | 47 ,, 26 ,, |
| Salop & Staffs | 55 : 1 earl included | | 28 ,, 11 ,, |
| Surrey & Sussex | 52 : 2 earls included | | 37 ,, 13 ,, |
| Somerset and Dorset | 133 | $145 = \begin{cases} 4 \text{ earls} \\ 48 \text{ in chief} \\ 93 \text{ others} \end{cases}$ 79 same as in A | 43 ,, 42 the same as in B |
| Yorkshire | | $143 = \begin{cases} 6 \text{ earls} \\ 102 \text{ milites} \\ 35 \text{ scutiferi} \end{cases}$ | 53 ,, 53 ,, |
| Lincolnshire | | 136 : 5 earls included | 67 ,, 44 ,, |
| Gloucestershire | | 63 : 4 earls included | 28 ,, 27 ,, |
| Hampshire | | $86 = \begin{cases} 1 \text{ earl} \\ 47 \text{ milites} \\ 38 \text{ others} \end{cases}$ | 51 ,, 50 ,, |
| | | Total : 573 | Total of five counties which are also in B list : 242 |
| | | | Total 935 |

If 2,750 barons, knights, or men of the status which required them to take knighthood, were to be found in all England, then the maximum of the cavalry arm would be about 8,000,

provided that—and these are important points—the king were
mad enough to try to raise his whole reserve at once; that
troopers could be found, not necessarily sub-tenants or small
landowners, but men of the type of the shilling soldier, in the
proportion of two to every knight; and that there were sufficient suits of armour and horses. Of course, in actual war the
cavalry was never so strong. At Falkirk we have already
seen that 2,400 is a reasonable figure, and Hemingburgh's
7,000 is impossible; but even 2,400 is double the strength of
the cavalry which fought in Wales. At Crecy about 2,400
men-at-arms of all ranks served, with perhaps 600 or more
light cavalry; at the siege of Calais, when a very special effort
was made to raise an overwhelming force, about 5,300 men-at-
arms, foreign mercenaries included [1]; the latter figures are
absolutely certain, the former as certain as most careful investigation can discover. Yet the myth that 40,000 English
cavalry fought at Bannockburn does not die.

I would refer once more to the extreme difficulty of pro-
curing horses. On the opening of the first two Welsh wars
officials were sent to France to purchase war-horses, which
were imported, not by hundreds or thousands, as would have
been necessary to satisfy the extravagant figures of myth or
fancy, but by mere tens. Only the barons and richest
bannerets rode the splendid 80 or 100, and even 120, marc
animals, the true *dextrarii*, slow but powerful shire-horses.
Other knights rode *equi*, priced at £15 to £30, and usually
the troopers of the king's household were equally well
mounted [2]. The rounseys of the ordinary troopers cost £5 to
£8 on an average, £12 or £15 occasionally in the case of the
best men of a retinue. The Beauchamp stud has become
famous in history because of the legend of the 'Kingmaker';
it is interesting to find that the Beauchamps in 1297 and 1298
possessed a larger number of highly priced horses than any
other family, one at 100 marcs, three at 80, two at 70, besides
almost equally valuable remounts. The question of the
armour has also been discussed above. Well-known brasses

[1] Gen. Wrottesley, *Crecy and Calais.*
[2] *Exch. Acc.*, esp. $\frac{6}{39}$ and $\frac{6}{40}$, inventories of 1298.

and seals give us the picture of a knight clad in chain mail from head to foot ; namely, in a mail hauberk with a hood attached in one piece, and mail breeches. The great helm was put on to cover the hood just before the moment of charging in tournament or in battle. The shields were kite-shaped. The weapons of offence were the long sword and the massive lance couched under the arm. In the case of the troopers the equipment must have been similar, but not necessarily so complete, as we see in comparing the first and second classes of the militia, and one imagines that a good deal of boiled leather was substituted for mail. The qualification of a fully paid trooper was that he rode a ' covered ' horse ; and one has to assume that even the £5 rounsey was strong enough to bear the weight of an armoured rider, not quite so heavy as the completely iron-clad knight, and of its own horse-armour. The expensive outfit tells against the English men-at-arms being very numerous.

The horsemen who took the king's pay provided their own arms and armour and horses. This is clear from the requirements of the Statute of Winchester and the evidence of the inventories. The king frequently gave valuable horses to favourite bannerets, and he gave the mounts of the members of his household. There are also entries in miscellaneous rolls of the presentation of pieces of armour, or whole suits, to members of the household. Being equipped from their own store, or by the leader of the troop, the paid horsemen were then recompensed by the crown for what they lost in war. It is to meet the claim for recompense for horses that the inventories were drawn up. A very curious and unique document of 1283 proves that, similarly, arms and armour lost on the king's service in war were made good[1] ; this record accounts for an issue of 200 shields, 140 headless lances, and 120 lance-heads. In the unpaid feudal host the loss fell on the baron or the retainer as the custom of each particular retinue dictated.

The question of provisions is also interesting. Crown officials went out in all directions to sweep in both food and

---

[1] *Exch. Acc.* ⅘.

material of war from the counties of England, where the sheriffs collected it, from Scotland and Ireland, and even from Gascony. The crown had the right of pre-emption, and bought at cost price, or even below cost price, for there was a standing grievance against pre-emption under Edward II and Edward III; then the supplies were retailed to the leaders of the retinues or of the infantry. The king was thus a middleman, and got the middleman's profit, a substantial sum of some thousands being put to his credit in the war budget[1]. We cannot determine how the men were paid in consequence, that is to say, how much of the cavalryman's 1s. or the infantryman's 2d. reached him in specie, and how much was deducted for food. Again, this refers to paid troops only. The relation of the feudal retainer to the baron did not concern the crown. The issue of stores in such cases where the documents enlighten us refers entirely to paid troops.

The royal household alone presents the features of a small standing force. All other corps, paid or feudal, were raised for special service, and were disbanded. But the *familia regis* was available for immediate service, and must have been invaluable as a nucleus of resistance against the Welsh while the others were being raised. It was composed of bannerets, knights bachelors, and troopers. The bannerets and knights frequently did work very similar to what the professional leaders of the paid squadrons did, I mean the Greys and Huntercumbes. They formed a permanent headquarters staff, and were detached for duty of every kind. They garrisoned the king's castles, and assisted in the government of the annexed parts of Wales; thus William Sikun was for many years governor of Conway. In a war they requisitioned and brought up relays of infantry and workmen, each knight having his special work. They superintended the transport, and escorted prisoners or hostages. Some seem to have been always near the king's person as his immediate staff. They had the ordinary pay, the bannerets 4s. and the knights 2s. But when on special duty the latter usually drew 3s., *in negotio regis extra curiam*. Whether the extra 1s. was in lieu of

---

[1] See below, p. 197.

rations, or to support the orderly who was attached to each knight on service, does not appear. When *in curia*, the members drew both rations and pay. Hugh de Turberville was a typical useful servant of the crown in this class. He had been Seneschal of Gascony, and had therefore some experience. In 1277 his name does appear, but his services are not known ; in 1282 he was a knight in the paid cavalry, then rose to be banneret, was engaged in recruiting infantry from the south-eastern marches, took Hereford's place as deputy constable, later on was custodian of Bere castle, and for a time was deputy Justiciar of North Wales. Richard de Boys was a ubiquitous arrayer and leader of infantry. Eustace de Hacche appears first as a trooper, and rose to be a banneret of great repute. A few Gascons were in the corps. William de Monte Revelli was constantly in England, and had lands by the king's gift. Other Gascons for a time joined the household after the great corps of mercenaries was disbanded in 1283. William de Cymry must have been a Welshman of a superior type, for the king marked his sense of his value by the gift of a horse worth 80 marcs, a most unusual price for the mount of a member of the household. Imbert de Monte Regali, commandant of all the crossbows in 1277, was a Frenchman of Royaumont, if names mean anything. Once a German name appears. The knights of the household mustered about forty strong in 1277, rather more in 1282 [1]. In peace there were about thirty at headquarters with the king. Those who were no longer needed for war services or for duty in garrisons received a small retaining fee, and immediately drew daily wages again when the next war broke out.

The troopers of the household, the *servientes regis ad arma*, *valetti regis*, *scutiferi regis*, as they are indifferently called, were quite distinct from those orderlies who were in attendance upon the knights of the household. They had a good status as the king's immediate followers, and had much the same duties as the knights. They received only the customary 1s. a day, but were in pay the whole year round, not merely for

---

[1] *Exch. Acc.* $\frac{3}{21}$, and other rolls quoted below.

the exact duration of the war. They also drew rations. Thus they were of a type superior to the ordinary retainers of the barons. Each had to maintain two servants or *garciones* and three horses, and pay at once sank to 7*d*. or 8*d*. if the stable were not up to the mark. There are frequent entries of sums paid for horses or for armour for their use. As much as £16 and more were paid for these troopers' mounts, and many a knight was worse horsed[1]. Their number varied as the need of increasing the corps grew. We can account for fifty or sixty in 1277, but the entries of their pay appear on different rolls, so that it is uncertain if the full strength is calculated ; some of them were mounted crossbowmen at this date. In 1282 sixty were sent up to the front immediately, and nearly 100 served during the whole of the second war. In peace small bodies of six or eight were told off to castles ; perhaps twenty or thirty were in personal attendance on the king. Several were kept together in one body during a war near the king's person when he took the field, and in a battle they fought in the charging line. At Falkirk the evidence of the inventories shows that several had horses killed under them. Some of them came from Rue and Crecy and Valery in Ponthieu ; others are called the Lombard, the Basque, the Gascon. Henry de Greneford was told off in 1277 to command the Macclesfield archers, and in 1295 the English foot crossbowmen. Kenrick Seys Waleys was a prominent trooper in 1277, had three horses given to him by the king and after the war took part in the administration of Wales ; he must have been nicknamed 'the Saxon' because of his adherence to England, was probably hated as a renegade, and was one of the officials against whose cruelty Llewelyn complained.

Such men formed the permanent household. But it would appear from the inventories that, as the reign proceeded, Edward increased his household for an important campaign. He added the retinues of some of the professional captains. Thus in 1296 Hugh le Despenser and Robert de Clifford had considerable troops *in hospicio*, and there served also Guy son of

---

[1] *Exch. Acc.* $\frac{3}{15}$, a miscellaneous roll.

the Earl of Warwick, and Humphrey son of the Earl of Hereford. In 1297 John de Drokensford, the controller, and Walter de Beauchamp, the steward, had troops of thirty-two and twenty-six lances respectively, and the Earls of Warwick and Lancaster were included in the household. In 1298 Lancaster's retinue was raised to forty-five, and Despenser's to fifty lances. In each of these campaigns there were separate rolls of the paid troops *non in hospicio*. I cannot find any similar increase of the household troops for the Welsh wars, and it seems to be coincident with the new troubles, and the need of raising larger numbers of paid cavalry to go to Scotland as a more difficult country to subdue. Also in these years the millenars or colonels of the infantry are sometimes entered on the household roll; in 1296 five from Yorkshire, one from Herefordshire, and one from Chester; in other years knights who may be inferred from other evidence to have been millenars.

The mounted arm was completed by the inclusion of crossbowmen. In 1277 there was only a small body of twenty, mostly foreigners, many of whom afterwards joined the household. In 1282 a dozen Gascon mounted crossbowmen joined before the large corps of 1,500, horse and foot, arrived to meet the crisis of the war. Apparently all the troopers of the Gascon cavalry had crossbows. They were evidently regarded as choice soldiers, and their wages were sometimes 1*s.* a day, more often 1*s.* 6*d.* In 1298 there were 106 mounted Gascons in the army, some just in time to take part in the battle of Falkirk, some too late. But there are no traces at this period of the English horse-archer. The hobelars were not yet a recognized corps, and even the name does not appear in the Welsh wars; the few unorganized light horsemen are styled *servientes cum equo discooperto*.

In the feudal host of 1277 a few light horse, fewer foot, and some camp-followers are entered as sent by tenants who owed a fraction of a knight's fee, or who held their lands by serjeanty on condition of performing a specified service. I make out the following list[1]:—

---

[1] *Parl. Writs*, vol. i, *passim*.

12 light horse, *cum equis discoopertis.*
8 foot sergeants.
1 mounted crossbowman.
4 archers, with a bow and 25 arrows each.
1     „     „     „     2     „
1     „     „     „     unspecified number.
1     „     „     without a cord.
1 sergeant to carry the king's bows.
7 boys with horses of low value, sacks, and spits.
6 men with spades or axes, &c.

It is a little startling to find that ill-equipped archers were actually sent to the muster and solemnly enrolled. The comedy of the feudal system is even further illustrated. One tenant owed a soldier bound to remain in the army as long as his provisions lasted ; he actually turned up with a piece of bacon, and ' as he quickly ate it up he forthwith retired.' Of course, the feudal system was never designed to provide infantry, or an army service corps, or engineers ; the figures above would only suit an army on the stage. Proper infantry and workmen could always be had if the king offered pay. Mr. Hewitt, whose splendid work on arms and armour will always be a classic, is occasionally rather weak when he describes infantry ; he makes one infer, though he does not actually state, that Edwardian foot were a mob of men who only remained in the army as long as their ammunition and provisions lasted. But these tenures are merely exceptional, and comic by being exceptional.

Among the infantry the crossbowmen were of a class superior to the mere *pedites.* The general repute throughout Europe of the crossbow was greater than that of any other bow at this date, and this was as true of England as of other countries. The men were organized into a corps apart. They drew at the least 3*d.*, frequently 4*d.* a day, and their vintenars 6*d.* Now an average good mechanic earned about 4*d.* ; foremen and small numbers of highly skilled smiths and masons, the most valuable workmen of the Middle Ages, earned 6*d.* ; unskilled labourers and the ordinary foot had 2*d.* The crossbowmen therefore ranked with skilled workmen.

The language of chroniclers, especially Trivet[1], who attributes entirely to this corps the victory of Conway, whereas in reality there were vastly more of the ordinary foot engaged, further proves their reputation. As elsewhere in Europe, they were of two classes, townsmen and mercenaries, chiefly from Gascony, but also from Ponthieu. But the weapon was never popular in England, never 'caught on,' so to speak. This was partly due to the national hatred of mercenaries and of the crossbow as their favourite weapon, witness Magna Carta, partly to the expense. It was extremely awkward both to carry and to load[2]. The ordinary 'one foot' crossbow was loaded by the soldier slipping a foot into a stirrup attached to the bulging part, and thus gaining a purchase by which he hauled the cord by main force over a trigger ; then he had to fit the bolt, to raise, and to aim. A 'two feet' piece was loaded by a similar effort, but by both feet giving the purchase without a stirrup; it was not so much used as the 'one foot,' being more expensive, and probably more awkward. The *balista ad turnum*, or *à tour*, was worked by a winch, and was only used for defence of walls. But, once loaded, the ordinary crossbow was very powerful and effective in the hands of a trained man, like the old musket or fusil. Very special training was required to procure precision and rapidity of 'fire,' and, in fact, the crossbowman had to be a professional soldier if he was to be of use in the field. Neither the crown nor the nobles could afford to keep large bodies of such professionals, let alone the fact that cavalry was the favourite arm. Mercenaries, though the system was hated, were used, but in very small numbers ; Edward had some 120 of them, horse and foot, in 1277, and the big corps of 1,500 Gascons was quickly sent away in 1283 after they had broken the back of the Welsh resistance. One can say that Gascony was the Hanover of the thirteenth and fourteenth centuries. Englishmen in a vague way resented the connexion, but probably they gave as grudging a consent to the employment of the useful Gascons as the Parliament

---

[1] Trivet, p. 335 (Eng. Hist. Soc.).
[2] Viollet-le-duc, *Mobilier Français*, v. 20, &c.

of George III gave to the enrolment of German riflemen. Native English foot were drawn from the militia of the counties. Raw peasants could not handle the mechanism without stiff training, for they were essentially militiamen, and not regulars. But as war succeeded war, such men could and did take kindly to the bow, a simple weapon and capable of improvement. Edward may have tried to get them to use the crossbow[1], for in 1295 he gave orders to raise many thousands of both crossbowmen and archers from the counties. If he was trying to do so, it was a great failure.

The professional crossbowmen of this reign were therefore very few, but were ready at short notice. They were either on duty in the king's castles, or were available for immediate mobilization like first-class reservists, and the same officers served in war after war. When once brought up to the front they all served to the end of a war, and then some of them went into garrison in the newly conquered or newly built castles. In 1277 some were already up in March; in the next July 250 were in the king's main army, of whom about 100 can be inferred to have been Londoners, fifty came from other parts of England, and 100 from Gascony and Ponthieu[2]. They first served, together with the mounted men and the choice archers of Macclesfield, under Imbert de Monte Regali in one brigade. Then they were split into detachments for service in Anglesey or on shipboard, and about 100 remained with the king. The majority went home on the conclusion of peace. Again, about 250 English cross-bows can be accounted for in 1282, and they were similarly broken up in various divisions of the army and fleet. In 1287 London and Bristol supplied eighty at quite short notice[3], and in 1296 London supplied fifty at the expense of the city for defence of the coast[4]. As the Scottish wars pro-ceeded the numbers of the corps increased. Besides that some ten or fifteen were on the strength of each castle in Wales, similar detachments were raised for garrison duty in newly acquired castles in Scotland, and 250 foot and a few

---

[1] *Parl. Writs*, vol. i. p. 270.    [2] *Exch. Acc.* $\frac{3}{11}$ and $\frac{3}{19}$.
[3] Ibid. $\frac{4}{17}$.    [4] *Parl. Writs*, vol. i. p. 278.

horse were in the field army assembled in the winter of 1297–8 [1].
A *factor balistarum* and an *atilliator quarellorum*—armourers
would be the modern term—were permanently maintained at
the Tower of London at yearly wages [2], while there was a
similar depot at Bristol from which men were drafted and
ammunition forwarded to the armies in South Wales.

The cost of crossbows and quarrels or bolts varied considerably. The average price of the ' one foot ' was from 3s.
to 5s., of the ' two foot ' 5s. to 7s., and the 'great ' *balista ad
turnum*, really a small engine, 9s. [3] The quarrels at one
time cost 34s. 4d. for 2,600, at another 10s for 1,000. Iron
heads were contracted for at 14d. to 16d. per thousand [4].
The question of ammunition was very important, and we
find that enormous supplies were brought up. In March,
1277, no less than 200,000 rounds were ordered [5], 150,000 for
' one foot ' and 50,000 for ' two feet,' for use in South Wales.
The same year Imbert bought thousands at a time for his
brigade at Flint [6]. In 1282 some 14,000 were sent to Rhuddlan, 10,000 to Chester, and 10,000 to Carmarthen, all of these
from the depot at Bristol [7]; 4,000 were first supplied to the
fleet, and 40,000 sent later in the year under an escort of ten
troopers as a reserve supply, from London. Next year
170,000 are accounted for as issued to both Gascon and
English crossbowmen in the Anglesey division of the army
only, and the Gascons had originally brought with them
70,000 [8]. Meanwhile, a bare 16,000 arrows were issued.
These figures represent a minimum of the ammunition used,
for missing documents probably would have given us many
similar entries. After the second war, when the castle of
Carnarvon was built, a consignment of 120 crossbows was
sent up from Bristol [9], twenty-four of them being 'two

---

[1] *Exch. Acc.* $\frac{1}{2}$.
[2] Issue of the Pell, 4 & 5 Edw. I.
[3] *Pipe Roll*, 10 Edw. I, under ' Bristol.'
[5] *Close Roll*, 5 Edw. I.
[7] *Pipe Roll*, 10 Edw. I.
[8] *Exch. Acc.* $\frac{3}{29}$ and $\frac{4}{5}$.

[4] *Exch. Acc.* $\frac{5}{15}$.
[6] *Exch. Acc.* $\frac{3}{15}$.

[9] *Pipe Roll*, 16 Edw. I (being the belated accounts of the thirteenth
and fourteenth years).

feet' pieces ; they were made of Spanish yew and whale-bone—horn was used as a substitute for yew, but not often, and not on this occasion—and a complete set of accoutre-ments, baldrics, &c., was also provided ; the quarrels amounted to 104,800, of which 16,000 were for 'two feet,' and be it noticed that this was a store of ammunition laid up in a time of peace. At the time of Rhys's rising, nine crossbows and 21,000 quarrels were shipped from Bristol to Carmarthen[1], and later 20 crossbows and 6,000 quarrels. All the details argue the importance of this small corps of professional soldiers.

The rest of the infantry were raised from the counties and the march. The first two Welsh wars had been fought before the Statute of Winchester was passed in 1285, but already a state of things existed which the statute systematized. The sheriff was at the head of the county militia of freemen. By the assize of Henry III the proper arms were fixed, including bows ; the statute provided that there should be a 'view of arms' by two officers called constables. The first duty of the militia was the defence of the county, the maintenance of order, and the pursuit of criminals when the 'hue and cry' was raised. When war broke out the arms were ready, and each man was equipped at his own expense, the county bore the expense of mobilization, and the crown paid wages from the date of the outward march. In 1277 occasionally the sheriff led his contingent to the war, but as the reign wore on the king appointed special officers to take over the men from the sheriff. Writs were issued authorizing them to raise a specified number of men ; such writs became more common from the war of 1282 onwards, and the system was in full force in 1294. The Commissioners of Array, as they came to be called, were usually experienced officers, and being often sent, war after war, to the same counties, they doubtless knew the right men to choose. The unit was a company of a hundred men, whose officer was a centenar or constable, mounted and paid at the cavalry rate of 1s. a day ; it may be that the constables who viewed the arms, and therefore knew

[1] *Pipe Roll*, 16 Edw. I.

the men, served in the army as centenars. The companies were divided into sections of nineteen, who received 2*d.* a day each, under vintenars or twentieth men at a double rate of 4*d.* The custom of the reign was to summon infantry from the counties nearest to the scene of action, Gloucestershire, Herefordshire, Shropshire, Staffordshire, Chester, and Lancashire. For some special reason Derbyshire and Nottinghamshire, for which there was one sheriff, were also called upon, and the reason is obvious, for the Sherwood foresters were notoriously good poachers and good marksmen. Worcestershire and Warwickshire are never found to have sent foot to Wales, unless, perhaps, they are sometimes included under 'divers counties.' Lincolnshire, Yorkshire, Westmorland, and Rutland sent once very small corps, and Wiltshire and Somerset once to a campaign in South Wales. The custom of requisitioning men for service near to their own county was evidently strict. When the Chester levies of both horse and foot were summoned *extra fines proprios* to go to South Wales in 1287[1], the regent, Edmund Earl of Cornwall, promised that it would be considered as a 'gracious service,' and not to be counted against them as a precedent.

Exactly in the same way the stewards of the lords marchers recruited an infantry of Welsh friendlies. A cardinal point to be remembered in Edward's wars is that he could command the services of the bow-armed Welsh of Gwent and Glamorgan, the descendants of those very same fierce fighters and bitter enemies of the family of Braose of whom Gerald de Barri wrote a century earlier ; and not only of Glamorgan and Gwent, but also of the marches of the coast, Gower, Kidwelly, Llanstephan, and Pembroke, in each war large relays being requisitioned from them. Whether the reason be that English rule was really lenient, so that it was natural for the men of the march to fight on the English side, or whether an inherent love of fighting was in itself a sufficient incentive, in any case these friendlies were always forthcoming. In South Wales the infantry which overcame Llewelyn's supporters was purely Welsh, except that a handful of English appear in 1282, being

[1] *Parl. Writs*, vol. i. p. 252.

probably drawn from the garrisons of royal castles. Also, in 1277 and 1282 large bodies of South Welsh were drafted off to the king's armies in North Wales, in 1277, indeed, actually outnumbering the English foot. In 1287 the former subjects of Llewelyn in Snowdonia and the Four Cantreds, Englishmen from all the border counties, and South Welsh friendlies, were massed to crush Rhys by an overpowering show of force ; but a few months later, when he broke out again, the South Welsh friendlies alone sufficed. In 1294 the men of Glamorgan, and probably of Gwent also, were in revolt, yet declared that they were against the Earl of Gloucester only, and not against the king, and this was just the year when the English foot of Wiltshire and Somerset were summoned, though there is no record of their services. On the other hand, the Welsh of the marches of Brecknock and Radnor revolted on every occasion ; it may be that the country was wilder and less easily tamed, or that the Bohun and Mortimer rule was harsh. Further to the north, again, the lords of Powys were bitter enemies of Llewelyn, and always fought for Edward ; in fact, they came to be much more English barons than Welsh princes, for the patronymic ap Gruffudd disappears and de la Pole becomes the family name, and they continually supplied Edward with foot.

As fast as Wales was conquered Edward demanded service from his late enemies as a pledge of their sincerity. Rhys yielded to Pain de Chaworth in 1277, and one condition was that he should raise his men to join the conquerors. In 1283 some princes of Cardigan surrendered, and at once were called upon to take part in the war on the opposite side. The men of Snowdon were brought down south in 1287, and the men of Anglesey in 1295. Pay was always given for such services, exactly on the same scale as to Englishmen and to the loyal friendlies, but the Welsh centenars were usually badly mounted, and received in consequence 6d. or 7d. in place of the usual 1s. Unpaid service was demanded from men who were fighting in their own march or county, pay being immediately given when they were brought across the boundary. Yet when some great undertaking was on hand, such as an important siege, pay was sometimes given even to the locals after a preliminary three days' service had been done, without pay, as a duty.

All the infantry, both English and Welsh, fought for short periods at a time, and fresh relays were continually being brought up. The Welsh were rarely out for more than a month at a time, and once we have definite evidence that the men of Gwent had a contract for a month. But in 1277 a picked body from Gwent and Crickhowell, and a similar picked body of English archers from Macclesfield, were in the field for a much longer period. The rest have the appearance of being an ill-combined rabble, some 15,000 being in arms at one time, 6,000 English and 9,000 friendlies. Training to act in masses over a wide area they can have had none, and it is not surprising that this great body was disbanded quickly, a few of the best being retained, and new relays coming in to relieve them. The rapid dwindling of the numbers upon many different pay-rolls suggests desertion and inability to bear fatigue and the strain of war. Disease must have been rampant when large masses of inexperienced men were herded together. Naturally we look for improved methods in the succeeding wars. The dry details of the pay-rolls point to an improvement in organization as experience grew, as Edward improved—practically created—his infantry. We can trace reform in organization, in the weapon of offence, and in combination of infantry with cavalry.

In the war of 1282 we never find 15,000 foot massed in one place, and only twice 7,000 and 8,000, who, however, were immediately split up into detachments. The king's own army usually included not more than 3,000 or 4,000, perhaps as many were in the Anglesey division, and 2,000 in the division of Chester or that of Hope. We can trace how the men, especially the English infantry, remained with the colours for longer periods, often for three months at a time, and they were bow-armed in increasingly larger proportion. But I believe that the most important improvement was in the organization. The millenary or unit of 1,000 comes definitely into evidence in 1282, though I cannot find the word itself in any document before 1296. The whole of the infantry indeed was not yet regimented by thousands, for in the division of Hope there were 2,600 archers arrayed merely in twenty-six companies or centenaries; but in 1295 in the chief field army there were about 3,000 men, and the pay-roll shows us that they were arrayed in three units of a thousand, each subdivided. A regular brigade of three regiments is obviously easier to handle than a mass of thirty companies. In this year we may say that the king had out the militia battalions of the Cheshire Regiment, the Lancashire Fusiliers, and the Shropshire Light Infantry, each under an accredited colonel, also a weak provisional battalion made up from 'divers counties'; the word millenary was not used, but each battalion was 1,000 strong, more or less. John de Merk was the colonel of the Cheshire, Thomas de Roshale, a sub-tenant of the Fitzalan fief, of the Shropshire, each of these being a knight, but it was not necessary for the millenar to be a knight. Naturally, the more frequently the same men were commissioned to raise their militia battalions, the better they would know their centenars and men, and would choose the best material. So, when the first war against Scotland took place in 1296, a Herefordshire and a Cheshire battalion went up to Dunbar, together with five from Yorkshire, the former being tolerably trained in war and the latter quite raw. The infantry in Flanders in 1297 was about 8,000 strong, and 4,000 of these were from Wales. In the February of 1298 Wales and the border counties furnished between 9,000 and 10,000 foot out of a total of 28,500 mustered at Newcastle, but of these 7,000 were sent home again at once. The next summer, in the campaign which ended at Falkirk, we know that 10,500 Welsh and 2,000 Cestrians and Lancastrians were summoned, and not a single infantryman from the northern counties of England. Hemingburgh's sweeping statement is well known; practically all (*quasi omnes*) the foot were Welsh. Now it is always fatal to take such a phrase literally, for one remembers *quasi castellum* and the bitter controversy resulting. But if we say that the flower of the infantry was drawn from Edward's old enemies in Wales, his allies of the friendly marches, and the oft-mentioned English counties, we cannot be far wrong. Unluckily there is no definite information from pay-rolls, but only from writs of summons, and though knights such as John de Merk appear on the horse-inventories they are not actually stated to be millenars. Meanwhile the Yorkshiremen and Northumbrians cannot have been the equals of these trained men, and the facts of the battle of Falkirk, the foot being brought up to restore the day after the first repulse of the horse, which was work possible only for trained men, prove that Edward was wise in relying on his organized and regimented soldiers who had learnt the art of war in Wales. It would be just to say that all other Englishmen were more raw and unwarlike in 1298 than the men of Chester and Shropshire in 1277, for the latter had had some experience against Llewelyn already, the former absolutely none before the wars against the Scots began. I would add that as Edward was organizing his foot in his Welsh wars, he took one step in the right direction towards providing uniform, an important factor in organization. In some miscellaneous accounts is found an entry of an order for cloth from which arm-pieces were to be made for infantry, and these were to be marked with the cross of St. George.

From the facts of Edward's wars, it would be difficult to believe that pugnacity was the inherent virtue of the Anglo-Saxon. The downright love of fighting and adventure for their own sake was the characteristic of the Norman, and the knight of this reign may have been rash and impatient of discipline, but he loved to fight and charge. The Anglo-Saxon had to be taught to fight, and those counties first became warlike which were nearest to the theatre of the war, the borders of Wales. These men may have had a considerable strain of Welsh blood in them; at any rate, they coalesced with the friendlies of the marches. Otherwise, we have seen how only the Sherwood foresters had a taste for fighting. But Edward was evidently hoping to create the taste in other counties by virtue of the 'view of arms' ordained by the Statute of Winchester. In 1295 he ordered to Winchelsea 25,000 foot of the counties from Dorset to

Norfolk, bowmen and crossbowmen[1]. This was the first time
that so great a levy was ordered, and if he imagined that the
whole body would have come to the muster organized and
skilled in the use of the weapons, he must have been indeed
sanguine. Most probably he ordered so many thousands in
the hope that the few good men among them would form an
efficient force. In 1294 and 1295 he was driven to the
expedient of taking criminals into his ranks for expeditions to
Gascony. In almost every campaign in Scotland we find
that the soldiers of Yorkshire and Durham and other counties
deserted. Thus in the winter of 1299–1300 both horse and
foot, who had been recruited and given a first instalment of
pay, deserted[2]. Edward had issued special writs ordering his
officers to treat the levies with courtesy and promise them
good treatment on his part, so that his anger at the desertions
was considerable, and the offenders were ordered to be imprisoned ; even the men of Shropshire and Derbyshire were
among the culprits. So we trace the same distaste for war to
the end of the reign, and of course through the next reign.
The panic caused by Bruce's raids into the northern counties
after Bannockburn is notorious, so that the midland and
southern counties were called, for the first time, to send
men to Scotland, because the northerners were demoralized.
Edward III had the greatest difficulty in sweeping men into
the ranks in 1333 ; Falstaffs and Shallows abounded in real
life, and convicted criminals and poachers had to be impressed[3].
Yet this army, collected with such difficulty, won a striking
victory at Halidon Hill. Here, I take it, is the turning-point.
The pardoned criminals and poachers—this was not a general
or unmeaning pardon, but each man's offence for which he
was pardoned is specified—had vindicated England's fighting
capacity. Wages now rose to 3*d.* a day. Still the English
had no reputation whatever, and Jehan le Bel is quite explicit
in showing how Crecy came as a surprise to all Europe.
Even after Crecy, desertions were frequent during the siege

---

[1] *Parl. Writs*, vol. i. p. 270.     [2] Ibid. pp. 326, 339, 344.
[3] *Scotch Roll* of 1333, *passim.*

of Calais [1]. Looking back through this string of facts, we can appreciate what difficulties were in Edward's way in 1277, how poor the material must have seemed, and how good the training which enabled him to organize, not indeed the foot of all England, but the foot of the half-dozen counties and the march. Of course, it was an organization suited to militiamen and peasants rather than to professional soldiers of a regular army; not the organization of a Marlborough or Frederick, but such as, let us say, the Boers have had.

With the improvement in organization goes the improvement in weapons. We have seen that the longbow was not a new weapon, the use of which was learnt during the Welsh wars. It was already in the hands of some proportion of the English and their allies, the Welsh of the march. The task before Edward was to improve his men in the use of it, to accustom them to get a longer and stronger reach, and to arm with it an increasing proportion of all his foot. The great mass of 15,000 foot in 1277 was partly bow-armed, partly spear-armed. If an entry in the roll styles a corps *sagittarii*, the next entry is sure to style it *sagittarii et lanceati*. Yet I wish to refer again to the two picked corps, 800 men from Gwent and Crickhowell and 100 from Macclesfield, who not only served longer than any of the other levies, but in every entry are invariably styled *sagittarii*, the Macclesfield men also drawing a special wage of 3d. a day *quia de terra Regis*. In the next war we find more men definitely and invariably entered as *sagittarii*, 2,600 at Hope, 1,000 at Rhuddlan. But it was useless to put such a weapon in the hands of inexperienced men, and one doubts if Edward ever tried to arm the whole of his infantry with it. It has been already noticed that there are to be found in the documents very few entries of the issue of arrows, while quarrels were issued in thousands to the very small number of crossbowmen. Twenty-four or twenty-five arrows went to the quiver; this is the number required by certain tenures, and when Bruce tried to create archery in Scotland, he ordered certain men to have bows and

---

[1] *French Roll*, 1345 and 1346, *passim*.

'schaphs' of twenty-four arrows [1]. If every man's original small stock or quiverful was supposed to last for his short period of service, the archers cannot be regarded as very valuable soldiers.   The bow, just like the rifle, required enormous quantities of ammunition.

The crossbow has already been compared with the musket, and the comparison is really not fanciful.   Each was awkward, but, by a stiff mechanical drill, professional soldiers could be trained to load, ram or fit the charge, raise, aim and fire, in several separate motions.   Each threw a heavy missile, which, at a short range only, brought the enemy to the ground by sheer weight, maiming and breaking if it did not kill.   The one reached its zenith during the crusades and the thirteenth century, the other under Marlborough and Cumberland, Moore and Wellington.   Meanwhile, the longbow and the rifle were known, but had not started on a career of development. These depended each on the application of a certain principle : the bow could be rapidly developed when once the right attitude was adopted, the rifle when once the inventor's art showed how the piece could be loaded.   The arrow, like the bullet of a Mauser or a Lee-Metford, has a long range and great penetrating power, but, being slight and thin, does not smash and bring down unless it hits a vital part.   But by way of compensation, rapidity of fire makes up for lack of weight, and both archery and rifle-fire dazzle and bewilder.   Lastly, each weapon depends less on a stiff mechanical drill than on freedom of the limbs and open order, while the limit of the efficiency of each is the limit of the supply of the ammunition.

The bow of Edward I was probably at first not much more powerful than the short bow of Hastings and Northallerton, but it was a longbow because it could be improved up to the standard of Crecy and Poitiers, whereas a short bow, drawn to the chest, does not admit of improvement.   It cannot have been up to that standard, for it was yet inferior to the crossbow, whereas in the fourteenth century it was superior in just the same proportion.   First comes the question of

[1] *Scottish Statutes* in the year 1318.

attitude.  The man has to stand sideways to his enemy, and this has the effect of making the act of aiming and the act of loading practically one motion ; he gets his aim at the same time as he exerts his strength [1].  Then comes the question of mastery and adaptation of the strength of the individual archer.  A strong man breaks too slight a bow ; a weak man is baffled by too strong a bow.  A maximum of energy is obtained when the archer, standing sideways and bringing both hand and eye into play, makes his maximum reach from outstretched left hand to right hand below the ear.  Back, shoulders, and arms are utilized, and both weight and strength are put into the bow.  But all authorities agree that a reach of a full yard is next to impossible, for the left arm must be curved to get the muscles into play and to prevent the string from touching the chest.  Let us next remember that men have rowed as well as shot from time immemorial, but both boating and shooting have their periods of relapse or perfection.  At the end of the nineteenth century, light-boat racing has been brought to perfection, as archery in the fourteenth ; but, let us say, the Red Indian had already perfected the use of a canoe, and various orientals—Persians, Parthians, Byzantines, and Turks—had already perfected their systems of archery.  Let us compare an English light boat and an English bow, as they come near to perfection when once a course of development has been started.  The secret is the same, conservation of energy to suit the machine.  Every limb and joint, muscles as well as sheer weight, training being added to natural capacity, must be utilized to suit the delicate craft which the boat-builder's art has by long experience enabled him to turn out.  So the archers had to train from one generation to another, develop their muscles, and apply both weight and strength to a simple and strong, yet springy and delicately poised instrument.  Light boat and bow alike baulk a novice, and cause him to misuse his strength.  The process of development was beginning in Edward's days, and the result was seen in his grandson's.  As suggested before, Robin Hood with a real six-foot bow is impossible in the

[1] Mr. Hereford George, *Battles*, esp. p. 51.

thirteenth century, but tradition attributed to him what was possible to the fourteenth-century archer, with all his training and experience. And it has yet to be said that a simple powerful bow was pre-eminently a weapon for peasant militia-men. There was nothing complicated in its mechanism, and no professional drill was wanted. The fourteenth-century English archer had probably as much or as little drill, beyond practising at the butts, as the Boer, but like him took kindly to his weapon. The parallel becomes more true when, some-where about 1333, or a trifle later, horse-archers were raised in the north of England. These men could not shoot from the saddle, for a solid foundation is required for the pull, but they moved quickly and dismounted to shoot.

In Wales and in Scotland the archers had not to meet an enemy completely clad in armour. If it is an axiom in military history that the fully developed longbow of Poitiers could penetrate chain-mail, whereas the less perfect bows of the Turks could not—for there are many passages in the chroniclers of the crusades which show that the arrows stuck in the mail, so that the wearer looked like a hedgehog with bristling spikes—it is equally clear that the badly armoured Welsh and Scots could not face the hail. We are especially told that at Dupplin Moor and Halidon Hill the archers aimed at the unvizored faces, *ita excaecaverunt et vulneraverunt in facie continuis ictubus sagittarum . . . vulnerati in facie et excaecati ideo cito faciem sagittarum ictubus avertere incepe-runt*[1]. Thus even the undeveloped bow of 1277 or 1282 could establish a 'funk'; the word must be pardoned for the sake of its expressiveness. The enemy either stood still, being unable to reply, or, charging blindly, were thrown into hopeless con-fusion. The arrows could stop a rush, not because they brought a man down, but because they made him wild as they hurtled round his ears, and if he was not hit in a vital part he was still useless. Very few soldiers have ever had the experience of facing both musket-shots and arrows, therefore the evidence of the few who have been under the 'fire' of each is all the more valuable; such evidence is conclusive that

[1] *Chronicle of Lanercost*, pp. 268, 273.

the arrows bewilder more than the balls[1]. Of course at Crecy the archers carefully aimed at and maddened the horses. Moreover, as we see at Agincourt, they were not defenceless when their arrows gave out, but joining in with their hand-weapons, especially as they were more nimble than the men-at-arms because they did not wear body-armour, could complete by a charge a victory of which they had laid the foundations by their shooting.

On the question of range and penetration, beyond the general fact that arrows could be driven through mail, I can adduce no clearer evidence than that of a modern amateur. Mr. Longman, writing in the 'Badminton' book of *Archery*, records his own longest shot as 286 yards, and that was a 'slashing loose'; to steady oneself to take aim lessens the range. We remember how Shakespeare's Old Double, on whose head John of Gaunt betted much money, could shoot an aimed arrow 240 yards, and a flight arrow 280 or 290. But the best professional soldiers of the fourteenth century could doubtless beat the modern amateur and the Elizabethan marksman, for Shakespeare's facts must be taken from his contemporaries at a period when archery was decaying, up to the traditional 400. Henry VIII, it is well known, would allow no practice range to be less than 220. Mr. Longman's best penetration was to pierce four pads and part of a fifth pad, each composed of forty-five stout sheets of brown paper, tied tightly to the trunk of a tree, at the short range of seven yards. On another occasion he drove an arrow into a solid oak gate-post, and the point was so firmly embedded in the wood to a depth of three-quarters of an inch that it had to be cut out.

The result of the improvement in archery is seen very much more in the English than in their Welsh allies. Whereas in the Welsh wars there is little to choose between them, whereas it was possible for Hemingburgh to assert that at Falkirk almost all the archers were Welsh, by the early days of Edward III the English had gained the greater reputation. In 1333 the men of Halidon Hill were purely English, some

[1] *Sepoy to Subadar*, edit. Colonel Norgate, p. 23.

of the contingents of foot were composed entirely, others mostly, of archers. The bow was the English weapon *par excellence*. In 1346 the Welsh who went over to France were still only half bowmen, half spearmen or daggermen; they had been so far distanced that 'Welshman' was a synonym for the man who, otherwise useless in battle, was sent out to kill the enemy who lay wounded or bruised on the ground. A writ is extant by which it is ordered that only those Welsh who were proved to be competent should be armed with bows. I believe that these competent ones were brigaded with the English and paid, like them, 3*d*. a day. But the typical daggermen were specifically styled Welsh, and never rose above 2*d*.

Edward I began to combine horse and foot in the field, and this development again was perfected under Edward III. He interlaced the two arms; how the archers were arranged we cannot quite make out, but are told that a crossbowman or an archer was placed between each pair of horsemen. It is notorious that he first riddled his enemy with arrows, and then rode him down. Orewin bridge and Conway were battles in Wales which presaged Falkirk. Curiously enough Edward was at neither Welsh battle, but was at the Scottish battle where the tactics were the same on a larger scale. The credit of the two preliminary triumphs of the bow must go, if some one leader has to be chosen out for the credit, to John Giffard. Of course the commander-in-chief and organizer, to whom the credit has to be given in the end— as, for instance, to Marlborough although Webb won the victory of Wynendael, to Wellington although Picton might deliver the decisive blow—was Edward himself.

What remained for the unknown men of genius who advised Edward III, men who at Halidon Hill avenged Bannockburn by using their wits, was to brigade horse with foot, to raise an ideal mounted infantry of horse-archers, and to dismount the knights in battle to form the centre of each brigade, with dismounted horse-archers and foot-archers on the wings. Mediaeval military science could go no further.

None of the actual fighting in Wales was on a large scale.

I should very much doubt whether more than 2,000 or 3,000 men, all told, were engaged in either of the two chief engagements. The task of the historian is not to record big actions, but the slow process of hemming in and wearing down the Welsh, and then the erection of castles to curb them. Edward was fighting against geography. His real skill is seen in his organization, not only of his men, but in a greater degree of his transport. He brought up carts and carters and woodmen who were impressed for the work and carefully guarded *ne fugerent per viam*, but paid for their services. He kept open communications by sea by means of a squadron from the Cinque Ports, and, when these ships were dismissed, by boats. He had relay after relay of workmen to cut through the natural barrier of forests, and made a road along the coast from Chester to Conway, fortifying his base at each stage by way of Flint and Rhuddlan. The axe was his weapon as much as the lance and the bow, even as now the spade is an auxiliary to the rifle. The conquest of Wales was effected by patience and resolution, which are not so interesting to record or to read, but which are more serviceable in war than dashing bravery in the open battlefield. Meanwhile, in spite of the preliminary difficulties, poor material, inferior weapons, short service, long spells of inactivity between war and war, and an apparent absence of military enthusiasm in the nation, except among those men who lived closest to Wales, Edward was creating an infantry tradition.

We know hardly anything of Llewelyn's men. Their tactics were of the guerilla type. They avoided pitched battles, sought cover in the forests and mountains, and loved to pounce upon convoys. They were very active and difficult to reach. Their chief weapon was a long spear, and one doubts if the Welsh of the north ever practised archery. Trivet shows very clearly that, as in the days of Gerald de Barri and of Simon de Montfort, the long spear was national. It is nature's weapon for poor and free countrymen. The North Welsh and the Scot had no need to copy each other's methods of war, and neither needed to imitate the Fleming. A long shaft of wood tipped with iron does not require

a genius to invent, and to believe literally from chroniclers
that one nation copied another in the use of the spear on
foot, whereas it was a coincidence of military needs which led
several nations at the same date to use the weapon against
cavalry—a weapon which has been used from time out of mind,
and is marked out by nature for use by masses of men—shows
a lack of acumen in a critic.   The only pictorial evidence of
the North Welsh soldiers is to be found in a book of contemporary Welsh documents, where the scribe has sketched three
Welshmen, two armed with spears, and one with a short bow
of horn, but none of them wearing armour [1].

When Edward wanted ships he had a legal call upon the
Cinque Ports in return for various privileges in self-govern-
ment.   In 1293 there was an investigation into the customary
obligations of the ports [2], and it was found that an unpaid
service of fifty-seven ships was due for fifteen days, the
voyage to the scene of the war not included.   Hastings and
her dependent membra, including Winchelsea and Rye, owed
twenty-one ships; Dover and her similar membra also twenty-
one; Hythe, Sandwich, and Romney five each.   In 1277 an
advanced squadron of eighteen ships was joined later on by
seven more, and one ship was sent by Southampton and one
by Bayonne.   In 1282 first arrived twenty-eight ships, followed
by twelve more and two great galleys.   I do not know if the
documents [3] have ever been used before; Professor Montagu
Burrows mentions eighteen ships only in the first war [4], but
the roll, barely legible in places, yet shows clearly a total of
twenty-five; in Mr. Laird Clowes' *Royal Navy* the first and
second wars are confused, the chroniclers are misquoted, and
no documentary evidence is used.   The facts are undoubted,
and the full fifty-seven were never sent to Wales.   The reason
has to be guessed.   Either Edward, in consideration of the
distance from Kent and Sussex to the Dee, of his own accord
accepted a quota of ships, or the natural desire to avoid the

---

[1] *Chapter House*, Liber A, pp. 327, 401, 410.
[2] *Red Book of the Exchequer*, ii. 715 (R. S.).
[3] *Exch. Acc.* $\frac{3}{14}$ and $\frac{3}{26}$.
[4] *Cinque Ports*, p. 117; no authority given.

performance of a full obligation led the authorities of the ports to shirk their duty, so that in later days an inquest had to be ordered. There is also another difficulty; in 1282 the period of the unpaid *servitium debitum* is written as forty days. The scribe may have had the feudal forty days running in his head, or he may have written *xl dierum* by a slip in place of *xv*; unluckily the figure only comes once, and afterwards he put *eodem servitio*. Or Edward may have really tried to exact forty days' service, but this is not likely. Other facts are fortunately clear. After the period of unpaid service the crews in each war received pay for about two months. Each ship carried a rector or sailing-master at 6*d.* a day, a constable or leader of the fighting men at 6*d.*, and nineteen sailors at 3*d.* Archers and crossbowmen, all drawing 3*d.* a day, were drafted from the army, 114 in 1277, and 350 in 1282, being distributed irregularly according to the size of each ship. As many as thirty of these marines served on one ship, an average of ten on several, and on some ships none. The two great galleys carried each a rector, two constables, and forty-seven sailors. There were two chief captains at 1*s.* a day in 1277, four captains and seven centenars of marines in 1282. Stephen de Penecester, the Warden of the Cinque Ports, was in chief command and drew the money; but he also appears as one of the registered knights in the retinue of the Earl of Norfolk. In 1277 he also drew the large sum of £600 early in the year, probably for preliminary expenses of equipment.

War service under the crown seems to have been always distasteful to the sailors. The ships were merely Channel traders, and there are many statements in the chroniclers that war dislocated trade. The men were keen enough to fight the Norman sailors, or the sailors of East Anglia, of whose rising importance they were inordinately jealous. Such private war was in support of their trade and profits, and they entered into it with a will. There is the instance of the celebrated· fight between the fleet of the Cinque Ports and the fleet of Yarmouth in 1297 [1] which seriously embarrassed Edward in

[1] Hemingburgh, i. 158; Trivet, p. 363.

the midst of his Flemish expedition. But it was irksome to the same men, however pugnacious they may have been, to give their services to the crown. In 1346 it is an un-doubted fact, though not sufficiently recognized in history, that Edward III and his army were left stranded in Nor-mandy simply because the fleet disappeared in complete defiance of orders ; the king gave leave to some masters to return to England with invalids and with the spoil of Caen, and promptly they all went off, so that the army had to proceed as best it could, and Crecy was as it were an accident [1]. Therefore we find that Edward I wisely did not try to keep his sailors with him beyond a certain period ; in both 1277 and 1282 the ships were dismissed towards the end of September after about two and a half months' service. Their task was to isolate Anglesey and transport a division of the army across. This work done, and communications by sea being kept open by a few boats requisitioned locally, the Cinque Ports men went home to their ordinary trade in the Channel. It is interesting to note the help given by privateers from Bayonne, one ship in 1277, fourteen in 1295. In the last war sea power was most valuable, for many castles were relieved and revictualled by sea long before the field army could penetrate through the Welsh insurgents. In fact, if one lesson of Edward's wars is that the feudal system of the period had to be supplemented by a system of paid troops, and a second lesson is the need to combine horse with foot in open battle, a third lesson undoubtedly is the importance then, as now, of sea power.

## NOTE ON SCUTAGE.

Although the greater tenants-in-chief were formally sum-moned to various campaigns to do feudal service, only on five occasions in the reign of Edward I was a levy of scutage granted by consent, viz. for the Welsh wars of 1277 and 1282, and the campaigns in Scotland of 1300, 1303, and 1306. All those who served, who paid in full their fines *pro servitio*, or who, though not actually in the army, were doing their duty

---

[1] *French Roll*, Aug. 5, 1346 ; 20 Edw. III, m. 21.

to the king elsewhere, were allowed to raise 40s. per fee from their sub-tenants. The permits were entered on 'scutage rolls' (*Misc. Chancery Rolls* $\frac{11}{10}$, $\frac{11}{11}$, $\frac{11}{12}$ are extant examples). This tells against the theory mentioned on p. 46, namely that a tenant-in-chief brought to the army only the number of knights which he owed for his demesne, for it would be against the interest of the crown to allow him to enrich himself in this way at the expense of the holders of the infeudated land. The formula, addressed to some sheriff, runs: 'Quia x per preceptum nostrum fuit nobiscum in exercitu nostro Wallie anno regni nostro . . . mo, tibi precipimus quod eidem x facias habere scutagium suum de feodis militum que de eo tenentur in ballia tua.' Ladies or guardians of lands in wardship were allowed the right, and Hugh le Despenser is an instance of a baron allowed it without having been actually in the army.

In 1292 there was a vehement complaint that tenants were being pressed to pay up arrears of scutage: 'graviter distringuntur et multipliciter inquietantur' (*Rot. Parl.*, vol. i. p. 80). The king answered that the rolls should be searched so that service could be proved.

In 1305 again there was complaint (ibid. p. 166), and again the answer was that service in 1300 and 1303 should be proved and the tenants quitted. We learn that the prelates, earls, barons, and others had sanctioned a levy of scutage of 40s. per fee for these two campaigns, to be taken within two years if Edward wished, and evidently the officials had been pressing even those who had fought.

Edward II made an effort to exact all arrears of scutage for all the five campaigns of his father, his argument being that service or other reasons for exemption had not been proved. 'Non ostenderunt quicquid . . . procedebatur ad exactionem et levacionem' (ibid. p. 384). It would thus appear that in spite of the careful drawing up of the marshal's roll at the opening of a campaign, or of the corresponding scutage roll on which the permits to levy on the sub-tenants were registered, some lords were too careless to offer their proofs. But probably Edward II was not worrying his tenants to pay the arrears of the two Welsh wars so much as those of the later Scottish wars.

In all these cases of permits or complaints the scutage is assessed at the regular 40s. scale on the full obligation, and I can find no mention of the forty-marc scale on a reduced obligation.

# CHAPTER III

## THE WAR OF 1277

WE traced the course of events in the first chapter down to the battle of Evesham. Earl Simon had been slain, and his partisans were proscribed and hunted down. The civil war was practically over. Yet the effects were still felt, and the crown was unable to enjoy a complete triumph, for it is clear that a sweeping general proscription was impossible. But looking only at what concerns us, namely the relation of the civil war to Wales, we find a new development in 1267. Earl Gilbert of Gloucester suddenly made alliance with Llewelyn and marched to London in arms[1], ostensibly, it would seem, making a parade of chivalrous intervention to stop the persecution of the Montfortian remnant, his late enemies, but really one would infer with the object of demonstrating to King Henry the importance of his own position as holding the balance of power; he had fought for the crown in 1265, but as an independent lord of the march he did not intend to let the crown become too strong, lest having beaten the Montfortians and the Welsh it should aspire to crush the special rights of the marchers themselves. Then diplomacy stepped in, for Henry invoked the aid of the crown's most potent ally. It was not for nothing that John had made his momentous surrender to Innocent III, or that Henry had allowed one Pope after another to dictate to England. The papal intervention brought the earl to terms[2]. He consented to give his bond of £20,000 for his future loyalty, the Pope to be the judge of the sufficiency of the

---

[1] *Brut*, p. 355 ; Trivet, p. 271 ; *Dict. Nat. Biog.*, vol. x. p. 380.
[2] Rymer, June 26, 1267.

security. As a matter of fact, next year at Prince Edward's own request the bond was remitted [1], but Rome had supported the crown in a serious danger.

Next the papal legate induced Llewelyn to negotiate. Conditions of peace were drawn up; the Prince of Wales was to do homage to the king [2]; he was to withdraw from lands to which he had no claim, for instance from Hawarden, but Robert de Monthaut was not to reconstruct a castle there for the next thirty years; the Four Cantreds were to be acknowledged to be Llewelyn's; 'the custom of those parts' was to regulate points at issue, chiefly points of allegiance and homage; and as to all debatable lands there should be future arbitration. It was rather a truce than a peace, for obviously there was not yet a final settlement. In 1269 Prince Edward, in 1270 other commissioners were sent to Wales to make a lasting peace; still nothing definite resulted [3].

The prince took the cross and was absent from England for four years. He must have added to his stock of military experience by seeing Eastern methods of fighting. On his return home through France as king he took part in the tournament which degenerated into a real battle, and is known as the 'little war' of Chalons. But it is of more interest to us to know that, landing in England as king in the August of 1274, he found the Welsh borders still unsettled. The state of unrest was intolerable, and sooner or later there was certain to be war.

Llewelyn evidently intended to prolong the unrest. It mattered little to him whether he was taking part in an English civil war as an adherent of the Montfortians, or taking advantage of the vague terms of an inconclusive peace. His object was simply to strengthen Wales while England was otherwise distracted and presumably weak, to profit by Edward's absence, and to defy invasion by getting ready beforehand. He had indeed retired from Hawarden, but refused restitution of Powysland to Gruffudd ap Gwenwynwyn on similar terms; to restore an old enemy and an ally of

[1] Rymer, July 16, 1268.          [2] Ibid. Sept. 21 and 29, 1267.
[3] Ibid. May 21, 1269; Oct. 16, 1270.

England would be fatal. Builth castle he had destroyed long before, but he retained the surrounding lands as well as the castle of Dolforwyn to the dispossession of Roger de Mortimer, and the marches of Elvael and Ismynydd to the dispossession of Ralph de Tony[1]. He occupied the greater part of Brecknock, refusing to submit to arbitration the claim of the Earl of Hereford. Not content with this he invaded Shropshire and occupied a third part of the barony of Peter Corbet[2]. Moreover, he had quarrels in his own family, kept his brother Owen in captivity, and drove David in exile into the arms of England. However, such masterfulness often defeats its purposes. By raising up new enemies and exasperating old ones he was storing up for himself disaster.

It was in the south that his masterful spirit led him to make his worst move. For a moment, in 1267, he had been allied to the Earl of Gloucester. By a new invasion of Glamorgan in 1270 he finally drove that holder of the balance of power to be royalist and anti-Welsh. The invasion was in connexion with the construction of Caerphilly castle. Built in the closing years of the reign of Henry III, Caerphilly 'is both the earliest and the most complete example in Britain of a concentric castle' of the type known as Edwardian[3]. The rings of walls and towers, the outer and middle and inner wards, argue the greatest skill on the part of the architect; more than that, they argue fear of Llewelyn. To build elaborately and to confess oneself to be on the defensive are signs of weakness. Indeed, Llewelyn showed that his power was not to be despised even by an Earl of Gloucester, for on the occasion of his incursion he refused to retire except on conditions[4]; Caerphilly was to be held by the Bishops of Lichfield and Worcester temporarily in the king's name, and a final settlement by arbitration was to be arranged next year at the ford of Montgomery. Further west rose a new castle at Kidwelly 'of the Edwardian or concentric

[1] *Close Roll*, June 5, 1277.
[2] *Rotuli Hundredorum*, 2 Edw. I, vol. ii. p. 113.
[3] Clark, *Medieval Military Architecture*, vol. i. p. 160.
[4] *Land of Morgan*, p. 135.

type, slightly modified from the perfect example of Caerphilly [1],' probably dating from the same period. Pain de Chaworth, as his father Patrick had been before him, was a strong royalist. Thus, both the uncertain waverer and the royalist were now arming against the Prince of Snowdon, who menaced the English ascendency in every direction. Yet one doubts whether Llewelyn really did himself any good by penetrating into South Wales. The independent Welsh of Cardiganshire and the inland parts of Carmarthenshire were neither united nor powerful. They could not hold their own against the lords marchers unless Llewelyn appeared in person to support them at intervals. Cardigan and Carmarthen were held for the king, and the line of march estates was unbroken from Pembroke to Monmouth. The true home of Welsh patriotism was in the north. Llewelyn effected little by his raids to the south, but he converted the waverers from being anti-royalist to be anti-Welsh.

The wishes of the government of England in favour of peace were pronounced, both during Edward's absence and after his return. It may have been that the wish to be fair to Llewelyn was genuine, or that war with Llewelyn was feared lest there should be a recrudescence of civil war. Whatever the reason, there was an almost painful yearning for peace at any price. The grievance of the Earl of Hereford against Llewelyn was investigated and found not to justify war [2]. Chance after chance had been given to the prince to appear to pay the homage, which would have been little more than nominal, according to the treaty of 1267. He had refused to submit debatable points to arbitration, that is to say, to complete the details of that treaty. He had shown his masterfulness as a Welsh patriot, dispossessing the lord of Powys and persecuting his own brothers lest they should form the nucleus of a pro-English party in Wales, raiding in South Wales, harrying and holding marches, and even occupying English soil. A finishing touch alone was needed. He, in the strangely illogical position adopted previously by himself

---

[1] *Medieval Military Architecture*, vol. ii. pp. 154, 161.
[2] C. T. Martin, Preface to *Peckham's Letters*, vol. ii. p. li (R. S.).

and earlier by his grandfather, was bent on doubling the parts
of patriot and ally of the discontented barons of England.
He meditated marriage with the daughter of Simon de
Montfort, which meant a policy of pure aggression. To
Edward the state of affairs was impossible ; with the most
honest wish to be pacific he could not allow a new Montfortian party to be formed, and it would be better to make
a national war on Wales than to allow Welsh aggressiveness
to stir up the embers of civil war in England. So Llewelyn's
bride was intercepted on her way to Snowdon, and preparations were made for war. Now things turned out differently
from what perhaps either Edward or Llewelyn expected.
The baronage was united, very many of the old Montfortian
faction are to be found serving the king in Wales, such as
Nicholas de Segrave, Baldwin Wake, John d'Eyvile, John
de Vescy, Geoffrey de Lucy, Robert de Ros, as well as the
trimming Earl of Gloucester, and it is clear that, fearing the
Welsh more than the crown, they refused to be drawn into
civil war. The Welsh patriot, it was at last recognized, could
not be the ally of the baronage. The declaration of a
national war upon Wales was determined by a full council
of prelates, earls, barons, and others, who simply stated that
Llewelyn's previous evasions and refusal to perform his
homage proved that his present attitude was dishonest, and
refused to give him another chance of performing it lest he
should again evade[1]. The same council authorized Edward
to call out the feudal host. This brings us to the November
of 1276.

Edward had learnt enough of the art of war to know that
an invasion of Snowdonia would be no light task. A substantial army had to be created, with an organized commissariat, and this meant time. Meanwhile, the defence of the
march and the west of England, and the recovery of what
Llewelyn had already seized, had to be entrusted to those
most interested and nearest to the scene of action, the lords
marchers and the tenants-in-chief of Shropshire and Herefordshire. Many barons were both marchers and tenants-

[1] *Parl. Writs*, vol. i. p. 5.

in-chief, and we have seen that Llewelyn had been most aggressive on the middle march of Powys, Radnor, and Salop. Edward appointed as his captains the most influential men of the north, centre, and south. The Earl of Warwick was commissioned on November 16, 1276, to take command at Chester, Roger de Mortimer at Montgomery, and Pain de Chaworth at Carmarthen, each of these bases being a royal stronghold, and the lords marchers being thus converted into royal officials[1]. Landowners of adjoining counties and those holding lands over the boundaries of the counties, *extra metas comitatuum*, were ordered to support them with all their resources. There was one corps available for immediate service, the *familia regis* or household. Some forty knights and seventy troopers were sent either to Oswestry on the one side or to Carmarthen on the other, and the majority of them were already up in the same November or December; they set to work at once, recruiting foot and collecting supplies[2]. The Earl of Warwick and Pain de Chaworth, also the Earl of Lincoln, were clearly authorized to collect men-at-arms at the royal wages; the evidence, as discussed above, justifies us in inferring that there were contracts, but of course the recruiting took time, and the cavalry were not up till the next January. Then Edward turned his eyes abroad. Both he and his barons sent agents to France to buy war-horses, *dextrarii* and *magni equi*, more than a hundred in all. Thirty of the choice mounted crossbowmen of Gascony were summoned. The custodian of the port of Wissant, near Cap Gris Nez, was advertised that the King of France had given leave for both mercenaries and horses to be shipped thence to England[3]. On December 12 writs were issued to call out the feudal levy of England, the summons being of the old-fashioned type. One set of writs, according to precedent, were addressed to the earls and greater barons individually, who were to come in person with their *servitium debitum*;

---

[1] *Parl. Writs*, vol. i. p. 193, from *Patent Roll*.

[2] *Exch. Acc.* $\frac{3}{21}$, and various entries in other pay-sheets, and *Patent Roll, passim*.

[3] Ibid. Dec. 7, 1276, and various dates onwards.

a second set went to churchmen and ladies, who were to send their contingents; and a third ordered the sheriffs to collect the bulk of the lesser tenants-in-chief[1]. The muster was for the 1st of July, 1277, at Worcester.

The pay-rolls of the war, and more especially some writs addressed to the lords marchers who were ordered to have no dealings with the enemy, show us the state of the march at this moment[2]. It must be remembered that the counties did not extend so far to the west as they do now, and in fact the border line was rather uncertain. Various lands, such as Ewyas Lacy, Clifford, Erdesley, the forests of Dean and Clun, were officially reckoned to be in Wales, though the sheriffs were often called upon to exercise their authority on the march side of the boundary under special circumstances[3]. Some of the landowners within the counties are included in the following list:—

| | |
|---|---|
| Lord Edmund of Lancaster, the king's brother, with John de Beauchamp as constable | Cardigan and Carmarthen[4] |
| Nicholas FitzMartin | Cemaes |
| The king's bailiffs, for John de Hastings (Marshal and Braose lands) | Cilgeran |
| William de Valence, Earl of Pembroke, by marriage with a granddaughter of William the Marshal | Pembroke |
| Roger de Mortimer (Marshal and Braose) | St. Clears |
| Earl of Hereford (Marshal and Braose) | Haverford |
| Guy de Brian | Laugharne |
| Geoffrey de Camville | Llanstephan : coast west of the Towy |
| Pain de Chaworth | Kidwelly (Cydweli) and Carnwyllion : east of Towy |
| William de Braose | Gower : west of Glamorgan |

---

[1] *Parl. Writs*, vol. i. p. 193, from *Close Roll*.     [2] Ibid. p. 195.

[3] e.g. *Close Roll*, June 5, 1277.

[4] See *Eng. Hist. Review*, Jan. 1895, esp. p. 32.

| | |
|---|---|
| The Earl of Gloucester and his sheriff (*vice-comiti suo*) | Glamorgan |
| The Earl of Gloucester and his bailiffs | Caerleon : W. Monmouth |
| The Countess of Gloucester : Matilda de Lacy, the earl's mother | Usk |
| The Earl of Norfolk, Roger le Bigod, through his grandmother, daughter and coheiress of William the Marshal | Strigul and Netherwent : S.E. Monmouth |
| Lord Edmund of Lancaster, by confirmatory grant, May 5, 1277; original grant, June 30, 1267 ; by confiscation from John de Monmouth, a Montfortian. | Ward of castle and honour of Monmouth |
| Same dates ; lands of Hubert de Burgh which had lapsed to the crown. | 'The three castles,' viz. Grosmont, Skenfreth, and White Castle, in E. Monmouth |
| Henry de Bray, steward for John de Hastings (Braose lands) | Abergavenny, Overwent |
| Grumbald Pauncefot | Crickhowell, E. Brecknock ; and custody of Forest of Dean |
| Reginald FitzPeter | Talgarth |
| John Pichard | Stradewy, valley of middle Wye |
| The Earl of Hereford (Braose and Bohun lands) | Brecknock and Hay |
| John Tregoz | Ewyas Harold |
| Geoffrey de Geneville, married granddaughter and coheiress of Walter de Lacy | Ewyas Lacy and Ludlow in Salop |
| Theobald de Verdun, married the other coheiress | Ewyas Lacy |
| Roger de Clifford | Tenbury |
| John Giffard, through his wife Matilda de Clifford | Clifford, and claim on Llandovery |
| Ralph de Tony | Elvael (Elveymusmenith) held by Llewelyn |
| Robert de Mortimer | Richard's Castle |

| Roger de Mortimer | Wigmore in Here- fordshire, Cleobury Mortimer in Salop, march of upper Severn, Radnor, but Builth held by Llewelyn |
| --- | --- |
| Richard Fitzalan, in wardship, future Earl of Arundel | Clun, S.W. Salop; and Oswestry, N.W. |
| Bishop of Hereford | Bishop's Castle, W. Salop |
| Peter Corbet | Caurs, W. Salop: a third of his land held by Llewelyn |
| John and Roger l'Estrange | Ellesmere & Knockin |
| Roger de Monthaut: in wardship | Hawarden and Mold |

We have a considerable amount of evidence which tells us how the various commanders fared during the interval before the king had prepared his main army of invasion. The Earl of Warwick expended £1,094 between January and May during 120 days [1], rather a larger sum than the Earl of Lincoln, as we shall see, drew for the cavalry at Montgomery; let us say that he had 120 or 130 lances in pay. The names of several of the knights are preserved, some of them losing horses in the king's service, the value of which was repaid, others having letters of protection [2]. There were some north-country barons, such as Robert de Ros and his sons from Yorkshire, Brian Fitzalan of Bedale, Roger de Clifford the younger, and Roger de Leyburn, who had married the coheiresses of the barony of Westmorland; John de St. John, Robert de Tateshale, and Aymer de St. Amand were bannerets who reappear in other wars; Reginald de Grey, an old royalist of the Montfortian wars, and his son John, Adam and John de Monthaut, whose kinsman, Roger, was heir to the barony of Hawarden, but was at this moment a minor, were Cestrians with a direct interest

---

[1] *Pipe Roll*, 7 Edw. I, last membrane (the war budget).
[2] *Exch. Acc.* $\frac{3}{15}$; *Patent Roll*, 5 Edw. I, *passim*.

in the war. It is not at all clear how much voluntary and unpaid service was done by the tenants of the county palatine; the king later on praised 'his men' of Chester [1], *non debent summoneri per breve regis in quo continetur quod homines regis de com Cestr fecerunt regi servicium suum regi debitum in exercitu predicto et plus quam idem servitium ad rogatum regis*; but tenants might do non-feudal service as a graceful act, and at the same time might be taking pay. David, Llewelyn's brother, was with this force. Foot could always be raised without trouble in the county palatine, but such stray entries which are found of payments to foot and to workmen are not dated. The work of recruiting and organizing would fall upon Guncelin de Badlesmere, the justiciar. We find him collecting the tax of a fifteenth, handing over sums to various royal officials for the payment of stipendiaries, and seizing corn in the king's name under the royal right of pre-emption [2]. But the only entry which refers to actual fighting is an order addressed to David and Guncelin, directing them to 'receive to the king's peace' the Welsh of Bromfield, the district corresponding to the southern part of the present county of Denbighshire [3]. Therefore there was some advance upon the middle Dee, and, as in the next summer Edward was able to march on Flint without any fear of a flank attack, we may assume that the Earl of Warwick drove the Welsh well back from the immediate west of Chester. One would infer that up to the arrival of the king and the main feudal army stores and men were being collected at Chester as the chief base. Workmen and crossbowmen, for instance, were found there by the king in readiness for an advance. There is an entry in the pipe roll of the year, undated by bad chance, of payments made to men of both these classes who were on their way to Chester [4].

The greater part of the earl's paid cavalry did not serve beyond the end of May. A further sum of £1,407 paid to

[1] *Pipe Roll*, 8 Edw. I, under 'Chester.'
[2] *Patent Roll*, Jan. 24, 1277.   [3] Ibid. Dec. 26, 1276.
[4] *Pipe Roll* 5 Edw. I, under 'Oxon.'

the Chester division represents the service done up to the January of 1278. Many tenants-in-chief, especially the Cestrians, whom the king himself certified as having done more than their *servitium debitum*, were in arms continuously, and were ready under the earl to be registered in the feudal army when the king, in July, came up from Worcester.

Of the army of the middle march under Roger de Mortimer there are more precise details. In this direction Llewelyn was fighting in person on the upper Severn, and the feudal tenants of Shropshire and Herefordshire turned out to do unpaid service before the year 1276 expired. Bogo de Knoville, Sheriff of Shropshire, had the chief management of raising men and supplies [1]; he was at present in command at Oswestry, a fortress which was now in the king's hands under the sheriff, as Richard Fitzalan was in wardship, and was a secondary basis only less important than Montgomery. His own retinue was composed of ten horse, and there were another ten horse and some foot in garrison, paid out of the revenues of various manors of the Fitzalan fief. Two knights and thirty-eight troopers of the royal household were up in December at Oswestry [2]. At Montgomery were Peter Corbet and Adam de Montgomery, with fourteen horse in pay and a dozen foot [3], while Llewelyn was out in the neighbourhood in the winter; *ante adventum comitis de Lincoln . . . dum princeps Wallie fuit in partibus illis cum exercitu suo.* The Sheriff of Herefordshire also came up to Montgomery. The fortifications of both castles were repaired and strengthened under a certain Master Bertram, the king's engineer. But the English did not remain on the defensive. Roger de Mortimer had with him, amongst other tenants, Robert de Mortimer, Roger l'Estrange, the elder Roger de Clifford, and Corbet when his services were not wanted in garrison [4]; what force of foot he may have requisitioned cannot be ascertained. First Llewelyn was driven out of Shropshire and Corbet's lands were recovered [5]. Then Powysland

---

[1] *Pipe Roll*, 5 Edw. I, under 'Salop.'
[2] *Exch. Acc.* $\frac{3}{15}$.          [3] *Pipe Roll*, 'Salop.'
[4] *Patent Roll*, protections; *Exch. Acc.* $\frac{3}{16}$.          [5] *Brut*, p. 365.

and the march of Elvael were reoccupied, but for the time
were held in the king's name by l'Estrange and Clifford[1].
This was a successful first advance which lasted into the
January of the new year, and on February 5 the king wrote
a warm letter of thanks for the 'spontaneous and gracious'
service done[2]: *non ratione alicuius servicii nobis ad presens
debiti sed sponte et graciose.* This service beyond doubt was
not paid.

By the end of January a powerful reinforcement arrived,
the paid squadron of Henry de Lacy, Earl of Lincoln.
Exclusive of the earl it was exactly 100 lances strong, and it
was subdivided into troops under some notable bannerets:—

| Bannerets[3]. | Knights. | Troopers. | No. of lances. |
|---|---|---|---|
| The Earl of Lincoln . . . | 6 | 23 | 30 |
| John de Vescy . . . | 4 | 10 | 15 |
| Otto de Grandison . . | 4 | 10 | 15 |
| William de Leyburn . . | 2 | 7 | 10 |
| Robert FitzRoger . . | 3 | 6 | 10 |
| John de Vaux . . . | 3 | 6 | 10 |
| Geoffrey de Lucy . . | 2 | 2 | 5 |
| John de Bohun . . . | 1 | 4 | 6 |
| Total : 1 earl and 7 bannerets | 25 | 68 | 101 |

Of these, Otto de Grandison had no feudal obligation, but
the others were all tenants-in-chief and men of position;
Lucy, Bohun, and FitzRoger, however, were not registered in
the feudal army of the next summer. Engaged on a contract
and paid for forty days at a time, the squadron served for
120 days down to the end of May. Meanwhile the household
cavalry had been reinforced up to five knights and forty-two
troopers. The strengthened army of 148 lances of all ranks,
with some proportion of the unpaid horse under Mortimer,
proceeded to follow up the previous successes, pushed along
the Severn and captured Dolforwyn castle, thence struck into
the valley of the upper Wye and reoccupied the lands of
Builth and its ruined castle[4]. I should take it that this marks

---

[1] *Patent Roll*, Jan. 26, 1277 ; *Close Roll*, June 5, 1277.
[2] *Parl. Writs*, vol. i. p. 196.
[3] *Exch. Acc.* $\frac{3}{12}$, a special roll for this squadron only.
[4] *Brut*, p. 365.

the limit of Llewelyn's previous aggression, for Radnor and
other castles would seem not to have been lost by Mortimer.
At any rate now the whole march was clear of the enemy.

The paid squadron was disbanded in May, though some
of the knights and troopers certainly, perhaps many of them,
were re-enlisted at the feudal muster in July at Worcester.
They had completely overthrown Llewelyn's power on the
Severn ; not only was the prince quite unable when the main
campaign opened to distract Edward by menace of a counter-
attack from Powysland, but also large drafts of friendlies from
the newly reconquered lands were sent up to join Edward's
army of invasion. The Welsh, not unlike the Boers, had
very little power of making a serious counter-attack beyond
vexatious, but from the military point of view useless, guerilla
raids. Again, like the Boers, they relied on the natural
difficulties of the geography of Wales and their own rapidity.
The mere fact that Warwick and Lincoln were able to do
so much before the king's advance, thus enormously helping
the king, argues a weakness in the Welsh defence. Doubtless
Llewelyn thought that as he himself and his grandfather had
previously defended Snowdonia, and then retaliated as the
English retired, he would be able to recover lost ground after
the failure of the main invasion. But Edward was organizing
well and was not going to fail. Therefore the Welsh really
lost their chance in not striking harder during just this
preliminary period, while the English preparations were being
made.

The services of Lincoln and his men not being required
after May, Mortimer continued to hold his command from
Montgomery as his base, and his work would have been
to guard and patrol the newly reconquered lands. He
received 800 marcs in all for the purpose of maintaining
troops in garrison down to the autumn [1] ; on a later occasion
we find that some twenty-five horse and eighty foot sufficed
to garrison his own castles of the march—Radnor, Cefnllys,
Dunawd, and Dolforwyn—but at this moment Dolforwyn,
together with Builth, was held in the king's name. Some

[1] *Exch. Acc.* $\frac{3}{16}$.

twenty horse more would suffice for Montgomery. He probably also had the feudal retinues of Robert de Mortimer and Peter Corbet as well as his own; for though all three registered the names of their knights and troopers with the marshal at the feudal muster of July, they did not serve in the king's army.   Bogo de Knoville, proceeding to join the king, turned over Oswestry to Roger l'Estrange, who also was entrusted with the ward of Dinas Bran on the middle Dee, and thus was in touch with the army of Chester [1].   Gruffudd ap Gwenwynwyn was restored as lord of Powys, yet restored unmistakably as a vassal of England under the control of l'Estrange as the royal official.   The march of Elvael was restored by Roger de Clifford to Ralph de Tony, who was now just of age [2].

Meanwhile the Earl of Hereford was fighting for his own hand, and with his own resources, in Brecknock.   It will be remembered that he had already lodged an ineffectual protest against Llewelyn's occupation, but he had been answered by the king's council that Brecknock was not a debatable land according to the treaty of 1267, and that it was doubtful if the Bohun family had ever properly conquered it according to the custom of the march [3].   Evidently he now took advantage of the pressure brought by Lincoln and Mortimer upon Llewelyn just to the north, and with his own forces, without crown pay of any kind, occupied the land he claimed [4]. Having done this he was free to appear in person at the feudal muster to do his duty as constable.

In South Wales Edmund of Lancaster, the king's brother-german, had received as marcher lordships both Cardigan and Carmarthen, but as he was not on the spot John de Beauchamp was his deputy and constable [5].   Pain de Chaworth, we saw, was commander-in-chief, and was already fighting against the Welsh of the Towy; the Welsh chronicler says the war there began in 1275, but the later autumn of

---

[1] *Close Roll*, July 18 ; *Patent Roll*, July 18 and 21.

[2] *Close Roll*, June 5.

[3] C. T. Martin, Preface to *Peckham's Letters*, vol. ii. p. li (R. S.).

[4] *Brut*, p. 365.        [5] *Patent Roll*, Jan. 23, 1277.

1276 is much more likely, as his dates are confused [1].   In the
January of 1277 Pain had up a good force, quite sufficient
indeed to overawe the inland Welsh, who were not formidable
when no longer helped by Llewelyn.   William de Braose of
Gower, Geoffrey de Camville of Llanstephan, Guy de Brian,
and John Giffard were in arms and had letters of protection ;
being lords marchers they with their mounted followers served
without the king's pay.   The paid squadron was seventy-five
lances strong under seven bannerets, whom we shall find
continually doing service in this part of Wales, and who for
the most part came from Devon and Somerset, where they
were tenants-in-chief.

| Bannerets [2]. | Knights. | Troopers. | No. of lances. |
|---|---|---|---|
| John de Beauchamp        . | 2 | 5 | 8 |
| Roger de Molis      .    . | 2 | 7 | 10 |
| Oliver de Dyneham .      . | 2 | 7 | 10 |
| John de Mohun      .     . | 3 | 6 | 10 |
| Alan Plukenet      .     . | 2 | 7 | 10 |
| Ralph Daubeny      .     . | 2 | 7 | 10 |
| William FitzWaryn        . | 1 | 5 | 7 |
| (Hugh Pointz, kn.) .     . | 2 | 2 | 4 |
| (Thomas de Moleton, kn.) | 2 | 4 | 6 |
| Total : 7 bannerets | 18 | 50 | 75 |

There were also sixteen knights of the household, each with
a trooper as orderly, and sixteen troopers of the household
ranked independently.   The 123 paid lances and the horse of
the lords marchers make perhaps a total of 160 or more.   No
foot can be found in pay, but Pain and other marchers doubtless produced some.   Some crossbowmen must have been
available from Bristol and the permanent garrisons of the
various castles, for an enormous quantity of ammunition was
ordered up for them [3].   Pain de Chaworth, having already had
some fighting with the South Welsh chieftains, was able in
January to undertake a strong offensive movement, and he
struck up the Towy.   Details of the campaign there are none,
but we know that by April 11 he brought Rhys ap Maredudd,
lord of the Vale of Towy, to submit and to surrender under

[1] *Annales Cambriae*, p. 104.          [2] *Exch. Acc.* $\frac{3}{13}$.
[3] *Close Roll*, March 12.

terms his castle of Dynevor on that river. The treaty provided that the castle and lands should be held in the king's name, and perhaps the king would ultimately restore them, but in any case would give Rhys full satisfaction [1]; he was to do homage and trust to the king's sense of justice, to grant to the English forces the right to march through his remaining lands, and even to give armed assistance to Pain if it should be required. Meanwhile he retained his castle of Dryslwyn, which lay on the Towy between Dynevor and Carmarthen. From this time onwards for the next ten years he was the constant ally of England, and there are no signs of wavering; yet it is curious that Llewelyn preferred a list of complaints in Rhys's name in 1282, alleging oppressive treatment at Pain's hands and brutal conduct towards his followers even at the moment while the treaty was being signed.

Two days later the cavalry pay-roll was closed, and the paid squadron, having served for two periods of forty days under contract, was disbanded. But the campaign was by no means finished. In the very same week we find troopers of the royal household requisitioning levies of foot from the friendlies of Gwent and of Pain's own march of Kidwelly [2]. Dynevor was well situated, being much further inland than Carmarthen and at a bend of the river, and formed a good base for a renewed advance. John Giffard was detached to occupy Llandovery higher up stream, while Pain himself penetrated into the wilder country to the east and occupied the castle of Caercynan. These new conquests were completed by the first week in June [3]. We find that a sum of £285 was immediately issued for the repair of the fortifications of both Dynevor and Caercynan, and John Penrhys, a tenant of William de Braose of Gower, was appointed to be custodian [4]. In June, word came from the king that his brother Edmund was going to take over the command with a detachment of the feudal host.

Reviewing these preliminaries we see that at least 300 horse

[1] *Rymer*, April 11, 1277.

[2] *Patent Roll*, April 9, 1277; *Exch. Acc.* $\frac{3}{15}$.

[3] *Patent Roll*, June 5, 1277.

[4] *Exch. Acc.* $\frac{3}{26}$; *Pipe Roll*, 9 Edw. I, m. 2.

were in pay at the three chief bases, and curiously enough
this is the ·exact figure given by the author of the *Flores
Historiarum* [1], a none too common instance of real accuracy on
the part of a chronicler.  Adding the household cavalry and
the unpaid men of the lords marchers and the tenants-in-chief
of the neighbouring counties we can calculate 500 lances.  All
the way along the line the outworks of the Welsh defence had
been carried, on the Dee, the upper Severn, the upper Wye,
and the Towy.  In the meantime Edward was mobilizing
and getting up stores, and the ships of the Cinque Ports were
on their way.  The really difficult part of the war was now to
begin.  Yet, as a matter of fact, the king's advance to the
confines of Snowdonia and the occupation of Anglesey took
barely more than two months; another two months saw the
conclusion of peace.  The Welsh collapse in contrast to the
previous menacing attitude of Llewelyn is striking.

On the 1st of July, the Earl of Hereford as constable, and
the Earl of Norfolk as marshal, were at their posts at Worcester
to register the feudal host.  The figures represent the entire
strength of the tenants-in-chief, whether they served with the
king in person or away from him.  Some men were registered
at Worcester and thence proceeded to South Wales, others
went direct to South Wales or had been there some time
previously.  Those who were already at Montgomery were
probably allowed to send in their names for registration
without coming in person, and those at Chester were entered
afterwards when the king moved up from Worcester.  Let us
assume from the arguments previously used that the tenants-
in-chief gave in the names of all knights actually serving with
them, but where knights only were registered a proportion of
troopers, about two or three to one, must be reckoned.  The
quotas of Edmund and of William de Valence have to be
added to the division of South Wales, and to complete the
cavalry arm we must also add the royal household, the few
mounted crossbowmen, David's bodyguard, and the retinues
of lords marchers, such as Pain de Chaworth, who only
registered the knights due for their English fiefs.  The figures

[1] iii. 48 (R. S.).

are therefore approximate, yet the margin of error is not likely to be large. The weakness of the force, which was fairly strong in numbers considering that this was Edward's first war, was that a great many of the men must have been utterly without experience ; Evesham had been fought twelve years earlier, and, except on the march, there had been even no skirmishing since the civil war. Moreover the units were not coherent. The earls' quotas of 'decent' strength, several barons' quotas of moderate strength, and a great many small units of two or three lances, did not constitute an organized brigade. Where each leader has his own independent retinue we would look in vain for subordination of commands.

| | Registered number. Knights. | Troopers. | No. of lances. | Total after additions. |
|---|---|---|---|---|
| A : with the king[1] : Earls . | 62 | 5 | 67 | 220 |
| Churchmen[2] | 13 | 39 | 52 | 66 |
| Others . | 112 | 183 | 295 | 364 |
| | 187 | 227 | 414 | 650 |
| B : with Roger de Mortimer . | 8 | 12 | 20 | 40 |
| C : with Edmund . . . | 33 | 55 | 88 | 160 |
| | 228 | 294 | 522 | 850 |
| Household and other details[3] . | | | | 150 |
| | | | | 1000 |

This gives the king for his field force at headquarters some 800 cavalry of all ranks. They would not have been all available for a charge if the Welsh had offered pitched battle. As fast as the army advanced men had to be told off to guard the line of communications, and parties were also detached for the work of a staff, bringing up infantry and guarding convoys, and in fact the whole 800 would not have been concentrated in one place except at the outset. Garrisons of castles were quite independent of the field army, whether those of the king, or those of the lords marchers.

The king left Worcester in the second week of July, and moving by way of Shrewsbury reached Chester on the 15th,

[1] *Parl. Writs*, vol. i. p. 197 seq.  [2] Two bishops sent knights only.
[3] *Exch. Acc.* $\frac{3}{17}$, $\frac{3}{18}$, $\frac{3}{21}$.

where he added to his army the feudal quotas of the Earl of Warwick's command. The fleet of the Cinque Ports reached the Dee just about the same time. A main squadron of eighteen ships was taken into pay at the end of July[1], and if the men served without pay for the customary period of fifteen days after arrival at the scene of action, they must have arrived in the middle of the month. Seven ships joined later, together with one from Southampton, and one from Bayonne. The twenty-six English ships carried two chief captains at a wage of 1s. a day, forty-eight masters and constables at 6d., and 608 sailors at 3d.; according to the recognized equipment of nineteen sailors to a ship, there should have been 494, and the extra 114 may be supposed to have been crossbowmen and archers drafted from the army. Stephen of Penecester, Warden of the Cinque Ports, was in command and drew the pay. The fleet was strengthened by eight tenders, boats purchased or hired locally, and manned by eight masters and forty sailors[2]. Assuming that the Bayonne crew, who were paid £8 for apparently a month's service, was composed of twenty men, we have a total of 726 of all ranks. The chief pay-roll shows an expenditure of £532 in wages. Letters of marque were issued, or rather the mediaeval equivalent, authorizing the sailors to plunder any of the Welsh except those who ' came to the king's peace [3].'

The infantry ready for service amounted to some 2,576 men[4]. David had 200 foot and twenty troopers of his bodyguard, all in English pay. John de Monthaut, of the family of Hawarden, and therefore an hereditary enemy of Llewelyn, had 1,000 mixed archers and foot spearmen of Chester, 120 of Lancashire, and 616 of divers counties. Bogo de Knoville, Sheriff of Shropshire and Staffordshire, had 640 of those counties. Imbert de Monte Regali was at the head of his full corps of about twenty mounted and 250 foot crossbowmen, together with the 100 archers of Macclesfield, who were clearly a picked

---

[1] *Exch. Acc.* $\frac{3}{14}$.                     [2] Ibid. $\frac{3}{15}$.

[3] *Patent Roll*, Aug. 5.

[4] All the following dates and figures from *Exch. Acc.* $\frac{3}{11}$, the main infantry pay-roll.

body of men and drew a special wage of 3d. a day *quia de terra regis*[1].

The plan of campaign was simple. Bromfield and the middle Dee, also the country round Hawarden, being already clear of the enemy, Edward's army could advance along the left shore of the estuary towards Flint and Rhuddlan. His rear was secured from attack, and he could by his ships keep open communications by sea. The point to which he was aiming was the mouth of the Conway. The knowledge of the failure of Henry II, and his own experience of twenty years back, warned him not to engage recklessly in the forests and hills of the interior. He knew the Welsh tactics, how they hung back from battle and loved to swoop down from cover upon the flanks of a slowly moving and baggage-encumbered army of invasion. Their country was suited to guerilla warfare, while the English armies were tied by the difficulties of transport. His plan, therefore, was to advance solidly from a strong base, cut through the forest while guarding his workmen with the full strength of his army, and then create a new base from which to repeat the process. It was obviously best to make this advance along the coast, and then to strike up the river valleys, fortifying posts provisionally during the campaign, where he could construct permanent castles afterwards when Wales was annexed. The co-operation of the fleet in conveying the heavy baggage and material was invaluable. The process was simple, or seems so to a peaceful reader. But a very little reflection shows that only great powers of organization and the strength of a resourceful country at his back could enable Edward to succeed. To war against geographical difficulties as well as a patriotic enemy needs genius. We have many parallels in English history. Thus Edward III, literally deserted by his fleet, had great trouble in cutting his way through to Crecy, then gained the most conspicuous success of his reign when, acting on sound military principles, he laid siege to Calais, the key by which he maintained afterwards his connexion with France. A mere blundering raid into the interior nearly brought the Black

---

[1] First mentioned in *Exch. Acc.* $\frac{3}{15}$, July 20.

Prince to ruin, but for the valour of the fighting men at Poitiers; the great invasion of 1359 was a hopeless failure, and so were John of Gaunt's later efforts. Scotland however gives a better analogy; the only true policy was to hold strong castles in the valleys and invade in force along the coast road, Newcastle being the Chester, and Berwick the Rhuddlan of the north; *mutatis mutandis* Dunbar was the Conway, the key of the defence. Without a fleet, or unless the enemy made some rash move and threw away the game, it was impossible to turn either position. But the Welsh were fierce and liable to despondency, the Scots infinitely more tenacious.

Thus Edward started from Chester on his first stage of path-cutting. 'Between Chester and Llewelyn's country lay a forest of such denseness and extent that the royal army could by no means penetrate through without danger. A large part of this forest being cut down, the king opened out for himself a very broad road for an advance into the prince's land, and having occupied it by strong attacks, he entered through it in triumph[1].' Within ten days he worked along the coast-line up to Flint, where headquarters were fixed on July 26, through the country which had been the scene of the disaster of Henry II. Next he made a base at 'Flint, near Basingwerk,' as the documents style it, and for over three weeks was engaged on the second stage. Enormous quantities of timber were brought chiefly by sea from Chester, together with ammunition and supplies, and there was a great train of carters, who had been impressed for the king's service, but were paid[2]. A strong post was thus made, though the works were but temporary and of wood, for there was no time to prepare stone. The leading magnates of Chester, with the justiciar Guncelin de Badlesmere, were employed here, as would be naturally expected from their knowledge of the country. Imbert, with his crossbows and the Macclesfield archers, had the post of honour in defending the works, and the purchase of great numbers of quarrels means that there was plenty to do in the way of beating off the Welsh. Mean-

---

[1] Wykes, in *Annales Monastici*, vol. iv. p. 272 (R. S.).
[2] *Exch. Acc.* $\frac{3}{15}$, the chief miscellaneous roll.

while, as the path-cutting and fortifying continued, the king crossed over the estuary and moved from place to place in Lancashire and Chester to superintend the transport service [1].

On August 16 Edward was back at Flint, and made a definite compact with David that the latter should have his share of whatever land was conquered from Llewelyn [2]. Then after three weeks and more had been spent in the creation of a base, he pushed on with the main army for Rhuddlan by the second section of the newly cut road. Headquarters were here on the 20th. Rhuddlan lies a little back from the coast up the Clwyd, and on its right bank—a good position from which to strike up the Clwyd southwards to Denbigh and Ruthin, or along the coast to Conway. One entry informs us, but the date is not given, that Ruthin was occupied. But the last stage of the main advance was towards Conway, and the woodmen were once more at work. Reinforcements were coming in. There remained under John de Monthaut and Bogo de Knoville 2,190 of their infantry, with David's 200, and 160 of the crossbows; drafts, both of archers and cross-bowmen, had gone on board the squadron to act as marines, and a garrison had been left at Flint. Lancashire, Derbyshire, and Rutland sent 1,860 new foot, and Chester 620. Thomas le Ragged brought 1,010 from the Peak, enrolled separate from the rest of the Derbyshire men probably because the honour of Peveril was mostly in the king's hands; they were paid 3d. a day while on the march, and 2d. after they had joined at Rhuddlan. This gives 5,680 English infantry. Soon Richard de Boys brought 9,760 foot from the march and adjoining districts of England, thus made up:—2,700 from Radnor and Brecknock under Howel ap Meyrick, who was constable for the king at Builth, and steward for the marches of the Earl of Hereford and of Roger de Mortimer; 1,580 under William de Hameldon from the march of the Earl of Gloucester and Lord Edmund; about 1,000 under Henry de Bray, steward of Abergavenny, including 500 from Overwent, others from Crickhowell and Talgarth and the neighbour-

[1] *Itinerary of Edward I* in MS. in Record Office.
[2] Rymer, Aug. 16, 1277.

K 2

hood; 700 from Powysland under Lewis de la Pole, son of Gruffudd; and other details from the Shropshire estates of Peter Corbet, Roger l'Estrange, Richard Fitzalan, and the Mortimers. Richard de Boys brought up the whole body by way of Oswestry. The centenars of the Welsh detachments were mostly mounted on uncovered horses, and had a wage of 7*d.* a day. The total of infantry at the end of August thus rose to 15,640, of which 9,000 at least I should take to be Welsh friendlies.

Meanwhile the forty days of feudal service had expired. According to one chronicler the king dismissed all the retinues of horse except those whom he wished to continue their service[1]. All the earls can be traced as remaining with him, and it must be supposed that they retained their unpaid quotas. But some cavalry was certainly taken into pay. There is an item of £721 paid to soldiers after the king's arrival at Flint, and as our infantry roll is quite complete, this money can only have been given to horse, volunteers out of the disbanded feudal retinues[2]. About 125 lances serving for eighty days to the end of October can be reasonably allowed. There is no extant writ to the effect that the king 'affectionately requested' non-feudal service according to the usual formula, but he probably did so by word of mouth. An affectionate request did not necessarily imply unpaid service in continuation of previous feudal unpaid service, but, as we have abundant evidence, was equally addressed to those who, after their feudal duty, took his pay. Various barons and good fighting men took out letters of protection in the middle of August or early in September[3], such as Robert Fitzwalter, Walter de Huntercumbe, Gilbert de Gaunt, and Nicholas de Segrave, and these would probably be the troop-leaders of a squadron taken in pay; and among the lords marchers Reginald FitzPeter and Ralph de Tony now seem to have joined the king.

Of a separate paid squadron under Reginald de Grey we have definite information. It was ninety lances strong, and

[1] Barth. de Cotton, p. 155 (R. S.).     [2] *Pipe Roll*, 7 Edw. I.
[3] *Patent Roll.*

forty-two days' pay was drawn immediately after the feudal days were over.   Most of the bannerets in command of troops had been previously serving in the Earl of Warwick's force at Chester.   I suggest that Grey recruited the squadron from the small incoherent units of the feudal levy, and especially from among his old, and many of them his constant, comrades in arms.   Recruiting them by contract, he was able to put on foot a body with duly subordinate commands and manageable because thus organized.   In any case the evenness of the figures is suggestive, and had Robert de Ros brought some knights and a full troop of twenty lances the strength would have been exactly 100.   But one point is to be noticed; because Grey's own troop consists of twenty-five, there is no ground to suppose that he had already been serving during the feudal forty days with that number, for his recognized obligation was only two knights.   The money paid was £256. As precisely that sum was handed over to the Earl of Norfolk for him to account for details later, it seems probable that the earl marshal was in chief command at Flint, and therefore his unpaid quota, twenty or thirty lances, should be added to the ninety[1].   The men formed a strong rearguard to hold Flint and its growing fortifications, as well as to patrol the forest road, and fifty crossbowmen and 850 archers were detached from the main army to act with them.

| Bannerets[2]. | Knights. | Troopers. | No. of lances. |
|---|---|---|---|
| Reginald de Grey  .  .  . | 5 | 20 | 25 |
| Robert de Tateshale .  .  . | 3 | 11 | 15 |
| Aymer de St. Amand .  .  . | 1 | 8 | 10 |
| Alex. de Balliol .  .  .  . | 3 | 6 | 10 |
| John d'Eyvile  .  .  .  . | 4 | 5 | 10 |
| Roger de la Zouche  .  .  . | 2 | 7 | 10 |
| (Robert de Ros, not present)  . | — | 10 | 10 |
| Total: 5 bannerets under Grey | 18 | 67 | 90 |

Further to the rear more horse and foot would have been maintained by the sum of £1,407, which we noticed was paid in gross to the ' garrison of Chester.'

The war was now at the last stage.   With his communica-

---

[1] *Pipe Roll*, 7 Edw. I; see below, p. 141.
[2] Ibid. 8 Edw. I, under ' Flint.'

tions protected by Grey's command, and probably a similar command at Rhuddlan for which he could spare plenty of foot at least, Edward pushed on through the last section of his forest road to the Conway. Headquarters were at Diganwy on August 29; the documents style the place 'Gannou.' Llewelyn had fallen back, and was now at bay to defend his inner mountain citadel. The Conway, deep and tidal, covered his immediate front; behind him were the heights of Penmaenmawr; further away to his right and rear the castle of Dolwyddelan, guarding the upper Vale of Conway, and the great mountain of Snowdon itself. Edward at Diganwy held the base of the promontory of Great Orme's Head, with the estuary of the Conway before him, but the fleet was at hand to effect a crossing. Just at this critical moment the numbers of the English infantry sank to 7,362 men with 120 crossbows; on September 3 there was a further fall to 2,125, with 105 crossbows. The explanation is, however, simple. Anglesey had been isolated, for the fleet had been available for at least six weeks. Edward's plan was to send a large force over to the island, and thus menace Llewelyn's Penmaenmawr position from the rear. By the infantry pay-roll we are only told that twelve horse, thirty-one crossbows, and 112 archers were sent across, quite an inadequate force; but the entry shows that some proportion of the main army was detached. The miscellaneous roll shows that £1,445 were paid for the expenses of the Anglesey division, being sufficient for 2,000 foot and some horse for two months[1]. John de Vescy and Otto de Grandison, accompanied by fourteen troopers of the household, commanded this division. Next it would seem that by far the greater portion of the Welsh friendlies were dismissed, for they rarely served for more than a month, and their numbers were quite unmanageable. In the second week of September, the king had with him at Diganwy a small but picked force of only 2,000 foot, men of Chester and the Forest of Dean, Bray's 800 of Gwent and Crickhowell and Monmouth, who are always entered as archers and were probably the best picked men, and the Macclesfield 100; the latter had now closed up

[1] *Pipe Roll*, 8 Edw. I, under 'Flint.'

from the rear, where they had previously been, and came for the first time on the chief pay-roll. Similarly the reduced body of horse would have been divided, perhaps 200 and most of the household being with the king, and 200 with John de Vescy in Anglesey.

The Welsh chronicler states that the English destroyed the harvest in Anglesey [1]. A century earlier Gerald de Barri had written that the island was the granary of Wales, while Snowdonia was given up to sheep-grazing. Curiously enough among miscellaneous payments we find that wages were paid to 120 *falcatores* at a rate of 4*d*. and 5*d*. a day, and 240 *messores* at 3*d*. and 4*d*., in just these two first weeks of September, also to the masters of four ships who carried them to Anglesey [2]. The corn or hay was therefore not destroyed, but was harvested for the use of the English army. The work of the fortnight upset Llewelyn's determination. Cut off from his granary, menaced by the fleet and the division which threatened to recross the Menai from Anglesey in his rear, confronted by Edward at Diganwy, he may well have felt despair. He had found that the English had closed in upon him by a slow and relentless march from Chester to Flint, Flint to Rhuddlan, Rhuddlan to the Conway river; their rear and flanks had been protected at each stage, they had secured a base at each step, and they were masters of the sea. They had refused to be drawn into the interior, where their communications could be cut, or his own Welsh could rush down upon them unawares. Between the jaws of the closing vice he felt himself unable to resist, for the traditional tactics of the Welsh were unavailing. Moreover, on his own confession, in later days he was singularly liable to alternate fits of energy and despair, 'the fear which may fall even upon a steadfast man.' So he was willing to surrender upon conditions.

The surrender must have suited Edward's plans. Though his was a good position, there were obviously certain elements of weakness. The bulk of his army was quite raw. He could not be sure that the feudal horse, who had already

---

[1] *Brut*, p. 369.   [2] *Exch. Acc.* $\frac{485}{19}$ and $\frac{3}{15}$.

consented to serve over the forty days, would care to remain with him much longer. An autumn campaign in the mountains would lead to sickness, and to attack Llewelyn's central position from two separate bases with an army of inexperienced men would be hazardous. It was good policy on his part not to goad an already yielding enemy into a mood of desperate defiance, and indeed in the next war Llewelyn and David defended the same ground to the bitter end in a spirit of sheer desperation. So on September 12 he drew back from Diganwy to Rhuddlan.

While negotiations were being carried on, Edward retained a force of foot at Rhuddlan, decreasing on September 16 to 1,600 with ninety crossbows. On September 23 a new relay of 1,930 came in from Oswestry under William de Hameldon, but only stayed for a week; they were drawn from Shropshire and Powysland. The Macclesfield 100 were still up to strength, but Bray's archers dropped out early in October. For service in October a few lords, among them Peter Corbet, who had been previously away from the king's person, took out letters of protection on joining him, and a hundred of Corbet's men, other hundreds of Mortimer's, Clifford's, and Lincoln's, were alone left at the beginning of November. Meanwhile some force was still kept in Anglesey, probably most of Hameldon's relay going over. A diminishing but still a strong body held the country round Flint; some fifty horse under Grey and Tateshale, thirty-six crossbows and 650 archers; and others were still maintained at Chester. The fleet was dismissed at the end of September. The king did not remain all this time at Rhuddlan, for we find him in October at various places, and once as far away as Shrewsbury, and he must have been personally superintending over a wide area.

Meanwhile Edmund had had an easy task in the south. Some of the feudal army joined him from the muster at Worcester, others apparently went direct to Carmarthen or had been already serving there in pay. The lords marchers who also held fiefs in England produced their quotas, not very large ones; for instance, William de Braose had three knights for his Sussex fief, Nicholas FitzMartin three from

Devonshire, and Geoffrey de Camville three.   Other tenants-in-chief who were in this army, but had no direct interest in the march, were John de la Mare, who brought six lances, and William de Greystock, who also brought six from Yorkshire and Cumberland.   Maurice de Berkeley with his son Thomas and one other knight came from Gloucestershire.   Each recognized *servitium debitum* of three knights would imply an actual troop of ten lances in all.   Adding troopers as usual, and the retinues of Edmund himself and William de Valence, I infer about 160 lances, and there are yet the mounted men of Pain de Chaworth and other marchers to be considered, so that a total of 200 is reasonable.   There is no clue whatever to the number of foot and crossbows with them.   The army pushed over the watershed to Cardiganshire, for Pain had already pacified the Vale of Towy.   Hardly any opposition was encountered, but we have hints of a good deal of plundering ; the custom was for the booty to be regarded as the king's property, and the heads of the retinues might buy from the king [1].   The campaign proceeded along the river Aeron, and on July 25 Aberystwith was occupied, where the foundations of the 'noble' castle of Llanbadarn were immediately laid [2]. Then when the feudal forty days were over, a letter was received from the king 'affectionately requesting' a continuance of service, which it was promised should not be counted to the prejudice of those who responded.   From notes appended to the marshal's register it seems that only about thirty men retired as they had the right to do [3].   The rest remained to harry the Welsh of the Aeron, and most of these would have been paid, for £400 are entered as forwarded to Edmund, £233 to Pain, £50 to his younger brother Patrick, and smaller sums to John de la Mare, Robert de Vaux, and others.   John Giffard, it is interesting to remark, owed £12 to the crown for non-service *pro vadiis servientium qui non deservuerunt.* The last Welsh chieftain who remained in arms fled away in September to Llewelyn, 'for fear of the English who were

---

[1] Certain entries in *Exch. Acc.* $\frac{3}{20}$.
[2] Trivet, p. 298 (Eng. Hist. Soc.).
[3] *Parl. Writs*, vol. i. p. 213 ; Aug. 8, 1277.

at Llanbadarn[1].' On September 20 Edmund returned to England, having disbanded the field army, and leaving Roger de Molis to command and to finish the building of the castle.

The details of the war are dry, but we decidedly have a good insight into Edward's methods. First we see his need of ready money. Justiciar and sheriff hand over to the royal paymasters sums out of the fifteenth which had been granted in 1275[2]. Urgent messages for remittances are sent to Ireland. On one occasion five barrels of specie are brought up on carts to headquarters at Chester[3]. The king requisitioned everything he wanted in the way of supplies as well as men, carts and corn and timber as well as carters and workmen, but he always paid. He gave the soldiers their pay every three or six days after they had joined, and while they were on the march to join him they drew it from the recruiting officer or millenar, who in turn got back his expenses from some official of the wardrobe, or else the sheriff of the county through which their route lay deducted the sum from the revenue of the county when he made up his accounts for the pipe roll of the year. Workmen were treated in the same way. Both soldiers and workmen were liable to impressment if the required number could not be made up otherwise, but while there is no direct evidence that compulsion was at this date necessary for the former, we have a clear instance in connexion with the latter, when a small escort of cavalry was told off to guard some sappers *ne fugerent per viam.* Impressed or volunteers, they were all paid, the skilled men of each trade usually at the same rate as the crossbowmen, 3*d.* or 4*d* a day, and the foremen 5*d.* or 6*d.*, while the few unskilled labourers who were requisitioned received 2*d.*, like the ordinary foot. Both classes had to be paid at short intervals because they had to buy their own provisions, the crown acting as middleman in collecting and retailing, therefore the urgent need of ready money is apparent.

The most interesting details are those connected with the

---

[1] *Brut*, p. 369.          [2] *Patent Roll*, May 22.

[3] Details chiefly in *Exch. Acc.* $\frac{3}{15}$ and $\frac{3}{19}$; occasional entries in *Pipe Rolls.*

path-cutting[1]. Certain knights of the household were told off to superintend each a special part of the work, some engaging or impressing the *fossatores* or woodmen, others surveying them while making the road. Walter le Jaye, Gilbert de Brideshale, and Peter de Brampton appear each in his particular sphere. In August, while headquarters were at Flint and the road was being cut through to Rhuddlan, 1,500 to 1,800 woodmen were engaged, besides 330 carpenters and 200 masons on the fortifications at Flint; in September, between Rhuddlan and Diganwy, 700 to 1,000 woodmen and 100 to 150 mechanics. Some of the trained miners of the Forest of Dean were brought up by a trooper of the household, also some charcoal-burners and quarrymen, and four or five blacksmiths. The other men came in relays from Lancashire, Chester, Shropshire, and Derbyshire, while masons and carpenters from Wiltshire, Somerset, and Dorset were similarly sent to Carmarthen and Dynevor. It was a gang of 300 woodmen from Hoyland that had to be specially guarded by cavalry lest they should desert. But the rapid alterations in the figures from week to week suggest that desertions were frequent generally, while the care exercised in making exact payments suggests a supervision which was fairly close. A decided touch of humour peeps out of the sheets of accounts. Once 8s. 9d., once 3s., we find solemnly entered as paid *e dono regis*, in special reward for good work *quibusdam fossatoribus bene laborantibus*. A total sum of £1,551 is accounted for by one roll in wages to workmen only, and other sums in various miscellaneous rolls.

Similarly interesting entries concern the foot[2]. Some Shropshire centenars on returning home received 10s. each, a Herefordshire man half a marc, and some wounded Glamorgan archers 40s. between them. A batch of 453 Shropshire archers received 37s. 9d., which works out at exactly 1d. per man or half a day's pay, to drink the king's health; and 250 from the lands of John l'Estrange and Lewis de la Pole had 38s. 4d., or nearly 2d. each. These *pourboires* (*ad potand*) occur with some frequency, chiefly to small bodies of archers and sailors.

[1] *Exch. Acc.* $\frac{485}{19}$.  [2] Ibid. $\frac{3}{19}$.

To recognize good service shows good sense on Edward's part, but the entries as one suddenly reads them on the roll are decidedly comic. An entry of another kind, journey money given to crossbowmen at the conclusion of the war, forty-eight of them returning home to London, thirteen to other parts of England, and sixty-six to Picardy *en route* for Gascony or homes elsewhere in France, is important as showing the provenance of these useful soldiers.

The budget of the war is complete. Master Thomas Bek, chief official of the wardrobe, accounted for the issue of most of the money in large amounts, and sent the account in to the Exchequer so that it appears on the last sheet of the pipe roll of 1279. He notes that various ' particular rolls ' will show the details, and fortunately the greater number of these are extant. Only the £1,021 sent to the army in South Wales, part of the money spent at Flint, and the expenses of some of the cavalry of the household are not accounted for. Both knights and troopers of the household, when they were serving away from headquarters, were paid by whoever for the time was commanding them ; thus several of them appear for some days on the pay-sheets of Montgomery and Carmarthen. The mounted crossbowmen of the corps were on a separate sheet for a full year. The item for food is very small, only £416, and one infers that this was the supply for the household, feudal lords and leaders of paid troops having to get up provisions as best they could. The figures should be compared with those of the next war.

PIPE ROLL, 7 EDW. I (last membrane).

£

*Milites et scutiferi*, Chester, Jan. to May, 1277, under the Earl of Warwick, 120 days . . 1,096

*Milites et pedites*, Chester, to Jan. 1278 . . 1,407

*Exch. Acc.* $\frac{3}{12}$ *Milites* at Montgomery, Jan. to May, under the Earl of Lincoln, 120 days . . . . 968

,, $\frac{3}{13}$ *Milites* at Carmarthen, Jan. to April, under Pain de Chaworth, 80 days . . . . . 715

Army at Flint, *post adventum regis*, August . 721

,, $\frac{3}{17}$ Mounted crossbowmen, May to November . . 126

,, $\frac{3}{11}$ Crossbowmen, archers, and foot-spearmen, July 18 to November 10 . . . . . . 4,762

PIPE ROLL, 7 EDW. I (last membrane, *contd.*).

| | | | £ |
|---|---|---|---|
| *Exch. Acc.* $\frac{485}{19}$ | Carpenters and mechanics, Flint and Rhuddlan . | | 1,551 |
| ,, $\frac{3}{14}$ | Masters and sailors of fleet, up to Michaelmas . | | 532 |
| ,, $\frac{3}{15}$ | Miscellaneous expenses . . . . | | 747 |
| ,, $\frac{3}{19}$ | Gifts to knights and others, value of horses, &c. . | | 1,633 |
| | Food, and fees of those collecting it . . . | | 416 |
| | 'Garrison' in Anglesey and Montgomery, plus some foot, autumn . . . . . . | | 2,300 |
| ,, $\frac{3}{16}$ | 'Garrison' in Flint, *post recessit rex* . . . | | 1,223 |
| | 'Garrison' in Carmarthen, autumn . . . | | 474 |
| | Howel ap Meyrick at Builth . . . . | | 100 |
| | Bogo de Knoville and others, bringing foot to Flint | | 541 |
| | Repaid to merchants of Lucca, part of loan . | | 988 |
| | Drawn by the earl marshal, who will account for the items (Grey's horse?) . . . . | | 256 |
| | | Total . | 20,556 |

Not entered on the *Pipe Roll*:

| | | | £ |
|---|---|---|---|
| ,, $\frac{3}{21}$ | Knights of the household . . . . | | 830 |
| ,, $\frac{3}{18}$ | Mounted crossbowmen . . . . | | 264 |
| ,, $\frac{3}{20}$ | Various lords in South Wales . . . | | 1,021 |
| | | | 2,115 |
| | *Pipe Roll*, 8 Edw. I : foot at Flint : autumn, 1277 | | 478 |
| | | Gross total . | 23,149 |

Besides the special war expenses the maintenance of the military members of the household in time of peace, these being the only standing troops of the period, cost on an average nearly £7,000; wages, gifts, purchase of horses and armour, payments in lieu of robes, &c., came on the king's private or wardrobe account [1]. When the ready money was not forthcoming, for the collection of the fifteenth was slow and arrears were considerable, recourse was had to Italian bankers. The fifteenth of 1275 should have brought in about £120,000; the thirtieth voted in 1283 yielded £55,000 immediately, and £8,400 of arrears came in gradually up to 1289 [2]; the fifteenth of 1290 yielded £107,500, without counting the sums due from Chester and Durham, and arrears were yet expected [3]. Customs yielded at this period £8,000 to £10,000 annually [4].

[1] *Pipe Roll*, 8 and 10 Edw. I, under 'Wardrobe.'.
[2] Ibid. 16 Edw. I.      [3] Ibid. 23 Edw. I.
[4] Ibid. 8 and 16 Edw. I.

Thus the crown could meet the expenses of the first Welsh war without much trouble.

Annexation of the whole of Wales was not Edward's policy. Llewelyn having yielded, and being likely to remain quiet under English supremacy, it was sufficient to bind him to do homage for his principality ; annexation followed the second and more desperate war after each side had called up all its reserves. There was a big war indemnity of £50,000, and an annual rent of 1,000 marcs on the English evacuation of Anglesey[1]. But these were soon remitted, and Anglesey was to revert to Edward if Llewelyn should die childless. Then Edward claimed, by reconquest rather than annexation, the country which he had himself held for a short time in 1254, and which had changed masters frequently but had never been permanently occupied by the English, namely, two of the Cantreds and Cardiganshire and Carmarthenshire. The other two Cantreds, Rhyfoniog and Dyffryn Clwyd, were awarded to David, Denbigh and Hope being the chief strongholds. Finally, Llewelyn was allowed to marry his Montfort bride at Worcester in 1278. The English commissioners who arranged the terms were Antony Bek, the king's celebrated secretary and future Bishop of Durham, another highly placed cleric, Otto de Grandison, and Robert de Tibotot. Grandison's name does not appear in the printed text of the treaty, but his services are clearly shown by a document which contains entries of money for the expenses of the commissioners[2]. The march was not touched by the treaty ; marchers who had been dispossessed by Llewelyn entered into their own, except where the king kept some castle to himself as having been conquered by his paid troops.

English ideas were to be introduced with all speed for the orderly government of the new territory. Most marked is Edward's determination to thin out the forests, and Welsh resentment thereat was very bitter. One order referring to the Mortimer march shows his reason, for the closely wooded districts were haunts of robbers, *quod tuto transeatur ubi*

---

[1] Rymer, Nov. 12, 1277 : from *Welsh Roll.*
[2] *Exch. Acc.* $\frac{3}{15}$, and *Welsh Roll*, Nov. 2, 1277.

*robberie fieri solebant*; free communication is the strongest evidence of order and civilization. Then the shire system and legal procedure in shire courts were introduced[1]. In 1278 commissioners, including the Bishop of Worcester, Pain de Chaworth, Henry de Bray, and Howel ap Meyrick, were appointed according to the legal formula *ad audiend et terminand omnes querelas* in South Wales. In 1280 the system of jury trial *per duodenam proborum et legalium hominum* was introduced. In 1280 a commission was appointed, consisting of the Bishop of St. David's, Reginald de Grey, and Walter de Hopton, to investigate the manner in which the king's ancestors were wont to govern the Welshmen, and they were to take evidence on oath from knights and freemen. Sittings were held at Chester, Rhuddlan, Oswestry, and Montgomery, and afterwards at Llanbadarn, so that the investigation was fairly wide. Of the results of the commission it has been said that 'if the evidence is true there can be no doubt that in the area of inquiry Norman-English procedure and law had already almost entirely ousted the Welsh customs; but there is reasonable ground for suspecting it. ... The survival of Welsh customs tends to confirm one's suspicions, but, on the other hand, the commissioners' questions dealt chiefly with procedure and the rights of barons and landed proprietors; and it may be urged that the supersession of Welsh law in regard to that part of the *corpus iuris* was not inconsistent with the retention of Welsh usages in regard to other parts, or as to holdings of land by inferior tenants in particular lordships[2].' The area of inquiry corresponds to the annexed Cantreds and to Cardiganshire, also to the march lands reconquered from Llewelyn on the borders of Chester and Shropshire[3].

But while it was a slow process to wean the Welsh to English ways, military needs showed to Edward the necessity of building strong castles at the strategic points. In the north Chester and Oswestry were no longer to be the frontier

---

[1] *Welsh Roll*, 6 to 9 Edw. I, *passim*.

[2] Rhys and Brynmor Jones, *Welsh People*, p. 350.

[3] Bridgeman, *Princes of South Wales*, p. 163.

fortresses, but Flint and Rhuddlan were erected to form the first line, being as it were the Strasburg and Metz of the period, while the other two were like Coblentz and Mainz in the second line. We have already seen how Flint was securely held from the August of 1277 by Grey with a strong detachment of horse and foot, and the work of construction then began. Not so much money was spent as in the construction of Rhuddlan, for not much more than £1,200 can be found to have been spent in wages[1]. The Justiciar of Chester had full control, although some of the chroniclers were confused on the point and imagined that David held the new castle. However, it is perfectly clear from the rolls that David only held the two Cantreds of Rhyfoniog and Dyffryn Clwyd, and Denbigh and Hope were his castles. In the other two Cantreds of Rhos and Tegeingl, a certain Howel ap Gruffudd was royal bailiff, under the supervision of the justiciar, soon to be succeeded by Nicholas Bonel. Hawarden, during the continued minority of Roger de Monthaut, was first held by Kenrick Seys, a prominent Welsh member of the corps of mounted crossbowmen, and later by the elder Roger de Clifford[2]. Possibly both Howel and Kenrick were connected with David, and we know that they rendered themselves obnoxious to their fellow countrymen by their masterfulness and tyranny, as though they were trying to court the favour of the English by excessive severity. Doubtless they were regarded as renegades. Yet it is to be noticed that they were succeeded in office by Englishmen, who, in their turn, were accused of being equally severe. Clifford is said to have controlled the land round Hawarden ' as if he were justiciar of all Wales[3].' This is an error. The new Justiciar of Chester, who succeeded Guncelin de Badlesmere in 1281, was not Clifford, but Grey. His sway extended from Chester over Flint, Rhos, and Tegeingl, the revenues of which he farmed for 1,000 marcs, and his own salary was

[1] *Pipe Roll*, 6 and 8 Edw. I, under ' Flint' or ' Rhuddlan.'

[2] *Patent Roll*, Oct. 15, 1277.

[3] Rishanger, p. 97 (R. S.). Many historians have written that Clifford was *the* Justiciar of Chester. I can find no authority except Rishanger's phrase *tanquam iusticiarius,* and that Grey succeeded Badlesmere in that office is undoubted.

£100, but Rhuddlan and Dinas Bran were held apart as special royal strongholds [1]. Grey, we have already seen and shall see throughout, was a strong man and a good soldier, while Guncelin, being not up to the mark as an administrator in an important position, almost disappears from sight.

The castle of Rhuddlan, an entirely new castle as we are expressly informed, was a very extensive and costly fortress. In two pipe rolls we find that over £11,000 were raised, partly from the revenues of Chester and the Cantreds, partly from three half-yearly payments of Llewelyn's tribute from Anglesey [2]. Nicholas Bonel first sent in the account, and afterwards William de Perton, under the supervision of Master James de St. George ; we can hardly be wrong in inferring that the latter was the chief architect and designer of the great Edwardian fortresses, and we shall find him later on engaged at Conway, Harlech, and Beaumaris as *magister operacionum regis in Wallia*, at one time drawing daily wages of 3s. a day, at another time a yearly retaining fee of 100 marcs. Close on £9,000 are entered as paid in wages to the masons, whether working on the castle, the fortifications of the town, or a great dyke and artificial harbour, *magnum fossatum in quo nunc est portus qui ducit a mari usque castrum predictum* ; for Rhuddlan was three miles up the Clwyd, and Edward's design was clearly to constitute a strong naval as well as military base. The main strength of the garrison in the autumn of 1277, and well into 1278, was formed by fourteen troopers of the household. A special officer was put in command to be responsible only to the king, for the Justiciar of Chester had no control, and I should take it that the architect St. George held the office. The solidity of the work was such that David was unable to take the place in his first wild outbreak in 1282, and Edward created here a large and well-organized base for the first part of the war of that year. Dinas Bran was also held by a special officer, namely Roger l'Estrange, at a salary of £100 [3]. The custody of Oswestry and the control of the Fitzalan fief generally, during minority,

---

[1] *Pipe Roll*, 11 Edw. I.        [2] *Pipe Rolls*, esp. 6 and 8 Edw. I.
[3] *Pipe Roll*, 12 Edw. I, under 'Wardrobe.'

belonged to the Sheriff of Shropshire, Roger Springhouse succeeding Bogo de Knoville in 1280 [1].

In the south it would seem that Edward at first intended that his brother Edmund should continue to hold Cardigan and Carmarthen, both the castles and counties. But obviously it was impossible to introduce the shire system as long as Edmund was a lord marcher, and therefore an exchange was effected ; he received valuable lands in Derbyshire by way of compensation, and turned over to the king all his rights over Cardigan and Carmarthen. Bogo de Knoville was thereupon appointed Justiciar of South Wales, June 10, 1280. A county court was now to be held on two consecutive days in every month at Carmarthen, at which the neighbouring marchers were to do suit and service, and all the lands of the lately independent chieftains, and even those of Rhys ap Maredudd, were included in the shires. Thus the custody of the castles devolved on Bogo as the royal official ; on the one side Cardigan and the growing works at Llanbadarn, on the other Carmarthen and Dynevor, Caercynan and Llandovery [2].

On the west coast, the 'noble' castle of Llanbadarn—i. e. Aberystwith, but it is invariably called Llanbadarn, though the village of that name is further inland—was to be the new base of the English ascendency beyond the Aeron, as Cardigan was *cis* Aeron. £918 were provided at first to the Earl of Lincoln, who had the work of superintendence [3]. Next William de Valence was in command, and there is extant a letter from him to Henry de Bray, of Abergavenny, demanding with some urgency a remittance of money lest the masons desert [4]. £1,400 were supplied from the wardrobe later on, and £200 extra were spent on a wall to surround the town of Aberystwith. Some of the material is recorded to have been sent up from Bristol.

Carmarthen, and to a much greater extent Caerphilly and Kidwelly, sank in importance as fortresses of the second line,

[1] *Pipe Roll*, 12 Edw. I, under 'Staffordshire.'

[2] *Carmarthen Charters*, pp. 10, 11, 45, and onwards ; *Eng. Hist. Review*, Jan. 1895, pp. 34, 35.

[3] *Pipe Roll*, 6 Edw. I, back of last membrane.

[4] *Eng. Hist. Review*, July, 1899.

while Dynevor became the new strategic centre on the Towy, with Caercynan inland to the east, and Llandovery higher up stream. Comparatively small sums were spent, which points to the castles being already in a good state of repair. Llandovery castle was entrusted to Giffard, who already had a claim on the town through his wife, which he contested at law against Rhys Vychan [1]. Bogo de Knoville had full control, farming the revenues of the counties and castles, Llanbadarn included, but not Builth, for 400 marcs a year [2]. He made a tour of inspection, but in the Easter of 1281 was succeeded by Robert de Tibotot, who stands out in the records and documents an administrator as much superior to Bogo as Grey was to Badlesmere. Tibotot was now, with William de Valence, the most conspicuous figure of the English ascendency for the next thirteen years in South Wales, and he had some status as a lord marcher by his marriage with a daughter of Pain de Chaworth. The latter had died in 1278.

On the central march Roger de Mortimer was in possession of the four castles already mentioned—Radnor, Cefnllys, Dunawd, and Dolforwyn—the latter having been restored to him by the king. Bogo de Knoville, after he had been superseded in South Wales by Tibotot, appears in a much more humble position as custodian of Montgomery. But the chief interest attaches to Builth. It will be remembered how Mortimer had lost castle and lands long ago to Llewelyn, the Earl of Lincoln had reoccupied the site with his paid forces, and so the crown claimed and retained it, making restitution of Dolforwyn, probably by way of recompense. As Llewelyn had destroyed the old castle, an entirely new one had to be built from the foundations. In 1277 the work began under Howel ap Meyrick, who was thus transformed from a steward of the Bohun and Mortimer marches into a royal official and constable, and he was responsible to no justiciar, but directly to the crown. His garrison was composed in 1277 of nine troopers and forty foot, decreasing next year to four troopers and ten foot, and later on he would have had to maintain the

---

[1] Bridgeman, *Princes of South Wales*, p. 170 (suit 10 Edw. I).
[2] *Pipe Roll*, 9 Edw. I, m. 2 ; *Welsh Roll, passim.*

defence out of the revenue of the lands. The details of the construction are extant in duplicate, and in the course of four years about £1,600 were expended[1]. The incomings were a fine of 20 marcs from a Welsh chieftain who was bound over to keep the peace; £250 from the revenue of Builth, the lands being held by Howel at farm; £200 *de hominibus de* Builth, apparently as a fine because they had helped Llewelyn; £550 from the wardrobe; £433 received in instalments from Henry de Bray as steward of the Hastings march during minority. A body of 120 axemen were engaged in cutting four 'trenches,' i. e. forest roads, for the security of travellers in the direction of Mortimer's castle of Cefnllys—a wise policy, because Builth was the most advanced English outpost in a wild part of Wales and in a neighbourhood much prone to revolt. The new castle, we are expressly told in the accounts of John of Radnor, who was apparently the architect at a wage of 1s. a day, was built with a great central tower and six smaller towers in the curtain (*turris cum sex turriclis*), and the drawbridge was guarded by two more big towers (*magnis turrellis*); mention is also made of a hall, a chapel, kitchens, smithy, and stables. The freestone was quarried in the Black Mountains on the boundary of Herefordshire, and wages were paid to quarrymen, carters, lime-burners—whose kilns were at Talgarth in the same mountains—charcoal-burners, masons, carpenters, smiths, and hodmen. During the four years of construction, the works were surveyed by the Earl of Lincoln, Roger de Mortimer, Otto de Grandison, and John de Vescy, and that success attended the efforts of the builders is seen in the fact that never was the castle captured, although it was isolated and often surrounded by a sea of revolt, and although Llewelyn himself invaded the valley of the upper Wye. Howel ap Meyrick lived just long enough to see the completion of the fortress. In 1281, on his death, his accounts were wound up by his son Philip, and lands and castle were handed over on November 28 to Roger l'Estrange. By this last change the custody of Dinas Bran became vacant, and was conferred upon the Earl of Surrey.

[1] *Exch. Acc.* $\frac{485}{20}$, $\frac{485}{21}$, $\frac{485}{23}$, and *Pipe Roll*, 8 Edw. I.

# CHAPTER IV

## THE WAR OF 1282 AND 1283

THE second war is chiefly remarkable because David reconciled himself to Llewelyn. The two brothers fought to the end. They defended Denbigh and Snowdonia with desperation, instead of being cowed by the first English advance up to the outskirts. They penetrated into Cardiganshire and Carmarthenshire, touched the Bristol Channel, and twice raised Brecknock and Radnor. The area of the war was so wide that Edward was unable to march straight on Snowdonia, and there had to be several months of preliminary fighting along the whole line of the marches. A second war usually presents similar features. The side beaten in the first thinks that enough had not then been done, the victors' tactics were not understood, and greater steadfastness as the result of experience and foresight will wipe out the galling sense of past defeat and inferiority. The second Samnite and Punic wars are good cases in point. But in reality England gained. The collapse of the Welsh after fifteen months of war was all the more complete in proportion to the obstinacy of their resistance. The resources of England were found to be reliable just because they were so severely strained, and this statement is really true in spite of the fact that in the south the infantry was almost entirely drawn from the Welsh friendlies, or that in the north the tide of war was not turned until 1,5co mercenaries were brought in from Gascony. The winter campaign is most instructive as showing Edward's dogged determination not to accept defeat. Once more is seen the extreme importance of co-operation between fleet and army, while something new is the combination in battle of foot and horse.

No special cause for the rising need be sought beyond the

natural wish for liberty and revenge. That Edward, from 1277 onwards, was combining fairness towards the Welsh with reasonable precautions for security accords with his character. But he did not allow for that restlessness and independence of spirit which sees tyranny in precaution. That the chief grievance was the conduct of his officials, not of the crown itself, is also clear. Doubtless they behaved roughly, and Llewelyn, in his remonstrances addressed to Archbishop Peckham, especially insisted on the wanton cruelty of the English administrators[1]. *Semper mittebantur iusticiarii et ballivi ferociores et crudeliores.* The crown was responsible for the acts of its servants. In fact we find a world-old problem : on Edward's side a policy of unionism and centralized order, on the Welsh side resentment of interference with liberty. Love of order degenerates into brutal repression, liberty includes even licence to rob and be lawless. A good instance in point is the custom of appropriating wreckage. The custom encourages deliberate wrecking, and Edward and his officials set their faces against it, inflicting fines and impounding the spoil. Again, the systematic cutting down of forests, because they were the haunts of robbers, became a grievance. Llewelyn brooded over his personal wrongs which wounded his pride and prestige. He had had to sign a paper at Worcester, on the occasion of his marriage, to the effect that he would not keep any man on his lands, that is within his acknowledged principality of Snowdon, without the king's sanction ; Edward seems to have meant English outlaws, Llewelyn thought that the reference was to his own Welsh subjects. He objected to being cited to appear in person at Montgomery, and it did not soothe his sense of injury to be told that pleas concerning tenants-in-chief were held at fixed places. In the annexed Cantreds, the chief complaint was that the old customs of Wales and the privileges which even Henry III had allowed were systematically violated. English legal process was being introduced, and the armed interference of Reginald de Grey accentuated the grievance. Robert de Crevecœur, a knight of the household ; Kenrick Seys, the

---

[1] *Registrum literarum Iohannis Peckham*, ii. 437, &c. (R. S.).

royal trooper who has been already mentioned and who must have been regarded as a renegade ; Roger de Clifford, and his lieutenant, are represented as armed spoilers and extortioners. The sons of Gruffudd ap Gwenwynwyn are similarly named as tyrants towards the Welsh who bordered on Powysland. In Cardiganshire and Carmarthenshire the introduction of the shire system was resented, and in particular the right of the Welsh themselves to appeal to the justiciar against their own Welsh overlords. But it is rather startling to find a list of grievances tabulated on behalf of the loyalist Rhys ap Maredudd ; some of his men had been murdered by Pain de Chaworth at the time of the treaty and surrender of Dynevor in 1277 ; John Giffard had claimed wrongfully some lands, and the case had been tried in the county court of Herefordshire, not even 'according to the law of the county of Carmarthenshire.' But as Rhys did not revolt, we cannot but suspect that the grievances were partly manufactured ; and if manufactured in his case, perhaps also in others. In general, it must be allowed that English ideas were galling, even if in the long run English rule might prove salutary. The right of appeal to the justiciar was evidently much hated, but it shows that the Welsh nobles were outraged in their feelings, not that the poorer Welsh were badly governed under English law. Revolts are commonly due to the offended pride of a local aristocracy, who, as their next step, try to make the rising appear to be national and unanimous. When we see in the course of the war how steadily the Welsh of the march still fought on the English side, how frequently the men of some district recently in revolt joined the English to go against their own countrymen, we suspect that Edward's rule was after all not very heavy or unpopular. In 1283 some tenants wished to migrate from a march and to live under the crown, and this can only mean that the justiciar, Robert de Tibotot, made the crown acceptable to the humbler classes of Welsh in the south. Of course the Welsh of Snowdonia and the Four Cantreds were anti-English throughout from prince to peasant.

Edward's answer, when the grievances were submitted in

the course of the war, was characteristic. The revolt was inexcusable, because there was no reference to himself[1]. Why
had not Llewelyn informed him of the brutalities of the
English officials, of the heaviness of English legal process
when contrasted with old Welsh custom? He had been ready
to investigate and do justice. *Omni tempore paratus extiterat
omni facere iustitiam conquerenti.* If the justiciar or the
county court were grievous, was there not the king as overlord
ready to entertain the supreme appeal? 'Statesmanlike, but
high-handed,' is the commentary of Mr. C. T. Martin[2], on
whose preface to Archbishop Peckham's letters I have not
hesitated to base my summary of this question.

Mr. Martin has some interesting passages upon the Welsh
character as revealed in the story of the wrongs. ' Llewelyn
signed the paper at Worcester,' he says, 'compelled by the
fear which may fall upon a steadfast man, *timor qui potest
cadere in constantem virum*, a curious phrase which occurs
more than once in the series of Welsh remonstrances, and
which suggests that the Welsh courage was of the uncivilized
order, fury without much self-control.' In Wales, abject submission to English tyranny was varied by hysterical outbursts
for revenge. There was not that systematic and constant
hostility as between two sets of good fighters who almost liked
each other. 'The Welsh march was not like the borders of
Scotland, where people of the same race and of equal prowess
plundered and fought, thanking each other for the sport they
had shown, which sport was governed by certain defined rules,
tolerably well kept on the whole.' The Scottish borderer
was of a different type. The Welshman, as in the days of
Gerald de Barri, was all for sudden onslaughts, and when
faced and beaten back was despondent.

The peace was broken by David, the somewhat pampered
ally of England. The chroniclers and contemporaries
generally were much struck by David's conduct. 'We had
welcomed him when an exile,' said Edward himself[3], 'nourished
him when an orphan; endowed him out of our own lands,

---

[1] Mr. Martin reads *inexcusabiles*, not *excusabiles*, which is meaningless.
[2] pp. xlv, &c.     [3] *Welsh Roll*, June 28, 1283.

and favoured him under the cloak of our wings, placing him among the greatest of our palace.' On David's side it might be argued that he had not received as much as he himself expected by the compact of Flint; Edward had given him lands, but not the principality of Snowdon or Anglesey; he had got Denbigh and a rich wife, but was treated as a vassal of the crown of England, having to submit to the indignity of appearing before the Justiciar of Chester to prove his title to certain lands, and an inquiry was actually being held in the January and February of 1282. It was injudicious on Edward's part not to satisfy him thoroughly, but the king thought that reasonable compensation had been given, even if the exact terms of the compact had not been fulfilled. At any rate, it seemed that having fought already against his brother, 'contrary to the character of his race (*contra morem gentis*), and being now forgetful of the benefits of the king, who had protected him against that persecuting brother[1],' he was an ungrateful traitor. On March 21, 1282, he swooped down on Hawarden. The night attack was quite unexpected. The garrison was overpowered, and Roger de Clifford was taken captive. The chroniclers seem to have confused what happened next, and thought that Flint and Rhuddlan were also captured. But Edward's proclamation of the 25th refers only to a slaughter in the town of Flint, and the castles were certainly not lost; all the facts of the war, and especially the entire absence of any expenses which rebuilding would have demanded, show that they were safe from David[2]. But besides Hawarden, he already possessed Hope and Denbigh; Ruthin and Dinas Bran had to be reconquered by the English, and therefore were now in his hands, though Dinas Bran had been garrisoned by l'Estrange quite recently. The calling of a 'parliament' to Denbigh and the acceptance of war by the Welsh probably belong to this date; Langtoft[3] says the next

---

[1] Trivet, p. 301.

[2] Compare *Brut*, p. 373; Trivet, p. 302; *Annales Monastici*, 'Wykes,' vol. iv. p. 287; 'Dunstable,' vol. iii. p. 290; *Flores Historiarum*, iii. 56. The most conclusive evidence is given by *Pipe Roll* 14 Edw. I, last membrane.

[3] Vol. ii. p. 180 (R. S.)

Christmas, but Edward had then got the place securely garrisoned by the English. By the end of March we may suppose that all the Cantreds were up in arms, and the revolt was established up to the confines of Chester, but the castles of Flint and Rhuddlan held out, and were in connexion with Chester by water.

Llewelyn remaining in the north, David rushed off to rouse the South Welsh. In conjunction with Gruffudd and Llewelyn, sons of Rhys Vychan and lords of Isgenen, he captured Llandovery and Caercynan on March 26 [1]. With Rhys ap Maelgwn and Gruffudd and Cynan ap Maredudd, he seized and destroyed Llanbadarn on April 9 [2]. He set before himself a sound policy when he destroyed the fortresses which were symbols of slavery to England. To attempt to hold them, and thus to allow himself to be blockaded till he was reduced by starvation, would have been to play into England's hands. Certain unsuccessful attempts were made by the English in April to reoccupy Llanbadarn, and in June both Llanbadarn and Caercynan, but David's purpose was accomplished. Cardiganshire and Carmarthenshire were up, and the English were driven back to their bases at Dynevor and Cardigan. The marches were indeed safe, though doubtless they were raided; but inland Rhys ap Maredudd alone remained loyal, *solus inter nobiles et magnates*, and that, too, though a list of grievances was drawn up in his name. Throughout Brecknock and Radnor also the rising must have been general, and around Montgomery, as is shown by the numerous orders to receive the insurgents to the king's peace. David returned northwards, having fired the train of revolt. The fury of the outburst, the dash from north to south and back again, were characteristic of Welsh methods. Edward, throughout this war, never knew where the next blow was going to fall, and he could only wear the Welsh down by patience and a slow advance.

The king knew about Hawarden by March 25 [3]. He at once sent word to his justiciars, ordering Reginald de Grey to take command at Chester, and Robert de Tibotot in South

---

[1] *Brut*, p. 373.    [2] *Annales Cambriae*, p. 106.
[3] *Parl. Writs*, i. 222.

Wales; the Sheriffs of Lancashire and Derbyshire were to aid the one 'with arms and horses and their whole posse,' the Earls of Hereford and Gloucester the other. Roger de Mortimer was to command at Montgomery, supported by Bogo de Knoville and other magnates of Shropshire. A council was summoned to meet at Devizes on April 5.

At Devizes various writs were issued. The Earl of Gloucester was appointed commander-in-chief in the south, superseding Tibotot[1]. The Earl of Hereford having demanded the emoluments of his office as constable, Edward ordered the Barons of the Exchequer to investigate the precedents[2]; they reported that the earl had the right, which his predecessors had enjoyed, to receive 2d. in the pound on all pay given to the king's stipendiaries, also to 5s. a day with perquisites if he dined outside, 3s. 6d. if he dined in the household. The full feudal levy was not called out, but six earls and other crown tenants individually were 'affectionately requested' to come to Worcester by May 17, thence to accompany the king 'at our wages,' *ad vadia nostra,* a phrase unprecedented in writs of military summons. Then loans to the amount of 12,000 marcs were contracted with various Italian firms[3]. The Earl of Warwick and Walter de Beauchamp were sent to France to procure horses. The ships of the Cinque Ports were ordered. Agents were sent to Ireland and Scotland to procure supplies, also to Gascony and to Ponthieu, which had since the first war come to Queen Eleanor as her inheritance. Jean de Greilly, Seneschal of Gascony, was summoned to supply twelve mounted and forty foot crossbowmen, a modest number.

A force of cavalry was rapidly concentrated on the borders as in 1277[4]. The knights and troopers of the household, under Amadeus of Savoy, were pushed up at once in April from Devizes to Chester, fifteen knights with thirty-one troopers in attendance, and sixty troopers paid separately. In May the ever ready Robert de Tateshale had out a troop of fifteen lances, and William de Audley and Robert Fitzwalter had also fifteen each, so that with smaller details Grey was in

---

[1] *Parl. Writs,* i. 222–4.  [2] Rymer, April 6, 1282.
[3] *Welsh Roll, passim.*  [4] *Exch. Acc.* ⅘, the main cavalry pay-roll.

command of some 160 lances before May was out, and must have been in a fairly strong position to confront the insurgents at Hawarden and Hope.   The task of creating a base, getting up supplies and infantry in readiness for the king, would fall on him.   More to the south, at Oswestry, where Roger Spring-house, who was now Sheriff of Shropshire, had command, £240 were paid for forty days' service, enough to satisfy 600 foot[1], and there was one troop of thirteen lances under John de la Mare.   Roger de Mortimer had his own train of eighteen and Otto de Grandison had seventeen at Montgomery, where also the Earl of Lincoln drew £255 for twenty days, let us say for 100 horse and 600 foot.   There are no details of the force at Builth under Roger l'Estrange, or in Brecknock under the Earl of Hereford, but each was holding his own against a widespread revolt.   John Giffard had been driven away from Llandovery.   Alan Plukenet by the end of April concentrated a squadron of over ninety lances at Gloucester under five bannerets, and brought them to the aid of William de Valence and Robert de Tibotot in South Wales ; pay for forty days was given in advance.   Thus within a month of David's capture of Hawarden over 200, within two months over 300, lances of the household and paid squadrons were in arms between Chester and Cardigan, local levies not counted or troops paid by sums of money entered in gross without details. More cavalry were on their way to the front in June, until over 600 of all ranks were up and in pay in' different parts of Wales.   The answer to the king's call must have appeared to him to be very satisfactory.

A considerable difficulty now arises.   Having reached Worcester in the middle of May, as he had given out, Edward proceeded to issue new writs of summons, calling out the whole feudal host of all three classes of crown tenants in the most formal and orthodox way, and appointing a rendezvous at Rhuddlan on August 2[2].   There is such a difference between the previous summons from Devizes and this new summons of

---

[1] *Exch. Acc.* $\frac{3}{30}$, the main infantry pay-roll.

[2] *Parl. Writs*, i. 225.   This helps to prove that Rhuddlan was not captured by David.

six weeks later that some explanation must be sought; the first writs were addressed to certain individuals, affectionately requested them to serve, and offered pay; the new writs were addressed formally to all tenants and demanded service on their allegiance. Be it remembered that at the end of the year 1276 the king gave to his feudal lords a full notice of six months, and later on, in the wars against Scotland, he invariably gave a similar long notice when he issued a formal summons; the present summons fixed the muster at a notice of little over two months. An explanation that he was dissatisfied with the numbers that responded to his call for paid service is weak, for some hundreds of men were up and more were pouring in. Did he make the first call as a temporary measure, intending in any case also to order out later the full feudal host? But in that case he would have issued both sets of writs simultaneously so as to give as long a notice as possible. Or was the war more serious than he first thought? The loan, the collection of supplies, the orders sent to the Cinque Ports, all point to the contrary.

To judge causes by the sequence of events leads often to wild imaginings, but it is a method which has its uses. The constitutional position of a monarch like Edward has to be viewed differently at different periods of his reign, as his difficulties with his barons are seen in different lights. Therefore the sequence-of-events method will give us an idea of his policy if we closely refuse to look at any further crisis, for instance the great crisis of 1297. In 1274 there had been a commission appointed to investigate the titles and franchises of the crown tenants [1]; the king had just come to the throne, and required to know the exact status of the feudal nobles. The results are recorded in the Hundreds' Rolls. Then came the first Welsh war, and the calling out of the feudal host in 1277. In 1278 was passed the Statute of Gloucester based on the Hundreds' Rolls; the tenants were called upon 'to show what sort of franchises they claim to have and by what warrant.' The Earl of Surrey—but one would like to believe that it was Gloucester—melodramatically produced the rusty

[1] Stubbs, vol. ii. p. 120.

sword of his fathers as his warrant[1]. Now in 1282 the
baronage had their first chance of showing what they thought
of the *quo warranto*. Gloucester and Hereford were to the
front in asserting at Devizes their claims, the Clare receiving
the command in South Wales, the Bohun demanding the
acknowledgement of his status as constable ; this done, they
did not object to the crown's summons of paid professional
soldiers in place of feudal. Lastly at Worcester, perhaps as
the result of pressure, the crown was constrained to call for
feudal service. That there is at least an *a priori* probability
that this theory is correct is seen in the general necessities
of the crown. Paid service was obviously to Edward's
advantage, and no less obviously the greater barons wished
to make him dependent during a war on their unpaid quotas.
They refused to descend to the level of stipendiaries, stood on
their rights by insisting on the performance of their exact
feudal obligations—for the king stood on his rights in examining their franchises—and equally determined to maintain their
march privileges. Further, it may be argued that neither
Gloucester nor Hereford had received writs of summons on
the Devizes model affectionately requesting them to serve for
pay, and it cannot be a coincidence that they, the two most
assertive barons, were just the very two in evidence there,
being bribed to consent to the crown's offer of pay to the
others. We should notice that Lincoln had twice already
raised troops for pay, but never again, except perhaps in
1295, can he be found fighting except with his unpaid quota,
and yet he was a notable loyalist. There is yet this to be
considered ; no evidence justifies us in assuming that at this
date a party of opposition had been formed, but the two
earls seem to have been personally opposed to the crown ;
when the troubles of 1297 began, and there was a real
organized party, one of the most noteworthy facts is that
the feudal writs of summons were issued for the war in Scotland in the most formal manner.

The king was at Chester in the second week of June and
took over the cavalry which had already been mustered.

---

[1] *Chronicle of Lanercost*, p. 168 ; see *Dict. Nat. Biog.*, x. 382 and lix. 366.

More troops came in during the month, some new, some
which had already been doing duty elsewhere, until close on
300 lances were in the headquarters army exclusive of the
household.  The following is the roll at Chester, with the date
when each troop first came into pay ; but, as just suggested,
many of the men may have been already serving under the
Earl of Lincoln or others, and were merely transferred to
the king's army, the troops of John de la Mare and Hugh de
Turberville being certainly cases in point, the one having
originally been brought to Oswestry and the other to Montgomery.

| Bannerets. | Knights. | Troopers. | No. of lances. |
|---|---|---|---|
| Robert de Tateshale, May 8 . . | 4 | 11 | 16 |
| William de Audley, May 22 . . | 3 | 12 | 16 |
| Robert Fitzwalter, May 22 . . | 3 | 11 | 15 |
| William de Ros, June 9 . . . | 3 | 11 | 15 |
| Nich. de Segrave, June 9 . . | 3 | 9 | 13 |
| John de la Mare, June 9 . . | 2 | 10 | 13 |
| Philip de Kyme, June 9 . . . | 3 | 8 | 12 |
| Ralph Basset, June 13 . . . | 2 | 9 | 12 |
| Will. le Butler (of Werington), June 14 | 4 | 7 | 12 |
| William de Say, June 2 . . . | 2 | 7 | 10 |
| Walt. de Huntercumbe, June 15 . | 2 | 7 | 10 |
| Roger de Molis, June 15 . . | 2 | 7 | 10 |
| Aymer de St. Amand, June 24 . | 2 | 7 | 10 |
| Richard de Bruce, June 24 . . | 1 | 8 | 10 |
| Will. de Leyburn, June 24 . . | 2 | 7 | 10 |
| John de Bohun, June 23 . . . | 1 | 8 | 10 |
| Geoffrey de Lucy, July . . . | 2 | 7 | 10 |
| John le Marechal, June 17 . . | 2 | 6 | 9 |
| (Ralph de Berners, kn.) June 9 . | 2 | 7 | 9 |
| (Hugh de Turberville, kn.) May 8 . | 3 | 5 | 8 |
| (John de Sudley, kn.) April 29 . | 2 | 6 | 8 |
| (Adam de Creting, kn.) June 2 . | 1 | 7 | 8 |
| Smaller bodies, 3 bannerets . . | 7 | 20 | 30 |
| Total : 21 bannerets . | 58 | 197 | 276 |

There would thus seem to be three squadrons of one
hundred lances each, a few of the troops being short of some
multiple of five.  But there is no clue as to how the troops
were grouped in squadrons, or how the commands were
subordinated.  It will be noticed that Grey's immediate
command is not entered, for his own men came under another
paymaster whose account is not extant, and we only know
that over £900 were paid to horse and £1,100 to foot in his

division under the head of 'garrison of Chester'; £900 would maintain about fifty lances of all ranks for nine months. A similar calculation has to be made if we wish to ascertain Mortimer's strength at Montgomery. Then various entries show that the Earls of Lancaster, Lincoln, Surrey, and Norfolk were with the king in June or July, presumably with their quotas, although the feudal period was not to begin till August. The paid cavalry, Grey's command, the household, and the quotas would amount to 600 lances at Chester alone; in the whole of Wales 800 must have been serving. The foot [1] on June 15 numbered 7,000, but there were only eighty-six cross-bows. All the men were from English counties, and their pay was the regular 2d. a day even in the case of the Macclesfield contingents. It seems that an increasing proportion of the foot were armed with bows, for the word *sagittarii* occurs more frequently in place of the *pedites* or *sagittarii et lanceati* of the first war. The total of 7,000 was not kept up, but there is an easy explanation, for drafts were sent out on special duty, so that the numbers at headquarters dwindled. Similarly, the number of crossbowmen varies. At different times we can account for a good many, but rarely more than fifty to eighty were with the king; the rest up to a total of about 250 were in garrisons, or on shipboard when the fleet arrived. Reference has been already made to the enormous amount of crossbow ammunition, 10,000 quarrels being sent now from Bristol, 14,000 soon afterwards, and 40,000 next September as a reserve supply from London. There must have been many crossbowmen continually in action in one place or another. The army now ready to start against David, who had returned from South Wales, was concentrated round Chester, partly at Shotwick on the Dee, partly at Newton and Shocklack further inland.

The main plan of campaign was as in 1277, but was more difficult to carry out. The king's advance was along the coast to Flint and Rhuddlan, but first David's forces, whose base was at Denbigh and outposts at Dinas Bran and Hope and Hawarden, had to be contained or crushed. Therefore

[1] *Exch. Acc.* $\frac{3}{80}$.

Reginald de Grey was ordered to work westwards up the Dee, where already one of his bannerets, Brian de St. Peter, was commanding an advanced post[1]. With him was Owen, Llewelyn's brother, to whom Edward had granted lands in the neighbourhood and whose tenants had revolted. David, true to his tactics and refusing to let himself be caught in a castle as in a trap, fell back at once from Hope, but not before he had partially dismantled the fortress and stopped up the wells, thus compelling the English to delay while they rebuilt[2]. On June 16 Grey was in possession. He appointed Hugh de Pulford as Constable of Hope, with a force of thirty-six horse under Brian de St. Peter, thirty crossbows, and 2,600 archers who, it may be noticed, appear from the roll to have been an unmixed bow-armed corps. Their services would be required to beat off attacks of David's Welsh from the hills while the castle was being repaired. Great numbers of workmen were brought up, chiefly in gangs of twenty, from the northern and midland counties; 430 woodmen at first, and another 300 in July, 340 carpenters and forty masons. We find them at work on the fortifications, throwing down an unsafe tower, clearing out the wells, and so on, and this went on throughout July and August. Meanwhile, the cavalry were reinforced by a draft sent by Edward from headquarters of the troops of Robert de Tateshale, Aymer de St. Amand, and Roger de Molis, and smaller details, with thirty more crossbows, so that the force now mustered sixty-three horse and sixty crossbows, but the archers under John de Monthaut fell to 960. As in 1277, the men serving under Grey were his frequent comrades, who knew him and also knew the country. But he could control a larger force with the £2,000 already mentioned, and doubtless extended his operations over a considerable area. At the end of June Richard de Grey with six lances occupied a castle which, though the entry is difficult to read, seems to have been Ewloe, lying considerably to the north and close to the estuary of the Dee[3].

---

[1] *Welsh Roll*, June 15.
[2] *Misc. Chancery Roll* $\frac{1}{2}$ a special pay-roll of the army at Hope.
[3] *Exch. Acc.* $\frac{4}{1}$, as before.

Hawarden was probably evacuated in July by David, and Hope was being made a forward base for a further advance inland.

While Grey thus covered the king's left flank, the main army operated between Chester and Flint. No details can be found of Edward's doings, and he was probably engaged in organizing his horse and foot as they came up, while the Earl of Norfolk was busy with the commissariat. He could put into the field 600 horse by the end of June, and foot varying in numbers, as drafts were told off to Hope and as new relays were brought in, between 3,000 and 4,000; the chief infantry officers were Richard de Boys, Thomas de Turberville, and Walter le Jay. I have seen a statement in certain histories of Wales that Edward received a severe check about this date; but, as not one single passage in the chroniclers to which reference has been made to support the statement really bears it out, I cannot help thinking that by a strange confusion the defeat of the Earl of Gloucester at Dynevor has been transferred and put to the king's credit, or discredit, in North Wales. Every defeat is clearly reflected in the pay-rolls, but at this date the numbers of the cavalry remain constant, beyond the slight wear and tear of the campaign, and the diminution of the foot simply coincides with the drafting of archers to Grey's command. The language of chroniclers is always loose and, unless carefully examined, is most misleading, but that this particular defeat was suffered at Dynevor and not near Chester or Hope there can be no doubt at all. The king reached Flint on July 7, Rhuddlan on the 12th. As was suggested previously, neither of these castles had been in danger of capture at the time of David's first outbreak, though perhaps the towns adjoining had been pillaged. The fleet was now coming up, for twenty-eight ships began a period of fifteen [1] days of customary unpaid service on the 10th. Edward's chief care in July was to secure his line of communication with Chester and to keep in touch with Grey, while organizing for a combined attack on

[1] If *xl dierum* in the documents is a scribe's slip for *xv*. See above, page 107.

Denbigh on the one side, and on Anglesey on the other. Reinforcements of horse would be expected to arrive at the feudal muster on August 2, and new relays of foot had been ordered for the same date. There was some anxiety about remounts, for the King of France had refused to allow shipments to England. An order was issued, and sanctioned by the council, that each owner of land to the value of £30 should keep a horse ready to be sent to the army on an emergency, and a subsequent modification allowed a compensating fine to be paid [1].

In the south when the Earl of Gloucester took up his command he found a paid squadron of horse ready for him, nearly 100 lances strong, which Alan Plukenet had raised and concentrated at Gloucester towards the end of April. All the troop-leaders were tenants-in-chief from the south-west counties of England, but only five of them were bannerets, and the troops commanded by these were stronger than the others. Their first instalment of pay appears on the main cavalry roll, being on a forty days' contract, and then they came under the paymaster of South Wales, who drew up a special roll of accounts.

| Bannerets. | Knights. | Troopers. | No. of lances. |
|---|---|---|---|
| Geoffrey de Camville . . . | 2 | 12 | 15 |
| Alan Plukenet . . . . | 3 | 9 | 13 |
| Hugh de Courtenay . . . | 3 | 8 | 12 |
| John de Beauchamp . . . | 2 | 9 | 12 |
| Ralph Daubeny . . . . | 1 | 9 | 11 |
| Nicholas de Montfort, kn. . . | 2 | 6 | 8 |
| William de Mohun, kn. . . | 2 | 6 | 8 |
| Henry de l'Ortiay, kn. . . | 1 | 5 | 6 |
| Simon de Montacute, kn. . . | 1 | 3 | 4 |
| Hugh Pointz, kn. . . . | 1 | 3 | 4 |
| John de Cogan, kn. . . . | 1 | 2 | 3 |
| Total : 5 bannerets . . . | 19 | 72 | 96 |

Geoffrey de Camville and his troop very soon dropped out and served without pay as soon as he neared his own march. But Robert de Mohun came with ten lances in June, and other small details nearly brought the squadron up to

[1] *Welsh Roll*, May 26 and June 22.

strength again. These men formed the backbone of the army in the south, and served for a long time. They were but slightly reinforced; indeed, on the contrary, the troops fell off in numbers, which is suggestive of rather severe casualties in the midst of incessant fighting. Several of the leaders, Courtenay, Montfort, Montacute, and Pointz, would seem to have been wounded, as their men served for some time without them. But we shall see that they were strengthened when the feudal forty days began in August. The lords marchers are not in evidence on the roll. Besides Geoffrey de Camville, we have occasional notice of the service of Patrick de Chaworth, brother of the late Pain, and William de Braose, or his lieutenant John Penrhys, and constantly levies of foot were raised from their marches, as well as from the more distant Gwent. William de Valence and his son had unpaid retinues, and of course the Earl of Gloucester must have brought a very considerable body of horse when he came to take command. Rhys ap Maredudd constantly gave armed assistance to the English, his services being probably far greater than an occasional grant of a few pounds would indicate. In May and June all the horse, paid and unpaid, amounting to some 150 to 200 lances, were concentrated around Carmarthen and Dynevor.

All the organization in this part of Wales fell to a certain extent on William de Valence, but more largely on Robert de Tibotot, the justiciar, who had been originally nominated to the command when the war broke out. Superseded now by the Earl of Gloucester, he nevertheless did all the work of a chief of the staff, being associated by the king's orders with the Bishop of St. David's[1]. He was the guiding spirit throughout this war, and again in the operations against Rhys in 1287 and 1288. The complete pay-roll which is extant gives minute details, and his work always appears beneath the surface of the dry entries[2]. But he was doing more than merely paying the soldiers in the field. He practically maintained the permanent garrisons out of his own pocket, thus materially helping the king's cause by enabling the ready

[1] *Welsh Roll*, May 24.　　　　[2] *Misc. Chancery Roll* $\frac{1}{?}$.

money to go further. The consequence is that the roll only shows us the field operations by recording the payments made to Plukenet's horse, to the levies of Welsh friendlies, and to occasional bodies of crossbowmen and English foot ; the latter were clearly in permanent pay in the castles, and were maintained by Tibotot's private account, then when they made their appearance in the field they came on the roll. We shall see that the king recompensed the justiciar when the war was over. There are no details whatever concerning the transport and provisioning of the troops, which work, too, doubtless fell to him to carry out. I think that very probably at this date, as we know was the case in 1287, Tibotot could call upon the Welsh under his control to do unpaid service in defence of their own districts for three days at a time.

Unfortunately, the first few membranes of the roll are so mutilated that we cannot assign any date to the earliest operations of the Earl of Gloucester. He was probably on the spot at the end of April and throughout May, for various orders came to him from Edward pointing out the line along which he was to attack the insurgents [1] ; he was to reconquer and hand over Llandovery to John Giffard, and to pacify the district of the Ystwith and reconduct the English settlers to Llanbadarn. We can trace an unsuccessful attempt to carry out the latter part of the programme, for a few artisans were fetched up from Bristol to Aberystwith, but the renewal in June of the orders of April shows that the earl had so far done nothing to reinstate Giffard. On June 11—this is the first legible entry on the roll—an expedition was set on foot from Dynevor towards Caercynan, which had been seized and destroyed, at least partially, by David early in April. A force was made up of 1,600 foot from the marches of Cemaes, Kidwelly, and Llanstephan, and of about fifty of Plukenet's horse, the rest being in garrison or patrolling round the base castles ; to these must be added the retinues of William de Valence, of some of the marchers, and of Gloucester himself. There was a week's raiding. Caer-

[1] *Welsh Roll*, April 14, May 24, June 2.

cynan, or the ruins of the castle, was occupied by fifty foot and some workmen, as if the intention were to rebuild for permanent occupation. Then the force, returning to Dynevor carelessly without scouts and loaded with loot, was attacked all of a sudden from the hills, and, there can be little doubt, was very severely handled by the Welsh at Llandeilo Fawr. Young de Valence, Pembroke's son, was killed, with other knights. The date was June 17, according to the *Annales Cambriae*[1], and this coincides exactly with the termination of the earl's operations as seen in the roll. As was said above, this defeat has been transferred by some writers to North Wales, by others to the next year, but the authority of the Welsh chronicler, corroborated by the roll and the clear language of the sober contemporary English chronicler, Wykes of Osney, is conclusive[2]. Trivet claims a victory for Gloucester, but acknowledges that he immediately evacuated Carmarthenshire[3], thereby encouraging Llewelyn, and this would be a queer proceeding if the victory had been real. One has heard on other occasions of an enemy retreating rapidly after a successful guerilla attack and an English commander claiming to have completely routed him.

The English in the south seem to have been almost paralyzed for the next six weeks. The paid cavalry, suspiciously reduced in number since the battle of Llandeilo, were divided into two bodies of about thirty-five lances each, one sent over to garrison Cardigan under Philip Daubeny, the other remaining under Alan Plukenet to hold Dynevor, while John de Beauchamp and his troop were probably at Carmarthen. The Earl of Gloucester vanished, probably to defend his own march. Everywhere the English were on the defensive. It was now that Llewelyn seized his opportunity, appeared one knows not whence, descended on the Vale of Towy, ravaged at will, especially on the lands of Rhys, and extended his attentions over the watershed to the district around Cardigan. Edward on July 2 issued orders that the tenants-in-chief of the south-west of England were to do their feudal service in South Wales in place of coming to him at Rhuddlan, as

[1] p. 106.          [2] p. 286.          [3] p. 304.

Plukenet's corps was already composed of Somerset and Devon tenants, this was equivalent to calling out a reinforcement from the same parts. At the same time the tenants-in-chief of Shropshire and Herefordshire were ordered to reinforce Mortimer[1], and some went on to Roger l'Estrange at Builth, which indicates that on the Severn and Wye the Welsh were active in consequence of the battle of Llandeilo, and under Llewelyn's energetic personality were taking fresh heart.

In the place of the self-asserting, but now discredited, Gloucester Edward appointed William de Valence[2]. We have seen that the new commander had always done his military service in South Wales, and he had been chiefly concerned in superintending the erection of Llanbadarn castle. Possessing but a small fief of ten fees in England, he owed his importance to his marriage with a granddaughter of the great William the Marshal, thereby succeeding to one-fifth of the Marshal lands, and receiving the title of Earl of Pembroke from Henry III. But he was one of the adventurers against whom there had been so much feeling in the days of Simon de Montfort. He was the son of King John's widow by her marriage with Hugh le Brun of Poitou, and probably the earldom was regarded as a gift due to favouritism ; therefore in official documents he is hardly ever given the title, but is plain William de Valence. He had, however, sufficient status as a lord marcher, and, to give him additional importance, Edward had previously given to him the wardship of the march of Gwent and Abergavenny, evidently a rich piece of country, and an absolute mine from which, during the minority of John de Hastings, ready money could be drawn to meet the crown's expenses. If he was a foreigner whom the proud earls wished to disown, he was at least a useful soldier and administrator, unlike Gloucester, and for the rest of the war worked successfully with Tibotot. During July, while Llewelyn was out, he and Tibotot were entirely on the defensive. Besides Daubeny's horse they had a small flying corps of twelve Welsh horse and nineteen foot to scour

[1] *Welsh Roll*, July 2.          [2] Ibid. July 6.

round Cardigan, and once for a few days they had out 650 foot to harry the land of Gruffudd ap Maredudd, besides making what seems to have been a new but weak attempt to reoccupy Llanbadarn, while Plukenet still held Dynevor.

At last reinforcements arrived. Some forty tenants-in-chief or their knights brought horse to do feudal service[1], and most of the men of the paid cavalry now disappear from the pay-roll. Besides Courtenay, and others already mentioned, there came a Grenville, a Raleigh, a Marmion, and men of similar good names. They were inserting between two periods of pay a period of feudal service with increased contingents. It may be mentioned that Geoffrey de Camville was at this time specially commended by the king because he had already had his troop out without pay, and was promised that it should not be counted against him as a precedent[2]; this may be taken to mean that a lord marcher was not expected to maintain an unpaid retinue from his English fief to do service on or near his march. Another interesting point is that the Sheriff of Somerset was severely blamed by the king for having on this occasion taken bribes from competent soldiers to avoid service and compelled weaker men to take their places. But if Shallows and Falstaffs then abounded in real life, all the more credit is due to the others who produced their retinues and did good work.

Edward pointed out, as the objective of an organized expedition, the occupation of the lands of Gruffudd and Cynan ap Maredudd in Cardiganshire[3], which were to be handed over to their cousin Rhys, the loyalist. William de Valence could command perhaps 150 or 160 lances for the field, besides garrisons. He drew a dozen crossbowmen from some castle, and requisitioned a force from Rhys, to whom he made small payments in reward. The foot were drawn by Tibotot from the march. The first 600 were concentrated at Cardigan in July, and brought across to Carmarthen early in August, then 500 foot were raised at Carmarthen; a week later there were forty-three mounted constables, of whom only seven rode

---

[1] *Parl. Writs*, i. 244.    [2] *Welsh Roll*, July 27.

[3] Ibid. July 28.

covered horses and drew the pay of 1s., and 2,000 foot, the same Cardigan men, plus 700 from Kidwelly, 360 from Gower, and 500 from Gwent. A few of the officers, a Roger de Mortimer [1]—it is not likely that this was the son of Mortimer of Wigmore, for the post was not worthy of him—Geoffrey Clement, and some seventy men were English. The whole force proceeded up the Towy to bring Llewelyn to action *ad occurrend Llew*, but no details of fighting are forthcoming. They moved by way of Llangadoc to pick up Rhys's contingent, thence turned westwards to Lampeter, and struck across the watershed to Tregaron, and so down the Ystwith to Llanbadarn. But that position was not yet permanently occupied, nor on their side did the Welsh try to defend it. Finally they moved along the coast to Cardigan, whence Daubeny sent out a few horse to meet them, and were soon afterwards dismissed. The expedition had lasted forty days to September 6, nearly the exact period of the feudal service, which was counted from August 2 to September 11. The result was apparently quite satisfactory as regards Cardiganshire, for, although Llanbadarn was left deserted yet for a time, there was no more fighting south of the Aeron of a serious nature. The feudal period over, Daubeny retained thirty horse once more in pay, belonging to the same contingents as before, those of Courtenay, Pointz, Montacute, and Montfort; and these soon dwindled down to twenty. Otherwise, he only sent out a few small scouting parties of Welsh friendlies. So far Cardiganshire was pacified, and probably Rhys entered on the rebels' lands.

But Llewelyn had not yet been beaten out of Carmarthenshire. A writ from the king addressed to John Giffard implies, indeed, that he was reconquering Llandovery [2]; but the maintenance of a strong garrison at Dynevor, considerably stronger than that at Cardigan, shows the country to have been still

---

[1] There was a Roger de Mortimer styled ‘of West Wales’ (*Close Roll*, Dec. 17, 1276). He appears in a subordinate post in the January of 1283 and in 1287. I shall designate him, when he appears again, as Mortimer of West Wales.

[2] *Welsh Roll*, August 16.

unsettled. The forty feudal days being over, Alan Plukenet took once more into pay two knights and thirty-eight lances, and had fifty or eighty Welsh foot and a dozen light Welsh horse throughout September. As John Penrhys returned back to Gower from Cardigan with his 360 foot, he put in a week's service at Dynevor, and the 700 Kidwelly men and seventy English joined for one day to make an attack on Gruffudd ap Maredudd, whose castle was destroyed and burnt. The Welsh foot received 1d. each for this excitement, and the English the usual 2d. In October 200 foot were in constant pay. Once we find extra levies summoned to bring in a convoy of treasure of 1,000 marcs. A trooper and six foot had escorted it from Lincolnshire to Chepstow, three troopers and twelve foot took it on to Cardiff and through Glamorgan, then 400 were requisitioned to take it past Swansea, 'because Llewelyn and his army were on the other side of the water,' and sixty finally brought it in safety to Kidwelly. Another treasure of 1,250 marcs, part of a loan from London, was convoyed on four pack-horses by two troopers and four foot to Bristol, and was then sensibly forwarded by boat to Carmarthen. At last, suddenly, active operations ceased at the end of October. The pay-roll shows that Carmarthenshire was as quiet henceforward as Cardiganshire had been since the second week of September[1]. The reason is clear: the crisis was becoming acute in Snowdonia, Denbigh had fallen, and Llewelyn had to fly northwards to help David. Without Llewelyn, the resistance of the South Welsh was feeble.

Meanwhile, the Earl of Hereford had been so busily engaged in holding Brecknock, in the midst of a revolt of his own tenants, that he was unable to join the king at the feudal muster at Rhuddlan, and had to depute his uncle to act as constable. There is absolutely no information of his operations, but from various facts of his subsequent career one would infer that he was not only subduing Brecknock; he seems to have claimed as his own, by the right of the sword, the lands westwards, between the watershed and the Towy, i.e. between Llywel and Llandovery, and thence southwards to Caer-

---

[1] Details as before from *Misc. Chancery Roll* ⅓.

cynan. As always, he served entirely at his own expense. If this view be correct, he must have been powerfully helping the English commanders at Dynevor. Just about the very date when Carmarthenshire began to quiet down, as Llewelyn went northwards to help David, Hereford also went to take up his duties as constable with or near the king.

At Builth, Roger l'Estrange was holding his own, but clearly with some trouble. There are no records of payments to his men, whom he probably maintained by utilizing the £100 which he owed to the crown out of the revenues of that march. We only know that he must have been hard pressed, for, doubtless amongst other reinforcements, he received the help of the two knights and six troopers of the Bishop of Hereford's feudal quota[1]. The men of Builth were always prone to revolt, but the castle was new and strong, and was never captured.

Roger de Mortimer was fully occupied in subduing the Welsh of the upper Severn and Radnor. Over £3,460 were spent, in about equal proportions, on the horse and foot of the army of Montgomery during the whole war, but the details of payments are wanting. However, we can pick up a few facts from the occasional entries in the chief cavalry roll. At the first outbreak in March, four knights and thirteen troopers were taken into pay at Montgomery as Mortimer's own *comitiva*; Otto de Grandison had as many in May; John de la Mare had a troop of thirteen lances at Oswestry; and the Earl of Lincoln brought in at least 100 horse, and some foot for which he drew a sum of £255. This would show that the enemy were in considerable force in that month; but as the king formed his main army, much of the cavalry was called off to Chester, particularly Mare and Lincoln, and also one of Grandison's knights. Mortimer seems to have had a normal troop of twenty lances, for his recognized quota was six knights, which would imply twenty men in all; his successor later on had also twenty, and so had his son in the Scottish wars; but he was certainly strong enough to put a larger body into the field if it were wanted. His own four chief castles

---

[1] Madox, *Exchequer*, i. 669.

were garrisoned at his own expense [1], Cefnllys and Dolforwyn
each by eight horse and twenty foot, Dunawd by five horse
and thirty foot, and Radnor by four horse and twelve foot ;
the money which he received from the crown must have been
devoted to offensive movements, and to the garrison of the
royal castle of Montgomery. The force maintained by the
sheriff, Roger Springhouse, at Oswestry, consisted of two
heavy and two light troopers, three crossbows, and sixty foot,
and the place was handed over in August to Edmund de
Mortimer, Roger's eldest son [2]. The younger son, named
Roger, received in June a grant of the lands of Llewelyn
Vychan, further north towards the Dee [3], and thus became
a lord marcher in his own right as Mortimer of Chirk ; such
a grant probably meant real service in war. In the same
direction, the sons of Gruffudd ap Gwenwynwyn were in touch
with Grey's division at Hope [4].

One sees from these facts that along a line from Builth to
Hope small detachments were holding castles and containing
the Welsh insurgents, being within supporting distance of each
other. It is extremely likely that when the forty feudal days
commenced in August, Mortimer made a strong offensive
movement at the same time when Valence and Tibotot moved
in the south, Grey renewed his advance from Hope, and the
king from Rhuddlan. A simultaneous move would baffle
the Welsh, who otherwise could rapidly reinforce each other
against isolated attacks. The Earl of Oxford and the feudal
tenants of Shropshire and Herefordshire were ordered to do
their service in the army of Montgomery, and Mortimer was
not the man to abstain from taking the offensive when the
means were offered to him. The Welsh were certainly less
troublesome in September and October in consequence of
some such move, for both Mortimer and Hereford were able
to spare foot to send up to the king, but when Mortimer died
in October they had not been altogether crushed. The sheriff,
on taking over the four castles after his decease, reported that

---

[1] *Pipe Roll*, 12 Edw. I, under 'Staffordshire.'
[2] Ibid.             [3] *Dict. Nat. Biog.*, xxxix. 135.
[4] *Welsh Roll*, June 5.

it was impossible to collect any revenue from the Welsh vassals, as the march had not yet been pacified[1].

We return to the king at Rhuddlan. In July he was in touch with his fleet. On July 10 the advanced squadron of twenty-eight ships had begun a *servitium debitum* of fifteen days, Rhuddlan being the naval base and chief depot[2], and on July 15 309 crossbowmen and archers were drafted from the army to go on board as marines. A few days later twelve more ships joined and two great galleys. The latter, which were of a type quite new in English warfare, came from Romney and Winchelsea, and carried each a master, two constables, and forty-seven sailors. The forty ships of the ordinary coasting-trader type, as usual, carried each a master and constable and nineteen sailors. The document in places is barely legible, but it seems that Hythe, Sandwich, and Romney each sent three, Hastings and Dover the rest; i.e. each capital Cinque Port, with its dependent membra included, contributed three-fifths of the full obligation. The marines were increased up to 350, crossbowmen and archers alike drawing 3*d.* a day, and after the first payment from the infantry roll they came on the naval roll. They were unequally divided, a few ships taking none, and one taking thirty. There were seven centenars of marines and four principal captains of the fleet. Originally 4,000 quarrels were served out, and a greater number subsequently. Seven boats were purchased on the coast and were manned by fifty-three men[3]. The total of the officers and crews in pay after the obligatory fifteen days comes to 1,347, and the bill to £1,404.

The Earl of Hereford, being still engaged in Brecknock, deputed his uncle John de Bohun to act as constable. The Earl of Norfolk was present in person with Geoffrey de Geneville as his assistant. These proceeded early in August to register the feudal levy at Rhuddlan, 123 barons and knights and 190 *servientes-ad-arma*; but the retinues serving in South Wales, at Montgomery, or at Hope were not entered[4].

---

[1] *Pipe Roll*, as above.  
[2] See above, p. 145.  
[3] *Exch. Acc.* $\frac{4}{6}$, $\frac{3}{29}$.  
[4] *Parl. Writs*, i. 228.

Churchmen sent fourteen knights and forty-five troopers, of which four knights and twelve troopers represented the Bishop of Durham. Norfolk, Surrey, Lincoln, and Warwick registered twenty-eight knights besides themselves, and their united quotas would come to 120 or more lances. Edmund of Lancaster again professed ignorance as to his exact obligation, but he had a retinue at headquarters, for John Giffard was one of his knights; the latter, however, was soon dispatched to reconquer Llandovery. A great many fines were immediately paid in lieu of service, representing some 100 fees. Meanwhile thirty-seven knights and seventy-four troopers were still on the paid list as far as can be ascertained, for the roll is here quite illegible in places. All the bannerets and tenants-in-chief, whose paid troops were given above, were doing feudal service with much smaller 'recognized' quotas than they had had in pay. Assuming that the feudal levy came to 500 lances in all, and adding the few paid troops and the household, we get about 750 all told at Rhuddlan, while Grey had perhaps 100 not far off, but himself registered them apart from the king's army.

A doubtful point is in connexion with the Earl of Gloucester. His name is not entered on the register, nor is any *servitium debitum* acknowledged by him; yet some knights, who are themselves registered as tenants-in-chief serving with the king with a few lances, are also stated to be in Gloucester's following. Such men may be supposed to have given a double service of eighty days, for the earl and for themselves. But where Gloucester was in person there is no means of deciding.

The infantry at headquarters numbered, from week to week in August, 3,360 men, then 4,420, then 6,160, and 8,180. They came from the border counties of England, Lancashire, and Derbyshire, and one small body from 'northern parts.' There was a contingent of 1,800 Welsh friendlies from the marches of Edmund of Lancaster, the Earl of Hereford, and Patrick de Chaworth; rather a large body, considering that the war in the south was at a critical stage. The commanders of the relays were Richard de Boys, Thomas de Turberville, Robert Giffard, Guncelin de Badlesmere, William le Butler of Werington, Walter le Jay, and William le Long, who all appear frequently as captains of infantry or knights of the household, and the unit of 1,000 is more constant than in the first war. Continuing the record week by week in September we find the 8,180 dropping to 6,400. Then Hugh de Turberville, who had previously been serving in the paid cavalry with eight lances, suddenly appeared with 6,000 men from the Clare and Bohun marches, dropping at once to 2,350. The total was thus raised to 8,600, then sank again to 6,860, and to 6,580. In the first week of October there were 5,700; in the third week 2,900, Turberville's corps having entirely vanished. Meanwhile there were extremely few crossbows, a score or two, with the king, but large numbers at Hope and on shipboard. Towards the end of September appeared the first body of Gascon mercenaries, forty-three foot and sixteen mounted crossbowmen under William de Monte Revelli. But though the figures vary so much, it does not mean that the foot were disbanded after very short service. They were simply drafted from Edward's main army to the armies on his flanks, one formed to cross to Anglesey under Luke de Tany, another still operating from Hope under Reginald de Grey, and yet a third under the Earl of Surrey. A full corps of 1,000 archers was encamped at Rhuddlan, and paid by a special household account[1]. One can infer that a total of 8,000 foot was continually maintained in the three armies, the king reinforcing Tany and Grey or Surrey from headquarters as he deemed necessary.

[1] *Miscellaneous Chancery Roll* $\frac{15}{12}$, 'Wardrobe and Household.' This is an interesting document, because it is the only printed record of the war (*Archaeologia*, vol. xvi, November, 1806, by Samuel Lysons). Mr. Hewitt has quoted from it, and Mr. Oman from him. But there are a few slips in the printed copy. Mr. Lysons has dated it 1281, but 10 Edw. I begins in November, 1281, therefore the payments were made in 1282. The point is not very important except that 1281 was a year of peace, when it would be startling to find 1,000 archers stationed at Rhuddlan. Both Mr. Hewitt and Mr. Oman repeat the error. The wages of two crossbow-armourers are printed as ii*d.* a day; the document has vi*d.* The eye is always liable to be dazzled by record-searching, and if any one can point out my own slips due to the same cause I should be grateful. Other dates and figures are from *Exch. Acc.* $\frac{3}{80}$ and $\frac{4}{1}$, as before.

Commanding the services of so powerful a fleet and army, and with his base at Rhuddlan so that they were in touch with each other, Edward planned his next step. The central idea was the occupation of the island-granary of Anglesey as in 1277. On August 18 Luke de Tany, late Seneschal of Gascony, was commissioned to take across a division, and the fleet was put under his orders[1]. He was to occupy the island, then construct a bridge of boats over the Menai to Bangor, and thus recross to take the Penmaenmawr position from the rear, when the king was ready to come up to the Conway river from the east. But the plan took some time to work out. The Welsh, instead of being cowed as in 1277, held out. David still held all the country of the Cantreds except the strip from Hope to Flint and the coast-line to Rhuddlan, and Edward dared not advance to the Conway so as to expose himself to be attacked on the flank by David. Therefore, while he maintained his connexion with Tany's division, as Rhuddlan was the base of both fleet and army, he designed to strike at Denbigh with his own division up the Clwyd, and Grey was to come across from the Dee to occupy Ruthin to the south. When Anglesey was occupied on the one side and the Clwyd on the other, it would then be time to concert the joint movement upon Penmaenmawr. Sea power alone enabled Edward to lay these plans.

Tany set to work towards the end of August. He first had to devote himself to overawe the Welsh of the south coast of the island and secure the harvest for his own use. No less than £3,540 were paid for foot and £3,761 for cavalry during the whole war for the Anglesey division alone. The men were gradually drafted from the king's army, perhaps some 2,000 foot at first, and more afterwards, and 200 horse. Hemingburgh, indeed, says that 300 horse were afterwards defeated in battle under the command of seven bannerets, but the evidence of our pay-rolls establishes clearly enough that seven bannerets would not have more than a squadron of 120 lances at the most. Having shipped across his advanced corps, and effected a lodgement on the coast, Tany would have proceeded

[1] *Welsh Roll.*

to construct his bridge. From August 23 down to the end of September there are signs of great activity at Rhuddlan[1]. Timber, iron, nails, boats, and material of other kinds were being bought, and wages were paid to the sailors of hired or purchased boats to carry over both men and material. A gang of sixty-three carpenters, whose wages were 3*d*. a day, three foremen at 6*d*., and a master-carpenter at 1*s*., were sent over in August; further details raising their number to 100, and a second complete gang of 100 with their foremen went in September. It is indeed only stated that some were destined for Anglesey, but one infers that all of them were sent, and the pay-roll was kept at Rhuddlan. All the forty ships and the two galleys were available to protect the work-men and transport troops, while the thousand archers and a dozen crossbows defended the naval base. The bridge must have been nearly completed by the end of September. Not only were a bare score of carpenters then at work, but the fleet also was withdrawn. It frequently happened that the wars of Edward I and Edward III dislocated the trade of the coast of Sussex and Kent, and grumbling arose. Therefore, if the bridge was completed there was no need to detain the ships, and they returned to their ports. A further sum of £590, which is entered as paid to soldiers 'in the ships round Anglesey,' probably refers to the archers and crossbowmen who remained in various boats retained to keep open com-munications by sea. The withdrawal of carpenters and ships can only mean that the bridge was ready, and that Tany was able to protect it. In October we find him bringing over to the island twenty-three lances of his own troop, and ten lances and eighty Westmorland foot of William de Lindsay. But Edward gave strict orders that there was to be no attempt to recross the bridge to the attack of Penmaenmawr, until he, being ready to come up on his side, should give the word.

By land the meditated attack was made upon the Vale of Clwyd. The king, with the Earl of Lincoln, operated from Rhuddlan; Reginald de Grey moved across from Hope. It would seem that the Earl of Surrey helped to distract the

---

[1] *Misc. Chancery Roll* $\frac{15}{2}$ ; see previous note.

Welsh by pushing along the middle Dee upon Dinas Bran. In the first fortnight of September Grey occupied Ruthin on the upper Clwyd, and Edward, making a flank march past Denbigh, joined hands with him there. Later in September, and again in October, the division under Edward and Lincoln overran the watershed between the Clwyd and the Conway, headquarters being at Llangerniew. Denbigh, thus surrounded, fell in the middle of October, and was securely garrisoned henceforward. Dinas Bran fell before the Earl of Surrey. These facts are deduced partly from the dates and places given in the pay-rolls, partly from the grants of the conquered lands to the three chief commanders, for Edward made such grants during the war in acknowledgement of real military service. Thus, on October 7, the castle of Dinas Bran, with the lands of Yale and Bromfield, but exclusive of Hope, went to the Earl of Surrey for four knights' fees[1]; on October 16 the Earl of Lincoln received two of the Cantreds, Rhos and Rhyfoniog, exclusive of Diganwy and certain coast lands up to the march of Rhuddlan, but including Denbigh, for the service of six knights; Grey received for three fees the Cantred of Dyffryn Clwyd, the upper part of the vale, including Ruthin. During these operations the king's infantry, as we saw, varied from a strength of 8,000 to 3,000, according as he detached men to reinforce Tany or Grey and Surrey. Perhaps a total of 8,000 would represent a maximum strength in all the four armies ; and if Tany had 200 horse, 500 or 600 may be allowed for the others. The feudal period being over, we find several of the previous troops coming once more on the pay-roll ; but only those with the king, some 200 lances on an average, are specified, and how large were the unpaid quotas with the earls can only be a matter of guesswork to determine.

The English now held the important strategic points east of the Conway, and David retired on Snowdon. The war had perceptibly quieted down in the south and on the central marches. Llewelyn had quitted Carmarthenshire to join his brother in defence of the mountain home. The Earl of Hereford had come to join the king, and from October 14

[1] *Welsh Roll*, under these dates.

he had been drawing his 5s. a day as constable. The entry in the cavalry roll reads *Constab Angles*[1], which may mean that he was sent to Anglesey; yet we do not hear that Tany was superseded. As the bridge was constructed, and the king had cleared the country up to the right bank of the Conway, the crisis was clearly reached, and a simultaneous joint attack upon Penmaenmawr was at last possible. Yet there was no hurry. Headquarters were on November 5 at Denbigh, a few days later again at Rhuddlan. Edward was consolidating his new conquests or organizing transport for his final move, and word had not yet been sent to authorize Tany to cross.

At this juncture Archbishop Peckham appeared, and tried to induce Llewelyn to negotiate. Various accusations were tossed to and fro[2]. Llewelyn presented his list of grievances as justifying the war; Edward declared that it was inexcusable, because he had revolted without first appealing to the crown, being himself always ready to hear and investigate. The archbishop even went up into the mountains to treat with Llewelyn personally, much against Edward's wish. Now Tany could not restrain himself. In direct disobedience of orders, whatever the immediate cause may have been— ambition to finish off the war without the king's co-operation, disgust at being superseded by Hereford, momentary anger against the Welsh, who refused to come to terms, or, as seems much more likely, and is acknowledged by the fairest English chronicler[3], in a fit of deliberate treachery during the peace negotiations—Tany put his troops in motion. On November 6, 'while the king was still at Conway, and had not yet made arrangements for crossing the bridge of boats, which was not as yet strong enough nor quite finished, some of our army, about seven bannerets and 300 men-at-arms, to acquire glory and reputation, crossed at low water. When they had passed into the lower slopes of the mountain, and were at some distance from the bridge, and when the flood tide had come

---

[1] This entry is very clear and is repeated, therefore it does not seem to be a slip for *Angliae*. If the constable had been actually at headquarters, his salary would have been 3s. 6d. a day.
[2] See above, p. 150.  [3] *Annales Monastici*, 'Wykes,' vol. iv. p. 290.

up so that they could not retire upon it because of the high water, the Welsh came down upon them from the mountains. Our men, panic-stricken at the sight of their numbers, preferred to face the water rather than the enemy. They plunged into the sea, burdened as they were with their armour, and were drowned all in a moment [1].' Luke de Tany was lost, and, as his treachery seems clearly established, he deserved his fate. Among other victims were Lindsay and the younger Clifford, son of Llewelyn's prisoner at Hawarden. William le Latimer, a 'most strenuous knight,' was saved by his charger swimming to land. But there are obvious errors in Hemingburgh's narrative. The king was not at Conway, but at Rhuddlan or Denbigh. The bridge was certainly completed, for otherwise there is no reason for the withdrawal of the carpenters and the fleet; this error has the appearance of being concocted to disguise the treachery and palliate the defeat. Also, 300 men-at-arms is much too large a body in proportion to seven bannerets.

The crushing defeat completely changed the state of affairs. The archbishop a week later abandoned his attempts to bring about peace. The spirit of the English must have been shaken, at least in the Anglesey division, and all that the king could do was to withdraw to his base and consolidate his position. His main army he concentrated in the Vale of Clwyd and in the chief fortresses of the Cantreds, which were now all the more important to him as rallying-places. He remained himself at Rhuddlan, with about 200 horse of the paid list, the household, the fifty Gascon crossbows, and 1,000 foot under John de Monthaut. Reginald de Grey and Gilbert de Brideshale held Ruthin with 200 to 400 foot. Richard de Bruce, brother of the Earl of Carrick. had thirty crossbows and fifteen archers at the higher rate of pay of 3$d$. a day, 500 other foot, and several workmen engaged on the fortifications at Denbigh. Butler of Werington held Flint and Chester. The Earl of Hereford, drawing his fee as constable, seems to have been still in Anglesey, and the [2]

[1] Hemingburgh, vol. ii. p. 10 (Eng. Hist. Soc.).
[2] *Misc. Chancery Roll* $\frac{1}{12}\frac{5}{2}$.

renewed employment of sixty carpenters suggests that an immediate attempt was made to repair the bridge of boats. There was a month's breathing space, while the king and all his force were on the defensive. Urgent messages doubtless now went to Gascony, to hasten the levy of mercenaries, and to call for larger numbers of them. As the first detachments of Gascons began to come in, during the early days of December, Edward issued writs to summon new English foot. He had grimly determined on a winter campaign. Pierre de Langtoft, a very popular rhyming chronicler, whom Knighton copied, thus puts it:

> Grevouse est la guere, e dure a l'endurer;
> Quant aillours est l'este en Gales est yver [1].

It is to be specially noticed that Edward made this decision to go on fighting, in the face of the victorious Welsh and in spite of the bad weather, as early as December 6 [2], a full week before he could have received word of Llewelyn's death, which so materially affected the war. Meanwhile, it was a natural thing for him to dismiss a great proportion of his foot during the period of waiting, for he did not want large numbers unless he was on the offensive, nor was it wise to weary out his troops uselessly.

Instinctively he felt that Llewelyn, having thus re-established his position in the north, would turn again southwards. On November 12 he sent writs to summon to the support of William de Valence those feudal lords of Devon and Somerset who had already served [3]. The instinct was true. But this time Llewelyn burst into Radnor and north Brecknock, not into Cardiganshire. It is said that Edmund de Mortimer and his brother, to please Edward, pretended to turn traitors, and so lured the Prince of Wales to his ruin [4]; this may refer to the supposed treachery which preceded the final battle. Nothing was really needed to direct Llewelyn to these parts, for everything was in his favour. Roger de Mortimer had just died, and Roger l'Estrange had succeeded to the command

---

[1] Vol. ii. p. 176 (R. S.).    [2] *Welsh Roll.*    [3] *Parl. Writs,* vol. i. p. 244.
[4] *Annales Monastici,* ' Osney,' vol. iv. p. 290.

at Montgomery, turning over Builth to John Giffard[1]; Hereford was still in Anglesey; the sheriff's report, already quoted, shows that the Welsh of the upper Severn had not yet been crushed. The defence devolved upon l'Estrange, but beyond the facts that he had twenty horse in constant pay, that the sheriff, Springhouse, had also twenty horse next year at the siege of Bere, and that 2,000 foot were then speedily levied from Shropshire, we have no means to determine the English strength. So, also, it is difficult to determine who actually commanded at the battle: Peckham says Edmund de Mortimer was there, with his 'household'; the monk of Osney also says Edmund, 'with a following neither small nor ignoble'; Hemingburgh says John Giffard, with whom was the younger Roger de Mortimer. I believe that the latter statement is true, for Edward showed peculiar favour to Giffard ever afterwards—favour so pronounced that it argues some very special service—and consistently throughout these wars Edward rewarded with grants of land just those very lords who had been of most use in the conduct of the war; thus the grant of Builth and Isgenen to Giffard, and the restitution of these same lands to him time after time, in spite of his having lost them in the various subsequent risings, argues that Giffard did some great service to the crown, such as the crushing defeat of Llewelyn. Not a single authority represents l'Estrange as present in person. But we may well suppose that the Mortimer brothers brought to the campaign a large retinue of horse. Another point on which information is wanting is the proportion of English foot to Welsh friendlies; if we judge once more by the details of next year's siege of Bere, we would infer that, except a contingent from Powys, practically all the foot were English of Shropshire, and had Tibotot gone out of his way to send up any friendlies from the south, there would be some record on his special pay-sheet. We are justified in putting the credit of the victory of Orewin bridge to an almost entirely English force.

If we accept the traditional site of the battle, we must picture Llewelyn as holding the hills above the Yrfon, a

[1] *Welsh Roll*, Oct. 30.

tributary of the Wye, not far from Builth[1]. He refused to offer battle on the lower ground, but kept to the heights and raided the country round[2], holding, however, with some force a bridge over the river. He had expected the local Welsh to deliver Builth to him, but had been disappointed ; not that they were unsympathetic, but the English held that castle very strongly. The Welsh account represents him as lured treacherously to a conference with the local chieftains, and this may have reference to the pretended treachery of the Mortimers, or else he may have been accidentally away from his army while scouting. At any rate, in his absence on December 11, a Welshman pointed out to the English a ford, by which some of them crossed the Yrfon and proceeded to seize Orewin bridge from the rear. The whole army then crossed, and ascended the heights beyond. The Welsh, taken by surprise, and having no orders in the absence of their prince, stood their ground manfully, and shot down upon the English, but, shaken by the archers who were interlaced with the heavy cavalry, then attacked in the rear by some of the cavalry who worked round and pushed higher up the slope behind them, they broke and fled. Meanwhile, Llewelyn heard the noise of battle and was hurrying back. One Stephen de Frankton came upon him, not knowing who he was, and ran him through the body as he was without his armour. Not until the dead were being despoiled was it found out that the dread Llewelyn was no more. The picture as given by Hemingburgh is complete. We see the difficulty of getting the agile enemy to stand to accept battle, the lucky turning of the position by the ford, the inability of the Welsh to plan a defence without the aid of Llewelyn, who was their one leader, or to stand up against the combined attack of foot and horse. It is noticeable that they had some missiles, which may have been used, not by Llewelyn's own northerners, but by the local Welsh who had joined his standard.

If the credit of the good tactics which won the victory has to go to John Giffard, it is possible to connect Roger

---

[1] *Annales Monastici*, 'Dunstable,' vol. iii. p. 293.
[2] Hemingburgh, vol. ii. pp. 11–13.

l'Estrange also with it.   A Stephen de Frankton reappears
in 1287 as a centenar of Shropshire infantry in command of
a company from Ellesmere[1]; now l'Estrange was lord of
Ellesmere, and Frankton is a village in the immediate neighbourhood, so that the commander-in-chief of the district is
connected with the battle through his neighbour, possibly his
sub-tenant.   Chroniclers, indeed, are not agreed upon the
name, nor on the rank of Llewelyn's victor.   He is said to
have been a knight, but that is a mistake.   If Stephen be the
man who dealt the fatal blow, it is at least satisfactory to
know his true status, but one marvels that he was not knighted
or substantially rewarded.

L'Estrange sent to the king the official bulletin of Llewelyn's
death, a dispatch which is laconic to the point of being
tantalizing[2]:—'Sachez, sire, ke vos bones gens les queus vus
auez assingne de vestre entendant a moy se combatirent av
Leweln le finz Griffin en le paes de Buelt le vendredy pchein
apres la feste seint Nhoilas, issi ke Leweln le finz Griffin est
mort et se gent desconfit et tote la flour de se gent morz,
sicum le portr de ceste lettre vus dirra, et le creez de ce
ke il vus dirra de par moi.'   The result must have tended
to hasten the complete reduction of all the neighbouring
march, and there are no signs of any more trouble near
Montgomery.

Simultaneously with Llewelyn's invasion of the upper Wye,
there was a feeble outbreak in Cardiganshire, and William de
Valence had to arm[3].   Some twenty to thirty lances came up
once more from Somerset and Devon, Pointz and Montfort
serving in person, and Courtenay sending a few men, so that
Daubeny's command at Cardigan was raised to about sixty
horse.   On two occasions in December 500 foot were brought
from Kidwelly by Patrick de Chaworth in person, but soon
retired.   Patrick himself died about this time, probably in
some skirmish.   From Gwent came 300 foot, of whom 200
retired after a three weeks' contract (this is the earliest undoubted notice of a contract for service), and the rest remained

---

[1] *Exch. Acc.* $\frac{4}{16}$.        [2] *Eng. Hist. Review*, July, 1899, p. 507.
[3] *Misc. Chancery Roll* $\frac{1}{7}$, as before.

on into January, while the Cardigan men raised to defend their own county were not paid. The insurgents were soon worsted. Then, on January 9, by the king's orders, Valence organized a retaliatory force of 1,500 paid foot of Cardigan and Cemaes, Kidwelly and Gower, with some of the cavalry, marched along the coast, and finally reached Llanbadarn on the 14th. Roger de Mortimer ' of West Wales,' in command of twenty horse and thirty foot, was made constable, this being a permanent reoccupation of the country north of the Aeron. Two chieftains, Rhys ap Maelgwn and Cynan ap Maredudd, surrendered and were sent to Edward, their expenses to the court being defrayed. They were pardoned and sent back to Cardiganshire by the king on the condition that they should defend the county against their former allies, and, indeed, we find one of them later on taking up arms in the cause of England. South of Merioneth there was no more fighting after January, though the other insurgents remained at large for a few months longer.

Our interest returns once more to the north, where Edward was strictly on the defensive during November. The victory of Orewin bridge materially lessened the ill effects of the disaster at Bangor, and chiefly because Llewelyn had been slain. David had not the same influence, though he is said to have called a Parliament of Welsh to Denbigh, and received promises of support ; if to Denbigh, it must have been before Llewelyn's death ; if after Llewelyn's death, it must have been to some other place, say Dolwyddelan. But before reviewing the next act of the piece, we have to consider two points, the special financing of the war, and the coming of the Gascons.

Nine months of continual fighting had exhausted the king's ready money. The fines in lieu of feudal service were not very valuable. Besides the 12,000 which he had borrowed at first, he had got at least another 15,000 marcs from the Italians [1]. ' Either the king or his chief adviser was reluctant to ask Parliament for money, and recourse was had to the old expedient of negotiating separately with individuals and com-

[1] *Welsh Roll*, 10 Edw. I.

munities instead of obtaining a national vote.' He called for a *subsidium* or loan, to which the cities answered very readily. London, for instance, sent 6,000 marcs, Newcastle 1,750, York 1,040, Lincoln 1,016, Yarmouth 1,000[1]. But the money was spent, and we remember how one convoy of treasure was anxiously escorted past Llewelyn's army near Swansea. A winter campaign 'fierce and hard' was at hand, and Parliament had to be faced. In January, 1283, a strange double Parliament met, one half at York to represent the province of York, the other at Northampton to represent that of Canterbury[2]. So many of the important barons being with the king in Wales, those who attended were chiefly churchmen and the less warlike barons, with four knights of each shire, and some members from boroughs. The clergy grumbled, for they had already voted large sums; the others voted a thirtieth. The royal officials set to work at once to collect it, making allowance for the loans already contributed and for all personal service in the army. Chroniclers tell us that the behaviour of the officials was 'moderate[3].' The totals which we possess show that the thirtieth brought in twice as much as the loan, that is to say, that the nation raised one-third of the money at first voluntarily, two-thirds after the vote. To finish off the money question, we know that some of the clergy individually paid small sums as if it were a voluntary gift, but Edward, provoked by their slowness as a body, did one of those high-handed things to which he was apt to be tempted. In the March of 1283 he seized the crusade-money lying at the Temple and various cathedrals. Archbishop Peckham stood very firm and Edward restored it, and in October the clergy voted a twentieth for three years[4].

The most interesting feature of this part of the war is the coming of the Gascons. They were born fighters, 'the Swiss of the thirteenth century,' Gascons and Béarnais, Bigorrais and Basques alike, and one would infer that Edward would have

---

[1] *Welsh Roll*, Sept. 12 and Oct. 18, and *Exch. Acc.* $\frac{4}{2}$.

[2] Stubbs, vol. ii. p. 114.

[3] *Annales Monastici*, 'Dunstable,' vol. iii. p. 295.

[4] *Exch. Acc.* $\frac{4}{2}$; Peckham's *Letters*, vol. ii. pp. 548, 635-8.

utilized earlier the services of these subjects of his duchy but for the expense and the usual jealousy of the Englishman against the foreigner. In April, 1282, he had merely requested Jean de Greilly, his seneschal, to furnish forty foot and twelve horse, and in September William de Monte Revelli had actually brought over forty-three foot and sixteen horse. There were other difficulties in the way. Gaston of Béarn had been in revolt, and only recently had he made his peace with Edward, doing homage with a rope round his neck. He now professed to be loyal, but wrote in the summer in rather a suspicious manner ; the King of France, as overlord, forbade the recruiting and transmission of soldiers for the war in Wales[1] ; there was friction between the Gascon lords and the English officials, and the latter, it was insinuated, were in the wrong. It rather looks as if Gaston were trying to avoid doing the service which was required of him. But, on the other hand, he certainly served with Edward's ally, the King of Castile, in the autumn and winter at Edward's wages[2]. Moreover, some others wrote from Bordeaux that, willing as they were to go to Wales, they neither could nor dared move after the French king's prohibition. The consequence was that, beyond a score of Gascons in the household and Monte Revelli's men, the mercenaries arrived very slowly. Another body of twenty-two arrived in October, others very early in December. The general impression that one has from the facts is that, after his first call in April, Edward had been trying to get up more Gascons during the summer, but the difficulties were considerable. Just a few were appearing in the early autumn, then came the disaster at the Menai, and there was a much more urgent call. Antony Bek and John de Vescy were at hand, for they had been sent to negotiate a marriage between Edward's daughter and a son of his ally, Pedro of Aragon, and they spared no expense to recruit and dispatch a large corps[3]. Money caused the previous difficulties to disappear. Contracts were made, large sums were paid down for equipment over and above the contract wages,

[1] Rymer, vol. i. p. 611 ; July, 1282.    [2] Ibid. 625 ; Jan., 1283.
[3] Ibid. Feb. 10, 1282.

and the troops were collected.   Within a month of the Menai defeat already a fair number was up, and by the end of January the whole corps was in Wales, the two royal agents returning to England with the last detachment.

The pay-roll, which is quite complete, is, however, most difficult to understand [1].  The figures given below are approximately right in all probability, and have been obtained by a consideration of two points: the contingents to which sums are paid in the gross are to be inferred as still in Gascony, and when details are first given with the payments, they have arrived in Wales; secondly, when various subordinates draw the pay, only by the closest examination of dates and figures can we avoid the error of adding in the same corps twice. I read that in December there were in Wales twenty-one knights, fifty-two mounted and 533 foot crossbowmen; the knights received 2s. a day, the mounted men sometimes 1s. and more often 1s. 6d., the foot 3d.   By the third week in January the whole force was up, forty knights, 119 horse, and 1273 foot.   In December a separate pay-roll [2] shows that forty other mounted crossbowmen were serving, partly Gascons and partly Picards, many of them the same men who had fought in 1277 under Imbert de Monte Regali, and as the cavalry roll informs us that this officer drew pay from the 1st of November, it may be guessed that just before Tany's defeat he had been commissioned to recruit his old troopers. The highest total in January comes to 210 horse and 1313 foot, inclusive of the contingents of Monte Regali and Monte Revelli.   All the best families of the south were represented. Some of the knights had been rebels with Gaston against Edward, some were descendants of those who had served Henry III [3].   D'Albret, indeed, was not represented, but Gaston sent his lieutenants.   There came in person the Counts of Armagnac and of Bigorre, the lord of Bergerac, Roger de Mauléon, Arnald de Gaveston, Pierre de Greilly, Pierre Amanieu, Captal de Buch, the Vicomte de Tarcazin, and Guichard du Bourg, ex-Mayor of Bordeaux.   They came

---

[1] *Exch. Acc.* $\frac{3}{27}$.          [2] Ibid. $\frac{4}{4}$.

[3] *Gascon Rolls*, 26 Hen. III and 7 Edw. I.

pompously, says Hemingburgh, and doubtless they both fought and swaggered as befitted the forerunners of d'Artagnan. Many of the contingents suffered severely in the war, losing a third or even half their numbers. It is to be noticed that their particular weapon was the crossbow, and they brought with them some 70,000 quarrels in twenty-nine barrels and twelve baskets[1]. The greater number had only a three months' contract, inclusive of the two journeys, but a few contingents remained on longer. Guichard du Bourg, who put in one month extra with 200 men, received a pension of 100 marcs a year for five years. Armagnac received £250 over his contract wages, Mauléon £146, Bergerac £133, and so on. Several individual knights stayed on in Wales during all the year 1283, and even into 1284, as members of the household. The total cost came to £7,618, and Imbert's forty men, who served a full year, received £979.

Edward had been, since Tany's defeat, holding various places along the line of the Clwyd with a reduced force of both horse and foot. On December 6 he had sent out writs to summon new English foot for a renewed advance in January, and doubtless the arrayers set to work to get the men with fresh zeal when they heard the next week of Llewelyn's death. Meanwhile, the cavalry was represented at headquarters by 100 to 120 horse of the paid list and the 150 of the household. Of course Edward put the Gascons into the field as fast as they arrived, without waiting for the English reinforcements. They would have been especially useful in restoring the tone of the Anglesey division, which was certainly shaken by the defeat. The Earl of Hereford in the new year returning to Brecknock, Otto de Grandison, joined shortly afterwards by his old colleague John de Vescy on his arrival from Gascony, took over this division. The various entries in the rolls of the issue of ammunition, of wages paid, and of the purchase and transmission to Anglesey of fodder, point to renewed activity. Whatever English troops remained in the island, together with the Gascons, whose advent may be considered as giving to them new courage, must have been engaged

<hr />

[1] *Exch. Acc.* $\frac{4}{5}$.

in strengthening the bridge of boats and effecting a strong lodgement on the mainland near Bangor.

By the third week in January, 1283, the king was ready to move again. The foot poured in, their numbers being in excess of what he had requisitioned, until 5,000 men were present. Richard de Boys brought 1,000 men from Shropshire, William de Ryther 2,000 from Chester, and Hugh de Turberville 1,000 from the south-east marches, the men of Gwent alone not appearing, but many of them were now serving in Cardiganshire. Turberville was promoted to act as deputy constable in Hereford's place at a special fee of 2s. 6d. a day. The horse came to about 400 lances, if we reckon the unknown retinues of the earls. Edmund of Lancaster, Surrey, Warwick, and, for the first time as far as can be judged, Gloucester, were at the front. Lincoln and Norfolk, with Reginald de Grey, were probably holding the Cantreds to cover the rear of the advance. All the 1,500 Gascons and Picards had arrived and were available, except those who had been detached to Anglesey. Eight hundred woodmen had been requisitioned. The army crossed the watershed from the Clwyd by way of Llangerniew to the upper waters of the Conway, and, a base being secured at Bettws y Coed, laid siege to the castle of Dolwyddelan. Edward thereby avoided the difficulty of crossing the Conway by its tidal estuary, and would be able to work afterwards down stream by the left bank. In the meantime he had to carry on the siege without receiving any help from Otto de Grandison and the Anglesey division, who were too far away to concert an attack with him, but yet could distract the Welsh by demonstrations from Bangor towards Penmaenmawr.

It would seem that Dolwyddelan fell very soon. The queen, who was at Rhuddlan, paid £5 each to two messengers who brought 'rumours' of its fall on January 24. William le Vavassour drew pay for some crossbows and foot in garrison there about the same date, and though these payments are discontinued on the chief infantry roll until two months later, it is possible that the men were paid in the interval by a different paymaster. There are no traces of any subsequent siege, and it may be surmised that the 'rumours' were correct. The mountain home was now pierced ; a sacred spot, the birthplace of Llewelyn the Great, had been captured. Edward could now securely move down stream when he chose, but he wisely dismissed the bulk of the infantry after a campaign of three weeks. He would not vex them by further efforts in winter, and as he had Dol-wyddelan in his possession he could at will renew the attack on Snowdonia when the weather was more favourable. But these three weeks had broken the back of the Welsh resis-tance.

Langtoft emphasizes the importance of the Gascon soldiery, who, he says—

> Demorent of le rays, rescayvent ses douns,
> En mores e mountaynes raumpent cum lyouns,
> S'en vount of les Engleys, ardent les mesouns,
> Abatent les chastels, tuent les felouns,
> Passez sunt la Marche, entrez en Snaudouns[1].

But their contracts were up, and a great many of them de-parted in February. Dolwyddelan was entrusted to Gruffudd ap Tudor as constable, possibly in reward for his desertion of David.

Edward was quiet for a short time, merely garrisoning his castles. Then he made another move in March, pushed on to Conway, and occupied the angle where he subsequently built his celebrated castle. Headquarters were at Conway for the rest of the war. There were serving now 600 Gascons of all ranks, some 300 to 400 English cavalry, and 1,200 foot in the king's army ; the latter rose to 2,800, and by the end of March to 5,000, for one week only. Grandison and Vescy spread out their division westwards from Bangor to Car-narvon, and soon penetrated to Harlech ; they always had some boats connected with their force, and so they kept com-munications open by sea. It would seem that the Conway valley and the Penmaenmawr heights were occupied thoroughly, and from Dolwyddelan and Conway, Bangor and Carnarvon

---

[1] Vol. ii. p. 180.

and Harlech, the English could penetrate as they liked into Snowdonia.  Very many small bands were sent out, mostly of Welshmen in English pay.  There was no more fighting, but a mere hunt after David, who went 'playing the fox' and 'skulking like a thief[1].'

Yet did Llewelyn's brother make one effort more for dear life.  He suddenly broke from Snowdonia into the even wilder country of Cader Idris.  He made a new centre of resistance at Bere castle, lying 'in a cwm rising out of the heart of Cader,' in an ideal position commanding the valley and passes, and approachable only from the south by way of Machynlleth.  It seemed as if another war had begun, and the English would have to create a new base, and cut their way as slowly and laboriously into Merioneth as they had done into Snowdonia.  Edward thought that a campaign in force was necessary, and he ordered his feudal lords to meet him early in May at Montgomery[2].  But as a matter of fact the forces of William de Valence from Llanbadarn and of Roger l'Estrange from Montgomery were quite sufficient, and Edward had neither to come south to Merioneth himself nor to send troops from his own army.  Probably no one saw just then that the exhausted Welsh were on the verge of a collapse.  Llewelyn might have prolonged the struggle, but David was not up to his level as a national champion.  Moreover, the winter campaign had been irksome to the English, but had been positively fatal to the starved Welsh, who had no resources at their back.

L'Estrange was the first to move to the siege of Bere[3].  On March 28 Roger Springhouse, Sheriff of Shropshire, provided a force of 100 woodmen and seventy-two mechanics under four master workmen, with an escort of eighteen crossbows and 112 foot.  Richard de Boys raised 1,000 Shropshire infantry with carters and other workmen.  Both the sheriff and l'Estrange had their own troops of twenty lances each, but there is no other record of horse, though Peter Corbet and Bogo de Knoville seem to have joined the expedition,

---

[1] Langtoft, *passim.*          [2] *Parl. Writs*, vol. i. pp. 245-7.
[3] *Pipe Roll*, 12 Edw. I, under 'Salop.'

and probably the Mortimers also. Reinforcements of foot
came in soon. On the other side, William de Valence concentrated 900 foot at Llanbadarn on April 12 [1]: whether he
had been originally ordered to co-operate with l'Estrange, or
whether he was summoned a fortnight later because the work
was too much for the Shropshire forces alone, cannot be
decided. On the 15th he was up in camp before Bere with
1,400 foot, men of Kidwelly and the other marches which
always furnished men. Two small flying corps were fitted
out to scour the mountains to catch David, who had not shut
himself up in the castle. Then to secure the coast-line another
and larger body of 560 foot was detached towards Harlech
to join hands with Otto de Grandison, and to overawe the
western parts of Merioneth from that base. Meanwhile new
relays brought up Valence's besieging force to 1,060 and
l'Estrange's to 2,000, but there were barely twenty-five crossbowmen and forty paid horse in all. A curious fact is that
on the arrival of Valence the Shropshire infantry were put
under the South Welsh paymaster, and so, for the first time
in the war, we have an exact record of their strength. Springhouse now retired, leaving only one of his knights with the
besiegers.

Hemmed in by an army of over 3,000 men, and finding David
unable to relieve them from the mountains, the Welsh of Bere
surrendered on April 25. Lewis de la Pole, son of the lord
of Powys, was put in command with a garrison of eight horse,
nine crossbows, and forty foot. More workmen were brought
up under Master Bertram, an engineer whose services have
been noticed on a former occasion, and the defences of the
castle were made good ; also new tracks were cut through
the forests. The two chief leaders kept the field for another
month. With foot varying from 1,200 to 2,400, as some corps
were disbanded or new foot came in from Shropshire, with
l'Estrange's score of horse, and another score brought by
Daubeny from Cardigan, they marched up and down the
lower lands of Merioneth, now occupying Towyn on the coast,
now Cymmer Abbey on the north side of Cader. At the end

---

[1] *Misc. Chanc. Roll* ¼, as before.

of May William de Valence withdrew to Llanbadarn, and, leaving a garrison of eight horse and forty-eight foot there under Mortimer 'of West Wales,' he disbanded the rest. L'Estrange continued to patrol Merioneth with his twenty horse and 100 foot throughout June, and then he too retired. Richard de Boys was now left at Bere with a garrison of twelve crossbows and twenty-eight archers. The whole of this campaign argues a considerable amount of skill, and it is clear that the English were learning the art of organization. From two separate bases they had plunged into a wild country, had captured a castle, and reduced the whole district in about two months.

Meanwhile Rhys ap Maredudd had again had out some of his men in Edward's service, either joining in the siege or patrolling Carmarthenshire in Valence's absence. Rhys ap Maelgwn had acted up to the conditions of his pardon, and attacked his old ally Gruffudd ap Maredudd with sixty foot in English pay. From the north the Earl of Hereford, having left Hugh de Turberville as deputy constable with the king, had come back to Brecknock, and apparently was engaged in stamping out the embers of the war on the upper Towy ; it was to him that Gruffudd and Llewelyn Vychan finally surrendered in the summer after news came of the capture of David [1]. It may be that Rhys ap Maelgwn and Cynan ap Maredudd broke out again later, for we find them afterwards prisoners in Bridgenorth castle [2].

The important capture was at last effected. David fled back from Merioneth to Snowdonia. Edward, finding that the great number of troops which he had summoned to join him in May, in anticipation of a prolonged campaign around Bere, were not required there, called them northwards. Leaving Edmund at Conway, he filled the valley and penetrated from Llanrwst and Bettws into Snowdon with 7,000 foot, of which Hugh de Turberville had raised 6,000. Throughout May and June 3,000 to 4,000 were still kept, and swarmed in search of David. The play was nearly over. The Welsh evidently offered to surrender of their own accord. We find

[1] Trivet, p. 308.          [2] *Pipe Roll*, 16 Edw. I.

in the pay-rolls that many hostages were given up, which means that the surrenders were made in abandonment of David. Small bodies of Welsh were sent out to join in the hunt, *ad querend David per totam Walliam*, and we infer that the capture was the price of their pardon by the king. Finally, he was caught and handed over *per homines lingue sue*, an ignominious end to the war which would have been impossible had Llewelyn lived. Edward announced the event in the writs dated June 28, by which he summoned his barons to Shrewsbury to discuss David's fate [1]. Early in September he was escorted through Rhuddlan by sixty archers, and his two sons, Owen and Llewelyn, were sent for safe custody to Bristol [2].

This chapter may be conveniently concluded by an examination of the expenses of the war. Very fortunately the two great rolls of payments to infantry and cavalry, by which we have been able to follow from day to day the movements of the king and his headquarters army, contain not only the details of that army, but also the gross expenses of all the other divisions. Two 'particular' rolls have similarly enabled us to know exact details of the forces at Hope and in South Wales. As the totals of gross expenses correspond exactly to the details of these two, we may clearly infer an exact correspondence in the other rolls which are lost. Rolls of miscellaneous expenses are not forthcoming. One membrane of one roll only is extant, but luckily the total sum expended is endorsed. The pipe rolls enable us to supply the total of wages paid to workmen of all kinds. A comparison of the credit and debit accounts would suggest that we have not even then made sufficient allowance for outgoings, and therefore I have appended the figures of the cost of building the new castles. Carnarvon and Conway were taken in hand in 1283, and small sums were being still expended on them in 1288 and even in 1290. The very costly reconstruction of Harlech was begun in 1285, the great expense being difficult to explain.

---

[1] *Welsh Roll*, 1283.    [2] *Misc. Chanc. Roll* $\frac{15}{12}$; *Pipe Roll*, 12 Edw. I.

### The Expenses of the War.

|  |  |  | £ | £ |
|---|---|---|---|---|
| *Exch. Acc.* $\frac{3}{30}$ | Payments to infantry at |  |  |  |
|  | Chester, 1282 . . . . . | 1,115 |  |  |
|  | With the Earl of Lincoln, May, 1282 | 255 |  |  |
|  | Oswestry, May, 1282. . . . | 240 |  |  |
|  | Hope, 1282 [1] . . . . . | 941 |  |  |
|  | Montgomery, 1282 and 1283 . . | 1,740 |  |  |
|  | Anglesey, 1282 and 1283 . . . | 3,540 |  |  |
|  | Soldiers in ships . . . . | 590 |  |  |
|  | Rhuddlan, 1283 . . . . . | 706 |  |  |
|  | Carnarvon and Criccieth, 1283 . . | 809 |  |  |
|  | Carnarvon, 1284 . . . . | 120 |  |  |
|  | South and West Wales, 1282 and 1283 [1] . . . . . . | 3,011 |  |  |
|  |  | 13,067 |  |  |
|  | Headquarters army and small details | 11,663 |  |  |
|  |  |  |  | 24,730 |
| „ | $\frac{4}{1}$ Payments to cavalry at |  |  |  |
|  | Chester, 1282 (including a few foot) . | 973 |  |  |
|  | Hope, 1282 [1] . . . . . | 246 |  |  |
|  | Montgomery, 1282 and 1283 . . | 1,721 |  |  |
|  | Anglesey, 1282 and 1283 . . . | 3,761 |  |  |
|  | Rhuddlan, Conway, Carnarvon. . | 162 |  |  |
|  | South and West Wales, 1282 and 1283 [1] . . . . . . | 1,681 |  |  |
|  | Various garrisons, 1284 . . . | 536 |  |  |
|  |  | 9,080 |  |  |
|  | Headquarters army . . . . | 8,606 |  |  |
|  |  |  |  | 17,686 |
| „ | $\frac{3}{26}$ Ships from Cinque Ports . . . . |  | 1,404 |  |
| „ | $\frac{3}{27}$ The Gascons . . . . . . . |  | 7,618 |  |
| „ | $\frac{4}{1}$ Mounted crossbowmen, 1283 . . . . |  | 979 |  |
| „ | $\frac{3}{29}$ Miscellanea : one leaf of details, total endorsed |  | 5,409 |  |
| *Misc. Chanc.* $\frac{15}{12}$. Household at Rhuddlan . . . . |  |  | 2,220 |  |
|  |  |  | 60,046 |  |
| *Pipe Roll*, 19 Edw. I, m. 28. Payments to workmen . . |  |  | 9,414 |  |
| „ „ *Ad operaciones castrorum* up to November, 1284 . . . |  |  | 5,795 |  |
|  | Carried forward . . |  | 75,255 |  |

[1] Extant.

|  | £ | £ |
|---|---|---|
| Brought forward . . . |  | 75,255 |

*Pipe Roll*, 19 Edw. I, m. 28, and 14 Edw. I, last membrane :

| | | |
|---|---|---|
| Carnarvon castle in 1285 onwards . . | 6,621 | |
| Conway . . . . . . . | 7,787 | |
| Harlech . . . . . . . | 8,167 | |
| Criccieth . . . . . . . | 332 | |
| Bere . . . . . . . . | 259 | |
| | | 23,166 |

Total of war expenses and cost of castles . . . . | 98,421

## THE INCOMINGS.

*Exch. Acc.* ½

| | | |
|---|---|---|
| Various entries, illegible . . . . | 6,709 | |
| From sheriffs of counties . . . . | 1,340 | |
| From bishops and towns . . . . | 2,165 | |
| Revenue from Wales, 1284 . . . | 72 | |
| Sale of David's plate, bridge material, &c. | 317 | |
| Money going to Alfonso, but taken back because he has died . . . . | 2,380 | |
| Remains of the fifteenth of 1276 . . | 500 | |
| Customs on wool, hides, &c. . . . | 22,916 | |
| | | 36,399 |
| The tax of a thirtieth . . . . . . | | 37,432 |
| A subsidy (loan) from border counties, London, and a few towns, religious houses, archbishops, and eight bishops *quasi de dono* (£1,393) . | | 17,926 |
| Fines *pro servitio debito* (the largest item is £141) | | 2,959 |
| Sale of provisions . . . . . . | | 8,902 |
| | | 103,618 |
| But, because some sums are otherwise accounted for, the sum total is endorsed as . . . | | 98,106 |

# CHAPTER V

## THE PEACE SETTLEMENT AND RHYS'S RISING

FROM July, 1283, onwards there was no need to keep an army in the field. There was no resistance, and Edward, having resolved on annexation, devoted his attention to castle-building. He chose the sites already occupied by his troops round Snowdon. Carnarvon and Conway now rose as the typical new Edwardian castles in North Wales as Caerphilly in South. Carnarvon was wrecked in 1294, and, when rebuilt, was perhaps planned on a grander scale than now. Criccieth and Harlech, Dolwyddelan and Bere, were old Welsh fortresses, of which Harlech was largely rebuilt on the Edwardian model. As this ring of posts round Snowdon became all-important, we hear less of Flint and Rhuddlan, which, however, were still crown property, being specially exempted when the king awarded the Cantreds to his nobles. Hope was granted to Queen Eleanor; Denbigh belonged to the Earl of Lincoln, Ruthin to Grey, Dinas Bran to the Earl of Surrey. It is in the new castles that we find the chief royal garrisons in the last part of 1283 and in 1284, eighty foot at one time in Carnarvon, forty at another in Harlech. Besides the garrisons Edward kept ten bannerets and forty-five knights in his pay as his administrative staff in the peace settlement[1], but no other force of cavalry beyond the troopers of the household and Imbert's forty mounted crossbowmen. William de Leyburn and William le Latimer, Butler of Wemme, Philip and Norman Darcy, Hugh and Thomas de Turberville, Walter de Huntercumbe, Bogo de Knoville, Eustace de Hacche, and others who had served in both wars

---

[1] At the end of *Exch. Acc.* ⁴⁄₇.

without intermission, whether with cavalry contingents or in command of infantry, continued their services as the king's professional captains; and of the foreigners, Pierre de Campan, a Bigorrais, Alex and Guy of the house of Bergerac, and a few others of the late commanders of the Gascon corps. The troopers of the household were divided among the fortresses, eight at Carnarvon, three at Conway, with a few archers at the higher rate of pay of 3*d*. Roger l'Estrange and Owen de la Pole were engaged in Merioneth and at Montgomery at bannerets' wages.

In 1284 a definite peace settlement was being made. The passing of the Statute of Wales and the birth of Prince Edward at Carnarvon enabled the king to lessen the pressure; he could appoint his officers as permanent administrators, and leave the Welsh to settle down under English rule. Gradually during the year he made his arrangements. In March the northern counties were settled[1]. The Four Cantreds, the castles of Rhuddlan and Flint, and the county of Flintshire came under the Justiciar of Chester, Reginald de Grey. Roger de Pulesdon, Sheriff of the new county of Anglesey, Richard de Pulesdon, Sheriff of Carnarvonshire, and Robert de Staundon, Sheriff of Merioneth, each at a salary of £40 a year, and their subordinates, the coroners and bailiffs of commots, were appointed under Otto de Grandison as Justiciar of North Wales. John de Havering was Otto's deputy at a salary of £40, and an exchequer was set up at Carnarvon as the new capital. Walter de Huntercumbe was given the custody of Bere, superseding l'Estrange; and Bere was considered as belonging to the administrative district of Carnarvon rather than to that of Montgomery. In August Dolwyddelan was entrusted for his lifetime to Gruffudd ap Tudor, who had already been in command there in 1283.

In September Edward commenced a royal progress through Wales, starting from Flint, and as he progressed he completed his arrangements. His most prominent officials accompanied him, William de Valence, Otto de Grandison, John de Vescy,

[1] Details in *Welsh Roll*, 12 Edw. I. Also the text of the statute, 12 Edw. I.

and Robert de Tibotot. In September Flint and Rhuddlan, Conway and Carnarvon, were constituted free boroughs, the population of such new places being largely English ; in each case the constable of the castle was to be ex-officio mayor. William Sikun (Chicoun or Cygoine) was already constable at Conway, and was reappointed at a salary of £190 with an establishment of thirty men, ten to be crossbowmen ; in the pay-lists of the wars he appears as a knight of the household. At Carnarvon John de Havering was constable, in addition to his deputy justiciarship, at a salary of 200 marcs and an establishment of forty men, fifteen to be crossbowmen ; a fresh supply of 104,800 quarrels, with 120 crossbows and accoutrements, was sent up to him from Bristol[1]. By November Edward was on the north coast of Cardigan Bay. Here he created Criccieth, Harlech, and Bere free boroughs on the same terms ; Criccieth was entrusted to William de Leyburn, and Harlech to Hugh de Wlonkeslowe, each to have £100 and thirty men ; Huntercumbe was reappointed to Bere, to have 200 marcs and forty men. Next year John de Bevillard took over Harlech, and Hugh de Turberville Bere.

On November 10 Edward reached Llanbadarn, and on November 22 Cardigan. The counties of Cardiganshire and Carmarthenshire were finally constituted under the control of Robert de Tibotot as justiciar. A special compact was made ; the king was in debt to Tibotot, as the result of war expenses and castle-building, and so, henceforward, he was to enjoy the revenues and hold the castles in good repair in compensation[2]. Thus he practically became Viceroy as well as Justiciar of West Wales, a position somewhat galling to the old chieftains, and more especially to the loyalist Rhys. The castles and various subordinate positions were entrusted to Tibotot's men, and so we have no details of crown appointments. Geoffrey Clement, who had already served under Plukenet at Dynevor, was the justiciar's chief official at Cardigan, Walter de Pederton at Carmarthen, and Roger de Mortimer ' of West Wales ' at

[1] *Pipe Roll*, 16 Edw. I.
[2] *Welsh Roll*, 18 Edw. I, July, 1290 (a writ of renewal).

Llanbadarn[1]. Plukenet is found working with Tibotot as before.

Passing to march lands the king came in December to Kidwelly, which was now held in wardship by Edmund of Lancaster for the infant daughter of Patrick de Chaworth, and thence to Gower. He probably found still smouldering the embers of an old quarrel between William de Braose and his tenants; in 1283 they had migrated to the royal lands of Caercynan[2], declaring that they would live under the king rather than under a lord marcher, and an inquiry had been instituted. Such a quarrel really gave to Edward the opportunity which he sought. Nothing is more marked than his wish to reduce the peculiar power of the marchers, and to put them on a legal footing similar to that of the crown tenants in England. Here, then, was a chance to break down the old claim that tenants of the march had no right to appeal to the crown against their lord. Moreover, the crown, as this incident shows, and the war of 1295 showed even more clearly, had the sympathy of the South Welsh tenants themselves, and therefore had a strong basis from which to attack the lords.

Up the Towy there was a question of considerable importance being agitated between John Giffard and the Earl of Hereford. We remember how Giffard held Llandovery since 1277, both by right of conquest and through his wife's claim; since the autumn of 1282 he had held the castle and march of Builth of the king at farm for £100 yearly. The king had also granted him the march of Isgenen, the land lying between Llandovery and the watershed which separates the Vale of Towy from Brecknock. In 1284 he was in full possession of all these lands, and we cannot be wrong in surmising that Edward was rewarding him by such grants, and by persistent favour shown to him in later years, for some great service done in the royal cause; the theory that he was the victor over Llewelyn at Orewin bridge suits well the facts of the case. He had also been serviceable to the crown when he had deserted Simon de Montfort, and fought for Edward

---

[1] See above, p. 194.　　　　[2] *Welsh Roll*, 13 Edw. I.

in the Evesham campaign. But not only did the lands of
Isgenen touch the march of Brecknock, which in itself would
be displeasing to the Earl of Hereford, but also the latter laid
claim to possession; he had received the final submission of
the sons of Rhys Vychan, and when they were dispossessed
he expected to receive Isgenen himself by march custom.
He had fought throughout the war most loyally, and if his
services had not been so conspicuous as Giffard's, that was
only due to lack of a similar opportunity. Edward was
clearly of a contrary opinion; he was rewarding the conqueror
of Llewelyn, and, moreover, was breaking down march custom
by showing that a royal grant was more valid as a title to the
possession of the land than the accidental fact that Hereford
had received the final submission of the Vychans. He did
not go up in person to settle the quarrel, but next year he
appointed judges *ad audiend et terminand*; that is to say,
legal process was to settle the disputes of the marches as
against the old custom of appealing to the sword in private
war. The award was in Giffard's favour.

Lastly, Edward's progress brought him to Glamorgan,
'which was recognized as belonging to the lordship of the
Earl of Gloucester, and he was received with the greatest
honour, and conducted to the boundary of his own lands by
the earl at his own expense.' Trivet's words are pregnant
with meaning [1]. The greatest and most assertive of all the
lords marchers treats the King of England as if he were
a brother potentate. The Clare lets the Plantagenet see that
here in Glamorgan is land not so easily reduced to the level
of an English barony. But the king has it in his mind that
sooner or later, by force or by diplomacy, even the Clare
shall yield. Each probably sees now more clearly than ever
the question which the wars against Llewelyn had inevitably
brought to the front. The one feared lest the conquest of
Wales might be intended to lead to the submission of the
march to the crown, and the other did really intend it.
A year earlier the marriage of Gloucester with the king's
daughter Joan had been discussed, and the dispensation of the

[1] p. 309.

Pope to authorize him to divorce his present wife was expected ; the marriage settlement will be seen later, for matters were not yet arranged.  Leaving Glamorgan now with the consciousness that the earl had been making a display of his power, Edward passed over to Bristol just before Christmas, and did not return to Wales until he came to judge in full court the Hereford-Gloucester suit in 1291.

Up to this time the king had maintained in his pay a permanent staff of sixty bannerets and knights and sixty troopers of the household at daily wages.  But we find the practice beginning of giving a fixed annual wage *pro feodo in loco vadiorum*[1].  The officers were put on a peace footing at a retaining fee, so to speak.  In 1285 a few, such as Daubeny and Turberville, at first continued to receive daily wages, over and above the sums which they might be drawing for the custody of castles, but for the last six months had the fixed fee.  The majority, however, had the fee for the whole year, 20 marcs each banneret, 10 marcs each knight.  Most of them were in posts of trust in Wales or on the borders[2].  There were forty-three troopers drawing the daily wage of 1*s.* in 1284, rather fewer on an average in 1285, all of them either in attendance as the king moved from place to place in Wales or England, or occupied *in negotio regis*[3].  In 1286 the retaining fee to the knights was still paid.  But when, in May that year, Edward crossed over to France, daily wages began once more for his train[4] ; he had thirty-eight bannerets and knights, some ten of them being Gascons or other foreigners, and twenty-two troopers, of whom almost all had been serving in the two Welsh wars.

It is not out of place to notice that 1285 saw the Statute of Winchester passed.  The experience of the wars probably suggested some need of a systematic inspection of the county forces, and of a legal power to be at the disposal of a sheriff when he raised the hue and cry.  Henceforward, arrayers receive the king's commission to pick and marshal infantry,

[1] *Exch. Acc.* $\frac{4}{8}$.                [2] Ibid. $\frac{4}{8}$.
[3] *Misc. Chanc. Roll* $\frac{20}{2}$ ; *Exch. Acc.* $\frac{351}{9}$.
[4] Ibid. $\frac{4}{13}$ and $\frac{351}{21}$.

and the sheriffs have to aid them, but practically there is very little difference between the contingents raised before and those raised after the passing of the statute, as far as numbers are concerned. It may be that the men were better equipped and more ready to serve in consequence of it, and the general organization was undoubtedly better.

While Edward was abroad and the Earl of Cornwall was regent, the old ally of England, Rhys ap Maredudd, rose in revolt. The fighting, comparatively uninteresting in itself, can be minutely traced from day to day in the records. There was a six weeks' campaign and a siege, and some 24,000 men in all were enlisted, partly from England, partly from Llewelyn's recent subjects in North Wales, but mostly from the marches and the loyalist districts, this being the largest force raised in all these wars. When they were disbanded, Rhys broke out again; there was another siege, but this time the local forces sufficed. Then he took to the mountains, and was not caught for a long time, but was no more dangerous. But beyond these facts, we get an insight into the constitutional questions of the day. As a result of the introduction of the shire system and the application of the Statutes of Wales and of Winchester, we find that the Welsh serving the king outside their own county receive pay, but in defence of their own county, not. However, if some great undertaking is on foot, they may be paid for service even in their county, after first doing a three days' unpaid *servitium debitum*; so the Carmarthenshire levies are paid for the siege of Dryslwyn and the relief of Dynevor, but, on the other hand, the Cardiganshire men receive nothing for the siege of Emlyn, except a small sum as a royal gift. With this may be compared John Giffard's tenure of Isgenen, for which he owed the service of one knight and a three days' *servitium debitum* of his bailiff and tenants. The Statute of Wales does not specially order such a service, but the documents show that it existed in fact. The war also led to quarrels between the lords marchers, and these in turn led to strong measures on the king's part towards the breaking down of march customs. Indeed, he gained over the lords, after 1292, a stronger ascendency than he had after the second war and the royal progress of 1284.

But the constitutional position of the lords marchers was not agitated till Rhys's rising was suppressed. The immediate point at issue was the constitutional position of the old Welsh allies of England. Now, in Powysland, the sons of Gruffudd ap Gwenwynwyn accepted the new position of affairs. Owen ap Gruffudd is no longer lord of Powys and an independent prince, but is Owen de la Pole of Welshpool, an English baron; he takes the royal wages as a banneret of the king's staff, just as does his neighbour, Roger l'Estrange; he and his brothers have their disputes concerning their ancestral lands, but these are settled by legal process. Rhys was *Dominus de Estratewy*, lord of the Vale of Towy. He evidently resented the introduction of the system of shires and hundreds, as two English chroniclers admit [1]. As a descendant of an old line of princes, as well as an invaluable ally of England, he had his grievance. And doubtless the peculiar position of Robert de Tibotot, being almost the king's viceroy rather than the king's official, was displeasing. At any rate, his general grievance was against Tibotot, and also against Alan Plukenet, for the two are classed together as *senescalli domini regis*, though what was the exact position which Plukenet held under Tibotot does not appear. It might be suggested that his special grievance, and a direct cause of war, was connected with the rival claims of jurisdiction over certain lands. In June, 1285, Rhys had married an English lady, Ada, sister of John de Hastings, the young lord of Abergavenny. He conferred on his bride the lands of Ostrelof and Mabwinnion, and Hastings conferred other lands, especially the castle of Emlyn, which formed part of his march of Cilgeran. Now, in the course of the war, Rhys began by ravaging Ostrelof, seized Emlyn at his second outbreak, and had the men of Ostrelof and Mabwinnion and Cilgeran ranged against him in the justiciar's army [2]. It is quite possible that

[1] *Annales Cambriae*, p. 109; *Annales Monastici*, 'Wykes,' vol. iv. p. 309; 'Dunstable,' vol. iii. p. 338.

[2] *Annales Cambriae*, and documents quoted below.

his wife's and his own tenants disliked his rule, or that Tibotot, as the king's representative, gave some decision on a question of jurisdiction which roused his anger. He was evidently also at feud with John Giffard concerning the march of Isgenen, which he frequently invaded in the war; and, lastly, it will be remembered that as far back as 1282, although he remained faithful to the English cause, he was even then supposed to have a grievance against Giffard about lands and jurisdiction. Whatever may have been the exact facts, Edward thought that matters could be adjusted, and wrote from Gascony promising justice. In February, 1287, the Earl of Hereford was commissioned to see that the peace was kept[1]. Hengham and other judges were to hear in May the alleged 'transgressions,' Rhys having already begun to take the law into his own hands. June 8 is the date definitely assigned to the first serious outbreak in arms.

The English had still been holding his former stronghold of Dynevor, while the chief seat of his power was Dryslwyn, which lies on the Towy four miles lower down. On taking up arms, he seems to have at once overrun Isgenen, driving back Giffard to Builth. He then seized not only Dynevor, but also Caercynan and Llandovery; so says the author of the *Annales Cambriae*, whose facts of this war, when tested by the documents, are always found to be correct. An English chronicler supports the statement, saying that Rhys captured a royal castle, where he left his wife[2]. Then he ravaged up to the gates of Carmarthen, eastwards up to Ostrelof and Swansea, which he burnt, and northwards to Llanbadarn, where he destroyed part of the town, but not the castle. One account says that he invaded England[3]; probably the march of Brecknock is meant, for he certainly occupied the watershed between Isgenen and Brecon.

The regent, Cornwall, being then at Westminster, wrote on June 14 to summon the barons to Gloucester by July 21. Meanwhile, he ordered Edmund de Mortimer and John

---

[1] *Welsh Roll*, 15 Edw. I.

[2] *Annales Monastici*, 'Wykes,' vol. iv. p. 309.

[3] Ibid. 'Waverley,' p. 405.

Giffard to defend Radnor and the upper Wye[1]. Then he
designated three points of concentration—Chester, Montgomery, and Hereford—from which troops were to converge
on Dryslwyn. The size of the forces ordered, and the fact
that North Wales and Chester, Derbyshire and Nottinghamshire, were laid under contribution, indicate that the rising
was considered to be serious. John de Havering was to bring
in the North Welsh, and such English troops as could be
spared, after allowance for the safety of the castles. Reginald
de Grey was to concentrate at Chester, and the promise was
given that the service of the Cestrians, who had never before
been summoned to march to the south, would not be counted
against them as a precedent, but as done 'graciously.' The
sheriff and lords of Shropshire were to rally round Roger
l'Estrange; they were specially thanked for their 'strenuous
aid' in the last war, and requested to show similar loyalty
now. There is no mention of a feudal levy, but only an
appeal to graciousness and loyalty. Time was short. Some
hundreds of woodcutters and workmen were ordered, but very
few were forthcoming; also, almost all the contingents of foot
were short of the numbers required. On the other hand, the
quickness of the various commanders was remarkable. Within
a month of the issuing of the orders, nearly 11,000 infantry
were actually on the Towy, having converged from four
different points to crush Rhys by an overwhelming display of
force. Most of the men were Welsh, barely more than one-
third English.

Of course, Tibotot was the first to move. Before any aid
could be expected from England, he took measures to preserve Cardiganshire from invasion[2]. Exclusive of foot serving
without pay in their own county, he had in pay two small
flying corps, six horse and thirty-six foot to patrol the country
south of the Aeron, three horse and twenty-four foot beyond
that river, between June 11 and August 10. Rhys is only
recorded to have made the one raid as far as Llanbadarn, and

---

[1] Dates from *Welsh Roll*, 15 Edw. I, mostly printed in *Parl. Writs*,
vol. i. p. 250 onwards.

[2] *Exch. Acc.* $\frac{4}{19}$.

Tibotot's efforts to keep him out of Cardiganshire seem to have been successful. With the first week in August, he was able to take in hand the defence of Carmarthenshire. On August 2 he concentrated at Carmarthen 560 Welsh of the loyalist districts, who received pay after doing a three days' *servitium debitum*, together with five crossbowmen and thirty English foot of the permanent paid garrison *retenti ad vadia regis*. Gradually the force rose to 2,000 foot, as men came in from Pembroke and Cardiganshire, a figure which represents the limit of what the loyalists of the south-west could do. I cannot find that Tibotot commanded any other English except the thirty-five just mentioned, but among his officers were Roger and Hugh de Mortimer and John de Knoville. This force the regent found waiting for him at Carmarthen.

The second army was concentrated under the regent's immediate command at Hereford, from July 21 onwards[1]. He intended at first to march straight to Carmarthen by way of Brecon, where he ordered a depot or market for supplies to be formed on July 23; at the same time he commissioned the Earl of Gloucester to take command in Brecknock, with a view to his ultimately joining in the march against Dryslwyn, *ulterius profecturus*[2]. But it would seem that a sudden invasion of Brecknock by Rhys upset these arrangements. Gloucester was busy against this new enemy during most of August, and the regent, instead of pushing across by the shortest route, made a wide detour through Monmouth and Glamorgan. The army started on July 28, marched by way of Usk, Newport, and Cowbridge, and so reached Carmarthen along the coast road on August 8. Out of 1,000 men originally ordered, Derbyshire and Notts sent 340, falling off later to 230; South Shropshire sent 500, and Herefordshire 1,280; the march of Monmouth added 360; from London came fifty-two crossbowmen, and from Bristol twenty-eight. The regent arrived at Carmarthen a few days ahead of his army. Between August 8 and 11 he rested there; on the 12th he moved up the Towy by the right bank, to lay siege to Dryslwyn, Tibotot's Welsh accompanying.

---

[1] *Exch. Acc.* $\frac{4}{17}$.       [2] *Parl. Writs*, vol. i. p. 252.

Grey and l'Estrange were not long in joining[1]. Grey seems to have started in a hurry, for his infantry were a few hundreds short, and he had only twenty woodmen out of the 500 who had been ordered. He left Chester with 500 English foot on August 6, picked up 500 Welsh of Ruthin and Denbigh, his own and the Earl of Lincoln's tenants, and halted at Llanbadarn. A day or two behind him came 300 of Queen Eleanor's men from Chester and Hope, with twenty woodcutters. John de Havering brought in 2,000 of Snowdonia and Merioneth ; the number is not stated, but an average payment of £18 10s. a day gives 2,000 men ; also, he brought 120 carpenters, masons, smiths, and quarrymen, the skilled English mechanics from the new castles, whose high wages varied from 3d. and 4d. a day for each carpenter to 5d. or 6d. and 7d. for the masons and foremen, twenty archers and twenty crossbowmen escorting them. Havering drew £50 to maintain the 'household' of Otto de Grandison, whose deputy he was, presumably the knights who formed the administrative staff of North Wales. Meanwhile, l'Estrange had raised the English of Shropshire and the marchers of Powys and Bromfield and Radnor, and joined Grey at Llanbadarn on August 10. The united force pushed on to Carmarthen, picking up 400 Cardigan men, who afterwards were added to Tibotot's army, and reached Dryslwyn on August 15. The total of nearly 11,000 foot was thus made up :—

| | | |
|---|---|---:|
| Grey | English of Chester . . . . . . | 700 |
| | Welsh of Snowdon and Cantreds . . . . | 2,600 |
| L'Estrange | English of Shropshire . . . . . | 1,000 |
| | Welsh of marches . . . . . . | 1,940 |
| Cornwall | English of South Shropshire, Derbyshire, and Herefordshire . . . . . . | 2,010 |
| | Welsh of Monmouth . . . . . . | 360 |
| Tibotot | Welsh of North Pembroke and Cardigan . . | 920 |
| | „ Carmarthenshire . . . . | 1,000 |
| | Crossbowmen . . . . . . . | 105 |
| | | 10,635 |

Besides the crossbowmen and mechanics, 3,740 only were

[1] *Exch. Acc.* $\frac{4}{16}$.

English.   One of the Shropshire centenars was Stephen
de Frankton, commanding the men of Ellesmere under
l'Estrange.

The numbers of the cavalry can only be guessed.   From
the patent roll we find that letters of protection were given to
150 barons and men-at-arms going to Wales.   In the Welsh
roll and one of the infantry pay-rolls are entries of various
sums paid, e. g. £200 to the Earl of Warwick, £160 to Surrey,
£60 to Norfolk, £300 to Edmund de Mortimer, £120 to Roger
de Mortimer of Chirk, £150 to l'Estrange.   Over £1,400 were
paid, in larger or smaller sums[1].   The Earl of Cornwall's own
following consisted, according to the patent roll, of eleven
knights, among them Walter de Huntercumbe.   The campaign
therefore marks a stage in the history of feudalism as a system
for raising cavalry.   There is no attempt to exact the *servitium debitum* of the feudal tenants, and instead of several
lords bringing each a few lances according to their tenure,
they group themselves under earls or other prominent commanders, to form fewer but larger units.   The first two wars
saw cavalry serving for pay before and after the legal forty
days of unpaid service, and this war sees even powerful earls
drawing large sums to maintain bodies of horse.   However,
there is no sign that the regent himself received pay for his
immediate following, nor did Hereford or Gloucester.   Of the
prominent soldiers of lower rank, we find Ralph Basset of
Drayton, Hugh de Turberville, Butler of Werington, Peter
Corbet, Norman Darcy, John l'Estrange, Bogo de Knoville,
William de Leyburn, all drawing sums from 10 marcs upwards.
Most of the lords marchers were serving, and men such as
Hugh de Courtenay and Hugh Pointz, who had letters of
protection, were doubtless in the retinues of some greater
barons.   Allowing for a period of six weeks, and assuming
that all the £1,400 represent payments to cavalry, for the rolls
dealing with the infantry are exhaustive, we may fairly estimate 500 paid horse ; adding Cornwall's and other unpaid
contingents, perhaps as many as 700.   They were not necessarily all at the same time at Dryslwyn ; for instance, the men

[1] All these sums are entered in *Pipe Roll*, 15 Edw. I, m. 1.

for whom Edmund de Mortimer drew £300 probably served in the march of Radnor.

While the army was being massed, and while Tibotot was guarding Cardiganshire and South Carmarthenshire, the task of confronting Rhys higher up the Towy obviously fell upon the Earl of Hereford, who had received a commission as far back as February.   He did everything that he had to do at his own expense, and the silence of both history and documents as to his operations is more than ever annoying.   But judging from later events, we may infer that he at least was contesting Isgenen and Llandovery, those lands of John Giffard to which he himself had once laid claim, and upon which he would descend immediately as he crossed the range westwards from his own march of Brecknock.   Meanwhile the regent had ordered Giffard to defend Builth.   Now the English army was ordered to move on Dryslwyn, through Brecknock, under the regent himself, and the Earl of Gloucester was in arms ready to go on with him (*ulterius profecturus*), but suddenly the troops had to be diverted by way of Monmouth.   This means a rising in Brecknock during Hereford's absence, probably the so-called 'invasion of England' of the Waverley annalist. The only man available to crush the rising and restore communications between England and the intended scene of operations at Dryslwyn was Gloucester.   Except under special circumstances it would be a gross breach of march etiquette to set a Clare to subdue a Bohun's revolted tenants, but there was now no alternative, and the regent had to give the task to the Clare.

We have an exact account of Gloucester's doings [1].   Between July 28 and August 10 he had 200 of the trained woodmen of the Forest of Dean at work cutting paths through the wooded mountains, and 100 of them somewhat longer.   A great force of foot was raised from his own vassals of Glamorgan and those of neighbouring marchers, not in crown pay at first, but put on the pay-roll on August 5, and these could be used to help in the path-cutting as well as to guard the workmen. His own men numbered 5,300, Edmund de Mortimer sent

[1] *Exch. Acc.* 4/18.

3,000, Hastings 600, Giffard 800, Tony 360, FitzReginald 300, Audley 100, while the loyal tenants of the Earl of Hereford from Brecknock and Hay were 2,000 strong. The total of 12,500 shows what the marchers could do when they made a special effort. This force, or the part of it under Gloucester's eye, was for a time just at the place where we should expect to find it, namely at Llywel, where the road now runs from Brecon to the Towy. The overflowing display of strength was successful, for the same document tells us that a treasure of £800 was safely brought from Hereford to Llywel for transmission to the army round Dryslwyn. Communication with England was clearly re-established. Meanwhile, another body of woodmen, 600 strong at first, rising to 650, and then dropping to 300, was engaged in cutting another path through from Glamorgan to Brecknock, by way of Morlais and the Taff Valley; this land was unoccupied, one infers, and later was the cause of great strife. By August 19 the work was done, and the foot of the marchers, having dropped down to 3,000 men, were disbanded.

The regent had, on August 15, round Dryslwyn his 10,600 foot and perhaps 600 horse. All the payments made to this force are dated from Dryslwyn. But, of course, even a large proportion of the men could have been spared to attack Dynevor, Caercynan, and Llandovery, while their official paymasters remained at headquarters. According to Wykes[1], the unnamed royal castle, where Rhys had left his wife, was blockaded and captured, but both the lady and the garrison were carried off under cover of darkness. Rhys never intended to let himself be caught inside a castle, and took to the mountains with his 'grave-riflers,' *cum vispilionibus suis.* We may conclude that these other fortresses fell some time in August without trouble; probably Grey and Tibotot did that part of the work, and subsequently formed a covering army against Rhys's guerilla attacks from the outside, while Cornwall's English army pushed on the siege of Dryslwyn. Havering's mechanics and sappers from the northern castles were set to work, and an engine was brought up. The bill

[1] p. 309.

for fitting it up, and buying hides, timber, rope, and lead, came to £14. Twenty quarrymen and four carters made and brought up the stone bullets. Other sums were paid for purchasing and making up pickaxes and other tools; woodmen and ditchers were also impressed, and both Huntercumbe and Leyburn appear in command of workmen. The mining and battering were in full swing between August 20 and 30, when twenty-six *fossatores* were paid *ad removend lapides et morttir ad caﬔllam et ad psternend murum capelle.* Now just at this very date the Earl of Cornwall's English soldiers of Herefordshire, South Shropshire, and Derbyshire were largely reduced in number; this is the only one of all the united divisions which suffered at all, losing over 700 men, more than a third of its original strength[1]. It is tolerably clear that they were conducting that part of the siege where the chief operations were going on, making a breach into the castle through the wall of the chapel, where indeed would be the most vulnerable point. Several chroniclers, moreover, say that there was a great disaster to the English, an undermined wall falling and killing many knights, and especially William de Montchensy, who, it may be noted, had only recently been outlawed, and was working out his sentence by fighting in Edward's service, in place of going into exile[2]. It is also a coincidence that the Earl of Gloucester came up with 3,500 new foot on August 29, just when the besieging force, knights and infantry alike, had been suffering loss at the breach[3]. Dryslwyn was either captured by renewed assaults, for 150 more infantry of the Herefordshire men were lost between September 1 and 4, or else was surrendered about September 5. On September 8 Alan Plukenet was made custodian of the place in Edward's name.

Each division retired on Carmarthen and was dismissed. The South Welsh at once disappear from the pay-sheets, the English and North Welsh received eight days' wages for the march home, counted from September 6, and Gloucester's men were paid a few days longer up to September 12. Rhys was

---

[1] *Exch. Acc.* $\frac{4}{18}$ and $\frac{4}{19}$, *passim.*          [2] *Patent Roll*, May, 1286.

[3] *Exch. Acc.* $\frac{4}{18}$.

at large, but evidently hoping that he was unable to resume the offensive the Earl of Cornwall returned to Westminster. There is a statement in the chronicle of Wykes of Osney, that Gloucester and other lords, secretly treacherous to the king as rumour went, persuaded the regent to make a truce.

Tibotot had now the task of making good the damage done by Rhys; for instance, we find that he spent £320 in this work at Llanbadarn[1]. He seems to have required more ready money than he could raise from the revenues of South Wales, which he had always drawn, and he accounted for about £600 in all to the officials of the Exchequer. Ten archers and twenty crossbows garrisoned Dynevor. Alan Plukenet, holding Dryslwyn under the crown, and therefore not being accountable to Tibotot, had a garrison of two knights, twenty-two troopers, twenty crossbows, and eighty archers[2]; only four of the horse and forty archers were Welsh, and amongst the Englishmen were several men who had been centenars in the besieging army and now volunteered to serve in garrison. He raised money by selling loot from Rhys's lands; for instance, seven bulls and fourteen oxen fetched 5s. each, and 126 cows 4s. each. The country seemed quiet, and the forty Welsh archers were dismissed in October. Whatever part of the lands of Rhys had been occupied by Tibotot, he garrisoned with his followers, and Roger de Mortimer 'of West Wales,' in particular, held Emlyn.

Quite suddenly, in the early part of November, Rhys broke out again and seized the 'new castle' of Emlyn. The castle had formed part of the dower of Ada de Hastings on her marriage with Rhys, and had been subsequently occupied by Tibotot, either by force or under the terms of the supposed truce. Mortimer was overpowered and kept captive by Rhys, and his garrison was slaughtered[3]. This done, the insurgents returned to the Towy, failed to seize Dynevor by a similar surprise, and laid siege to it instead. The Earl of Cornwall made light of the new rising, for the insurgents had recently been crushed by a great display of force, and could not have

---

[1] *Pipe Roll*, 16 Edw. I.            [2] *Exch. Acc.* $\frac{4}{20}$.
[3] *Annales Cambriae*, p. 110.

great resources. Moreover, the lords marchers, especially Gloucester and probably Hastings, who was much attached to Gloucester and who may have resented the retention of Emlyn by the justiciar, thinking that it ought to have been returned to him on being wrested from Rhys, were unwilling to move. Therefore, the regent simply wrote to them ordering them to remain on their marches, and see to the security of their own castles [1]. Offensive measures were left to Tibotot, who received merely a reinforcement of a few crossbowmen from London, and, with the aid of the Welsh loyalists, the justiciar speedily relieved Dynevor and retook Emlyn by siege. Rhys had also once more induced the men of Isgenen to rise.

Tibotot organized his relief expedition at the end of November [2]. He had out between 1,200 and 1,300 Welsh foot of Cardigan, Kidwelly, and Gower, these latter doing the usual three days' unpaid service before receiving pay. With the foot, fifteen light horse, and a few of Plukenet's men picked up at Dryslwyn en route, he relieved Dynevor on December 2. The next day he advanced up the Cothi to Brechfa *ad querend Rees*. Between December 4 and 7 he had only 400 Cardigan men in pay round Carmarthen *ad explor et custod*. From December 8 to 16 he was back at Dynevor, raiding up the Towy and accepting the surrender of the men of Isgenen. For one day he paid ten horse and 240 foot of Carmarthen *ad explor super Rees*, another day 765 foot under Henry of London, while six horse and thirty foot garrisoned the newly surrendered lands of Isgenen. Meanwhile Plukenet raised his garrison at Dryslwyn to forty-eight horse and thirty-eight crossbowmen, including the newly arrived Londoners. All other service, since the relief of Dynevor, was unpaid because in the county. From December 28 we find the converse; the siege of Emlyn being undertaken, the men of Carmarthen were immediately admitted to pay, those of Cardigan served as a duty.

William de Braose, son of the lord of Gower, on December 28

---

[1] *Welsh Roll*, Nov. 14.
[2] *Exch. Acc.* $\frac{4}{1}$, and *Pipe Roll*, 16 Edw. I.

concentrated seven horse and sixty-three foot of his own following, besides three heavy and eighteen light horse from elsewhere, two mounted and nineteen foot crossbowmen, and
400 foot. On January 1, 1288, they were already blockading
Emlyn *circa novum castrum ne illi de castro exirent*, and the
unpaid force of Cardigan was brought up by Geoffrey Clement.
The castle lies on the Teify not far above Cardigan. The
engine which had done the damage at Dryslwyn was brought
up by an escort of twenty horse and 463 foot, who were also
Braose's men. Within five days it was hauled to Cardigan by
way of St. Clears and Cilgeran, forty oxen and four four-
wheeled wains being used ; at Cardigan it was taken over to
the right bank of the Teify and repaired, and thence hauled
by sixty oxen into the camp before Emlyn by January 10.
The carting, with the hire and keep of the oxen, cost 45*s*.
*excepto auxilio patriae*. The wages of blacksmiths and cost of
materials used in the repair, including 4*s*. 6*d*. paid for pig's fat
for grease, came to 70*s*. Men were employed to pick up 480
stones on the beach below Cardigan and transport the same
by boat to Llechryd on the river, and thence to carry them on
120 packhorses to the camp, thus earning 48*s*. Ten mechanics,
Welsh, and therefore paid only 2*d*. a day, and twenty-four
woodcutters, were employed in making a bridge and hurdles
for an assault, and two master workmen at the end of the
siege received a marc each. The whole bill for the engine
and siege-works came to over £18. By January 10 the
besieging force had been reinforced up to sixteen heavy
and thirty-eight light horse, twenty-one crossbows, and 923
foot in pay, and the Cardigan volunteers ; by January 20 the
castle fell. As not a single man was missing out of the paid
portion of the army, it would seem that the surrender was
peaceable, and probably the engine and the 480 great stones
upset the tenacity of the defenders. A force of twenty-five
horse was left behind for a few days to help the Cardigan
men to hold and pacify the country, and the rest were
disbanded.

The justiciar thought fit to award £10 to the Cardigan men
for their assistance in the siege, and in hauling up the engine.

*Et sciendum ; quia bene et fideliter deserviebant domino regi et propriis sumptibus, precepit dominus R. de Tybotot eis dari £10 de curialitate et de dono domini regis, et ut facilius posset eos attractare si dominus rex eorum auxilio alias ibi vel alibi indiguerit.* The money was paid through Geoffrey Clement, *ad opus peditum ex Cardigan qui permanserunt in obsessione novi castri sine vadiis.*

Meanwhile since December a small party had been out in the mountains 'to search for Rhys.' After the fall of Emlyn two of the centenars of the besieging force and seventeen light horse pursued the search up the Towy to Llangadoc, while sixty foot scoured the forests (*de bosco in boscum*) between January 25 and 28. Then twenty-four other horse and 480 foot joined in, forty of whom came from the lands of Rhys's wife. They also took hostages from the lately insurgent parts of the interior. But after January there are no further entries in Tibotot's pay-roll, except when in April a convoy was forwarded from Carmarthen to Dynevor. For the rest of 1288 and all 1289 we only have Alan Plukenet's pay-roll of his garrison in Dryslwyn, from which we see that the northern parts of Carmarthenshire were gradually reduced[1]. Rhys gave no more trouble, surprised no more castles, but was at large till 1291. So harmless was he that in 1289 Plukenet reduced his strength to a handful of troopers, twenty crossbows, and thirty archers, and was himself frequently absent. Finally retiring in 1290, he handed over the castle and lands to Philip ap Howel ap Meyrick, son of the late steward and custodian of Builth.

The general superintendence of the pacification of Carmarthenshire and Cardiganshire was given in 1288 to the Earl of Hereford and to Edmund de Mortimer. Other lords marchers, such as the Earl of Gloucester, were merely ordered to look to the safety of their own castles and dwell on their estates in readiness. The Prior of the Hospitallers was sent to report on the general state of Wales, and inspect the fortifications[2].

---

[1] *Exch. Acc.* $\frac{4}{23}$.

[2] *Welsh Roll, passim.* I have seen in some histories that Gloucester was made chief commander, but this is an error.

In 1289 a writ was sent to warn all concerned that Rhys was likely to escape to Ireland. It is not stated that he actually got away to Ireland, but Wykes insinuates that the Earl of Gloucester was treacherously conniving at his escape, and offering him an asylum there. We also find William de Valence warned against receiving him at Kidwelly, and William de Braose in Gower. All we know for certain is that he was at last caught and sent to the king for sentence at York; Edward was not in York at all in 1290, but passed through in April, 1291, on his way to Norham[1].

The possessions and castles of Rhys were occupied of course by Robert de Tibotot, and in 1290 the agreement which the latter had with the crown was renewed. He was to hold all the castles of Cardiganshire and Carmarthenshire as before, drawing the revenues and appointing the officials in recompense for the crown's debts to him, for a further term of four years, Dryslwyn and Emlyn included[2]. John de Hastings, as noticed before, probably expected to get back Emlyn, but the crown argued that he had not legally entered into possession when it was handed over to Ada, being still in wardship; thus the crown, having conquered the castle by arms, kept it. This argument was used when a younger John de Hastings claimed possession as Ada's nephew[3]. Tibotot retained his position till 1294, when the agreement was once more renewed, just before he was ordered to the war in Gascony.

During these few years of peace we find a few changes made among the officials. John de Havering was summoned to Gascony, where he was appointed seneschal[4]. Hugh de Turberville in 1288 took up the vacant deputy justiciarship of North Wales in the continued absence of Otto de Grandison, and a few months later William de Grandison succeeded him. Turberville then went back to Bere, where he died in 1293 while in the enjoyment of various privileges which mark the king's appreciation of his services, and henceforward his widow

---

[1] *Patent Roll.*     [2] *Welsh Roll*, July, 1290.
[3] Bridgeman, *Princes of South Wales*, p. 199.
[4] *Welsh* and *Patent Rolls, passim.*

had a pension of £20 yearly. Robert Fitzwalter was there-upon made custodian of Bere. In 1293 Robert de Staundon became Justiciar of North Wales. Under him we still find Will Sikun as Constable of Conway. Walter Haket now held Criccieth. Harlech was held for a short time by James de St. George, the architect; the accounts, previously quoted [1], show that it cost as much to reconstruct Harlech as to build the entirely new castles of Carnarvon and Conway. Afterwards Vivian de Staundon, the justiciar's son, was made constable. In 1288, in Powysland, there was a general settlement of disputes between Owen de la Pole and his brothers; when he died, the custody of the lands of Machynlleth was granted to the Countess of Derby, during the minority of the heir, and the castle of Welshpool to Roger l'Estrange.

The budget of this short war shows a total expenditure of £10,606 [2].

|  | £ |
|---|---|
| Payments to infantry and workmen . . . . | 6,116 |
| „ „ feudal lords for cavalry . . . . | 1,400 |
| Cost of garrison of Dryslwyn after capture . . . | 1,936 |
| Expenses of siege of Emlyn . . . . . . | 554 |
| Repairs and new works at Llanbadarn . . . . | 320 |
| „ „ „ Carmarthen . . . | 169 |
| Garrison at Dynevor . . . . . . . | 111 |
|  | 10,606 |

[1] See p. 196.
[2] *Pipe Roll*, 15 Edw. I, m. 1, and 17 Edw. I, m. 1 and 2. The totals correspond exactly to the figures of the special pay-rolls of the war.

# CHAPTER VI

## THE CUSTOM OF THE MARCH

RHYS was yet at large when the question of the rights of the lords marchers, after having loomed for a long time in the distance, came prominently to the front. Both king and marchers must have long foreseen that the custom of private war would have to be settled, now that the power of the Princes of Snowdon had been extinguished. Edward was determined to enforce the doctrine that the dignity of the crown was to be respected. Private war was a relic of an unsettled age, an anachronism in fact. In place of fighting a dispute to the end, as in days when the king's power did not extend to Wales, the marchers were to submit to legal process, and if they argued that march custom did not sanction the imposition of law over them, they were to learn that the king was above both law and custom. Edward returned from Gascony in the summer of 1289. His prompt action in suppressing lawlessness of any and every kind was remarkable; it is now that he dismissed and ruined the corrupt judges, and set himself to compel the sheriffs to put an end to riots in their counties. To break down the custom of the marches was as much part of his policy as to make impossible the recurrence of wanton outrages like the riot at Boston fair. Moreover he had a golden opportunity, for the crown could effectually interfere when the marchers were fighting each other.

The central figure of march privilege was Earl Gilbert of Gloucester. He had practically the position of an independent earl palatine[1]; there was his *Curia Comitatus*, which Henry III had been forced in the Siward case to acknowledge

---

[1] Rhys and Brynmor Jones, *Welsh People*, p. 348.

as independent of the *Curia Regis*[1]; under him was his own *vicecomes*, his sheriff or deputy; he had 'a complete *imperium in imperio*[2].' In matters clerical he claimed to have sole authority over the see of Llandaff[3]. When his bailiff stopped one of the Braose family on the public road in 1281, and the latter appealed to the *Curia Regis*, the earl challenged the jurisdiction and would not answer to the *quo warranto*[4]. When the king passed through Glamorgan in the royal progress of 1284, he entertained him as though he were a brother sovereign potentate. And such a position influenced the Clare's status as a feudal baron of England, as Mr. Clark has so clearly pointed out. A baron who owed to the king the service of more than 450 knights, in addition to being lord of Glamorgan, simply held the balance of power in any crisis against the crown. In 1288 he led the baronage in refusing to grant a subsidy while the king was still absent in Gascony[5], *nisi prius personaliter viderent in Anglia faciem regis.* Rumour (*ut vulgariter dicebatur*) may have lied when it asserted that he treacherously put pressure on the Earl of Cornwall to make a truce with Rhys, or that he offered Rhys an asylum on his lands in Ireland; but even lying rumour represents what contemporaries think a man capable of doing. Moreover, in that war against Rhys, though it is an error to imagine that he was in chief command, he had out an enormous force of foot from his own lands and those of his brother marchers, Edmund de Mortimer and John de Hastings particularly, as though he was showing to the regent Cornwall what he and his neighbours could do of their own resources.

An interesting question had been long discussed between Edward and the earl. He was to divorce his wife and marry the king's daughter, Joan Plantagenet. The marriage settlement had been arranged as far back as 1283[6]; he was to surrender his lands in England, Ireland, and Wales, so that he and Joan might be enfeoffed therein with remainder to the

---

[1] Clark, *Land of Morgan*, p. 2–4.     [2] Ibid. p. 33.
[3] Ibid. p. 143.     [4] Ibid. p. 137.
[5] *Annales Monastici*, 'Wykes,' vol. iv. pp. 311, 316.
[6] *Land of Morgan*, p. 139.

heirs of their bodies. The papal dispensation was slow in coming, but it came at last, and with it the necessary freedom.

The other chief actor, the Earl of Hereford, had not been hitherto actively defiant of the crown. He was rather sullenly obedient, for he knew that he had not so strong a status as Gloucester's. There was nothing so far against him. He had served in the wars of 1277 and 1282 with his quota of knights, partly performing his duty as constable with the king—and we remember that he successfully demanded in 1282 the fee attached to his office—partly reconquering in his own name and with his own resources his rebellious tenants of Brecknock. Like Gloucester he never took the king's pay for himself, except as constable, or for his mounted retinue, though his son and one knight were in pay in 1283, and would be again in 1296. But the frequent risings in Brecknock prove that his power as a marcher was not very great; moreover the crown claimed from him the service of twenty-six knights for the lands he inherited from the Braoses, and it was decided, in 1274, that he had never conquered Brecknock so thoroughly that he could call upon Llewelyn to withdraw under the treaty of 1267. Though he was clearly a man who insisted on his rights and claimed the custom of the marches to settle disputes by private war, he was not powerful enough alone to defy the crown. One cannot avoid feeling some sympathy with him in the great dispute which he now had with Gloucester, and throughout our examination of the facts to be narrated we must forget entirely that in future years, exasperated by the treatment now meted out to him, and strengthened by powerful confederates, he was going to be the perverse and rebellious Hereford of 1297 and 1298.

It is Hereford's grievance which first attracts our attention in 1289, his old grievance against John Giffard, which had been intensified by the circumstances of Rhys's rising. Giffard held Llandovery, the castle and march of Builth, and, lastly, the march of Isgenen which bordered on Hereford's own lands, and the king's favour to him was pronounced. Hereford's grievance was that he himself had conquered the Vychans, and ought to have received Isgenen. The question of these lands was being disputed in 1284 when the king made his royal progress ; it was referred to law, and the answer was in Giffard's favour. The king's grant was a more valid title to possession than the accidental fact that the Welsh of that part had made their final submission to Hereford. Thus the earl found an upstart planted both on the north and on the west of his own march of Brecknock, an upstart who had been an opportunist in the civil war, who was masterful and a good soldier, but whose services to the crown were in his eyes no greater than his own ; the feeling of irritation was but natural. Then came the trouble with Rhys ; first Hereford was empowered to keep the peace before the outbreak ; when war began, he was on the spot to serve the crown, but whatever service he did, and wherever he did it, he fought entirely at his own expense. The probability is that he had the chief part in confronting Rhys before the Earl of Cornwall appeared, and that he reduced Giffard's revolted tenants of Isgenen, perhaps also of Llandovery and Builth ; certain it is that Giffard was one of Rhys's worst enemies, and all the known facts point to Giffard's lands as being a chief theatre of the war in the June of 1287. Then in the July there was a sudden outbreak in Brecknock, but Hereford was too busy elsewhere. So it would seem that the regent, wishing to reduce Brecknock speedily so as to establish a secure line of communication through from England to the Towy, gave that strange order to Gloucester to undertake the work, and only extreme urgency could justify such a gross breach of march etiquette when a Clare was set to hunt in a Bohun's preserve. The documents inform us that Gloucester had a great force of infantry and woodmen engaged in road-cutting between Brecon and Llywel, that is near where Hereford's and Giffard's marches met ; and again around Morlais, just where Hereford's and his own met, the land being wild and overgrown, and the exact boundary doubtful. Finally, the siege of Dryslwyn over, Hereford was commissioned in the November to guard Carmarthenshire, and more particularly to hold the revolted but now reconquered lands of Isgenen. By march custom he would claim that Isgenen was his by a double right of the sword, but by a strange irony under the same custom he was in danger of losing to Gloucester the southern strip of Brecknock. It was hard that, after doing his duty to the crown elsewhere at his own expense, he should lose a part of his own land.

In 1289, before the king had returned from Gascony, Hereford was in arms to assert his claims against Giffard. In the May of that year Hengham[1], who is noticeable as one of the corrupt judges whom Edward was shortly to degrade, was commissioned to hold an inquiry into the homicides and trespasses which had been done. The award was entirely in favour of Giffard, for in the October Edward, being now in England, definitely confirmed Isgenen to Giffard, who indeed died years later in full possession[2].

But meanwhile there was the more important war raging openly between the two earls—with what result and with the employment of what forces we do not know, for the present fighting was dwarfed by the events of the next year. Gloucester had been building a fort at Morlais, which lay on a small tributary of the upper Taff. The fort, indeed, is never once named in the *précis* of the great suit, but, as Mr. Clark shows[3], 'it is certain from the general tenor of the evidence' that it was Morlais castle—no temporary erection of wood, but a strong stone castle, the style of which 'points with tolerable certainty to the later period of the early English style or to the close of the thirteenth century.' Again, the general tenor of the evidence shows that the boundary was vague; that Gloucester was claiming a debatable strip, *ubi nunc est contencio*, up to the foot of the Beacons, i.e. claiming the land up to the watershed between his and Hereford's marches as belonging to Glamorgan; that it was a lawless country swarming with lawless brigands; and that each earl was engaged in stocking his side of it as though to prove effectual occupation, for the number of cattle and sheep on the pastures was very large. Evidently the road-cutting of 1287 first opened out the scene of contention. It may be added that, when Gloucester had been thus engaged, all his foot and

---

[1] *Patent Roll*, May 12.  [2] *Welsh Roll*, Oct.

[3] *Medieval Military Architecture*, vol. ii, under ' Morlais.'

woodmen were in royal pay; thus one would have expected that the king would put in his claim to the dispossession of both, but of this there is no sign.

The king was in deadly earnest to stop the private war. Our first definite fact is a strongly worded royal proclamation on January 25, 1290, formally calling on the earls to abstain from active hostilities. As if in a spirit of open and immediate defiance, Gloucester's men on February 3 raided into Brecknock, two leagues beyond the castle, killed some of Hereford's men, and carried off spoil; they were led by the earl's bailiffs, they marched under the earl's banner, and, as was the custom of the marches, he received a third part of the loot. He was distinctly cognizant of the raid after the fact. The bailiffs were John de Crepping, William de Valers, Richard le Fleming, and Stephen de Cappenor; Mr. Clark draws attention to the names, for three of them, it is shown, were not Glamorgan men but imported officials; Fleming might be from Glamorgan, but the name is too common for us to be certain [1].

Edward patiently overlooked for the time this sheer defiance of his proclamation. He was bent upon carrying through his long-cherished design of marrying Gloucester to his daughter. The papal licence had at length arrived. Gloucester surrendered all his lands into the king's hands in April, the marriage took place on May 2, and on May 27 writs were issued for the restitution. But the new enfeoffment was 'much less favourable to him than that set forth in the *praelocutio* of 1283, being to the husband and wife jointly for life, with remainder to the heirs of their bodies, and remainder over to her heirs, instead of, as before, to his heirs [2].' Such a settlement was all against the earl. It would hardly be too much to say that Edward intended to reduce him by his marriage, which might appear to be a bribe to make him loyal, but was really a punishment. He practically received back Glamorgan

---

[1] A *précis* of the whole case was drawn up and copied into the *Welsh Roll* of 20 Edw. I. I had written my narrative before discovering that Mr. Clark had already given the facts in his *Medieval Architecture*, and subsequently I have checked my account by his.

[2] *Land of Morgan*, p. 142.

and Usk on the same terms as Clare and Gloucester. This new status of inferiority he seems to have understood, for his next act was dictated by a spirit of defiance similar to the previous one. As the royal proclamation had been immediately followed by a raid into Brecknock, so now the restoration of his lands was followed by a second raid on June 5. The prompt coincidence of a raid following both the proclamation and the new enfeoffment argues premeditation.

The facts of the second raid were undoubted. The earl was entirely cognizant, *bene scivit de depredationibus*. Again the men were under his banner, and yielded up to him a third part of the spoil. Crepping was not actually present, but consented to it, and got his share of the spoil, and the other three bailiffs led.

A third raid took place in November, and for the third time there is a coincidence. We remember that the earl had a dispute with the crown concerning the see of Llandaff; on November 3 a settlement was made, the earl fully admitting the king's rights *propter privilegium regium et corone dignitatem ad quam specialiter pertinet episcopatuum vacantium custodia*; the bishops are declared to have always held their temporal barony of the crown and not of the Clares[1], and in enjoying the temporalities of the bishopric during voidance, after the death of the late bishop, the earl was usurping the king's rights. The third raid was a prompt answer of defiance after this surrender of his claim over Llandaff.

About the same time the brigands of the debatable lands of Morlais were active. They were mere brigands, for whom neither Gloucester nor Hereford was personally responsible. They committed robberies and also sacrilege. All four of Gloucester's bailiffs, however, had their share of the brigands' loot, except in the case of sacrilege, *exceptis bonis inventis in ecclesia eo quod de roberia facta in ecclesia neque comes neque ballivi sui aliquid sciverunt*. Yet was Gloucester morally responsible, not only because the bailiffs were his representatives and were cognizant of the brigandage after the event,

---

[1] *Patent Roll*, Nov. 3, 1290; *Land of Morgan*, p. 143.

but also because the bad example of men of high position is usually imitated by scoundrels. Gloucester was indeed acquitted afterwards by the jury on these meaner charges, but he had undoubtedly given a direct incentive to crime.

Hereford was the plaintiff at law. He had evidently suffered considerably, and he had obeyed the king's orders not to wage private war, for there are no signs that he continued to attack Giffard in prosecution of the other quarrel. The proclamation of January had been addressed to Gloucester in particular. Our sympathies go with Hereford. The lords marchers then sympathized with Gloucester, for he was voicing their own thoughts on the question of march privilege. I would submit, however, that no organized defiance of the crown existed as it undoubtedly existed in 1297 and 1298. Two powerful lords had been fighting, one continued to fight defiantly *contra pacem et post inhibitionem*; there was general lawlessness, and the body of neighbouring marchers thought that private war was the privilege of their order. Such facts cannot substantiate any theory of combined action against the king. This was his unique opportunity for interfering and breaking the custom, especially as Hereford could not possibly combine with Gloucester to support it, for he was the injured party and had appealed to law. The king saw that he could introduce legal process into the march once for all, there being no ground on which combination against him was possible. The irony of the situation is very strong. When men want to fight each other as they please, they cannot ally themselves together against the controlling power. So Edward, having his chance, determined that the suit should go on, even if Hereford, being frightened of the consequences, should wish to withdraw his plea; and in striking at the custom, after patiently waiting for the marchers to drop it in obedience to his orders, he struck hard.

Early in the year 1291 the Bishop of Ely, William de Valence, and two regular judges were commissioned to hear the case, but were to confine the inquiry to the facts of the year 1290, as committed after the definite royal proclamation. The Sheriff of Berkshire was ordered to summon the Earl of

Gloucester, Robert de Tibotot to summon the incriminated bailiffs, to appear at Ystradfellte in Brecknock on March 12, and a jury was to be produced from Herefordshire, Cardiganshire, Carmarthenshire, Gower, Kidwelly, Ewyas, and Grosmont. But next the king reflected that perhaps the Earl of Hereford might try to withdraw, or that there might be collusion[1]; in fact, it looks as if he had received some hint that there was a muttering among the marchers. To drop the suit would be to the prejudice of the honour of the crown. Therefore, somewhat later, for the new orders gave but a short space for obedience, he gave very precise and definite orders to the judges to collect the magnates and others of the marches, excusing not one of them for non-attendance ; the verdict was to be obtained from them on their oath on the book, for the case touched the honour and dignity of the crown. No stronger means could have been adopted to impress solemnly on the whole body that the king was in earnest to carry through the case. He was aiming to secure, out of their own mouths, a definite condemnation of their own custom of private war. Evidently each lord marcher was summoned by a special writ, together with their stewards and some of their tenants. The trial would then be impressive in the extreme.

[1] ' Praeterea Dominus Rex animadvertens postea quod transgressiones et iniurie predicte, si sunt facte post inhibitionem factam predicto comiti Glouernie ne prefato comiti Herford aut hominibus suis molestiam iniuriam aut gravamen inferret, per non prosecutionem utriusque eorundem comitum vel per collusionem intra eos factam forsitan remanere possent impunite, idem Dominus Rex per alias literas suas patentes mandavit prefato episcopo et sociis suis quod, licet contigerit prefatos comites vel eorum alterum a prosecutione vel defensione negotii predicti se subtertrahere velle, tum quod si quid inde factum esset vel attemptatum in preiudicium seu contemptum vel etiam lesionem corone sue et dignitatis regie vel contra pacem et post inhibitionem suam predicto comiti Glouernie post tempus supra dictum, pro statu et iure regis per predictum episcopum et socios suos inde rei veritas inquireretur. Et ideo eis mandavit quod per sacramentum tam magnatum quam aliorum proborum et legalium hominum de partibus Wallie et comitatibus Glouc et Herf per quos rei veritas melius sciri posset cuiuscunque conditionis fuerint, ita quod nulli parceretur in hac parte, eo quod res ista Dominum Regem et coronam et dignitatem suam tangit, super premissis inquirerent veritatem.'

On the appointed day, Hereford the plaintiff appeared, but neither Gloucester nor his bailiffs. John de Hastings, Roger de Mortimer, John FitzReginald, Theobald de Verdun, John Tregoz, and Geoffrey de Camville answered to their writs of summons, together with Robert de Tibotot, the royal stewards, who were Tibotot's subordinates, Lord Edmund's stewards from Monmouth and the three castles, and the Sheriffs of Herefordshire and Gloucestershire. An adjournment was ordered to Llanthew (Landou) near Brecon two days later. Mr. Clark reasonably infers that the judges wished to give Gloucester every opportunity, and they probably had an inkling that he would be contumacious. Moreover, the notice given to the lords marchers had been short.

At Llanthew all the same men were present, and Edmund de Mortimer had profited by the two days' grace, and was able to appear in person, but Gloucester was still absent. First the judges wished, in accordance with the king's orders, to empanel a jury of the lords marchers themselves. The book was tendered to John de Hastings and the rest[1]. Hastings, though young, was put in the first place as being the most considerable lord next to the two earls; he was particularly attached to Gloucester. Unanimously they refused to swear. Such a course, they said, was absolutely unprecedented. The judges did their duty, pointing out that

[1] 'Dictum est ex parte Domini Regis Ioanni de Hastings et omnibus aliis magnatibus prenotatis quod pro statu et iure Regis et pro conservatione dignitatis corone et pacis sue apponant manum ad librum ad faciendum id quod eis ex parte Domini Regis iniungeretur; qui omnes unanimiter respondent quod inauditum est quod ipsi vel eorum antecessores hactenus in huiusmodi casu ad prestandum sacramentum aliquod coacti fuerunt. Dicunt et quod nunquam consimile mandatum Regis invenit in partibus istis nisi tantum quod res tangentes marchiam istam deducte fuissent secundum usus et consuetudines partium istarum. Et licet prefatis Ioanni et aliis magnatibus expositum fuisset quod nullus in hac parte potest habere marchiam Domino Regi, qui pro communi utilitate per prerogativam suam in multis casibus est supra leges et consuetudines in regno suo usitatas, ac pluries eisdem magnatibus ex parte Regis coniunctim et separatim libroque eis porrecto iniunctum est quod faciant sacramentum, responderunt demum omnes singillatim quod nichil inde facerent sine consideratione parium suorum.'

even a lord marcher held his march under the crown; that is to say, that the king's commands swept away their special privileges, for he was above both law and custom. The doctrine of the royal prerogative could not have been put more clearly. Several attempts were made to break down their obstinacy by appeal to them as a body and to each individually. Each one refused to swear without consultation with his peers. None appears to have been the prime ring-leader, though Hastings was addressed first.

The doctrine of the royal prerogative having thus been strained by the judges without effect, they next examined into the reasons why some marchers or their servants were absent. Roger Pichard presented himself, but the writ had been made out in a wrong name, and he could not be admitted—a curious instance of mediaeval red tape. Geoffrey de Geneville proved that he was not a lord marcher, for he had enfeoffed his son Peter of all his lands in Wales; this was allowed as a bona fide transaction, and indeed Geoffrey was a loyal man, as he showed afterwards in 1297. It was proved and admitted that Hastings' steward of Abergavenny had received no writ, and that the lands of Edmund de Mortimer were too far distant for him to have had time to produce any of his tenants. Roger de Mortimer [1], the court admitted, held his lands under Hereford, and could not act. John Tregoz and Theobald de Verdun produced neither steward nor tenants, the latter rather defiantly adding that his tenants could not be bound to serve on a jury; *calumpniavit libertatem suam quo ad hoc quod dicit quod homines de terra sua non debent hic iurare.* The king remembered Verdun's impertinence on a later occasion. William de Braose had not yet received his lands from the royal officials since his father's death. Kidwelly was held in wardship for the heiress of Patrick de Chaworth by Edmund of Lancaster, whose steward was therefore responsible; the fact was known to the judges, and it was not necessary to insert it in the *précis.* The Earl of Norfolk and John Giffard are not mentioned at all, and the reason is clear; for Norfolk

[1] Chirk was far off in the north, and presumably Roger was summoned as holding some small piece of land, not as lord of Chirk.

also had a lawsuit with Gloucester on a question of march rights, and Giffard had recently been embroiled with Hereford. This completes the list of the marchers. Finally, a jury of twenty-four was got together from the tenants of the obedient lords and from other men produced by Tibotot and the royal stewards, by Edmund's stewards, or by the Sheriffs of Gloucestershire and Herefordshire.

The case proceeded. The Sheriff of Berkshire and Robert de Tibotot proved that they had ordered the defendant earl and his bailiffs to appear, and contempt of court was manifest. The facts were investigated, and found to be as stated above ; Gloucester was at least cognizant of the three raids by receiving after the event the due share of the spoil *prout decet dominum tempore guerre habere secundum usum et consuetudinem marchie* ; his bailiffs were absolutely guilty. As regards the cases of brigandage, Gloucester was acquitted ; the bailiffs were pronounced guilty of cognizance after the event, except as regards the robbery from the church. It was found that some of Hereford's men had been killed, number unknown ; 1,070 head of cattle had been raised, fifty horses and bulls, and countless numbers of sheep and pigs. Mr. Clark notes that the land must have been as heavily stocked then as now, which probably means that the earl wished to prove effectual occupation by putting as many animals as possible to pasture. Damages were assessed at £100. The judges reported to the king, after having formally and distinctly in the king's name forbidden a renewal of private war.

The king was in court at Amesbury in Wiltshire early in September. But in spite of the reiterated prohibition by the judges, more disturbances had taken place on the debatable ground. The king would also have to consider Gloucester's absence in contempt. So he gave out that he and the council of archbishops, bishops, earls, barons, and others would take the case at Abergavenny at Michaelmas. The sheriffs and stewards were to produce a new jury as before. The scene, when the day came, must have been more impressive than ever ; one of our strongest and most law-loving kings was in full court, sitting in judgement on the proudest of the old

Norman aristocracy, on the deep and difficult question of the royal prerogative to override custom. Hereford appeared, and was not examined on the old case, which had gone in his favour. But had he offended in the interval since the verdict of Llanthew? The new facts were these. Some of Gloucester's men were pasturing plough-oxen on the land which Hereford claimed, *in quadam placea de qua contencio est*; thereupon John Perpoint, Constable of Brecon, with a large body of followers came and drove them off, chased them over the border into Glamorgan, killed some men, and carried the animals with them into Brecknock *ipso comite de Herford nullo sciente*. When he heard of it, he ordered restitution, provided that security was given that the debatable land should be recognized as his, *capta securitate de hoc quod in terra sua depasti fuerunt*; yet the animals were still kept in Brecknock, and some were even slaughtered. A second time there was a similar scene. One thing was clear; Gloucester was absolutely guiltless of complicity, and his men had acted like robbers over whom he had no control. Likewise, Hereford was so far guiltless; he had arrested his own men whom he had understood to be responsible, and kept them still under arrest; he had made open proclamation, in churches and public places, that the royal prohibition of private war was to be obeyed. Neither earl was responsible for brigandage, even if the knaves lived on his land, for he was not aware of their names; *latrones sunt et vagabundi nec aliquid habentes nisi de latrocinio suo, et quidam eorum in terris eorundem comitum sunt residentes et domos habentes, sed de nominibus eorum penitus ignorant*. So far, indeed, Hereford was blameless, but Perpoint was his recognized servant and constable; further than that, he had himself destroyed his own case, a very strong one, by retaining the cattle until security should be given that the debatable land was really his. It was a fatal piece of stupidity, but stupidity does not excuse contempt of court. The question simply amounted to this: did Hereford think that the crown was so weak that he must take the law into his own hands to protect himself? A lord marcher had no right to be so stupid, for he was simply prejudging that the land was his, *maxime cum placitum adhuc pendens est de ipsa terra que est origo et occasio totius mali.* That was contempt.

Whether Edward had got something in the background against Hereford, whether he had suspected him of collusion by wanting to withdraw his original plea, whether he was glad to catch him at last guilty of contempt, though far less guilty throughout than Gloucester, cannot be known. It is dangerous to read between the lines of a document 6co years old. Hereford, even if out of mere stupidity, had set march custom against the crown's prerogative ; had in a fit of momentary impatience simply given himself away. The king, with the whole council of prelates and barons, pronounced that he had acted contumaciously [1], in defiance of the prohibition claiming to do in the march what he would not have dared to do in the kingdom of England, was liable to punishment, was to be committed to prison, and was to have his lands confiscated into the king's hands. Perpoint and four other servants, most of them Welshmen, were also committed to prison.

The court proceeded to examine Gloucester, who had not dared to disobey the call to appear before the king in person. Perhaps he was cowed by the king's clear determination to get to the bottom of the case, perhaps he hoped to find the prelates and barons of the council sympathetic. In any case he dropped his defiance and made trivial excuses. Two questions were put to him : could he explain his absence from the first trial ? and could he prove himself not responsible for the three raids of 1290 ? First, he put in a plea on a point of law ; he had been absent because the writ summoning him had been irregular. The court brushed aside the argument.

---

[1] 'Et quia hec omnia audacius et presumptuosius per ipsum comitem et homines de Breghennok fiebant, credentes quod per libertatem suam marchie possent evadere e pena et piaculo que merito incurrisse debuissent si extra marchiam alibi in regno talem excessum perpetrassent, et sic puniendus est dux libertatis, tam in re illa que sibi et suis temeram prebuit audaciam delinquendi, quam in persona ipsa, propter contemptum et inobedientiam Domino Regi factam contra inhibitionem predictam, constitutum est quod idem comes committatur gaole et libertas sua de Breghennok cum pertinentibus capiatur in manum Regis.'

Then he protested that he knew that the jury would be prejudiced against him, for the men had been summoned from lands which he and his father Richard had conquered for the king and the king's father ; therefore he would not have obtained justice from his enemies, his conquered enemies. The court held that as he had been absent it was too late to cast reflections on the jury ; *quod non possit vel debeat pars absens admitti ad calumpniandum personas aliquas iuratorum.* This was a sound decision, for he should have appeared and then challenged. Secondly, he argued about the raids. The February raid had taken place immediately after the original royal proclamation, before he had had time to order obedience ; that of June, while his lands were still in the king's hands, he and Joan not having yet been enfeoffed under the new settlement. The court held that he had had ample time to forbid his men in each case ; and as for the second in particular, there had been nine clear days between the restitution of the lands on the new enfeoffment and the raid. Lastly, he changed his ground, and argued that the new enfeoffment itself changed his status ; coming between the proclamation and the November raid it absolved him from obedience, for he was on a new footing as regarded the crown, and there had been no new proclamation.

*Dicit quod bene recolit Dominus Rex qualiter ipse ante diem illum* (November) *feoffaverat eundem comitem et Iohannam uxorem eius de tota terra de Morganon cum pertinentibus, per quod quidem feoffamentum idem comes una cum eadem Iohanna uxore eius sumpsit statum novum, per quod intendit et credit quod ab inhibitione prius sibi super premissis facta pure et omnino per admissionem illius novi status exstitit absolutus.*

The court refused to admit the argument of a 'clean slate.' The proclamation had been originally addressed to the earl personally, regardless of the conditions of his tenure ; *inhibitio prius sibi facta in pleno parliamento tenet et ligat semper comitem . . . facta enim fuit persone ipsius comitis et non terre.* The king claims by his prerogative that he has to be obeyed whatever may be the landed status of the baron. The feeble defence may be explained by the fact that Gloucester was already cowed, as suggested above, or it may be that he had deliberately planned the raids in such a way as to be able to shuffle out of his responsibility, a sort of mixture of defiance and chicanery.

Then accepting the finding of the jury of Llanthew as to the facts, the court pronounced that Gloucester was responsible for all three raids; his men had been led by his responsible bailiffs under his banner, and he had received his customary share of the spoil. In law he was guilty of complicity after the event. Morally he was undoubtedly guilty of cognizance before the event, for the circumstances were suspicious, and his servants must have known his will; but law cannot proceed on moral certainty, and it was quite sufficient for the king's purpose to catch him on the proved complicity afterwards. The sentence was worded exactly as in Hereford's case: he had acted audaciously and presumptuously, expecting to be acquitted by the custom of the march, and doing what he would not have dared to do elsewhere in the kingdom; therefore he was to be committed to prison, and all his lands would be confiscated. His four bailiffs were also imprisoned.

Promptly certain nobles came forward to offer themselves as bail: Edmund, William de Valence, the Earl of Lincoln, and John de Hastings for Gloucester; Reginald de Grey, Robert de Tibotot, Robert Fitzwalter, and Walter de Beauchamp for Hereford. Seven were stanch loyalists, and there is no significance in their attitude. They simply acted out of personal friendship. Yet in the one case of Hastings it is remarkable to find so young a man giving security for an older and war-tried earl; personal affection may have been the motive, or as a marcher he may represent sympathy with a victim of a king who broke march custom. William de Valence, it is to be noticed, had been one of the original judges. The king consented to release the earls on the guarantee that the sureties would produce their persons the next January at Westminster for final sentence. Each earl was allowed to be surety for his servants, who were also released.

Finally, after another short adjournment, the king pronounced in his council that all Gloucester's lands in Glamorgan were confiscate[1]; but as he had married the king's daughter, who had been enfeoffed conjointly with him, as he only held his lands for life and could not lose more than what was his own, therefore to prevent the loss of her inheritance to Joan and her issue, the whole council decided that the confiscation should take effect only for Gloucester's natural life, and that he should be again committed to prison at the king's will. The same formula was used for Hereford, except that a special note was added that his offence was not so deeply rooted in disobedience, and his wife is mentioned as a kinswoman of Queen Eleanor, who indeed had arranged and welcomed the marriage; therefore Brecknock was to be confiscate for his life only, and he was to be recommitted to prison at the king's pleasure[2]. Similarly the bailiffs were imprisoned. Probably the king gave the hint to the nobles, who had been sponsors previously, when he thought that they had been long enough

[1] 'Tam ipsi Domino Regi quam ceteris prelatis et magnatibus et singulis de concilio suo videtur quo ad comitem Gloucestrie quod libertas sua predicta, videlicet totum regale in terris suis predictis de Morgannon, cum pertinentibus pro se et heredibus suis forisfacta est ratione delicti predicti, set quod idem comes duxit in uxorem Ioham filiam Domini Regis nunc que quidem Iohana tantum habet in predicta libertate et in omnibus aliis libertatibus terris et tenementis ipsius comitis quantum et ipse comes habet, cum de libertatibus terris et tenementis sint coniunctim feoffati, per quod idem comes nichil habet seu habere potest in libertatibus terris aut tenementis predictis nisi ad terminum vite sue, nec idem comes Gloucestrie plus potest forisfacere quam suum est, nec esset iuri consonum quod ratione delicti ipsius comitis predicta Iohana uxor sua aut eorum exitus qui in nullo deliquerunt exhereditarentur, dictum est eidem comiti Glouc per consilium et iudicium Archiepiscoporum Episcoporum Comitum Baronum et totius concilii Domini Regis quod libertas sua predicta de Glammorgan, videlicet totum regale in eisdem terris, remaneat Domino Regi et heredibus suis ut forisfacta tota vita ipsius comitis, et idem comes retornetur prisone et inde redimatur ad voluntatem Domini Regis.'

[2] The special words in Hereford's sentence are: 'Sed quia videtur Domino Regi et eius concilio quod transgressio de qua idem comes Herefordie convictus est non est ita carcans nec tantam penam requirit quantam et facit transgressio predicta de qua predictus comes Gloucestrie convincitur, et quia idem comes Herfordie desponsaverat consanguineam Domine Regine consortis Domini Regis nunc, et quod quidem maritagium ipsa Regina fecit et acceptavit,' &c.

in prison to purge their contempt. Edmund, Valence, Lincoln, and Hastings again petitioned for Gloucester's release; Tibotot, Fitzwalter, and two new sponsors, Thomas de Berkeley and John Filleul, came forward for Hereford. The Clare was allowed to redeem his body for 10,000 marcs, Crepping for 500, Fleming for 30, Cappenor for 20, and Valers for 15. The Bohun had only to pay 1,000 marcs for his *transgressio non ita carcans*. Glamorgan was taken over in the king's name by Walter Hakelute[1], and Brecknock by Roger de Burghull, Sheriff of Herefordshire. But the king's honour had been vindicated, and restitution was made to both earls in the July following, to date from the 13th of that month[2].

So ended the drama of the humbling of the earls. Gloucester lived for three years and a half longer, doubtless a sadder and a wiser man, and he left by Joan a son and three daughters ; the latter divided his enormous property when the son fell childless at Bannockburn, so that no future Clare had a chance to rival his sovereign. Hereford lived with a rankling sense of injury to be the partner of the Bigod in a new and, as far as he was concerned, successful defiance. But the most interesting point remains unsolved, as Mr. Clark points out. We are simply kept in the dark as to the disposal of Morlais castle, for neither the *Inquisitio post mortem* of Gloucester's land nor that of Hereford's contains any mention of it, and we are driven to suppose that the king made some special and permanent confiscation of the debatable castle and land. Early in the sixteenth century they were held for the king.

The great trial is of such absorbing interest that we are tempted to overlook other cases of breach of the king's commands. Yet these other cases have their importance. John Giffard was an offender, and once had out his men under his banner near Gloucester ; we do not know the reason nor the result. A barren entry, attached to the very much condensed abstract of the Gloucester-Hereford case, tells us *item placitum contra Iohannem Giffard et homines suos pro vexillis displicatis apud Gloucestriam*[3]. He certainly lived to do

---

[1] *Patent Roll*, Feb. 19, 1292.    [2] Ibid. May 7 and July 15.
[3] *Abbreviatio Placitorum*, p. 227.

the king more service in war, service of a particularly useful nature.

The Earl of Norfolk also had his grievance against Gloucester, which explains why he had not been summoned to Llanthew and does not appear once in the great trial[1]. Some of Gloucester's tenants of Usk did suit to Norfolk; in consequence the Clare retainers invaded the lands of Netherwent and Strigul *vi et armis*, and carried off goods and chattels. The case was brought to law, but with the king's express sanction was allowed to be dropped. *Et sedati sunt.*

Hereford had a dispute with Roger de Mortimer, his tenant, concerning some lands in Brecknock[2]. It came twice before Roger de Burghull, the same official who had held Brecknock during the few months of confiscation.

Theobald de Verdun was prosecuted by the Prior of Llanthony, on account of various wrongs inflicted after the royal proclamation of January, 1290. The case would seem to have been pending when Theobald appeared with other lords marchers at Llanthew[3], and so the point arises whether he was justified when, on that occasion, he refused to produce his steward and tenants to serve on the jury. More likely he was acting contumaciously, as I suggested before, hoping that there would be a combination of lords marchers which would render the king impotent to stop all private war. The severity shown by the king leads us to suppose that he was defiant in his lawlessness. The case came on at Michaelmas in 1291; he was condemned to imprisonment, and to the confiscation during lifetime of all his lands of Ewyas Lacy, and the sentence was confirmed about the same time that Hereford and Gloucester were finally condemned[4]. He redeemed his body for £500. The confiscation took effect on February 19, 1292, and restitution was made on June 18[5]. At precisely the same time he is found to hold a letter of protection as going to Gascony, which suggests that he was purging his contempt by

[1] *Abbreviatio Placitorum*, p. 286.
[2] *Patent Roll*, Feb. 1292, and Dec. 1293.
[3] See above, p. 230.    [4] *Abbreviatio Placitorum*, p. 227.
[5] *Patent Roll.*

absence abroad. In 1297 the king was again severe on him[1];
he had pleaded that he was infirm and therefore unable to
follow the king to the war in Flanders, and his son was
recently dead ; he was told that his second son was of an age
to join the army, and that son must serve. It is a unique
instance of compulsion put upon a tenant-in-chief to serve
abroad or to send a deputy. Royal pay indeed was promised,
but there must be some special reason, such as a remembrance
of Theobald's previous contempt, which explains the special
severity.

It seems but a natural corollary to Edward's resolute policy
of crushing march privileges that he should immediately
attempt to tax the marchers. In the autumn of 1292 he
extracted promises from several of them that they would grant
a fifteenth[2]. Valence, Gloucester, Norfolk, Hastings, and
Giffard, amongst others, promised, and in the north Roger de
Monthaut[3]. It was a distinct innovation, and although he
made a formal promise that payment would not be reckoned
as a precedent, it was a clear step towards making the lords
understand that march land was but as other land. It can
hardly be doubted that Edward was irritating his barons,
however much he might feel himself justified in crushing what
appeared to conflict with the dignity of the crown. He was
creating a spirit of resentment which would explode to his
great injury in the matter of the *Confirmatio Cartarum.*
Then in the days of Edward II, when the lords marchers
found him to be so much weaker than his father, they
naturally resumed their march privileges, and these flourished
down to the Tudor period.

---

[1] *Parl. Writs*, vol. i. p. 295.    [2] *Patent Roll*, Oct. and Nov., *passim.*
[3] Nov. 27, 1293.

# CHAPTER VII

## THE LAST RISING; MADOC, MAELGWN, AND MORGAN; 1294 AND 1295

IN 1294 there were no signs of disturbance in Wales, and Edward had his attention fixed on France. There had been the war in the Channel between the English and Norman sailors, and the King of France had intrigued in Gascony, inveigling Edmund into surrendering the strong places. Parliament was summoned, and writs were issued in June, feudal indeed in form, but addressed only to the fighting barons and bannerets, calling them to Portsmouth by the 1st of September[1]. Two points of great interest are seen. The first is the summons of Scottish nobles, on whom Edward had a claim since the accession of Balliol and his act of homage. Secondly, foot were difficult to raise in England, for the English peasant was not warlike by nature, and unless he lived in the counties near Wales had no experience; he had no reputation whatever in the eyes of Europe, nor that spirit and love of adventure which fifty and sixty years later sent his grandsons to Crecy and Poitiers. Therefore Edward is said to have issued proclamation for the first time in his reign to criminals and outlaws, offering them pardon and calling on them to take the royal wages[2]. For the same reason also he called for Welsh contingents. Grey was to raise men from Flintshire and the Four Cantreds, Staundon from the three new counties of North Wales, and the order in either case was dated August 30[3]. Tibotot's two lieutenants, Walter de Pederton and Geoffrey Clement, were to

---

[1] *Parl. Writs*, vol. i. p. 259.　　[2] *Flores Historiarum*, vol. iii. p. 89.
[3] *Parl. Writs*, vol. i. p. 203.

raise men in the south and the marches. It was obviously easier for the king to coerce the newly annexed Welsh than his English subjects, while the issue of these writs for infantry, being so much later than those sent to the leaders of cavalry, suggests that the Welsh levy was determined on simply because no other foot could be procured.

The command of the expedition to Gascony was given to John of Brittany, Earl of Richmond, and to assist his inexperience the king joined with him John de St. John and Robert de Tibotot, *ei consiliarios . . . milites prudentes et in bellicis rebus expertos*[1]. St. John already held the post of Seneschal of Gascony in succession to John de Havering. The choice of Tibotot was distinctly wise, for he had shown great powers of administration in South Wales, and indeed represented in his person the English ascendency. He may have been appointed on purpose to lead the Welsh contingents in France; and, in any case, his removal did not prejudice his position as justiciar and receiver of the revenue, for on June 10 preceding he had had his peculiar powers reconfirmed to him, and in his absence Clement and Pederton were merely his deputies responsible to him[2].

The dates show the connexion between the expedition to Gascony and the new Welsh rising. The first detachment of English, having been summoned for September 1, are said to have set sail at Michaelmas[3], without taking any Welsh on board. The levies raised by Grey and Staundon had been ordered to be at Shrewsbury on September 30[4], which is the exact day of the Welsh rising as seen from various rolls, and immediately, on October 1, a report was circulated that Geoffrey Clement and Walter de Pederton had both been murdered by 'certain malefactors and disturbers of our peace.' William de Camville was at once appointed as deputy Justiciar of South Wales, Tibotot having already sailèd beyond recall; his father, Geoffrey de Camville, was to assist him[5]. Four days later one body of Welsh, which Pederton had raised, having by that date reached Winchester

---

[1] Trivet, p. 331.      [2] *Welsh Roll*, June 10 and Oct. 1, 1294.
[3] Trivet, p. 332.   [4] *Welsh Roll*.   [5] *Patent Roll*, Oct. 5, 1294.

on the way to Portsmouth, was turned back.  The king had, therefore, knowledge of their disaffection, but probably thought it a trifling matter.  The second English detachment, under Edmund of Lancaster and the Earl of Lincoln, was still under orders to proceed to Gascony; the Earls of Hereford and Arundel, Robert Fitzwalter, Fulk FitzWaryn, John Wake, and others had letters of protection as forming part of the expedition; on the 10th and 12th Wake received certain licences from the king in view of his intended absence in Gascony.  On the 14th judges were appointed to try a case in South Wales.  Then on the 15th it was seen that the disturbance was not merely the work of a few malefactors, but that a serious rising was to be faced.  Writs were flying all over England to call the barons to Worcester to a military council in view of a Welsh war, and Edward, able, as he always showed himself, to keep his eyes on one thing at a time, countermanded this second division for Gascony.

Thus the cause of the rising is not far to seek.  Restlessness and impatience of restraint would be cause enough, but the plain fact is the compulsory enlistment for service over the sea.  Arms were put into the hands of the Welsh by the English themselves.  Moreover, Tibotot had been withdrawn, Robert Fitzwalter had left Bere castle, and such prominent marchers as the Earls of Hereford and Arundel were going to the foreign war.  John Giffard had weakened himself at Builth by sending some of his men[1].  The least spark was necessary to set Wales aflame.  The murder of Clement may have been unpremeditated—it is to be noticed that the rumour of Pederton's murder was false[2]—and an act of this kind would be quite enough to excite to further effort men armed and coerced for an unpopular war.  But the general impression we receive from the documents is that the rising all over Wales was premeditated.  The explosion at Cardigan, at Builth, and at Bere, each of which castles was blockaded in the absence of its constable, at Denbigh where the Earl of Lincoln's men rose, and at Carnarvon where Roger de Pulesdon was killed and the castle destroyed, was simultaneous, although the English

---

[1] *Parl. Writs*, vol. i. p. 266.        [2] Ibid. *passim.*

received news of each outbreak at different dates. In each direction the war was officially dated as from September 30.

Other grievances the Welsh may have had. When quiet had been restored next year[1], John de Havering and William Sikun were commissioned to investigate the alleged wrongs which had been endured in North Wales at the hands of English officials since the annexation. It was quite in accordance with Edward's principles first to crush, then to investigate, for his wish to deal fairly by the conquered is undoubted. The officials on the spot were more oppressive than the king, and it was they who suffered, Clement and Pulesdon now, just as Clifford in 1282. But there was no list of grievances presented in 1295, such as were submitted to the archbishop in 1282. The one main exciting cause was the levy for foreign service.

Contemporaries, and also a future generation, were much struck by Edward's inability to prosecute war energetically in France. Langtoft, the rhyming chronicler, uses pretty strong language against the Scots and Welsh who prevented him from making a display outside this island:

> Escoce soit maudite de la mere De
> Et parfound ad deable Gales enfoundre;
> En l'un ni l'autre fu unkes verite.

A chronicler of Edward III repeats a prophecy, one of those prophecies after the event which sum up public opinion[2]. Edward the grandfather is represented as saying that he could not give the time to save Gascony, but that a day would come when a king would reign, munificent, merciful, affable, brave, in fact possessed of all the virtues, who would humble France. Meanwhile, he had to labour under a charge of something like cowardice. But he was right to put his whole mind to the one task lying before him. France and Gascony might wait, for the Welsh insurgents had to be suppressed at all costs, then Balliol, then Wallace. Unionism was a greater task than foreign conquest, yet not so showy.

The general impression which we gather of this rising is that it was totally unexpected, and therefore at first equally

---

[1] *Patent Roll*, Sept. 1, 1295.
[2] Bridlington chronicle in *Gesta Edwardi Secundi*, vol. ii. p. 94 (R. S.).

successful. Experienced men, such as Geoffrey Clement and Roger de Pulesdon, were surprised and slain. Such important central fortresses as Builth and Bere were almost without means of resistance, and the borders were more or less drained of men who were going to Gascony. But the worst was probably soon known. After the first dashing onslaughts the Welsh were not able to effect surprises, and if many of the lords of the march were at or on their way to Portsmouth, at least they could be soon recalled. Edward's promptness and experience were not at fault, and in fact the speed with which he was concentrating an army, issuing letters of protection to scores of lords and knights, and utilizing all the resources of England, is as noticeable as the lightning-like fury of the Welsh outburst. Equally striking is the wide extent of the rising ; but in this connexion Edward's experience taught him where and how to concentrate his forces to the best advantage, and he at once fixed on Chester and Cardiff and Brecon as the bases of the English armies.

As early as October 9 Reginald de Grey had fifty horse and 5,000 foot under arms. He probably controlled Flintshire, and saved Flint and Rhuddlan from the fate of Carnarvon, throwing troops into each castle so that the garrison of the one was raised to twenty-four horse, twenty-four crossbows, and 120 archers, and of the other to four horse, twelve crossbows, and twenty-four archers ; also a few workmen under Richard, the engineer, strengthened the walls and repaired the artillery[1]. On October 15 the king ordered his barons to send their men to one of the three bases, and themselves to appear at a council at Worcester next month; he did not call out the feudal array, but affectionately requested, and at the same time named commissioners to raise foot, not only in the usual counties but also in Cumberland, Westmorland, and Yorkshire, a sure sign that he was hard pressed to find men, and considered the war to be serious[2]. On October 18 he definitely knew that Bere was in danger. He now sent up the Earl of Surrey to Chester,

---

[1] *Exch. Memoranda*, 27 & 28 Edw. I, m. 5.
[2] Dates in *Welsh Roll*, 22 & 23 Edw. I.

ahead of the other countermanded barons from Portsmouth, and issued letters of protection to very many of the rest. On October 20 came an order for the transference to Wales of the supplies collected at Portsmouth[1]. On October 25 John de Havering was ordered to see to the revictualling of the northern castles by sea, a sign that the enemy already surrounded them by land, and the Constable of Bristol was to supply him with the means. The Earl of Lincoln, one of the commanders destined for Gascony, was up at Denbigh by November 11, probably starting so rapidly that none of his followers were entered on the roll as having letters of protection. But Edmund was more leisurely, being engaged in superintending the transference from Portsmouth, and seems to have first proceeded to Westminster to join his brother, in place of going straight to Wales. During October and a fortnight of November the king was in London. A Parliament met at Westminster on November 12[2], composed only of the magnates and four knights from each shire. They voted a tax of a tenth on movables. The towns, not being represented in Parliament, made separate bargains with the crown. That very day the royal officials were sent out to collect the money 'with the least possible loss and burden to the people of the realm[3].' Also by the advice of Parliament Edward appointed commissioners to 'take bond of all persons charged with offences,' if they would volunteer to serve at the royal wages against Wales, and subsequently in Gascony. Then he set out for Worcester to meet his council of war, and lay there from November 21 to 25.

The Welsh roll, 23 Edward I, contains nothing but long lists of names of those to whom letters of protection were issued for the war. It will be remembered that some few protections are entered on the patent roll of 1277, and a good many on that of 1287; also during the series of wars in Scotland a great many are entered on the special Scotch rolls. Of course not every soldier had a protection, and, on the other hand, the clerk who drew up the roll of the year did not

---

[1] *Exch. Acc.* $\frac{5}{8}$.  [2] Stubbs, vol. ii. p. 127.
[3] *Patent Roll*, Nov. 12, 1294.

necessarily enter the names of all those who actually had them. For instance, we now find only nine troopers of the household mentioned. When we can make a comparison with the extant cavalry pay-roll of 1295, or with the inventories of horses in 1298, it is seen that usually about one-third, occasionally a much smaller proportion, occasionally as many as two-thirds or three-quarters of the men-at-arms of some retinue, had protections. But in the particular instance of the campaign of 1294 I believe that some retinues are entered in full, those of the Earls of Lancaster and Warwick in particular, for the figures correspond very well in their cases to the undoubted numbers of their retinues in other wars. Robert de Tateshale had protections for his son and seventeen followers, which was rather more than his normal strength in 1282. But the Earl of Lincoln, who had already pushed up to the scene of war, had hardly any. I suggest that the clerk of the roll entered at various dates the names of all the followers who then and there were in their leader's retinue with the king, and the reason why the list is so full, being much more exhaustive than those of the rolls of most wars, is that the retinues were already in arms for Gascony. Also an examination of the dates is helpful. Surrey had nineteen protections on October 15, thence to Christmas seven more: now we know that he was sent forward to Chester ahead of the king, and it would work out very well that he started with, let us say, twenty to thirty lances of his own retinue, and was reinforced later by ten or more. John de Berwick, commissioner of array for the infantry of Shropshire, and his followers had protections dated Worcester, November 24, the very date and place where the foot would be expected to join the king. Next year John de Merk had his protection on April 23, precisely the day when a body of 1,000 foot of Chester first appear in the solitary infantry roll which we possess; a casual entry elsewhere proves that he was the millenar or colonel of the Chester men, and the coincidence strikingly suggests that the millenars are entered just when they brought their foot up to headquarters. Therefore we are justified in using the roll of protections to enable us to mark the times and places, and this is fortunate, as we have extant only one pay-sheet of infantry next year, and one of a single squadron of horse.

A general conclusion is that Edward, between the middle of October and Christmas, raised 900 lances, partly from barons or bannerets on the Welsh borders, partly from men mustered for the war in London, whence he himself marched to the rendezvous at Worcester, but mostly from the countermanded army at Portsmouth. This figure makes liberal allowance for the cavalry who had not received letters of protection. Garrisons and the retinues of the marchers may perhaps raise the total to 1,000. The lances may be thus apportioned to the various parts of Wales, the arrayers of infantry and their mounted staffs of six or eight troopers each not counted. It will be seen that new men have appeared since the last war, Hugh le Despenser being especially noticeable.

|  | With protections. | Possible total. |
|---|---|---|
| *In South Wales*:— | | |
| Under William de Valence, including Alan Plukenet, Ely Daubeny, Nich. de Carew, John de Columbers, John de Cogan, John de Rivers . | 28 | 50 |
| Under Earl of Norfolk, including Hugh Pointz, Thomas and Maurice de Berkeley . . . | 28 | 50 |
| Under Roger de Molis, William de Braose, Geoffrey and William de Camville, and other marchers . . . . . . . . | – | 50 |
| | | 150 |
| *In Brecknock, Builth, Montgomery, &c.* :— | | |
| The Earl of Hereford . . . . . . | 12 | 40 |
| The Earl of Arundel (including Fitzwalter) . . | 8 | 40 |
| Roger l'Estrange and Edmund de Mortimer . . | 5 | 40 [1] |
| John Giffard . . . . . . . . | 3 | 30 [2] |
| | | 150 |
| *In Glamorgan*:— | | |
| The Earl of Gloucester . . . . . . | 5 | (?) |
| *In advance of the king in North Wales* :— | | |
| The Earl of Lincoln . . . . . . | 1 | 30 [1] |
| The Earl of Surrey (afterwards reinforced) . . | 26 | 50 [1] |
| Reginald de Grey . . . . . . . | 9 | 50 [2] |
| | | 130 |

[1] Average numbers in other wars ; see pp. 60 and onwards.
[2] Numbers actually in pay ; see pp. 244, 252.

| With the king:— | With pro-tections. | Possible total. |
|---|---|---|
| Edmund of Lancaster . . . . . . | 50 | 50 |
| The Earl of Warwick . . . . . . | 25 | 25 |
| Robert de Tateshale . . . . . . | 19 | 20 |
| Hugh le Despenser . . . . . . | 15 | 15 |
| Peter de Mauley . . . . . . | 15 | 15 |
| John Wake . . . . . . . . | 15 | 15 |
| Walter de Beauchamp, *senesch. hospicii* . . . | 12 | 25 [1] |
| William de Mortimer . . . . . . | 10 | 10 |
| John de l'Isle . . . . . . . | 10 | 10 |
| The Earl of Cornwall . . . . . . | 2 | 45 [1] |
| Walter de Huntercumbe . . . . . . | 8 | 15 [1] |
| Smaller details *cum rege* . . . . . . | 120 | 225 |
| | 301 | 470 |
| Total in whole of Wales (excluding Glamorgan) . | 421 | 900 |

Taking South Wales first, we see that the Earl of Norfolk
and William de Valence were in command, while Roger de
Molis was appointed marshal of the army; however, he was
certainly not in authority over them, as the number of letters
of protection issued to their followers shows. As in previous
years, the crown tenants of Devon and Somerset were ordered
to serve here[2]. I take it that the recorded retinues of each of
the two earls, twenty-eight lances strong, were not commen-
surate with the ordinary feudal quotas of each, but, including
as they do Pointz and the Berkeleys and others, represent
a paid squadron of some hundred lances. The lords marchers
may have contributed another fifty. Thomas de Berkeley and
Walter de Pavely, having protections dated October 18 under
Norfolk, were in November commissioned to raise foot in
Wiltshire and Somerset[3]; similarly, Alan Plukenet, who was
with Valence on October 14, the earliest date of a protection
for the Welsh war, was told off to raise foot in Gloucestershire.
We may infer a total army of 150 lances and 2,000 foot.
Some of the latter would be quite inexperienced, for Somerset
and Wiltshire had never previously sent infantry to Wales.

[1] Average numbers in other wars ; see pp. 60 and onwards.
[2] *Parl. Writs*, Oct. 15, 1294, vol. i. p. 265.
[3] *Welsh Roll*, 22 Edw. I, Nov. 22.

Probably the march was disturbed as much as the rest of Wales, for we have always seen that otherwise the infantry of Welsh friendlies was quite sufficient in 1277, in 1282, and, after the first outbreak, in 1287. Bringing up English foot to South Wales argues a serious rising. But we have absolutely no details. The head of the insurgents was ' a young man of the name of Maelgwn, under whom the Welsh of the west did much harm in the neighbourhood of Pembroke and Cardigan[1].' The tenants of John de Hastings are also known to have been in revolt[2], but there is nothing to show whether the men of Cilgeran near Cardigan or those of Gwent are meant. The widow of Geoffrey Clement fled to Llanbadarn, and it may be, therefore, that Cardigan was captured when her husband was killed. Llanbadarn was blockaded later, for Roger de Molis had time to throw himself into the place ; the Welsh with all their numbers were unable to reduce the castle, but it was completely cut off from relief by land, and only saved by sea from surrender by starvation. The war was probably spasmodic but serious, and next spring, but a very short time after the insurgents had been pressing hard against Llanbadarn, the rising collapsed suddenly before the king marching southwards.

Though the fighting is but scantily illustrated, some interesting points stand out. Among Norfolk's knights is to be noticed one John ap Adam, one of the very few Welsh adherents of England of whom we have knowledge from time to time. He may have come from the earl's own march of Strigul. He was enfeoffed by right of his wife, just about this very date, of land in Somerset and Gloucestershire, was returned in the sheriffs' lists as holding land over the limit of value which required the accepting of knighthood[3], and was frequently summoned to fight against the Scots. He took his position as an English lord, *dominus de Beverstone*, an entirely unique position, for even the Pole family were not so completely anglicized.

---

[1] Trivet, p. 333.

[2] *Patent Roll*, Aug. 24, 1295 (a writ of pardon).

[3] *Parl. Writs, passim* ; Ormerod, *Strigulensia*, p. 98.

When Geoffrey Clement's widow was under shelter at
Llanbadarn against the rebels, John FitzReginald of Talgarth
took advantage of her defenceless state and harried her lands;
at least, next year she accused him of so doing. The lady
appears to have been of a masterful nature, and was herself
accused of dispossessing and injuring the widow of Griffith
de la Pole. It matters little who was in the wrong in either
case. But the way in which the typical lord marcher maintained his aggressive nature, and sought to conquer land for
himself even in a period of rebellion, is highly characteristic.
Such quarrels were doubtless common enough in the lawless
days of the march, but Edward had set himself to stop them
by introducing legal process. Each of these two suits was
referred next year to regular judges [1].

But more important is the case of the Earl of Norfolk.
In October he had been ordered to South Wales, and most
of his followers had their letters of protection dated that
month. On November 21, at the military council at Worcester,
he must have protested against what was a breach of his
rights. Edward thereupon promised in the most formal
manner that, in sending the earl marshal away from his royal
person to a different part of Wales, and in appointing Roger
de Molis to be marshal of the army in that same part, he did
not intend to set up a precedent to the prejudice of the earl.
He pledged himself explicitly to observe the earl marshal's
hereditary privileges. Why Edward was so anxious to send
Norfolk to South Wales does not appear; perhaps he feared
a rising in Netherwent, as Glamorgan had also broken out
against the Earl of Gloucester. The episode is of intense importance as explaining the 'go or hang' scene of 1297. More
than this, I should argue that Norfolk had given previously
no sign of being an opponent of the crown; he was not now
offended with the king, but only wanted a guarantee that his
rights would not be violated in the future. But in 1297 he
formed with Hereford a regular party of opposition. I have
dwelt on the point, partly to show how the Welsh wars affected
the future, partly to draw attention to the king's formal

[1] *Patent Roll*, Aug. 18 and Sept. 1, 1295.

promise, which I have not seen quoted by any historian in connexion with the great crisis. By considering it, one can better appreciate Norfolk's bitter, and otherwise unintelligible, defiance. The following is the text, which has been calendared but not, as far as I know, reproduced in full before [1].

' Rex omnibus quos etc. salutem ;

'Cum mittamus hac vice dilectum et fidelem nostrum Rogerum le Bigod comitem Norff et marescallum Angliae una cum dilecto avunculo et fideli nostro Will. de Valenc. comite Pembroke ad partes SuthWall in expeditionem nostram contra Walenses inimicos et rebelles nostros, et constituerimus dilectum et fidelem nostrum Rogerum de Molis marescallum exercitus nostri in expeditione illa quamdiu nobis placuerit, nolumus quod missio eiusdem comitis marescalli a latere nostro ad partes praedictas seu huiusmodi constitutio marescalli eidem comiti marescallo vel heredibus suis cedat in preiudicium vel trahatur in consequentiam in futurum.'

A neighbouring theatre of revolt, as just mentioned, was Glamorgan, which had been quiet in all previous wars. The reason is probably to be found in the celebrated trial of 1291, for the tenants would be likely to understand that their earl was reduced from his high estate by imprisonment. We may guess that the outbreak occurred in the same month, seeing that Cardiff was one of the bases to which troops were ordered. The leader was a certain Morgan, or Rhys ap Morgan [2], whose ancestors had been dispossessed by the Clares. The interesting point is that he declared himself to be in arms only against the Earl of Gloucester, not against the king. He is said to have completely driven the earl out of his lands, and to have occupied the castle of Morlais itself [3], and one need not be surprised to hear that this debatable land attracted the insurgents. One account has it that only the more powerful vassals successfully resisted their lord [4], and the lesser men were conquered. But there is no authority for supposing that royal troops fought in Glamorgan. We shall see that when Edward came

---

[1] *Patent Roll*, 23 Edw. I, Nov. 24, 1294.
[2] Trivet, p. 333.  [3] *Annales Monastici*, ' Worcester,' vol. iv. p. 596.
[4] Ibid. ' Dunstable,' vol. iii. p. 387.

south in the next June he spent very little time there, and merely took over the lands into his own hands, so it would seem that the earl had not done much to reconquer them, but that the insurgents, true to their profession, promptly submitted to the king. It may be that the revolted tenants of Hastings were the men of Gwent close at hand. Langtoft's words are worth quoting[1]:

> Le counte de Gloucestre, ne say la chesoun,
> A perdu en Suth Wales more et mansioun ;
> Morgan li surquert, li fet destruccioun.
> Mes al rays Eduuard volt Morgan si ben noun.

In Brecknock we know no more than that the Earl of Hereford was engaged in pacifying the insurgents at his own expense, but details as usual are wanting[2]. The castle and town of Builth were blockaded by the Welsh insurgents, and a garrison of three heavy and three light horse, twenty crossbows, and forty archers were holding out for six weeks. John Giffard organized a relieving force of ten knights, twenty troopers, and forty light horse, who made five attempts to cut their way through to the castle, and were finally successful about November 12[3]. Next January both Hereford and Giffard joined the king at Conway.

As regards Merioneth and Powys, the siege or blockade of Bere castle was at first serious. Robert Fitzwalter, the custodian, was recalled from the expedition at Portsmouth, his absence having doubtless encouraged the rising, and the castle being insufficiently provided with means of defence. On October 27 Edward wrote somewhat anxiously to direct the Earl of Arundel, Fulk FitzWaryn, Roger l'Estrange, Bogo de Knoville, and Peter Corbet to undertake a relief expedition to save Bere, *cuius salvationem cupimus toto corde*[4]. The subsequent silence of documents and chroniclers alike argues that the relief was effected. Next year Fitzwalter and Corbet joined the retinue of the Earl of Warwick under the king, and when Edward came to those parts in July he merely

---

[1] Vol. ii. p. 218.          [2] *Welsh Roll*, Nov. 23, 1294.
[3] *Pipe Roll*, 24 Edw. I, m. 16.          [4] *Parl. Writs*, vol. i. p. 264.

marched quickly through Powys, without turning aside into Merioneth.

In the north was the greatest danger. The Earl of Surrey, we saw, was sent up to Chester on October 18, and his grandson, Henry Percy, serving as his banneret, and twenty followers had letters of protection dated October 15. The Welsh were under Madoc, son of the late Prince Llewelyn, and the first among them to rise were doubtless those who had been raised for service in Gascony. They ravaged the king's manor of Overton in Flintshire[1]. But their chief exploit after the first explosion was the seizure of Carnarvon, Roger de Pulesdon being off his guard and suffering for it with his life ; the date must be quite early, and there is nothing to show whether Madoc was concerned in the surprise or put himself at the head of the movement afterwards. Carnarvon was of course destroyed, lest the Welsh, being entrapped, should be besieged in their turn and thus caught. Simultaneously the Earl of Lincoln's tenants of Denbigh had risen. To stem the revolt the earl had apparently too slender a force. If he relied on his presence and authority to overawe his tenants he was soon undeceived, for they encountered him near Denbigh on November 11, and drove him out with serious loss[2]. Nothing more could be done until the king arrived. Meanwhile Rhuddlan and Conway were safe, even if they were cut off from England by land, and Reginald de Grey had raised a considerable force to protect Flintshire, though his 5,000 foot did not serve for very long. Criccieth and Harlech were threatened the next year, but we do not hear of their being attacked now. In all these cases we see the enormous importance of sea power. The castles held out as long as provisions could be brought up by ship, and John de Havering and his comrades, backed by the authorities of Bristol and Ireland, did their work in revictualling them.

The king concentrated at Worcester towards the end of November some 350 lances, new levies, or the men from Portsmouth. Henry de Greneford, a royal trooper and now chief leader of crossbows, had about sixty or seventy of that

---

[1] *Patent Roll*, Jan. 3, 1295 (a writ of pardon).      [2] Trivet, p. 333.

corps, if we judge by the evidence of the next year. John de Berwick brought in foot from Shropshire, and Osbert de Spaldington from Gloucestershire; and if, as is extremely likely, the eight men entered as having letters of protection with the former were his centenars, the Shropshire contingent was 800 strong. Then moving by way of Shrewsbury, and probably hearing that Bere was not in danger, so that he did not need to divert his march into Merioneth, Edward arrived at Chester before December 5. He picked up the contingents of the Earls of Surrey and Lincoln, and some reinforcements which increased other retinues, Edmund's and Tateshale's for instance, making his cavalry total about 600 or rather more, but I cannot trace where the foot of Chester joined him. Then instead of following the coast-line to Flint and Rhuddlan, he struck inland, obviously with the design of first crushing the insurgents of Denbigh, who had routed the Earl of Lincoln. He marched south to Wrexham, where he had his head-quarters for a few days from December 11, and where Hugh de Cressingham joined with foot from Lancashire and the more distant counties. On December 15 he turned westwards to cross the watershed between the Dee and the Clwyd by way of Llandegla, struck the head waters of the Clwyd at Derwen on December 18, and pushed down stream by Llech in Ken-merch, past Denbigh to Henllan. A few more troops joined him now, notably a body under Reginald de Grey, who we may suppose had been on duty at Rhuddlan, and came up stream to meet him. It would seem that he was satisfied that he had overawed the Welsh of Denbigh, for he arrived in person at Conway about Christmas. Hemingburgh and Trivet, the latter giving most details of the campaign, tell us that the army was scattered. We can imagine Edward established at Conway at the end of the year with the leading division, while the rest were still spread over the valley of the Clwyd and the coast-line under the Earl of Warwick.

The chroniclers continue the story[1]. After Edward had welcomed at Conway the Archbishop of Canterbury, he pro-ceeded further to the west. The Welsh roll enables us to fix

---

[1] Hemingburgh, vol. ii. pp. 58, 59; Trivet, p. 335.

the date; he was at Bangor on January 7 and 8, 1295. He had still with him only the van of his army, and had too rashly penetrated into a difficult piece of country which the Welsh knew only too well how to defend. The spurs of Snowdonia running northwards from Carnedd Llewelyn, and forming between Conway and Bangor that Penmaenmawr position which was the centre of the operations of 1282 and 1283, gave the Welsh an admirable cover from which to attack his flanks and rear. They rushed down and captured the whole of his commissariat train, presumably on January 9 or 10. He was forced to retire on Conway, and there submit to the indignity of a siege. It was not a very serious matter in itself, for walls could always defy the Welsh when there was no chance of effecting a surprise, but supplies ran short to a dangerous extent, the whole of the commissariat train having been lost. Floods and a high tide added to Edward's anxiety, and prevented him from getting in touch with the Earl of Warwick and others who were to the rear. While he was resolutely holding out, but feared starvation, he refused to appropriate to his private use the one small cask of wine which was in the castle. Water mixed with honey had to take the place of wine for the king, as well as for his men. The chroniclers were particularly struck with this circumstance, as though it was the chief feature of the blockade of Conway, and of course in the Middle Ages and right down to quite recent times, in the absence of a scientific process of filtering water, an army was quite dependent on an adequate supply of wine or beer. Throughout Edward's reign the documents frequently contain entries concerning the arrival of casks from Gascony.

Relief was not long in coming. Hemingburgh tells us that 'soon' the waters subsided, the rest of the army came up and routed the Welsh. Trivet with more detail tells of an important victory of the Earl of Warwick, which he describes immediately after the fact of the blockade of Conway. The language of this chronicler undoubtedly implies that the loss of the train, the blockade, the victory and relief came one after the other within a short time. And we have the following reason for fixing the date exactly. On January 24 the king[1], 'wishing to show his gratitude to John Giffard, has taken him under his special protection and defence on account of his bodily infirmity, and also because quite recently he and his men have powerfully aided the king in the king's Welsh expedition'; *regi potenter subvenit hiis diebus.* It is not too much to assume that Giffard had pacified the march of Builth and had now come north; Hereford also, some of whose followers had protections dated January 7, had probably come up after pacifying Brecknock. We can picture to ourselves the Earl of Warwick's position. He hears of the blockade of the king at Conway, at once closes up the rear of the English army which is spread out eastwards, picks up the corps of Giffard and Hereford, catches the Welsh unawares, and, by defeating them in pitched battle, relieves the king and castle. Giffard is wounded in the battle, and receives the king's special thanks. On these data the battle near Conway may be assigned to a day or two before January 24.

Trivet's description of the victory is a veritable *locus classicus* to all who wish to trace the development of infantry tactics. 'The Earl of Warwick, hearing that the Welsh were massed in great numbers in a certain plain between two forests, took with him a picked body of men-at-arms, together with crossbowmen and archers, and, surprising them by night, surrounded them on all sides. They planted the butts of their spears on the ground, and turned the points against the charging cavalry so as to defend themselves from their rush. But the earl placed a crossbowman between each two men-at-arms, and when the greater part of the spear-armed Welsh had been brought down by the bolts of the crossbows, he charged the rest with his squadron of horse, and inflicted upon them a loss greater, it is believed, than any which had been experienced by them in the past wars.' What we know of the constitution of an Edwardian army precludes the idea that the crossbows alone did all this injury; archers must be added. But the passage is invaluable to the student of war. Naturally we compare the details of that other fight at Orewin

[1] *Patent Roll.*

bridge, and the whole series of Scottish battles. Two problems faced an English general: first, to bring to action an enemy who moved lightly and resolutely refused pitched battle in his native country, admirably suited as it was for guerilla tactics; secondly, to combine horse and missile-armed foot to the best advantage. The spear is nature's weapon for brave and hardy men massed together in self-defence. Any one can hold firmly a shaft of wood tipped with iron, but the cavalry lance or sword or axe can only be wielded by a comparatively trained soldier. The spearmen can stand but cannot manœuvre; for Macedon in ancient, Switzerland and Germany in mediaeval days, alone have produced a professionally trained race of pikemen able both to stand and to charge. If, then, the English commander has got his enemy at bay, it is his task to restrain his cavalry from an insensate rush upon the hedge of points until the missiles have been brought into play. However few in numbers were the crossbowmen in the army, however weak the bow of this date, however undisciplined the archers, they must in time break up an unmoving enemy. But Trivet implies that Warwick began this fight with cavalry, and only interlaced with them the crossbows (and the bows) when the Welsh resisted the first rush. The lesson of Falkirk is the same. The pride of the mounted arm would insist upon leading. Not even yet were foot and horse systematically combined, and it required the tremendous defeat of Bannockburn to bring home to the generality of English knights that horse alone cannot win battles against spear-armed infantry. Orewin bridge and Conway, and Falkirk but three years and a half later, are steps in a process of evolution towards ideal tactics. The few crossbowmen are considered more serviceable than the archers, but the tendency is towards perfecting a missile weapon. As experience grows, the bow ousts the crossbow as the best arm for infantry; as training begins to tell, the bow becomes longer and stronger, and the archers become more apt in its use. Thus, though the words of the chronicler, and the evidence of the high pay given to the crossbowman, show that he was the more important soldier in 1295, this battle near

Conway is a link in the chain leading up to Crecy, where indeed the longbows triumphed over both crossbows and cavalry.

If it be right to assume that John Giffard was the leading spirit at Orewin bridge, and was consequently highly honoured by Edward, it is a strange coincidence that he was also at this battle and again was specially distinguished by Edward. It appears as if he was the chief exponent of combined infantry and cavalry tactics, and taught the Earl of Warwick how to win a notable victory by employing methods used so successfully by him twelve years before in a different part of Wales.

One more point may be considered. The Earl of Warwick cannot have had a very large force. He was only bringing part of the army to the relief of Edward and of the other part blockaded at Conway; and he surprised the Welsh with only a part of this part. Similarly at Orewin bridge the English army does not appear to have been numerically strong. At Dupplin Moor in 1332 against the Scots, as on the most famous field of Agincourt, the victorious army which produced the deadly effect was very small. But size, under the circumstances, means little when good combined tactics are used. Heaven fights on the side of the big battalions when the armies are equally well handled, but a small, good fighting machine, like a well-bred terrier, will beat a bigger, equally brave, but awkward enemy. Again, the battle shows that the Welsh of Snowdon had never learnt the use of missiles. These northerners were as distinct from the southerners of Gwent as in the days of Giraldus Cambrensis, and they allowed the English to learn and develop archery, while they themselves clung to the use of the long spear. The battle of Conway was, moreover, a purely English victory; there is not a trace of southern friendlies being up in the north at this date.

After being relieved Edward seems to have withdrawn for a time to Denbigh, and Edmund remained at Conway during the whole of February and March. The place was quite safe, and communication with England was open, for the number of writs entered on the patent roll shows that the ordinary business of government was easily carried on. Also, having avenged the loss of his baggage and momentarily overawed the Welsh, he dismissed some of the contingents forming his field army and concentrated the rest on the fortresses. It was needless to exhaust the strength of the English by winter campaigns, so he stood on the defensive as in the winter of 1282. A new field army was formed in March. Meanwhile, something could still be done by sea. Provisions were being continually brought round [1]. We have documents giving details of two Bristol ships [2] plying from December to April between that port and Dublin and Conway, the much-needed wine and oats being the chief items of their cargo, and of another squadron of three ships engaged in the same task [3]. Fourteen ships of Bayonne, which probably originally came with wine, received at Conway from Edmund of Lancaster in the king's name letters of marque [4]. They were licensed as privateers to divide in equal shares the plunder obtained from the king's enemies. The policy of resting the portion of the army which had not been dismissed, and of reconstituting the commissariat train during some two months, was distinctly wise. But writs were out in February calling for volunteers for the cavalry.

During this interval a considerable number of documents, mostly loose single sheets of parchment done up at random, give us an account of proceedings on the west coast. How far Criccieth and Harlech were in danger at the first outbreak in the autumn does not appear. Between January and April, 1295, successful expeditions were undertaken for their relief. Robert de Staundon had been quite cut off from England except by sea. He had no force on which to rely except the garrisons in the castles, the English settlers in the small towns of Criccieth and Harlech, and a handful of six Irish and nine loyalist Welsh horse who probably acted as a patrol [2]. Robert Hacket was now Sub-constable of Criccieth ; Vivian de Staundon, the justiciar's son, of Harlech. In January Edward commissioned Richard de Havering to

---

[1] *Exch. Acc.* $\frac{5}{5}$.    [2] Ibid. $\frac{5}{18}$.    [3] Ibid. $\frac{5}{19}$.
[4] *Patent Roll*, Feb. 16, 1295.

conduct a relief expedition[1]. A ship and three barges were freighted in Ireland with provisions and crossbow ammunition, and the sailors, together with eighteen crossbowmen and three archers serving as marines, were in pay from January to April. They were discharging their cargo at Harlech on March 31 and again on April 6, at Criccieth on April 3 and 11. Out of 5,000 quarrels, 1,700 were sold to various crossbowmen, and 800 later on in Anglesey, 2,500 therefore remaining for the two castles relieved. Havering reported that at Criccieth, beyond his relief supplies, there were thirty carcasses of beef and 109 of mutton in store.

Llanbadarn came within the sphere of action of the commanders in South Wales[2]. Roger de Molis himself was stationed there, and was in February blockaded and cut off. The king from Conway, and William de Valence from Carmarthen, sent orders to the Constable of Bristol to throw in relief, provisions, 5,000 quarrels, a dozen crossbows, and cords for a year's supply. A ship or two barges were to be manned *de bones gentz et vigerouses et de arbalestriers, quar le chastel et les gentz qui leurs sont sront en pil si hastif remedie ne soit mis.* The receipt of the stores was acknowledged by Roger de Molis on April 12, and again in June. The document giving the information is the bill which the Constable of Bristol sent in to the Exchequer officials, and in 1296 there were £398 still owing to him. The Gascon, Welsh, and Scottish troubles, all coming upon Edward at one time, caused the crown to run into debt.

The field army, reconstituted towards the end of March, was ready to renew operations in April. It is more than ever difficult to determine the strength of the cavalry. Letters of protection were issued to men who had not served in the autumn, or renewed to those who had served; others had been already in arms elsewhere in Wales, and now joined the king's army, while others yet again may have continued to serve with him without reissues. He had in all 250 horse with protections. The largest retinue, that of Edmund, was

[1] *Exch. Acc.* $\frac{5}{17}$.    [2] Ibid. $\frac{5}{19}$.

composed of sixteen knights and twenty-nine troopers.
Warwick by this time had thirty-eight lances of all ranks,
including four bannerets, Ralph Basset, Robert de Scales,
Robert Fitzwalter, and Peter Corbet, who had protections, and
he must have had sixty or seventy lances in all. Surrey and
Henry Percy had eighteen with protections, probably thirty
or more in all. Hugh le Despenser has dropped out. The
Earl of Hereford, of whose followers eleven had protections,
certainly seems to have been at headquarters; a writ was
tested by his banneret, Nicholas de Segrave, as deputy constable, during his probably temporary absence. Walter de
Beauchamp, steward of the household, had no followers entered
on the roll, but his normal retinue was twenty-five lances.
A new-comer was Antony Bek, the warrior bishop, but with
only two followers with protections. But the most interesting
cases are those of John de Hastings and the Earl of Gloucester,
the former with twenty-one and the latter with six : were they
now for the first time up with the king? The presumption is
that they were, for those barons who were still in South Wales,
Valence, Norfolk, Molis, Plukenet, and others, had new protections entered only for themselves, or at most one or two
bannerets. It would be intelligible if we supposed that
Edward, finding that the men of Glamorgan had been successful against the earl, and the men of Gwent or Cilgeran
against Hastings, yet knowing that Morgan professed loyalty
to the crown, called the two up to him, and intended himself
to pacify those insurgents later on. In Gloucester's retinue
were John Wake and John Lovel, who in the autumn had
commanded independent units of horse.

The Earl of Lincoln, I take it, was not with the king, but
was holding Denbigh and the Clwyd. Only three of his men
had protections. One of these was Robert de Tateshale, who
had never before served under the earl's banner, and may now
be supposed to have had his troop up to the strength of the
previous autumn, some twenty lances. Similarly, the Earl of
Arundel may be taken to have remained on duty on the
borders of Shropshire.

The only definite evidence of cavalry in this war is given

by a pay-roll of Grey's squadron [1]. He concentrated in March
at Rhuddlan, and thence brought to headquarters, 108 lances
in six troops. Very few of the men had protections. One
banneret served for forty days, one for 110 days, but the
majority for about nine weeks, and there is no certain evidence
of a contract, which however probably existed. Their numbers
continually dwindled during the campaign, an indication of
casualties in action.

| Bannerets. | Knights. | Troopers. | Total. | No. who had protections now or last autumn. |
|---|---|---|---|---|
| Reginald de Grey   .   . | 8 | 26 | 35 | 10 |
| Roger de Monthaut and William de Mauley   . | 2 | 16 | 20 | 2 |
| Richard FitzJohn   .   . | 3 | 13 | 17 | 3 |
| Walter de Huntercumbe   . | 3 | 9 | 13 | 7 |
| Philip de Kyme.   .   . | 2 | 10 | 13 | 8 |
| Ralph Pipard   .   .   . | 1 | 8 | 10 | 3 |
| Total : 7 bannerets   . | 19 | 82 | 108 | |

The details of the squadron are interesting because on February 10 the king, after the relief of Conway, had called for
volunteers from the class of the £40 landowners, and from
those below that limit who had the requisite arms and horses ;
this had been a call for cavalry to take the king's pay [2].
*Quod prompti sint et parati cum equis et armis ad eundum in
obsequium nostrum et morandum ad vadia nostra ad voluntatem nostram quandocunque super hoc ex parte nostra per
spacium trium setpimanarum fuerint premuniti . . . et eciam
quod qui non habent quadraginta libratas dumtamen habeant
equos et arma ad vadia nostra admittentur.* Grey had therefore answered the call by recruiting a full squadron from the
men who were thus warned. Also the earls, recruiting some of
the bannerets in addition to their ordinary retinues, had raised
similar squadrons, Warwick having Fitzwalter and Corbet as
his troop-leaders, Lincoln having Tateshale, and Gloucester
having Wake and Lovel. The cavalry total at headquarters

---

[1] *Exch. Acc.* $\frac{5}{18}$.        [2] *Parl. Writs*, vol. i. p. 267.

comes to about 325 lances, of which we have definite evidence, perhaps 600 in all.

The king renewed offensive operations, having the whole of Grey's squadron, a good proportion of the other cavalry, about seventy crossbows under Henry de Greneford, and nearly 2,000 foot from Lancashire and Chester. The infantry pay-roll at this time is complete ; the sheets have in a curious way been separated, and are found in two bundles ; but they are the work of the same paymaster, and can be read continuously[1]. The men of Lancashire were up first, and as they dropped out new relays from Chester took their place, with a few of 'divers counties.' The archers of the household, or bodyguard, numbered twenty-five, and Huntercumbe had a special body of a dozen *per preceptum regis*. For a fortnight in March and a week in April, headquarters being still at Conway, the army was engaged in subduing the Welsh of the valley ; on April 9 and 10 it moved to Bangor, and the retinues of Edmund, Warwick, and Hereford joined. There may have been a movement towards Carnarvon, but no attempt was yet made to reconstruct the castle. On April 15 Anglesey was occupied, and headquarters fixed at Llanfaes. Edward imme-diately ordered the construction of Beaumaris castle, William de Felton being constable, and Henry de Lathom having a small squadron of ships to patrol the straits[2]. He forced 600 Welsh of Anglesey to join his army. Surrey and Hastings now joined with their horse, the Lancashire foot were 600 strong, the Chester foot 950 rising to 1,160, and divers counties 280. Quitting Anglesey on May 6, for the next three weeks the army scoured the country round Dolgelly, and pushed along to Harlech and Towyn ; it will be remembered that Richard de Havering had already re-lieved and revictualled the castles of this coast six weeks earlier. By the end of May only 200 of the Lancashire foot remained ; a Lincolnshire corps of 193 retired, but relays brought the divers counties' total to 525 ; the men of Chester were reinforced up to 1,300, and 600 came from Shropshire, soon reinforced to 800. The crossbowmen now mustered 100

---

[1] *Exch. Acc.* $\frac{5}{16}$ and $\frac{5}{18}$.    [2] *Pipe Roll*, 6 Edw. II, last membrane.

strong, but Grey's horse lost, by withdrawal or by casualties, twenty of their number. The evidence of the chroniclers is to the effect that the Welsh were starved into a surrender, and the rapid movements of Edward's army point to a typical collapse. Within two months and a half the war had been finished off in Snowdonia and Anglesey, and along the coast of Merioneth. Amongst the miscellaneous documents is a list of the names of seventy-four hostages taken from Carnarvonshire and Merioneth. But it may be doubted if Madoc had yet made his surrender, for the same chroniclers say that he was pardoned on condition of sending men to fight the South Welsh, but the infantry pay-sheets show that the Anglesey foot alone were serving. The truth would seem to be that the English arms were generally and speedily successful since the advance; the losses of the Welsh are undoubted, but the final submission of the leaders was not yet.

Before the close of May, Edward was able to advance into South Wales, the army consisting of ninety-four crossbows, 150 foot of Lancashire, 1,200 of Chester, and 1,000 of Shropshire. The Anglesey Welsh, reduced in number to 570, were dismissed after the first week in June. Grey's cavalry had dropped off, with the exception of Huntercumbe's dozen lances. But Edmund and Warwick and others remained[1], and the king was now in touch with Pembroke's and Norfolk's available forces. We find him occupied for a week at Llanbadarn. Roger de Molis had been already successfully revictualled by the care of the Constable of Bristol, and however closely the Welsh had pressed upon Llanbadarn in the spring, just as in the case of their attacks upon Criccieth and Harlech, they melted away before the rapid advance of the English army. The dates point to an utter collapse of the rising in Cardiganshire. On June 2 and 3 Edward was at Cardigan, then at Emlyn. Another week took him across Carmarthenshire, where seventy foot joined him from Carmarthen and 370 from the lands of Ralph de Tony. On June 10 and 11 he was on the watershed crossing over to Brecknock by Llanddausant and Llywel.

[1] *Exch. Acc.* $\frac{5}{18}$ (notes of provisions sold to several leaders at Llanbadarn and Cardigan).

On June 14 and 15 he was at Merthyr Tydfil. What had happened in the course of Morgan's rising is conjectural. Edward now took over the whole of Glamorgan into his own hands, accepted the submission of the insurgents against the wishes of the earl, and appointed Walter Hackelute as royal custodian of the country[1]. As a matter of fact the lands were restored to the earl and to Joan his wife the next autumn[2]. This business did not take a long time to finish. Returning to Brecon on June 16 the king pushed through into Powysland, lay at Welshpool on June 21 and 22, and thence marched straight back to Conway by June 30.

He had now no further task than to provide for the construction of the castles of Carnarvon and Beaumaris. On July 9 and 10 he was at Carnarvon in person; on July 10 he crossed over to Anglesey, where the work had already been begun under William de Felton. By July 21 he was back again at Worcester, exactly eight months since he had opened his campaign, and early in August at Westminster.

John de Havering was commissioned, as Justiciar of North Wales, to see to the peace settlement and to the work of castle-building, and was to have the same fee that Otto de Grandison had drawn[3]. On July 17 he took up his duties at Oswestry with a personal following of four horse and twenty crossbows[4]. First he visited Criccieth and Harlech, and made a register of the garrisons; at Criccieth he found that Robert Hacket had thirty-six men, of whom five were citizens of the English town, and only two were Welsh; at Harlech Robert de Staundon had thirty-seven men, twelve being English citizens and one Welsh. In each case Englishwomen were registered 'on the strength' of the garrison. But henceforward the documents, scanty at the best, quite fail us. In a Welsh chronicle of later date it is asserted that Madoc, being still in arms, made a successful raid into Shropshire, and was at last brought to surrender by Havering[5]. The statement

---

[1] *Annales Monastici*, 'Worcester,' vol. iv. p. 526.
[2] *Patent Roll*, October 20, 1295.
[3] Ibid. Sept. 3, 1295.　　　[4] *Exch. Acc.* $\frac{5}{18}$.
[5] David Powell's *Caradoc*, p. 272 (edition of 1832).

may well be true, and indeed one English authority has it that Havering, after the king's departure, received the final submission, and so it may be granted that Madoc made this last despairing effort[1]. All accounts agree that the Welsh, after great suffering, were beaten down to utter exhaustion.

The war is fairly typical of its kind. The English had preliminary checks at Denbigh and Bangor, besides the first losses in the outbreak at Cardigan and Carnarvon. There was a pause while the resources of England were being brought into play, and then the reconquest was easy before the king's rapid march. Edward did not show himself vindictive towards Madoc, whom he kept in captivity. His sense of justice led him to include, in his instructions to Havering, the task of investigating, together with William Sikun, who remained for many years Constable of Conway, the grievances of the Welsh against the English officials since the annexation[2].

'Rex dilectis et fidelibus suis John de Havering iusticiario suo North Wall et Will Sycum constabulario castri sui de Aberconwey salutem ; Quia ex gravi querela hominum communitatis North Wall accepimus quod vicecomites ballivi et toti ministri nostri de partibus illis eisdem hominibus varias transgressiones iniurias extorsiones oppressiones et dampna gravissima a tempore quo terra illa in manus nostras devenit intulerunt et adhuc de die in diem inferre non desistunt ad grave dampnum et depaupertatem hominum communitatis illius manifestam, volentes igitur quod eisdem hominibus omni iustitia subveniatur in hac parte assignavimus vos iusticiarios nostros ad inquirend per sacramentum proborum et legalium hominum de partibus illis . . . et ad iusticiam inde faciendam secundum legem et consuetudinem partium illarum.'

Nevertheless the rising had complicated Edward's foreign relations. France profited, and the English efforts in Gascony were feeble. The knowledge that France was ready to embarrass Edward by any means at home led Thomas de Turberville[3], a knight who had seen service in Wales in 1277

---

[1] *Annales Monastici*, ' Dunstable,' vol. iii. p. 387.

[2] *Patent Roll*, Sept. 1, 1295 ; 23 Edw. I, m. 9, back.

[3] Hemingburgh, vol. ii. p. 60.

and 1282, to buy his release from captivity by promises of treachery, happily frustrated. French ships harried the southern coasts in 1295, and it was French influence which caused Balliol to throw off his allegiance. As a result of the general upset of his foreign policy we find Edward seriously straitened for money. Previously he had paid his way with ease, and if indeed he was tempted in 1283 to lay hands on crusade money, he was able to make restitution without being thereby bankrupt. But now, in spite of two large grants by Parliament in 1294, and another again in 1295 when the model Parliament sat, he was unable to get out of debt. Small sums were owing to Grey and other cavalry leaders, and to the Constable of Bristol. The tightness of the money market is more particularly illustrated, however, in connexion with the castles. An Edwardian fortress was a serious piece of work, planned on a grand scale. The mediaeval mason was no jerry-builder, but a solid worker who required proportionately high pay. Edward was not the man to stint his servants, and he was keenly enough interested in the building. Therefore, if complaints were made that the work was being hindered for want of money, it is certain that the king was really straitened.

Three letters are extant concerning the castle-building[1]. They are all on one sheet of parchment, being the official copies made by some clerk. John de Havering first sends a covering letter, asking the Treasurer and Barons of the Exchequer that the money assigned for the work of Carnarvon may not be diverted to Beaumaris ; the construction of Carnarvon is much in arrears, and it is more dangerous to send money by sea to Anglesey than by land to its proper destination ; 650 marcs have been stopped by the officials of Beaumaris. Havering's letter is not dated, but he clearly writes on February 26, 1296, from Conway, whither he has come to take the treasure, but finds that the Beaumaris people have impounded it. He sends with his protest a report from Walter de Hereford and Hugh de Leominster, the overseers or clerks of the works at Carnarvon, 'written at Conway this present 26th of February.' First, the walls of the town of

---

[1] Part of *Exch. Acc.* $\frac{5}{18}$.

Carnarvon had been taken in hand, and had been completed by September 10 last. The men had then been put to work at the castle, and up to November 27 they had been paid only £100 and at least £400 were owing, but they have gone on building to the present. The wall within the moat has been begun, and four towers in the wall; for a distance of 10 perches it is now 24 feet high, for another 8 perches it is 12 feet high, with a uniform thickness of 15 feet. Since the July of 1295—the date at which Edward was in person on the spot, and the work had actually begun under his eye —£1,466 have been received from England, and £782 from the revenues of North Wales. But besides workmen's wages and the cost of material, there are also the garrisons of Carnarvon and Criccieth to be paid, together with the crews of two barges, victuals to be bought, and Havering's fee of £220 to be satisfied. Twenty men-at-arms, forty crossbows, and a hundred foot are guarding the works, while at Criccieth the constable has ten crossbows and twenty foot.

The officials responsible at Beaumaris, under William de Felton, are James de St. George, whom we have now frequently met as an architect, and Walter de Winchester, who is presumably the overseer. They also write from Conway, but a day later. They have been ordered to report on their work from time to time, and now beg to submit to the Treasurer and Barons of the Exchequer that the work, during the whole of the winter and up to the present, has been very costly, £250 being wanted every week. Four hundred masons are at work, some cutting and others laying the stones (*quatre centz macheons quei tailleurs quei couchours*), 1,000 less skilled artisans (*menus oueriers*) making mortar and lime, &c., 200 carters, and thirty smiths and carpenters: 160 carts and wagons are in use, and thirty boats bringing up the stone. There is a garrison of ten men-at-arms, twenty crossbows, and 100 foot [1]. The debt is already over £500. But a great deal has been done; the wall of the castle is in places 28 feet high, and at the lowest 20 feet; ten towers have been commenced outside, and four inside; four great gates have been

---

[1] Later we find eighteen crossbows and fifty foot (*Exch. Acc.* $\frac{6}{1}$).

hung, which are locked at night (*qui sont closes de lok chescune noit*; the scribe's knowledge of Norman-French here breaks down), and each will have three portcullises. A forty-ton vessel fully laden will be able to sail at high tide up to the biggest gate in the face of any Welsh enemy (*maugre tous les Galeys*). The writers almost sadly say that if they cannot have the money they want, well, so be it, let them have further orders and they will cut down the expenses, if this is really to the king's advantage; *si par auent'e vous sentez ɋ no' ne peusseoms tantz deñs auoir, le no' mandez et no' mettroms oɗours a vostre volunte selonc ce ɋ vous verrez ɋ mieutz soit pur le ꝓfit ñre seigñ le Roy.* They conclude by reminding the treasurer that Wales may be apparently pacified, but Welshmen are Welshmen, and an English officer has to know them well, and to be on his guard in case the king's wars in France and Scotland continue, which Heaven forbid; *mais vous sauez bien ɋ Galeys sont Galeys et vous les deuez bien conustre et sont a duter de tāt le plus si les Gerres de France et Descoce veysent auant ɋ dieu ne voille.* In any case money must be sent—this in a postscript after the letter has been closed and dated—because, however much has been done, it will be of little value if more is not done; *car tāt come ilyad fait uncore poy vaut si plus ny soit fait.*

There is a human interest, and a pathos almost, in these letters which the ordinary lifeless documents lack. The pride of the master-builders, the reputation of the king's captains, is at stake. There is rivalry between Carnarvon and Beaumaris. Carnarvon castle is not far advanced, but the walls of the town had to be built first; the twenty-eight feet of wall and ten towers and gateway of Beaumaris take the pride of place over the lesser extent of wall and four towers of the other. But perhaps the best touch is the Englishman's tone towards the Welshman. 'We do not intend to be caught napping again,' the last letter seems to say; 'we know now his treacherous character, and we judge him for what he is worth; he will not take by surprise this splendid castle with its gateway on the sea.' One wonders what ultimately became of the 650 marcs. The officials of Beaumaris were in possession when Havering wrote, but the tone of their letter a day later makes one think that he had wrested the money from them. His authority, one would have thought, extended over all North Wales, but here he is only responsible for Carnarvonshire. In course of time, however, the money was forthcoming from the revenues of North Wales, from Ireland, from the proceeds of taxation in Yorkshire. The works of Beaumaris were finished in 1298 at a total cost of £7,041, besides the maintenance of Felton's garrison of ten or twenty horse, twenty crossbows, and 100 archers[1]. The town of Carnarvon was rebuilt and walled at a cost of £1,024, and the castle was rebuilt and finished in 1299 for £4,393[2].

Robert de Tibotot, returning from Gascony, resumed his place as Justiciar of South Wales on the old conditions in 1298, but he died the same year. Walter de Pederton succeeded him[3]. But in 1300 John de Havering was made justiciar of the whole of Wales. In the meantime Reginald de Grey, whose services the king required in his campaigns in Scotland, gave up the justiciarship of Chester to Richard de Mascy. Finally, in 1301, Prince Edward was created Prince of Wales and Earl of Chester.

During the period after Tibotot's death we have some facts of the normal peace establishment in South Wales. The revenue of the country brought in £634 yearly. Llanbadarn castle was held by John de Scudamore as constable, with a garrison of fifty men at a yearly wage of a few shillings together with rations. Ralph le Blunt held Dryslwyn with twenty-four men, and drew £40 yearly; Henry Scurlach, a Welshman, held Dynevor on similar terms; Richard Wroth, at Emlyn, had 40 marcs. At Cardigan and Carmarthen there was no garrison beyond the constable of each place and a watchman and doorkeeper. Caercynan is not mentioned at all. The up-keep of the six castles and occasional repairs came to £360 yearly[4].

---

[1] *Pipe Roll*, 6 Edw. II, last membrane.
[2] Ibid. 29 Edw. I, m. 24.     [3] Ibid. m. 51, 52.     [4] Ibid. m. 35.

# CHAPTER VIII

## EVENTS LEADING FROM THE WELSH WARS

A CHAPTER on Edward's subsequent military undertakings, and on those political questions which affected the military situation, is not out of place as a pendant to the tale of the Welsh wars. The importance of the crisis of 1297 is emphasized when one can trace a connexion between the earls' grievances and the king's treatment of them in Wales. On the other hand, the details of the armies raised for service in Flanders and Scotland show not only how Edward used his previous experience so as to equip stronger forces for more arduous tasks, but also how he utilized the conquered Welsh, the friendlies of the march, and the Englishmen of the border counties, as being his best material for war. The evidence at our disposal is curiously different from what we used in the preceding chapters. The infantry or the cavalry pay-roll is now not often extant, and in its place we have the horse-inventory. Certainly we knew already, from entries in miscellaneous rolls, that in the Welsh wars the king refunded the value of a horse lost in his service, but now we find the complete inventories made of the value of each single horse, together with a description of its points and colour, the valuation being taken either at the outset of a campaign or when a retinue joined an army during a campaign. Only the mounts of the members of the household and the paid cavalry are entered, and feudal quotas are not touched. The general result is that most retinues are found to be of greater strength than in the Welsh wars, but small units of four or five lances are still found ; and I infer that the king increased his household during a war by the addition of specially raised troops, often of considerable strength, for instance the fifty lances of Hugh le Despenser. The system was beginning to spread by which a baron contracted for the maintenance of a troop, so that on the outbreak of war he had the men ready to take the king's pay; this we know was the relation between Aymer de Valence and the Berkeleys. Also we find in many cases the horses of the mounted officers of the infantry valued together with those of the cavalry proper, and finding certain horsemen designated in a roll as centenars or millenars, we may take it that the other officers' names are in the same roll but not specially designated. Thus John de Merk, when he has his own horse and those of two troopers valued for a campaign, is probably the millenar of the infantry of Chester with the army. Then a great many names of *socii* in small units of two or three or half a dozen are entered independently, the county whence they came being usually added. Such men may be centenars of foot, but not always, for the southern counties were never called on to send men to Scotland at this date, and many *socii* are southerners. They were mostly, I believe, independent volunteers below the £20 limit, that is to say mounted men belonging to the second class of the national militia under the assize of arms. Others were the king's household troopers or special bodyguard, *servientes regis ad arma* or *valetti regis*; others, again, are recognized by their names to be leaders of squads of crossbowmen, for instance Henry de Greneford. Lastly, the mounted servants of the household are entered, and in the figures given below I have as carefully as possible excluded all the cooks and butlers and clerks from the fighting strength. I have analysed five inventories: one of the household troops in Scotland in 1296, two of the household and paid cavalry outside the household in Flanders, and two similarly of the cavalry of Falkirk; but it has to be remembered that all the horse in Flanders were paid, and therefore we have an exhaustive roll, whereas the unpaid quotas of the earls and the Bishop of Durham have to be added to the paid horse of Scottish campaigns.

In 1296 Edward addressed writs of summons to several

barons individually, and also called upon all landowners at the £40 limit to be in readiness with arms and horses in case they should be required to take the field[1]. There was a 'marshal's roll' of the rest of the paid cavalry, but we only have the household inventory extant. I have added up precisely 300 lances, 54 bannerets and knights, 146 troopers of their retinues, and 100 independent horsemen or *socii* in small groups[2]. The most important retinues are:—

|  | Knights. | Troopers. | Total. |
|---|---|---|---|
| Hugh le Despenser . . . | 3 | 21 | 25 |
| Alan Plukenet . . . . | 2 | 11 | 14 |
| Robert de Clifford . . . | 2 | 11 | 14 |
| John d'Engayne . . . . | 3 | 9 | 13 |
| Walter de Beauchamp . . | 2 | 9 | 12 |
| Peter de Chanent . . . | 2 | 7 | 10 |
| Adam de Welles . . . | 1 | 6 | 8 |
| Thomas de Berkeley . . . | 1 | 6 | 8 |
| Alan de Waldeshef . . . | — | 7 | 8 |
| Robert FitzPain . . . . | 1 | 6 | 8 |

Guy, son of the Earl of Warwick, and Humphrey, son of the Earl of Hereford, were present with a few *socii*, neither of them having been knighted. The advent of these young nobles and such new men as Despenser and Clifford introduces us to a generation which had not fought against Llewelyn. Henry de Greneford and his fifteen *socii* would represent a corps of at least 160 crossbowmen. There were five millenars of Yorkshire infantry and one from Westmorland, and though John de Merk and Osbert de Spaldington are not named as millenars, they probably had contingents from Chester and Herefordshire; thus there would be some 8,000 foot, but there is no sign of a Shropshire contingent, and only one body of 300 Welsh of Brecknock can be traced. The horse and foot of Durham, the horse of the marshal's roll, and the feudal quotas would give a total of perhaps 1,000 horse and 10,000 foot, all told. Hemingburgh[3] says that the division which was sent forward under the Earl of Surrey and won the battle of Dunbar was composed of 1,000 horse,

---

[1] *Parl. Writs*, vol. i. pp. 275, 278.    [2] *Exch. Acc.* $\frac{5}{23}$.

[3] Vol. ii. p. 103.

exclusive of another 100 of the Bishop of Durham, and 10,000 foot, while the king remained behind at Berwick with presumably as many or even more. Such figures strike one as being far too high ; in fact the numbers given by Hemingburgh for the battle seem to me to be suitable for the whole army, of which only the advanced guard was actually engaged. Twenty-four ships accompanied the army[1].

No sooner have we entered on the fateful year 1297 than we feel the air murky and heavy with disaffection. The clergy began by refusing to grant money in January ; we need not pursue the question of the bull *Clericis Laicos*, nor Edward's measures of coercion, except that in July, as a punishment, he ordered certain clerics to produce their feudal contingents for a campaign over the sea, this being a formal summons[2]. Towards the end of February occurred the scene of Hereford's and Norfolk's defiance, and the king laid hands upon the wool and hides[3]. The feeling of irritation which the two earls, each of them an hereditary official, manifested towards the king was very natural. I cannot help thinking that the reason of Norfolk's outburst has not previously been adequately explained, but when it is remembered that he had been formally and explicitly promised by the king in 1294 that he would not be again sent away from the royal presence, which was an acknowledgement that his legitimate place was in the king's headquarters army, his bitter animosity is more intelligible. Hitherto he had not been contumacious, but now he was led by his personal grievance, in resentment at being ordered to Gascony, to make himself out to be a popular champion against the crown. Hereford's attitude also becomes clearer, when we admit that he had been very hardly treated in 1292. Dr. Stubbs has pointed out that the fact of his imprisonment must have embittered him, but the details of the celebrated trial make us understand better why he was so embittered ; he had been in the right all through his case against Gloucester, he* had obeyed the king and was sure of a verdict in his favour, but at the last moment had put him-

---

[1] Hemingburgh, vol. ii. p. 97.     [2] *Parl. Writs*, vol. i. p. 283.
[3] Hemingburgh, vol. ii. p. 121.

self in the wrong by detaining some of Gloucester's cattle unless security were given that the debatable land was really his. Technically, he had been beyond all doubt guilty of contempt of court. Yet Edward hardly acted wisely in punishing so severely, by imprisonment and subsequent fine of 1,000 marcs, what was after all little more than a technical offence. Thus both Norfolk and Hereford had in the first place a personal grievance. Then they insisted on the strict letter of the feudal law in refusing to go to Gascony while the king went to Flanders. *Vires adquirit eundo.* Their opposition became subsequently a national and constitutional question. Resistance to a demand for feudal service over the sea led, by a natural train of thought, to a similar resistance against John on the same ground, and so the mind runs back to Magna Carta. It must be allowed that some rankling sense of injury was underlying what appears on the surface to be a petty question ; that Edward's heavy taxation was a grievance as far back as 1288, when the Earl of Gloucester voiced the opposition ; that Norfolk and Hereford would not now have been able to form a party if the feeling against the crown had not been general. But Edward might have avoided a crisis in this particular year by treating the earls tactfully at the first. By his strong insistence he fanned a flame of disaffection which might otherwise have died out. It is curious that the strongest of the opponents of the crown, namely Gloucester, had died recently, and one wonders how the question would have been worked out had he been alive to support the other two.

It is difficult to decide if Edward really found trouble in raising his army to go to Flanders. The figures below would show that a very fair force of cavalry was raised. Perhaps the foot were backward, so that Welshmen had to be enlisted. But the chief grievance was at first connected with the expedition to Gascony, where matters had been going badly, and if service in Flanders was also made a grievance it would seem to be by an afterthought. The course of the altercation may have run in this way. The king tries, in answer to the two earls and to their voiceless but numerous allies among the barons, to insist on his right of demanding feudal service. His opponents know that the conditions of such service have been largely modified by compromise, the principle of a quota has been admitted, and payments have been made to all cavalry serving before or after the customary forty days, except as regards the earls' quotas. They must know that the king prefers to have paid troops, because they are more manageable and more amenable. But he has begun to demand feudal service since their defiance. So now they, though willing to do feudal duty this side the Channel because it is derogatory to an earl's status to take money, will answer the king by using his own arguments against him. All service beyond the Channel must be paid, or otherwise 'Magna Carta is in danger,' a very specious war-cry. 'Eodem anno post multas et varias altercationes concessit dominus rex omnibus qui debebant sibi servitia et omnibus viginti libratas terrae habentibus non teneri ire secum in Flandriam nisi ad vadia et pro stipendiis dicti regis[1].'

I have suggested this line of argument because from the facts of the Welsh wars, and from the very many writs concerning military service, especially those relating to the class of £40 or £20 landowners who were liable to be called on to take knighthood, it is clear that up to this year payments were customary and recognized. For instance, the writs of summons to the expedition to Gascony in 1294 were, in appearance, formal demands on feudal allegiance[2]; yet would Edward have really tried to compel to serve without pay a limited number of tenants-in-chief, the very men who in Wales were invariably the bannerets in command of paid troops or squadrons? Surely such compulsion would be a gross injustice to good soldiers, if they alone were liable to unpaid service, while others were not compelled. Therefore such formal writs cannot but have been mere invitations to professional soldiers to raise cavalry for the king's pay, though couched in feudal language. Then we have the instance of Theobald de Verdun, whose case has been discussed previously, but when we have a definite case in point we have to make the

---

[1] Stubbs, vol. ii. p. 150.  [2] See above, p. 77.

most of it. Theobald was under the royal displeasure, for he had been one of the contumacious marchers of 1291; he was now ordered to send his son to serve in his place, both as a duty and a punishment, but his service would be paid. Therefore it is impossible to argue that the offended earls were now, as the quotation above would seem to show if it were taken out of its context, insisting for the first time on payment for service in order to embarrass the king. They were rather turning against him his own weapons.

The sequel is graphically described by Hemingburgh. The king, on the advice of a certain baron, reconciled himself with the archbishop, and then constituted him, together with the loyal veteran, Reginald de Grey, as guardian to the youthful Prince Edward. The barons and people with raised hands swore allegiance to the prince as heir and successor, and Edward in return apologized for the seizure of the wool. But while some prayed publicly for his success, others cursed in secret. Then Hereford and Norfolk were deposed from their offices, for they had withdrawn themselves from court, and, considering this the last straw, they sent a message to the king, who was on the point of sailing, that they demanded the confirmation of the charters. Certain barons were trying to act the part of mediators, but the final answer was that the king could not discuss the charters without a full council, part of which had remained in London, and part had already sailed for Flanders. 'If the earls choose to accompany me, it will please me much; but if not, I request that they will not injure me, or at any rate my kingdom, in my absence.' Then he set out, and the two formed a party to insist upon the confirmation, and to prevent by arms the collection of the tax which they declared to be illegally claimed.

Counting those contingents which arrived in Flanders after the king, up to January of the next year, I make the cavalry of the army 822 strong[1]. There were 127 bannerets and knights, 475 troopers of their retinues, and 220 unattached lances. I have included all the mounted men except those who are obviously mere servants or clerks, and from the true

[1] *Exch. Acc.* $\frac{6}{28}$, $\frac{6}{37}$.

cavalry arm must be deducted the millenars and centenars of
foot. The following are the more important retinues :—

| | Knights. | Troopers. | Total. |
|---|---|---|---|
| Aymer de Valence . . . | 8 | 41 | 50 |
| John de Drokenesford . . | 3 | 29 | 33 |
| Geoffrey de Geneville . . . | 4 | 23 | 28 |
| Walter de Beauchamp . . | 4 | 22 | 27 |
| Guy, son of the Earl of Warwick . | 5 | 22 | 27 |
| William de Leyburn . . . | 5 | 17 | 23 |
| (Earl of Lancaster) . . . | 2 | 19 | 21 |
| William Tuchet . . . . | 4 | 12 | 17 |
| John de Benstede . . . | 2 | 13 | 16 |
| Adam de Welles . . . | 2 | 11 | 14 |
| Peter de Chanent . . . | 2 | 11 | 14 |
| James de la Planche . . . | 2 | 10 | 13 |
| Robert de Tateshale (son) . . | 2 | 9 | 12 |
| Gilbert de Gaunt . . . | 1 | 10 | 12 |
| Robert de Scales . . . . | 2 | 8 | 11 |
| Walter de Teye . . . . | 2 | 7 | 10 |
| John Husthwaite . . . | 1 | 8 | 10 |
| John d'Engayne . . . . | 3 | 5 | 9 |
| Edmund de Stafford . . . | 1 | 7 | 9 |

Of the largest of these retinues we have interesting information. William de Valence had died about a year before, and
Aymer, in spite of his youth, had already been summoned
to Parliament. On July 2, 1297, he formed his retinue to
proceed to Flanders by making a definite contract with the
Berkeleys[1]: Thomas, the father, was to maintain four knights,
two esquires for himself, one esquire for each knight, and four
valets; Maurice, the son, was to maintain two knights and
seven esquires or troopers; in times of peace they were to
draw a fixed sum of money with robes and diet, in war the
customary wages of bannerets and knights, plus an extra sum
of 100 marcs if the campaign were abroad. In our inventory
we find both the Berkeleys and their six knights, but forty-
one in place of the covenanted seventeen esquires and valets,
the retinue being increased for war. There is no question
of feudal obligation. A young baron with a taste for war
simply creates a squadron of his own at a retaining fee,
and puts his services at the disposal of the crown. It is the

[1] Bain, *Calendar*, vol. ii, no. 905.

nearest approach in this reign to the very common contract of Edward III. Next we know that Thomas was created constable of the army in Hereford's place, yet he was Valence's soldier by contract; one would think that the king intended to give the office to his young cousin, but saw that it was better to trust the more experienced banneret. The fifty lances practically represent the constable's troop and a baron's private retinue thrown into one, and raised in strength for the war. Valence was unable next year to defray all the expense, and was in debt to the Berkeleys; yet it might have been expected that the crown would maintain the whole troop, and I suppose that the king's pay did not go far enough.

John de Drokenesford was the controller, and Walter de Beauchamp was the steward of the household. Geoffrey de Geneville, who had already in 1282 acted as assistant to Norfolk, was now marshal in Norfolk's place; hence the strength of his troop beyond what one would expect of his status as a not very prominent marcher lord. The Earl of Warwick did not accompany his retinue, though his horse, one of the splendid 100 marc animals of the Beauchamp stud, was valued as if he were going to sail; he had fallen ill suddenly and died next year. Guy, his son and heir, led the retinue both now and next year. Thomas of Lancaster did not accompany his retinue, which was of unusual proportions, only two knights out of twenty-one lances. Tateshale, Gaunt, and Stafford, also Alan Plukenet's son and Robert de Tony, neither of whom had been yet knighted, and Miles Pichard, represented the rising generation. John de Kenesse, a knight of Holland, served as a mercenary with seventeen lances. Henry de Beaumont, a French mercenary, was doing his earliest service under a King of England, and afterwards he was a most invaluable soldier, fought at Falkirk and Bannockburn, Dupplin Moor and Halidon Hill, was probably a chief leader in the military reforms of Edward III, and married a Scottish heiress. Richard Siward and Simon Frazer were Scots, and three Welsh chieftains, Rhys Vychan and Gruffudd and Cynan ap Maredudd, were probably working out their pardon and redemption from captivity, being mounted on sorry nags of 3 to 7 marcs each.

The foot were very largely Welsh. The writs of summons only show that 2,000 were requisitioned from Cardiganshire and Carmarthenshire, and 750 from the march. The inventory gives us the names of twenty-three centenars from every part of Wales, five from Cardiganshire, one from Carmarthenshire, one from Builth, three from Powys, thirteen from North Wales and the Cantreds. But I doubt whether the first two countries sent a body 1,400 short; also other lords marchers than John Giffard may have produced men. Young Alan Plukenet and Robert de Tony with their nineteen *socii* probably led the other Welsh, thus raising the numbers of the centenars to forty-four, and the Welsh foot to 4,400. John de Merk probably had a corps from Chester; four *socii* from Shropshire may represent 400 men, and the four knights and twenty-seven valets of John de Berwick may represent 2,700 foot from other parts of England. Thus we have a possible total of 8,500 infantry. Hemingburgh[1] says that the French dared not attack Edward's army, because there were among them many archers, and not only the French who were their open enemy, but also their own allies the Flemings, had good cause to fear them, for they plundered the citizens of Ghent and Damme somewhat ruthlessly.

I venture to give my own idea of the signification of what passed in England during Edward's absence. We saw that Hemingburgh states that the Archbishop of Canterbury had been reconciled to the king, and appointed as chief adviser to the young Prince Edward, together with Reginald de Grey. But the former did not act in that capacity, for we find his name only in one of the writs of the time, and he doubtless went against the king's interests as soon as his back was turned. The chronicler's mention of Grey shows that he was regarded as the chief military member of the council; other members were the earls who remained in England—Cornwall, Surrey, Warwick (who had intended to go to Flanders but was invalided), and Oxford—John Giffard, Henry de Percy,

[1] Vol. ii. p. 159.

Alan Plukenet, John Tregoz, John Lovel, Guncelin de Badlesmere, John de Cobham, Adam Gurdon, and certain clerics
and judges. It may be taken that all these men were loyal
to the crown; more than that, I suggest that such good
warriors were left in England on purpose that they might give
their military service in case the recalcitrant earls, who openly
were defiant and in arms, should become too overbearing,
for otherwise they would have gone on the king's service to
Flanders. Surrey and Percy were, however, in Scotland.
The first act of the council was to call to a *colloquium* at
Rochester some 220 knights and others by September 8;
they were to come with arms and horses[1]. Very many of
them were quite unknown men; others were veterans of the
Welsh wars, such as Camville, Pointz, and Pipard; just a few
were obviously men of the Hereford and Norfolk faction, such
as John de Segrave and Edmund de Mortimer. Ostensibly,
the purpose of the *colloquium* was to deal with the defence of
the coast against a possible French descent, but one is tempted
to read between the lines, and surmise that armed resistance to
the two earls was discussed. However, the ostensible purpose
was alone in evidence, and Guncelin de Badlesmere and John
de Cobham were commissioned to lay plans for the defence
before the meeting[2]. Meanwhile most of the members of the
council were, by writs of September 5, summoned to London
for September 30[3]; Grey did not receive a writ because he
would have been at court and engaged in sending out the
writs to others. On September 9—that is to say, the day after
the Rochester *colloquium*, and therefore probably in pursuance
of some plan there determined—other writs were sent to the
Earl of Arundel and some forty men of inferior rank to come
on September 22 with arms and horses, but no rendezvous
is given[4]; Arundel, there can be little doubt, was loyal.
On the same day the Archbishop of Canterbury, various other
ecclesiastics, Hereford and Norfolk themselves, John and
Nicholas de Segrave, John Lovel, Robert FitzRoger, Fulk
FitzWaryn, Robert de Tateshale, Edmund de Mortimer, and

---

[1] *Parl. Writs*, vol. i. p. 296.    [2] Ibid. p. 298.
[3] Ibid. p. 55.    [4] Ibid. p. 296.

Alan de la Zouche, were all summoned for September 30 to London[1] ; they were not told to come with arms and horses, and they would seem to represent the party of opposition. This 'Parliament' was then put off to October 6, for on September 15 two knights from each shire were summoned to London at the new date to receive their copies of the *Confirmatio Cartarum*, which the council had clearly advised the prince to issue.

But here comes a new fact. On September 16 a completely fresh series of orders was issued. The Earls of Cornwall, Warwick (who had recovered from his illness), and Oxford, Giffard, Tateshale, FitzWaryn, FitzReginald, Wake, Brian, Camville, and others, were to appear on the very same October 6 at London in arms[2]. The list is remarkable. The name of Marmaduke de Twenge is included, but we know that he was in Scotland, and this fact alone is important. Tateshale and FitzWaryn are clearly now recognized as being loyal, for their inclusion in a previous list pointed to previous suspicions of their loyalty, and it would be repugnant to our ideas to find Tateshale arrayed on the side of the recalcitrants against his old comrade Grey, and against the son of the king whom he had served so well in Wales. Next appears a long list of sheriffs in the case of some counties, special arrayers in the case of others, who were to bring knights and valets at the royal wages[3] ; the rendezvous was to be London, and the date October 6. Here is no question of coast defence. Cobham and Badlesmere were the Kentish arrayers, and one does not bring armed men from Kent to London to protect the coast. Neither was the purpose to send a reinforcement to Edward in Flanders, for never is London the point of concentration for a foreign expedition, but invariably a Cinque Port or Southampton or Portsmouth is chosen. It remains that no explanation will suit these writs except that Grey and his fellow councillors intended to fight the two earls and their party, possibly, or indeed probably, intending at the same time to issue honestly the *Confirmatio Cartarum* as they promised.

But events were moving very fast. William Wallace was

---

[1] *Parl. Writs*, vol. i. p. 56, &c.    [2] Ibid. pp. 56, 300.    [3] Ibid. p. 299.

in arms. Edward had known this before he set sail for Flanders, had made light of the revolt, for indeed few prominent Scots joined Wallace, and had merely ordered Surrey to raise the soldiers of counties beyond the Trent. It may be remarked, by the way, that with so many knights and troopers in Flanders, others in arms with the two earls or against the two earls, and so much excitement being attached to the political question in England, not many men were available to send against Wallace. The usual myth of an army of many thousands serving in Scotland may be quite safely disregarded; however, Surrey with the troops at his disposal—Percy, Huntercumbe, Twenge, and Cressingham being the only prominent bannerets whom we know to have been with him—was beaten at Stirling bridge on September 11, just at the moment when Grey and the council were thinking of enrolling troops for a civil war. The disaster was known in London before September 28, for on that day the Sheriff of Notts and Derby was ordered to send his knights and valets up to the north, in place of sending them to London by October 6. The sequel is notorious. Hereford and Norfolk appeared at the city gates with 1,500 mounted followers and a choice infantry—the number is enormous, and nearly as large as the total of cavalry which fought next year at Falkirk, but Hemingburgh's figures always are big[1]; they refused to enter until they were allowed to secure the gates with their own men, and finally received the *Confirmatio* on October 10. It can hardly be disputed that on the one hand England was saved from the bloodshed of civil war by a serious defeat in Scotland, and on the other hand that the crisis in England, nearly ending in civil war, prevented the council from at once moving to nip in the bud the equally serious crisis caused by Wallace. I suggest that neither is English constitutional history studied aright without some acknowledgement of Wallace's influence upon the charters, nor is the tale of Scottish independence adequate unless it be remembered that an English constitutional question prevented an immediate revenge.

[1] Vol. ii. p. 147.

The action of the council was, if we consider the difficulty of the circumstances, very creditable. It was clearly on their advice that the young prince consented to confirm the charters, and the same day, October 10, on their intercession, he promised to intercede in his turn with the king his father to reinstate them in his favour [1]. All their partisans were also to be pardoned; John de Ferrars alone is mentioned, but we cannot be far wrong in adding at least Nicholas de Segrave, Edmund de Mortimer, and John de Hastings as attached to Hereford, and John Lovel, John de Segrave, Robert FitzRoger, and Alan de la Zouche as attached to Norfolk. A previous list of names may represent those who first were thought to be of the party, but we saw that Tateshale and FitzWaryn returned to the royal cause, if indeed they had ever left it; John Lovel was of the council, and ought to have been loyal. Both loyalists and recalcitrants now set to work to take in hand the war in the north, for Wallace had been raiding in Cumberland and Northumberland, pretty severely too. At first orders were sent to Robert de Clifford, Brian Fitzalan, and other north-country magnates to rally to the Earl of Surrey, while the Sheriffs of Yorkshire, Notts, and Derby were to send up the troops that they had enrolled in view of a civil war [2]. But Surrey and Henry de Percy had evacuated all the positions in Scotland, in fact they had come down to London and were present at the pardoning of the two earls. Therefore Clifford and Fitzalan were on October 18 commissioned to defend the marches as best they could with local help, while preparations were made for getting up to Newcastle a very large force of both horse and foot. Meanwhile the king was calling for reinforcements to join him in Flanders, so that the council must have been hard pressed to find enough men.

Some 29,000 foot were called out from Wales, Chester, Shropshire, and the northern counties, to be at Newcastle early in December [3]. In his Welsh wars Edward had established the principle of fighting through the winter. But

---

[1] *Parl. Writs*, vol. i. pp. 61, 62.     [2] Ibid. p. 300.

[3] Ibid. p. 304.

the service was evidently unpopular, the levies came in very slowly, and new writs were issued fixing the end of January for a rendezvous, again at Newcastle. Ralph Fitzwilliam, who was temporarily in command while awaiting the return of the Earl of Surrey, had with him for the last fortnight of December and all the month of January not more than 2,000 local foot, fifteen mounted and sixty foot crossbowmen, and six north-country knights with forty troopers[1]. The bulk of the foot arrived in the first week of February, some of the contingents having taken two or three weeks to march up. By this time the Earl of Surrey and many other barons were at Newcastle. Thomas de Roshale brought in 1,700 foot from Shropshire, the Earl of Hereford *duxit secum* 120 Welsh of Brecknock, the Earl of Norfolk similarly 100 from Strigul, and Arundel 600 from Powys and Clun. Percy had 1,400 northerners, besides the previous 2,000. Yorkshire, Lancashire, and Westmorland produced 10,000 more. But the men of Chester and Snowdonia were late, and Surrey was instructed to advance without them; 3,000 Cestrians and 4,000 Welsh were paid for the march out and home again without fighting. The total of infantry without them comes to 16,000 on February 9; new relays brought the figure up to 21,500, but soon it dropped to 18,000 and to 15,000 again, and in March to 10,000 and 5,000. Meanwhile the great lords, both the recalcitrants and the loyalists, joined Surrey's army. A force of 500 horse was raised in December in the king's pay; of these Surrey himself raised 100, Norfolk 130, Hereford 90, Gloucester 100, Warwick 30, and Percy 50, and they were authorized to levy 200 more if necessary[2]. The Earl of Arundel and William le Latimer were also in pay with twenty-seven knights and 110 troopers[3], together with 110 independent troopers ranked as *socii*, who were mostly in units

[1] *Exch. Acc.* $\frac{7}{2}$.

[2] Bain, vol. ii, no. 1044; taken from *Exch. Memoranda*, 26 Edw. I, m. 106. Mr. Bain has made a slip, a very rare thing for him; December, 26 Edw. I, is December, 1297, not 1298. Ralph de Monthermer was now Earl of Gloucester, having married Joan Plantagenet, widow of the late earl.

[3] *Exch. Acc.* $\frac{7}{2}$, as before.

of ten or twelve; Arundel's own troop was exactly forty lances, and two of his knights were John de Seton and John de Kirkpatrick. Thus the cavalry total comes to 750 lances at least. The foot crossbowmen were reinforced up to 250 men, the largest number that I have met at one place during this reign, except just at the very outset of the first war of 1277.

The earl advanced to the border and relieved Roxburgh. Then he fell back to Berwick, and so passed the remainder of February and all March. Beyond the relief of the English besieged in these two castles, the Scots retreating and declining battle, he effected absolutely nothing, and Edward landing from Flanders in the middle of March sent orders that the army should be withdrawn. During April and May 1,000 to 2,000 foot, 50 to 100 horse, remained in pay on the defensive. Guy of Warwick, having returned with Edward, immediately went straight up to Berwick for garrison work with twenty-five paid lances.

I have given these details because this is the largest army of which I have found record, 21,500 foot exclusive of the 7,000 who were turned back; and though that high total was maintained only for a few days, 18,000 on an average served for over a month, and 10,000 for six weeks. But large as it was, it was equally feeble. Beyond the 1,700 men of Shropshire and 820 Welsh of the march, it must have been composed of men of a very raw type, extremely unwieldy, and doubtless reduced day by day by diseases which would have been rampant in the early spring in crowded quarters. Edward called back Surrey from his advance from some such cause as the inherent rottenness of the troops. He planned to make a better advance with better troops in the summer, and he was issuing the writs to summon new foot just when Surrey was dismissing the last of his rabble.

As this new army was destined to win the victory of Falkirk, the writs of summons must be quoted, there being unluckily no extant pay-roll[1]. Edward requisitioned from—

---

[1] *Parl. Writs*, vol. i. p. 312.

| | Foot. | | Foot. |
|---|---|---|---|
| North Wales . . . . | 2,000 | Cardigan and Carmarthen . | 2,300 |
| Four Cantreds . . . | 700 | Cemaes . . . . . | 200 |
| Anglesey . . . . . | 500 | Brecknock . . . . | 400 |
| Earl of Surrey's lands . . | 400 | Kidwelly and Monmouth . . | 300 |
| Chirk and Powys . . . | 600 | Glamorgan . . . . | 1,000 |
| Edmund de Mortimer's lands . | 600 | Abergavenny . . . . | 400 |
| Builth . . . . . | 500 | Gower . . . . . | 300 |
| Matilda de Mortimer's . . | 300 | Total | 10,500 |

One thousand English were requisitioned from Chester, and one thousand from Lancashire, but not a man from Shropshire, doubtless because Thomas de Roshale and his men had served for full two months in the spring. It is highly probable that Hemingburgh was quite right when he wrote that practically all the infantry of this army was Welsh; 10,500 out of 12,500 would be *quasi omnes*. The writs were repeated six or seven weeks later, when a second time exactly the same number of men were summoned, and as the two sets of writs are on different rolls, patent and close, one can assume that no others were issued. From the horse-inventory I cannot find that any English millenars were present from other counties, except Peter de Tadcaster, who may have had some Yorkshiremen, but the same inventory shows that he was not up till after the battle of Falkirk. Robert l'Engleys, the Westmorland millenar of the spring of this year, was now one of Clifford's knights. On the other hand, John de Merk and Peter de Dunwich, who commanded the foot of Chester and Lancaster on other occasions, are both found on the roll. So also are John de Havering, who had four knights and twenty valets, and may be taken as commanding the North Welsh, he being still justiciar ; William de Felton, Constable of Beaumaris, with thirteen valets, similarly commanding the men of Anglesey and perhaps the Cantreds ; and Robert de Tony, with two knights and fifteen valets, who, having been knighted since the campaign in Flanders, may have led the South Welsh. Roger de Mortimer of Chirk, Hugh de Mortimer, whom we have already met as a subordinate officer of Robert de Tibotot in Cardiganshire, Thomas Earl of Lancaster, and other marchers and earls who were in the cavalry of the army, would have detached some of their followers to lead their respective contingents of marchers. We may assume that the 250 crossbows of Surrey's late army were available, while the mounted mercenaries of Gascony would have been accompanied by another corps of foot crossbowmen, say 250 or 300 strong.

The cavalry rolls [1] are more than usually interesting. The horse are in greater numbers than in Flanders, but fall very far short of the 7,000 that Hemingburgh would persuade us were present. Many of the retinues had been reconstituted since the king had returned from Flanders, new knights and troopers being enrolled under the barons and bannerets of that army; new retinues were added, and several young men had been knighted in the interval besides Robert de Tony.

|  | Knights. | Troopers. | Total. |
|---|---|---|---|
| Aymer de Valence [2], with Thomas and Maurice de Berkeley . | 8 | 41 | 50 |
| Hugh le Despenser . . . | 10 | 39 | 50 |
| Thomas, Earl of Lancaster, and Henry, his brother . . | 9 | 34 | 45 |
| Robert de Clifford . . . | 8 | 26 | 35 |
| Walter de Beauchamp. . . | 5 | 21 | 27 |
| John de Havering . . . | 4 | 20 | 25 |
| John de Drokenesford . . . | 3 | 20 | 24 |
| Ralph Pipard . . . . | 3 | 17 | 21 |
| Roger de Mortimer . . . | 3 | 17 | 21 |
| Robert FitzPain . . . . | 4 | 15 | 20 |
| John de la Mare . . . . | 4 | 13 | 18 |
| William de Leyburn . . . | 3 | 13 | 17 |
| Robert de Tony . . . . | 2 | 14 | 17 |
| John de Boutetort . . . | 4 | 12 | 17 |
| Robert de Monthaut . . . | 3 | 12 | 16 |
| Nicholas de Audley . . . | 3 | 12 | 16 |
| Hugh Bardolf . . . . | 3 | 11 | 15 |
| Adam de Welles . . . | 2 | 12 | 15 |
| John de Benstede . . . | 2 | 12 | 15 |
| William de Felton . . . | — | 13 | 14 |
| Peter de Chanent . . . | 3 | 9 | 13 |
| John Tregoz . . . . | 2 | 10 | 13 |
| William de Cantilupe . . . | 2 | 9 | 12 |
| Eustache de Hacche . . . | 2 | 9 | 12 |

[1] I have quoted these rolls in the *English Historical Review* (January, 1898), but on looking them through more carefully I find that the figures must be slightly altered, yet not so much as to alter the argument that the force falls short of the traditional total.

[2] *Exch. Acc.* $\frac{6}{39}$ and $\frac{6}{40}$.

| | Knights. | Troopers. | Total. |
|---|---|---|---|
| John de Beauchamp . . . | 2 | 9 | 12 |
| Hugh de Courtenay . . . | 2 | 9 | 12 |
| Ralph Basset . . . . | 2 | 9 | 12 |
| Thomas de Furnival . . . | 2 | 7 | 10 |
| John d'Engayne . . . | 2 | 7 | 10 |
| William de Grandison . . | 2 | 7 | 10 |
| John de Rivers . . . . | 1 | 8 | 10 |
| Henry de Beaumont . . . | 2 | 7 | 10 |

There were still several quite small retinues, many of them belonging to knights of the household who would be on staff duty, or, if present in battle, would be probably grouped together. The unattached lances come to 280, many of them being the *valetti regis* or troopers of the household.

There was a Gascon corps in the army, twenty-five knights and eighty-one valets, presumably mounted crossbowmen as in 1283, of whom rather less than half were up in time for the battle. The most noticeable name is that of Amanieu d'Albret, whose house was not represented in 1283, and who now brought two knights and thirteen valets. The Captal de Buch had a small retinue of one knight, Oliver de Lafitte, and five valets. Reynaud de St. Quintin was a Flemish mercenary with two valets. We know that the men stopped some little time in England, and when they went home they left their debts behind them, whether really straitened for means or defrauding their tradesmen we do not know [1]. The captal, for instance, left £37 unpaid, of which he owed 42s. to his landlord, 8s. to his chandler, and 6s. to his barber. But, on the other hand, I would remark that all the mercenaries, the Gascons, the Fleming, and Henry de Beaumont, were in the thick of the fight at Falkirk, losing several horses there besides other horses elsewhere, which shows that they were put to good use as serviceable soldiers, even if in money matters they were somewhat lax.

The following figures are as accurate as I can make them by careful counting :—

---

[1] Delpit, *Documents Français en Angleterre*, nos. 56-8.

|  | At Falkirk. | Joined later. |
|---|---|---|
| Bannerets and knights . . . . . | 214 | 17 |
| Troopers of retinues . . . . . . | 642 | 49 |
| Unattached lances . . . . . . | 258 | 26 |
| Gascon knights . . . . . . | 10 | 15 |
| Gascon troopers . . . . . . | 32 | 49 |
|  | 1,156 | 156 |
|  | 156 |  |
|  | 1,312 |  |

Thus the English cavalry, mounted officers of the foot included, were just over 1,200 of all ranks in pay. I take it that all these were in the king's main army, and not on garrison duty.

When we come to examine the unpaid quotas, our only evidence being the lists of letters of protection in the Scotch roll, we cannot be sure that we are not reckoning some troops which may have been elsewhere. Many soldiers had protections in the spring which were renewed in the summer, others had them in the spring or the summer only, and some, as we know from the inventory, were too late to take part in the battle. I have made out the following list, taking all those who were attached to important retinues, and it must remain a doubtful point whether all were in the main army :—

| The Earls[1]. | | Bannerets. | |
|---|---|---|---|
| Norfolk . . . . | 50 lances. | Latimer . . . . | 10 lances. |
| Monthermer . . . | 46 ,, | Wake . . . . | 10 ,, |
| Surrey . . . . | 46 ,, | Tateshale . . . . | 7 ,, |
| Angus . . . . | 22 ,, | Fitzalan . . . . | 5 ,, |
| Hereford . . . | 14 ,, | Segrave . . . . | 4 ,, |
| Lincoln . . . . | 14 ,, | Grey . . . . | 3 ,, |
| Warwick . . . | 13 ,, | Ferrars . . . . | 3 ,, |
| Oxford . . . . | 12 ,, | D'Eyvile . . . . | 3 ,, |
| Arundel . . . . | 4 ,, | Bruce[2] . . . . | 2 ,, |
|  | 221 |  | 47 |

[1] *Scotch Roll*, 26 Edw. I.

[2] 'Robert le Brus dom Vallis Anandi.' This was a war against the Scottish patriot, Wallace. The Earl of Carrick wrote early in July, three weeks before the battle, requesting that letters of protection might be renewed to three knights.

The Bishop of Durham had protections for twelve followers; Brian de Jay, Master of the Temple, for two; John of Brittany and John de St. John, lately returned from Gascony, for one each; and amongst others, Peter Corbet, Walter de Huntercumbe, and Edmund, Baron of Stafford, for themselves only. With Norfolk were Robert FitzRoger, John Lovel, John de Segrave, and John and Reginald de Cobham; Percy was with Surrey; Ferrars and Nicholas de Segrave were with Hereford, thus raising his small troop to decent strength, and Latimer with Arundel; Tateshale with his son may, as in 1295, have been with Lincoln. Grey had been called up from Chester, as the services of so useful a soldier were not wanted there, and he gave his justiciarship over to Richard de Mascy. He must have been drawing pay as he always did, and therefore I suggest that he was in a separate command on the border or along the lines of communications, in which case he would draw pay and have his horses valued by some special officials. In the case of the great feudatories the question is different. Though we have seen that the king's young nephews, Thomas and Henry of Lancaster, and his cousin, Aymer de Valence, were in the paid cavalry, and though a cry had been raised that all troops taken over to Flanders must be paid, yet at home the earls still stood on their dignity to do feudal service only. Loyalists and recalcitrants were alike in serving as a privilege rather than a duty. There is nothing to show how far the quotas actually corresponded to the letters of protection. The first three quotas seem to be strong enough. Gilbert de Umfraville, Earl of Angus, was not likely to have had a stronger troop than twenty-two lances. But the retinues of Hereford and Lincoln must be raised, probably by the inclusion of some of the bannerets and their men, as suggested above; Guy of Warwick, who by his father's death was now earl, must have had as many as twenty-five or twenty-seven lances, as in Flanders or recently at Berwick. Arundel and the bishop are clearly inadequately represented, but twelve lances formed a fair troop for Oxford. Making a calculation to allow for the retinues of John of Brittany and Brian de Jay, and the extra strength of these earls who had few protections, and supposing that some of the bannerets had their independent troops not under the earls, we might assign 1,000 lances. Or, to make a large margin, let us say 1,100, so as to give, with the 1,300 paid horse, 2,400 in all. Not all the number was necessarily at Falkirk.

But before the army was concentrated in Scotland the constitutional question was again discussed[1]. Hereford and Norfolk would not promise to serve until the king had once more bound himself to observe the charters. Edward was unwilling to pledge his word again, as he had already signed in Flanders. There was thus a deadlock, until the loyal earls pledged their word for the king. Then the feudal quotas were put in motion. I have no new light to throw on the campaign or battle. I have maintained throughout that Hemingburgh's figures are too high, and to follow him literally we must assume that Wallace's Scots must have been some 300,000 strong. Common sense tells us to reject them all. But this does not in the least affect our belief in his accuracy as regards the tactics of Edward in the battle, for his account is too precise in details to be passed over. Geoffrey le Baker of Swinbroke is an historian of the battles of Edward III of the same type; he gives impossible figures for Halidon Hill, for instance, but he is by far the best historian of military matters of his time, simply because he is precise in his statements. From Hemingburgh, viewed as a better historian than statistician, we have a fine picture of the advance of the cavalry ahead of the king and the foot, the leading brigade checked by a swamp and compelled to make a detour, the second brigade coming round on the right and so getting first into action, the Bishop of Durham trying to restrain the knights so as to allow the king to come up, the impertinent retort of Ralph Basset, the consequent repulse from the four great circles or schiltroms of Scottish pikes. Then the foot were brought up, probably a few hundred English and Gascon crossbowmen, many Welsh, and a couple of thousand English archers, who riddled the circles until the horsemen charged in successfully. It is a picture of a successful

---

[1] Hemingburgh, vol. ii. pp. 173–80.

Bannockburn, the foot being utilized and not wasted in the rear. From our inventory we know which troops of the paid cavalry suffered most. Henry de Beaumont lost his own horse and three more out of a troop of ten, Clifford lost eight out of thirty-five; these two were again comrades in arms in 1314, and were signally unsuccessful on the eve of Bannockburn. Eustace de Hacche lost five horses, Robert de Scales three, Robert FitzPain five, John de la Mare four, John de Boutetorte five, the Earl of Lancaster eleven out of his big troop of forty-five, Hugh le Despenser eight, and Aymer de Valence five out of fifty, one of the latter being Maurice de Berkeley's horse. John de Merk and William de Felton, whom I have taken to be millenars, lost each his own mount. The royal troopers also suffered considerably. In all 111 horses were killed, much the greater proportion being those of the household. But Ralph Basset, in spite of his boasting, had not a man dismounted, which looks as if he did not try to charge home.

Yet was the campaign of 1298 unsuccessful. Though Wallace's force was cut up at Falkirk, another body of Scots crossed into Cumberland to make a diversion, and Edward had to come back to Carlisle in September. Each year up to 1303 the same facts are seen: there may be a summer campaign, more or less successful in appearance, but the English army cannot keep the field in the autumn and winter, while in 1299 and 1302 there is not even a summer campaign. Scotland would never be conquered until the same policy could be followed as in Wales. The war must be fought to a finish without intermission. This Edward certainly intended to do. He brought up the courts of the King's Bench and the Exchequer to York, so that he might fight on and yet have at hand the means to carry on the ordinary business of the central government. But many causes combined to hinder him.

It is quite a commonplace of history to contrast the tenacity of the Scot with the alternate fury and despondency of the Welshman, also to find the tenacious spirit of patriotism in the commons rather than in the nobles of Scotland. The 'humiliating record' of the actions of Bruce is undoubted[1]. Yet the treachery of the Earl of Carrick, of Wishart of Glasgow, of Simon Fraser and others, embarrassed Edward more than open enmity, and behind the opportunism of the leaders—a less contentious word than treachery—was the unbroken national spirit of a people first aroused by Wallace. In contrast we remember that there was no really national resistance in Wales, and the cause of Gwynedd was lost with the death of Llewelyn. Then the geographical problem presents itself. The strongly marked natural features of Snowdonia, deep and narrow valleys, commanding ranges or clumps of mountains, seemed to defy attack; yet the preliminary difficulties being once overcome by an energetic king, relying on the resources of an England unvexed by civil strife, which resources were certainly not overstrained, an organized army, an efficient transport, a fleet co-operating and securing the estuaries so as to enable him to strike up stream, the Welsh were at last penned in and starved. The area of the main resistance in North Wales was small, and the configuration of the coast gave to the English a chance to surround Snowdonia, then to dominate it, when conquered, by a few castles in commanding situations. On the other hand, in the lowlands of Scotland the preliminaries seemed to be easier, the valleys being broader and the ranges of moorland less steep. Edward could easily penetrate into Scotland, but then the difficulties began, for he could not drive his enemy into a corner by seizing a few strategic points. The invaders, not the defenders, were starved in the long run. The control of the coast helped him less, and thus he had to secure a very large number of castles inland at long distances from the sea. Much larger garrisons were required for these than for the Welsh castles. So the financial question became serious, for both men and provisions had to be brought from England[2]. The Scots would not yield, no revenue was forthcoming from the districts apparently conquered, and the cheap method of farming the country, just as Giffard held Builth

---

[1] Sir Herbert Maxwell's *Bruce*, p. 121.
[2] Bain, nos. 1084, 1115, 1153, 1223.

and Tibotot Carmarthenshire and Cardiganshire, was inapplicable. The resources of England were too severely strained to endure the steady drain in men and money, whereas the revenues of Wales sufficed to maintain the castles in peace, and the money voted in 1283 covered the expenses of the longest Welsh war. In 1282-3 Edward fought for fifteen months, in 1294-5 for eight months without intermission, except when he paused for a moment while waiting for reinforcements; his one continued effort in Scotland was that of 1303-4.

Also he was now distracted from Scotland by his embarrassing relations with the Pope and with France, and by his wish to recover what he had lost in Gascony. But what weakened him most seriously was the action of his nobles; indeed this was the main cause of his delay in conquering the Scots. There had been no gradual absorption of a wide belt of march during the two centuries since Hastings. Thus he had no energetic race of lords marchers on whom he could rely, who would fight as the other marchers fought Llewelyn, for their own profit rather than as a duty owed to the crown of England, and who would produce relays of friendlies to act as an efficient infantry, side by side with the levies of the border counties of England. The English barons had always been ready for a Welsh war in summer or winter, unless we except the alleged treachery of the Earl of Gloucester in collusion with Rhys ap Maredudd; they knew that Llewelyn alone benefited by civil strife in England, and both marchers and feudal tenants who held no march, Montfortians and royalists, served in Wales as they remembered Lewes and Evesham. But the barons who were backward in fighting the Scots either were of a new generation which knew not the lesson of the Montfortian troubles, or else, as in the case of Norfolk and Hereford, had their peculiar grievances growing out of the Welsh wars, and refused to serve in a fresh series of wars in Scotland without a definite guarantee. The bannerets of the professional type, Huntercumbe, St. John, Latimer, and others, were ready to serve, but Edward could not make an army from their retinues alone when the great feudatories were recalcitrant, though they sufficed to occupy the castles. Not only Norfolk and Hereford, not only Norfolk after Hereford's death towards the end of 1298, but a strong party of opposition, of which Norfolk was the spokesman and from which he derived his power, called for the reconfirmation of the charters. Two earls defying Edward on their own resources would have been soon crushed, and the existence of an organized opposition is clear. Lastly, on turning to the levies of infantry we must acknowledge that Edward had very poor material. He did not again, after Falkirk, bring up large forces from Wales and the march, Chester and Shropshire, for obvious reasons. The men of Cumberland and Northumberland were not very efficient for an invasion of Scotland, for they were afraid to leave their homes lest they should be devastated by retaliating raiders. The men of Durham and Yorkshire constantly mutinied and deserted. Only the foot of Lancashire, small numbers from Derbyshire and Notts, occasionally smaller numbers from Chester and Shropshire, seem to have been properly organized and good fighters, and willing to keep the field for more than a few days; and these are the counties from which we have always expected to find good material because of their earlier Welsh experiences.

All these causes operated together against Edward, from the September of 1298 onwards. Doubtless it was advisable to send home the Welsh and border infantry, but the Durham contingent simply deserted [1]. Norfolk and Hereford professed to be angry because they had not been consulted concerning the bestowal of certain land, and at Carlisle, whither the English army had retired, they set their faces against an autumn campaign, alleging the great fatigue of the war and the loss in men and horses [2]. Edward could not insist upon their remaining in arms, for their forty days had expired. Moreover they had already tasted the sweets of power, they cared nothing for the war, but were glad to find that Edward's eagerness to unite England and Scotland put a weapon into

[1] G. T. Lapsley, *County Palatine of Durham*, p. 128.
[2] Hemingburgh, vol. ii. p. 182.

their hands by making him dependent on them and their party. He gave way, and on September 24 and 26 ordered a new muster at Carlisle on June 6, 1299[1]. He himself yet lingered on the frontier, but there was no fighting this winter, except when raiding parties were organized from the castles held by the English, Edinburgh and Stirling, Berwick and Roxburgh, being the most important.

Edward did not summon this army for 1299 by formally feudal writs; he only called the earls and certain great tenants on their allegiance, there being nothing to prevent any from taking his pay, and volunteers were called for from the £40 class *a nos gages*[2]. However the army was never mustered. The lords would not march until Edward had once more confirmed the charters, and this he was reluctant to do, as it would be tantamount to his confessing that they were in the right in doubting his word previously given. Then he compromised by a confirmation with a saving clause *salvo iure coronae*. Was he dishonest in putting off the opposition in his wish to save the royal prerogative? Hardly so, for he was contending for something higher than the recalcitrants. He had admitted in 1295 the principle that 'what touches all should be approved by all'; he had accepted the confirmation of the charters by his son in his name in 1297, and had allowed the loyalists to pledge their word for him in 1298 before the army marched northwards. He was undeniably in earnest so far. What he stood out for when he added the saving clause was the retention of a supreme power, a power which could be used to dominate Parliament or a clique of barons for the national good. That certain barons merely formed a clique to assert their own interests, without any care for higher interests—union for instance—is proved by the events of these few years, and by his son's unhappy reign. There was no such thing as public opinion, and the crown alone could safeguard the nation by maintaining its prerogative as against a baronage, whose specious cry of 'Magna Carta in danger' virtually meant 'we wish to dominate England.' But unfortunately, as said above, his very eagerness to conquer and

---

[1] *Parl. Writs*, vol. i. p. 317.　　　　[2] Ibid.

unite Scotland was a weapon in their hands. Four times in
the course of the year the muster of the army was postponed [1].
The year was lost and the castle of Stirling fell, a strange
sequel to so striking a victory as Falkirk. Then Edward
gave way further, and reconfirmed the charters without the
saving clause. An army of some kind was got together in
December. We have no direct evidence of its numbers, and
only know that 16,000 foot were summoned from the northern
counties, Derbyshire and Notts, Shropshire and Staffordshire,
but none from Wales and Chester. As it was winter, Edward
ordered his officers to promise that the men 'should receive
such courtesy, beyond their customary pay, that they would
acknowledge themselves satisfied with his treatment of them.'
But the season was late, the men deserted *en masse*, and
letters were sent out to the sheriffs ordering the arrest and
imprisonment of those who could not trust their king [2].
Worse than the behaviour of the foot was the open revolt
of all the military tenants of Durham, who told their bishop
that they were bound by their tenure only to serve in defence,
and could not be forced to cross their boundaries, the Tyne
and the Tees, in a war of aggression [3]; Ralph de Neville and
John FitzMarmaduke de Twenge are named as the ring-
leaders. A second time Edward had to forgo his winter
plans. He was simply forced to another surrender, and on
December 30 he ordered a feudal muster for June 24, 1300,
at Carlisle, the writs being issued in the most formal manner.
In March he issued the *Articuli super Cartas*.

It is not likely to be an accidental coincidence that a
summons for strictly feudal service was made about the same
time as Edward's surrender of the saving clause. Most of
his professional captains being on duty in Scotland in the
army of occupation, he had to call for feudal service to create
an army of invasion, which was just what Norfolk and his
party wanted. This was the first full feudal summons since
1282 [4], one set of writs going to the earls and individual
tenants, a second to clerics, and a third to the sheriffs, who

---

[1] *Parl. Writs*, vol. i. pp. 321-6.     [2] Ibid. pp. 329, 339.
[3] Lapsley, loc. cit.     [4] *Parl. Writs*, vol. i. p. 327.

were to raise quotas from the lands of ladies, of wards, and of the lesser tenants. Edward urgently demanded that the quotas should be larger than what was customary. A scutage was subsequently imposed, though it was disregarded as much as those of the first two Welsh wars. However, Edward still claimed his right to summon also the £40 class to serve for pay[1]. In summoning foot he directed the sheriffs and special commissioners to punish the late mutineers, authorizing imprisonment for the December desertion and compulsion for the new levy; John de St. John and Robert FitzRoger were told off as chief superintendents of this work[2]. The number requisitioned was again 16,000, from the same counties as before except Shropshire. No foot was summoned from Wales and Chester; yet Richard de Mascy, who was the newly appointed Justiciar of Chester, John de Havering, who was now Justiciar of all Wales, Bogo de Knoville, apparently the latter's subordinate in South Wales, and Philip ap Howel, Constable of Builth since Giffard's death, were all directed to enlist troops for pay (*purchacer bone eide et convenable*).

I offer my calculations as to the number of both the horse and foot of this army, because it is the only army of all these years the strength of which in each arm can be calculated within reasonable limits, and because it can be compared with the army of Falkirk. Each comprised about 2,000 horse and 10,000 foot, more or less, which is therefore the approximately normal strength of an Edwardian force towards the end of his reign. This admitted, even if there were no other arguments, the legend of the 40,000 horse and 60,000 foot of Bannockburn becomes the merest poetic figment.

The only document concerning the cavalry is a horse-inventory of the household[3]. There were nineteen bannerets, attended by an aggregate of 243 lances, giving an average of thirteen to each banner. Knights bachelors of the household, arrayers and arrayed of the £40 class—Hugh de St. Philibert had five knights and twenty-one troopers of this class and the class below it—and horse drawn from garrisons in Scotland,

---

[1] *Parl. Writs*, vol. i. p. 330.  [2] Ibid. pp. 340–3.

[3] *Exch. Acc.* $\frac{8}{23}$.

amounted to thirty-eight knights and 121 troopers. Troopers of the household and *socii* who came in small groups from the counties gave 120 independent lances. The total was 522. Now, in a celebrated poem on the siege of Caerlaverock [1], a professed eye-witness gives a gross total of 3,000 lances under eighty-seven banners; but if the above-mentioned nineteen and the king's own banners are deducted, the remaining 2,478 horse under sixty-seven banners would be at the excessively high average of thirty-seven to a banner. A quite reasonably high average of twenty-two would give a total of 1,474, and adding on the 522 of the household we reach approximately 2,000. It is always to be carried in mind, when we read mediaeval history, that eye-witnesses may be accurate in other respects but have an invariable knack of exaggerating figures. Next one has to doubt whether all the bannerets were in the main army during the whole of the short campaign. Thus, the poet says that Robert de Clifford was at the siege, yet in the horse-inventory we find only one of his knights and two valets registered; the twenty-two horses of Walter de Huntercumbe were valued a fortnight after Caerlaverock fell. Probably the 2,000 horse were serving not all in one place, but would represent the whole army of invasion in different parts of Scotland, irrespective of the troops who still remained in the garrisons after some of these latter had come to join the king. I have purposely reckoned a fairly high average to each banner because of the previously mentioned summons of the king for quotas above the ordinary, and so the eighty-seven may have given nearly the same total of lances as the whole force at Falkirk. There were four brigades; the first, under the Earl of Lincoln, the young Earl of Hereford as constable, and John de Segrave doing the marshal's work for Norfolk, who made some excuse for non-attendance, comprised sixteen banners; the second, under the Earl of Surrey, the Earl of Warwick, and Aymer de Valence, fourteen banners; the king's main body of thirty-four banners included those of John of Brittany, John of Bar, the Count of Laon, Amanieu d'Albret, Patrick of

[1] Edited by Sir Nicholas Harris Nicolas, esp. p. 62.

Dunbar and a few other Scots, Clifford, Despenser, Courtenay, and other well-known lords; the fourth was under Prince Edward, Thomas and Henry of Lancaster, the Earls of Gloucester and Arundel, and included the seven banners and 160 lances of the Bishop of Durham, who was not present in person.

The following is the table of the infantry[1]:—

| Summoned for June 24. | | At Carlisle, July 1. | At Caerlaverock, July 10–5. | Remaining in August. |
|---|---|---|---|---|
| 5,000 | Yorkshire. . . . | 2,912 | 2,932 | 919 |
| 2,000 | Lancs (Blackburn incl.) . | 267 | 1,327 | 1,026 |
| 2,000 | Cumberland . . . | | 940 | 346 |
| 3,000 | Notts and Derby . . | 386 | 900 | 289 |
| 3,000 | Northumberland . . | | 788 | 570 |
| 1,000 | Westmorland . . . | | 732 | 31 |
| 16,000 | | 3,565 | 7,619 | 3,181 |
| | Ireland . . . . | 306 | 361 | 306 |
| | Chester . . . . | | 307 | 167 |
| | Staffordshire . . | 137 | 216 | 188 |
| | 'Garrison' of Lochmaben | | 487 | 430 |
| | ,,      ,,   Roxburgh . | | 103 | 93 |
| | ,,      ,,   Berwick   . | | | 785 |
| | | 4,008 | 9,093 | 5,150 |

One sees that the counties furnished, a week late, less than a quarter of the proper complement originally requisitioned, and finally less than a half. A few further details from the roll will be found instructive. Only one thousand foot came from Lancashire, but they were arrayed in ten even companies of a hundred, and lost men by the ordinary wear and tear of war, not by desertion; the odd 327 came from Blackburnshire and were ranked separately. The three companies from Chester and the two from Staffordshire were also of even strength. The Westmorland men were at first raised in ten companies, but several being short of the full hundred were amalgamated; this county produced three-fourths of the complement, a comparatively high proportion, but the men soon fell away. The Yorkshiremen were over 2,000

[1] *Exch. Acc.* $\frac{8}{20}$.

short and were very irregularly arrayed, some companies
being seventy strong and some over 200. The crossbowmen
were twenty-eight in number, twenty-four in one body, three
from Lochmaben, one from Roxburgh. Clearly the crossbow
was losing its great reputation as a weapon in the field owing
to the proved superiority of the longbow at Falkirk, though
for many years yet to come it was retained for castle defence.
A dozen hobelars came from Ireland; the word was certainly
first used in Ireland for lightly equipped scouts, and was then
applied to similar light horse on the borders of Scotland
in these wars, for I can find no trace of it in any document
concerning Wales.

This army, having been slowly concentrated, and continuing
to receive reinforcements for some days after it quitted Carlisle, sat down before Caerlaverock on July 10. After a short
but fierce resistance, in which the besiegers lost considerably,
as both the poem and the horse-inventory admit, the castle
was surrendered on the second day; for, if some of Edward's
material in men was poor, his artillery was strong. Immediately desertions occurred among the foot, especially of
Yorkshire and Westmorland. On July 15 Edward was com-
plaining and ordering imprisonment[1]. He called for new
relays from Yorkshire, and the greater proportion of these in
turn deserted *en route*, the paymaster making a note on his
roll that certain centenars were in camp without any men,
*quia repatriaverant sine licencia*. It is pleasant in contrast to
notice the loyalty of the foot of Lancashire and Staffordshire.
One can understand why reinforcements had to be called up
from various castles, even from distant Berwick, weakening
their 'garrisons'—which word may be taken to refer to the
Scottish friendlies of the districts, for the garrisons proper of
these places were much smaller than the figures given above.
With foot dwindling to 5,000 Edward kept the field to the
end of August, marching through Galloway with Caerlaverock as his base. But the outcome of the campaign was
distinctly meagre, the capture of a single castle, and it can
hardly be wondered that he wrote angrily, *expedicio nostra*

---

[1] *Parl. Writs*, vol. i. pp. 343, 344.

*iam multipliciter extitit retardata.* The conquest of Scotland could not be achieved by a two months' holiday outing. In 1301 again there was a two months' campaign up the Tweed and across to Peebles and Glasgow, and the result was again meagre [1]. This army was 6,800 strong in infantry when it started, small contingents coming from Herefordshire, Worcestershire, and Gloucestershire, as well as from Shropshire and Derbyshire: 12,000 was the number summoned. The cavalry strength is unknown, and it was not a feudal muster for which a scutage could be demanded. The year 1302 was also blank.

Edward had clearly hoped for better results when, after his surrender on the charter question, he had called for feudal quotas beyond the customary strength. It seemed as if his abandonment of the saving clause and issue of the *Articuli* were useless. In a Parliament at Lincoln in the February of 1301 he gave away yet more [2], once again and finally confirmed the charters absolutely, and even dismissed his minister, Walter de Langton, to appease the insatiable opposition. Anthony Bek, on whom he had expected always to rely, having his own worries because the tenants of Durham obstinately protested against military service, turned suddenly against the king and declared the earls to have been in the right in their original demands. The Pope's claim that Scotland was a fief of the holy see, and therefore should not be invaded by the English, was of course pressed by the implacable Robert de Winchelsea. But the tide at last turned. The celebrated letter of the entire baronage to the Pope, controverting his claim to any authority over Scotland, marks the turning-point. Certain barons may have loved to worry Edward so as to gratify their spite or personal pride, but the body of barons was opposed to this outside interference. Bek was crushed by the confiscation of the temporalities of his see. In course of time even Winchelsea was exiled. But far more important was the case of Norfolk. In 1302 he surrendered his lands, his earldom, his marshal's office, receiving them all back from the king for lifetime only. What does

---

[1] Bain, no. 1229.          [2] Stubbs, vol. ii. p. 158.

this mean? Hemingburgh[1] gives what might be called an official excuse: the Bigod wished to spite his brother and spoil his inheritance, having no son to whom to hand on his honours, and so he begged the king to accept this temporary surrender. The explanation is paltry. The whole transaction has the air of being an act of vengeance on Edward's part. Before and after the death of Hereford there must have been a considerable party supporting Norfolk; that party being appeased by the way in which Edward had yielded on the matter of the charters, incensed at the papal interference, perhaps somewhat ashamed at having weakened Edward's military schemes, deserted the ringleader, and then Edward, finding Norfolk defenceless, simply stripped him of all his power. And so we come to the end of the career of a man whom we have traced through the Welsh wars and subsequent events, who was probably not remarkable for ability, but was by his office and the force of circumstances pushed to the front, and who has a more conspicuous place in history than many an abler man simply because he 'would neither go nor hang.' Lincoln, the gallant loyalist, had been since 1300 in Gascony. Surrey does not appear to have taken up arms again since that same year, and died in 1304. Thus all the great feudal warriors who faced Llewelyn have disappeared.

It only remains to add that 'in 1303 the true conquest of Scotland began[2].' A feudal army was collected and a scutage was afterwards claimed, but we have no evidence of the strength of the horse beyond an incomplete marshal's roll. Foot, at one time 5,500 strong, then 7,000, then 3,760, served the king from May to the end of August, but ready money ran short and he got into debt. Some of the pay due in September and October was not given till the next April[3].

---

[1] Vol. ii. p. 224.

[2] Professor Tout's phrase. I have largely profited by his twelfth and thirteenth chapters, adding the corroborative facts from Mr. Bain's *Calendar*, or from my own research in cases where the latter's abstract of some document seemed to me to be too scanty.

[3] Bain, no. 1599.

But at least he maintained some force during the winter, and next summer besieged and recaptured Stirling. The details of the siege train of thirteen great engines and the pontoons brought from Lynn are more interesting than those of the foot, which indeed present no special features. From our previous facts the constitution of an Edwardian army has been fairly illustrated. Scotland conquered at last, Wallace caught, a scheme of government introduced, France giving no more trouble, and the fortresses of Gascony restored to him, Edward seemed to have accomplished his life's work. The brawling bands of armed ruffians in England were suppressed after the issue of the writs of *trailbaston,* and one would not be far wrong in assuming that these men were chiefly the deserters from his armies in the Scottish wars. Had not Edward been near to his death Scotland might have been held as Wales was, Bruce's effort nipped in the bud, and the civil troubles and dishonours of the next reign avoided. But the tenacious Scot and the unpatriotic and assertive baron of England were alike too powerful for the second Edward. The cause of unionism was won only so far as the annexation of Wales was concerned.

# APPENDIX

## I

### NOTE ON THE DEATH OF LLEWELYN

WELSH tradition, I am assured, has always maintained and still maintains that Llewelyn was the victim of treachery. Who was the traitor? His brother David is vaguely accused, but not by any contemporary. The men of Builth, I am told, receive nowadays the odium for the deed according to the most widely spread tradition; but one looks in vain for confirmation, for on the one hand the Welsh of the surrounding country were so continually rising against the English, and on the other hand the town of Builth was so securely dominated by the strong castle which always defied attack, that neither countrymen nor townsmen deserve to be called traitors. The Welshman who pointed out the ford by which the English army got to the rear of Orewin bridge was but an individual traitor, and thus his action ought not to condemn any large class of Welshmen. It remains that the accusation against Edmund and Roger de Mortimer has most weight. It will be remembered that their father had been a Montfortian, and therefore an ally of Llewelyn, in 1258; he was a kinsman of the Welsh prince and was suspected of having connived at his conquest of Builth; then he went over to the royalist side, and was formally acquitted, after investigation, of the supposed connivance (see p. 25). Yet in 1281 he and Llewelyn entered into a compact for mutual support *contra omnes mortales cum toto posse tam tempore gwerre quam pacis*, but with this saving clause, *salva fidelitate in omnibus Domino Regi Anglie liberis et heredibus suis debita et penitus illesa* (Chapter House, *Liber A*, p. 364, back).

This alliance is a valuable fact as showing the intimacy between the cousins, in spite not only of the saving clause but also of the persistent way in which Mortimer fought against the Welsh in both wars. That Edmund and the younger Roger should call Llewelyn into Radnor after their father's death would doubtless seem to him to be quite natural.

My attention has been called to a passage in the *Annales Londinienses* (*Chronicles of Edward I and II* in the Roll Series), in which Edmund of Lancaster is said to have commanded the army which destroyed Llewelyn. No other chronicler mentions him, and I strongly suspect that *Edmundus frater regis* should be read *frater eius*, i. e. Roger de Mortimer's brother Edmund.

From Stephen's *Literature of the Kymry* (edit. D. S. Evans, 1876) I extract some of the striking and pathetic lines of the ballads of contemporary bards. Llygad Gwr wrote an ode about 1273 in honour of Llewelyn when he was at the height of his power after the civil war, when Edward was crusading, and much march land and even English soil was overrun by the Welsh :—

' About Tyganwy he has extended his dominions. . . .
He is a brave prince whose territories extend to the Teify. . . .
The shields of his men were stained with red in actions brave
From Pulford to the furthest bounds of Kidwelly. . . .
The lion of Gwynedd and its extensive white territories,
The governor of the men of Powys and the South,
Who has a general assembly of his armed troops at Chester,
Who ravages Lloegria (England) to amass spoils.
In battle his success is certain,
In killing, burning, and overthrowing castles.
In Rhos and Penvro and in contests with the French
His impetuosity uniformly prevails ' (p. 346).

The following, on Llewelyn's death, is from the bard Gruffudd ap Yr Ynad Coch :—

' Woe, ye tents of Cadwaladr, that the obstructor of the flood is pierced !
It is my lot to complain of Saxon treachery. . . .
A lord I have lost, well may I mourn,
A lord of a royal palace, slain by a human hand,
A lord righteous and truthful : listen to me.
I soar to complain. Oh that I should have cause !
A lord victorious until the eighteen were slain.
A lord who was gentle, whose possession is now the silent earth.
A lord who was like a lion, ruling the elements. . . .
Where shall we flee ? to whom complain
Since our dear Llewelyn's slain ? . . .
A head which, when severed, was not avenged by Kymry '
(pp. 370, 371).

We notice that here is no complaint of Welsh treachery, no accusation against the men of Builth, and thus our suspicions of Edmund de Mortimer are confirmed. 'The eighteen' may be either Llewelyn's corps-leaders, or perhaps eighteen attendants who accompanied him away from his main army. But beyond such facts of detail, we receive from these two extracts a picture of the lion of Gwynedd as the sole hope of Wales—the one hero who could unite the South and Powys and Snowdonia, whose loss was irreparable, and who, from the English point of view, was the aggressive neighbour and treaty-scorning prince, whose arms penetrated into England, and whose power had to be curtailed if the kingdom was to be at peace.

## II

### MADOC'S WAR

A CASE tried in the court of Grey's lordship of Ruthin sheds much light on the cause of the rising of 1294. The details are to be found in the *Ruthin Court-Rolls*, edited for the Cymmrodorion Society by Mr. E. A. Roberts, and also in an article written by him in *Y Cymmrodor*, vol. x. p. 182. I venture to give my explanation of the case, adding afterwards a transcript of the Latin.

Grey is lord of the barony, his superior officer is the constable, and William le Crother, as other evidence in the same roll shows, is a subordinate and presumably an Englishman. The business on hand is to make a return of names of available soldiers in view of a levy of Welsh for the expedition to Gascony; probably it is a preliminary inquiry, not an actual enlistment of men then and there. Under the constable's orders one Iorwerth ap Kenwric, on Whit-Sunday in 1294, calls upon Thomas ap Gilth Crist to give in his return of his men, but then, to show that he is only making the demand on compulsion, he proceeds of his evil will to curse the constable's beard and eke his head : 'Our constable will have to order me more than once before I will go to France.' Likewise he swears that before the middle of the month the said constable and all the other English will hear such rumours that they will not desire to come into Wales again. William reports the seditious language. Iorwerth is summoned to appear before the court of the barony on the next Thursday, but disobeys. On William's evidence he is condemned in his absence to a fine. In giving the Latin I have retained the abbreviated form of those words only of which the translation is doubtful, my interpretation of this strange and humorous passage being purely conjectural.

William le Crother gives evidence: Iorwerth interrogavit de Thom hom̄ suū redd suū (hominum suorum redditum suum), et dicit (William) quod per preceptum Conestabularii erat ista interrogatio facta, et tunc ipse (Iorwerth) ex male voluntate maledixit barbam Constabularii et postea caput si non preciperet (William or constable) iterum ire in Franciam, et iuravit quod ante mediam mensem Constabularius et ceteri Anglici habebunt rumores tales quod non desiderent amplius reintrare in Walliam.'

Here we have mutterings before the storm, threats of vengeance and revolt, which however would fall on deaf ears, for *rumores tales* were probably common. A difficulty is indeed caused by the date; this scene of cursing occurred at Whitsuntide, and Edward did not formally summon Welsh infantry till August 30. Yet Grey may have had a private warning to prepare his men, or at least to take some preliminary steps, weeks earlier.

We saw in the text that Grey raised 5,000 foot, some few loyalist Welsh perhaps included, as soon as ever the revolt was evident, and Edward marched by way of the Clwyd and Ruthin when he invaded Wales in person. The men of Ruthin did not all rise in revolt, though Madoc appeared in person to rally them. Next August, 1295, another court was held, but very few cases of rebellion were heard. One William ap Howel, who remained true to Grey and joined the king's army, accused a neighbour of breaking into his house in his absence 'in the time of Madoc ap Llewelyn'; and then in his turn he was accused of stealing a cow from a woman whose husband had joined Madoc, which crime the court held to be justifiable, and the cow was confiscated to Grey as lord of the barony. Another man was fined 6*d*. for cutting down a tree by Madoc's leave 'at the time when the said Madoc made himself lord.' Yet the rest of the work of the court was simply concerned with little everyday disputes, just as if there had been no war. Whatever revolt there was in Dyffryn Clwyd was not serious, and lasted but a short time. Justice seems to have been evenly administered in Grey's court. The following is a curious case of even-handed justice :—A jury of six English and six Welsh try one Henry de Riggebi whom Cadwgan accused of stealing his horse; they say that Henry took it without leave, but did not steal it; so he is fined, but Cadwgan is also fined for 'false clamour' (*Y Cymmrodor*, as above).

## III

### CASTLES IN WALES

In giving a brief note on this subject I would say that it is almost impertinent to praise Mr. G. T. Clark's splendid work, and merely remark that sometimes a date which I have gleaned from some roll corresponds with the date of construction which he fixed from the evidence of the style of a castle. As regards Harlech, however, the Edwardian additions are shown by the great expenditure of money to have been very considerable, practically equivalent to entire reconstruction.

First one notices the contrast between the Welsh and the Norman fortress. The Welsh chieftains must have learnt the art of building in stone from their invaders—not a very good policy, for the mountains were their best fortresses—but they built in lofty and inaccessible places in self-defence. The Normans built chiefly out in some plain to overawe a district. Tourists know well the sites of Harlech and Dolwyddelan, but out of their beat in a grand situation is Bere, which must have presented, when untouched by decay, the ideal picture of an eagle's nest dominating its valley. The group of three in South Wales, Dryslwyn, Dynevor, and Caercynan (locally called 'Castell Cennen,' but spelt as in the text by William Owen) must have been designed by one man, or by the members of one family.

The descendants of Rhys ap Tudor did not show much cousinly affection towards each other; they fought the Normans or each other, made alliance with the Normans or with the Princes of Gwynedd against each other, and ruined their cause by making impossible a spirit of unity. But at some time when the family was united, the three castles were planned. Dryslwyn and Dynevor look the one to the other at a distance of four miles, each on its steep hill over-hanging the Towy on the north bank. Caercynan signals across to both over an intervening range of heights, being five miles to the south-east of Dynevor. Dryslwyn is the lowest of the three, yet the original castle was protected on three sides by an almost precipitous ascent, and even on the fourth the ground was steep; after the English occupation a series of wards was added, each with its dry moat, extending down the fourth side. Dynevor keep now frowns grimly through trees, but then occupied an open plateau on top of a hill, precipitous towards the river, steep on the reverse side; the subsequent additions formed a long rectangle stretching over the plateau, then half of the castle was dismantled and a new curtain and a drum tower were built to make good the gap. In the case of Caercynan, at a distance no one can tell which is castle and which is rock. It stands on a limestone crag on a spur jutting out into a valley, and looks up and down, with a clear view of the sides of the ranges which form the valley, so that surprise would be impossible. It was designed purely for defence, as a last refuge if both Dryslwyn and Dynevor fell. Compact and small, it sat four-square amid the outcrop of rock, yet not occupying the whole of the top of the crag. English hands have added one circular tower at an angle, also an extra ward to cover the one gateway on the least impregnable side; on the far side is a sheer fall of some 300 feet.

On the other hand the chief Norman castles lie comparatively low. The great square keep of Chepstow, dating from the days of the early occupation by the Clares, seems to rise naturally out of the rock which is precipitous to the Wye, but the Bigod of our period, who also has the honour of having built the Tintern Abbey which all know so well in place of an earlier foundation, made great additions. He created a large ward along the slope from the keep down to the city moat, the main gateway with great towers in the Edwardian style being much below the old part. Two more small wards were added on the other side up the rock, and then the ridge was cut by a deep dry moat. Thus the whole castle is as it were a tongue in four sections, one side being the rock with its sheer fall into the river, the other separated from the town by a natural gully, the tip coming almost down to the level, and the root cut off from the rest of the ridge. Thus Chepstow seems to stand high by the accident of the ground, but was far from being a mere work of defence. Even the Clares' keep dominated the river: the finished castle of Bigod commanded town and country.

Abergavenny castle is, as regards situation, the typical fortress of a marcher lord. Placed on a gently rising piece of ground, it was so erected as to look down the Usk southwards and up the Usk westwards, whilst it faced, at some considerable distance, the mouths of three valleys running from the north and east; in fact the castle is the centre of a low basin into which the routes of that part of Monmouthshire all converge. We can picture the fierce lords of Braose ready at their centre to meet the wild rushes of the men of Gwent along one or another valley. But while the situation is charming, the ruins of the castle are poor and spoilt to form a pleasure garden, good for the citizen of modern Abergavenny but disappointing to an historian. Still one can make out the site of a keep, completely separated from the rest of the castle by a moat; then in Edwardian times another ward was built to cover the gap between the keep and the old ward.

Kidwelly castle lies on the bank of a little tidal river, and dominates a plain between the mountains and the sea. This bank is not lofty, but is tolerably steep. The old square keep was planted almost on the edge. Llewelyn is said to have destroyed it, but such ' destruction ' means nothing more than a partial dismantling and burning of the woodwork of the interior. The elder Patrick de Chaworth, towards the end of the reign of Henry III, reconstructed it on a new plan. Taking the partially wrecked keep as his starting-point, he erected an outer wall to form a large arc to another point up the river, the steep bank thus forming the chord; the towers in this wall form semicircles outwards, and are open inwards. Then an inner ward was built on the same chord as its base, so that the archers could dominate the outer wall if the enemy should carry it. Later a very beautiful chapel was added, built on the river bank at right angles to the wall of the chord. Compact and workmanlike, beautiful in colour and in design, the new castle was too strong to be captured, especially as the walls of the town formed a third and outer ring. From it Pain de Chaworth, the younger Patrick, and the Earls of Lancaster, one of whom was guardian to the latter's heiress and another married her, dominated the surrounding march and levied Welsh friendlies to join the armies of England.

Caerphilly castle reminds one in some degree of the Coliseum, grim, gigantic, ugly in its ruins, displeasing in colour, yet a monument of engineering genius. Undoubtedly begun by Gilbert of Gloucester while Henry III was yet king, designed on one plan by one master mind, it must have taken years to complete. Much of the work is said to be of the fourteenth century, when the Despenser had the same ambition to be an overpowering ruler which the Clare showed in the thirteenth. Ostensibly Caerphilly, like Abergavenny, on a low spit of ground (which the architect converted into an island) dominated an open plain into which valleys converged from every quarter, and thus overawed the inland parts of Glamorgan, which the Clares had never conquered so completely as the flat piece of coast-land. Yet one is tempted to think of the ambitious Gilbert giving orders to his architect to devise an enormous and impregnable stronghold with an unexpressed idea at the back of his mind that he wanted to have the means of defying his king.

Llandovery castle is of the small and compact kind. Whatever the Cliffords may have built there in past days, the castle of John Giffard, when he occupied the upper part of the Vale of Towy by right of conquest and by right of his wife's inheritance from the Cliffords, was quite new. A mere mound is crowned by an oval work, round towers and a curtain.

The royal castle at Builth was also absolutely new, for Llewelyn clearly destroyed here the old Mortimer castle. Not a stone is now standing. One would think that one was visiting some circular ancient British entrenchment. The top of the grassy mound shows where stood the central round keep of which our documents speak; a circular moat gives the site of the curtain and six towers of the middle ward; a circular outer moat indicates the advanced ward where two towers, doubtless like, but smaller than, those of Chepstow, guarded the main gateway. It must have been a perfect specimen of a concentric castle, exactly occupying its mound, having no weak side, small enough to be defended by a reasonable garrison of sixty or seventy men. Kidwelly pleases one's sense of proportion in the same way, but, as was seen above, is not perfectly concentric. Caerphilly is a square within a square, with an enormous additional outwork. The word 'concentric' only expresses the general idea of a fortress within a fortress, or of one ward commanding another ward, it being immaterial whether these are round, or oval, or rectangular with round towers at the angles, or even exterior to each other in a figure-of-eight shape. But Builth is truly concentric. I have sketched this group of castles partly because of the variations of the Edwardian type, partly because the old Norman work of pre-Edwardian days was enlarged and added to by those very barons of the Edwardian epoch whose doings are the subject of this book.

## IV

### CAVALRY AT FALKIRK

Too late to make full use of the details for insertion in the text of this book, I was led to consult a document (*Harleian MSS.* No. 6589) which is distinctly serviceable. It is a copy, dated 1606, of a 'rolle brought from Paris in 1576.' Internal evidence strongly suggests that the details are correct, for the bannerets are found brigaded in the same 'battles' with just those earls with whom we expect to find them, e. g. Tateshale with Lincoln, Percy with Surrey, and the king's bannerets are the same as those whose horses were valued by the two inventories. The roll gives us the names of 110 earls, barons, bannerets, and of these it has forty-eight in common with the inventories; there remain sixty-two banners under which the unpaid cavalry was ranged. The forty-eight in question are known to give 684 lances of all ranks, an average of fourteen lances to each banner. But on various grounds I should put the average of an unpaid retinue a trifle higher; Huntercumbe[1] is known to have had from sixteen to thirty lances year after year in these campaigns in Scotland, as the banneret sometimes of the Earl of Surrey, sometimes of the Bishop of Durham; John de Segrave contracted with the Earl of Norfolk[2] to maintain five knights and fifteen troopers as his banneret; and we remember that Valence and the Berkeleys had fifty lances under three banners. Allowing eighteen on an average to each of the sixty-two banners we obtain a total of 1,116 lances, and adding the 1,312 paid horse we have a grand total of 2,428; but I would repeat that we cannot be at all sure that every man was up in time to charge at Falkirk; some must have been on the lines of communication, and in the inventories mounted officers of foot are clearly included. It is a curious coincidence that careful investigation leads one to conclude that Froissart was right in fixing 2,400 as the total of the heavy cavalry who followed Edward III to France and fought at Crecy[3]. I would add that our new evidence divides the horse at Falkirk into four brigades, though Hemingburgh assigns only three. I have met the same discrepancy elsewhere, and suggest that a slight confusion easily arises if the king took a fourth or reserve brigade out of his own central body. The first included Lincoln, Hereford, and Norfolk, as Hemingburgh says; the second was led by the bishop; in the third the king had the two young Lancasters, John of Brittany, John of Bar, Guy of Warwick, the Gascons, Despenser, Clifford; the fourth was under Surrey, and with him were Gloucester, Arundel, Oxford, and Valence.

---

[1] *Rot. Parl.* vol. i. p. 194.     [2] Dugdale, under 'Norfolk.'
[3] General Wrottesley, *Crecy and Calais*; I have made a calculation in *Eng. Hist. Review*, Nov. 1899, p. 767.

# I. ROYAL FAMILY AND CONNEXION
## WITH BARONAGE

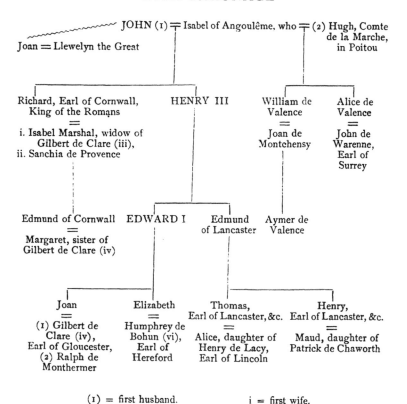

JOHN (1) = Isabel of Angoulême, who = (2) Hugh, Comte de la Marche, in Poitou

Joan = Llewelyn the Great

Richard, Earl of Cornwall,
King of the Romans
=
i. Isabel Marshal, widow of
Gilbert de Clare (iii),
ii. Sanchia de Provence

HENRY III

William de
Valence
=
Joan de
Montchensy

Alice de
Valence
=
John de
Warenne,
Earl of
Surrey

Edmund of Cornwall
=
Margaret, sister of
Gilbert de Clare (iv)

EDWARD I

Edmund
of Lancaster

Aymer de
Valence

Joan
=
(1) Gilbert de
Clare (iv),
Earl of Gloucester,
(2) Ralph de
Monthermer

Elizabeth
=
Humphrey de
Bohun (vi),
Earl of
Hereford

Thomas,
Earl of Lancaster, &c.
=
Alice, daughter of
Henry de Lacy,
Earl of Lincoln

Henry,
Earl of Lancaster, &c.
=
Maud, daughter of
Patrick de Chaworth

(1) = first husband.          i = first wife.

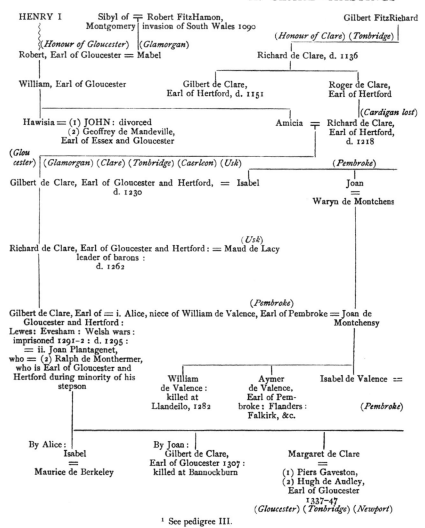

HENRY I    Sibyl of ⊤ Robert FitzHamon,                    Gilbert FitzRichard
           Montgomery │ invasion of South Wales 1090
                                                    (*Honour of Clare*) (*Tonbridge*) │
   *(Honour of Gloucester)* (*Glamorgan*)
Robert, Earl of Gloucester = Mabel              Richard de Clare, d. 1136

William, Earl of Gloucester        Gilbert de Clare,              Roger de Clare,
                                   Earl of Hertford, d. 1151       Earl of Hertford

                                                                    │(*Cardigan lost*)
  Hawisia = (1) JOHN: divorced              Amicia = Richard de Clare,
           (2) Geoffrey de Mandeville,               Earl of Hertford,
           Earl of Essex and Gloucester              d. 1218
*(Glou*
*cester)* │ (*Glamorgan*) (*Clare*) (*Tonbridge*) (*Caerleon*) (*Usk*)        (*Pembroke*)

Gilbert de Clare, Earl of Gloucester and Hertford, = Isabel          Joan
                d. 1230                                              =
                                                            Waryn de Montchens

                                        (*Usk*)
Richard de Clare, Earl of Gloucester and Hertford: = Maud de Lacy
             leader of barons:
                 d. 1262

                                        (*Pembroke*)
Gilbert de Clare, Earl of = i. Alice, niece of William de Valence, Earl of Pembroke = Joan de
  Gloucester and Hertford:                                              Montchensy
Lewes: Evesham: Welsh wars:
imprisoned 1291-2: d. 1295:
 = ii. Joan Plantagenet,
who = (2) Ralph de Monthermer,
who is Earl of Gloucester and      William         Aymer          Isabel de Valence ==
Hertford during minority of his    de Valence:     de Valence,
       stepson                     killed at       Earl of Pem-
                                   Llandeilo, 1282  broke: Flanders:   (*Pembroke*)
                                                    Falkirk, &c.

  By Alice: │              By Joan: │
        Isabel           Gilbert de Clare,        Margaret de Clare
          =              Earl of Gloucester 1307:        =
  Maurice de Berkeley    killed at Bannockburn    (1) Piers Gaveston,
                                                  (2) Hugh de Audley,
                                                      Earl of Gloucester
                                                          1337-47
                                              (*Gloucester*) (*Tonbridge*) (*Newport*)

                    ¹ See pedigree III.

MORRIS

# —VALENCE—BIGOD

de Clare, summoned into South Wales by Henry I on the dispossession of
Arnulf of Montgomery

(*Cardigan*) (*Pembroke*)

(*Usk*) (*Pembroke*) (*Cilgeran*) (*Netherwent: Honour of Strigul or Chepstow*)
Gilbert de Clare, Earl of Pembroke; heir to his uncle Walter, who founded Tintern Abbey

Richard de Clare, Earl of Pembroke, 'Strongbow,' d. 1176,
invasion of Ireland

Isabel de Clare = William the Marshal, Earl of Pembroke: d. 1219: five sons in turn
held earldom and office of marshal: the last, Anselm, died in 1245.

(*Cilgeran*)

Eva
=
William de Braose
(*Overwent*)

(*Netherwent: Strigul*)

Maud, = Hugh le Bigod, Earl of Norfolk
eldest
daughter

Eva de Braose
=
William de Cantilupe

Roger le Bigod,
Earl of Norfolk 1225,
Marshal *jure matris* 1246

Hugh le Bigod

Eva de Cantilupe
=
Henry de Hastings, d. 1268

Roger le Bigod, Earl of Norfolk
and Marshal: Welsh wars:
defied king in 1297: Falkirk:
dispossessed in 1302: d. 1306
(*Netherwent: Strigul*)

John de Hastings[1],
ward of William de Valence:
Welsh war 1294
(*Cilgeran*) (*Overwent: Abergavenny*)

Ada de Hastings = Rhys ap Maredudd,
rising of 1287

Elizabeth de Clare[2]
=
(1) John de Burgh,
(2) Theobald de Verdun
(*Clare*) (*Usk*)

Eleanor de Clare = Hugh le Despenser, exec. 1326
(*Glamorgan*)

Hugh le Despenser:
ranked as Earl (of Gloucester)
and received earl's pay at Crecy and Calais

[2] See pedigree VII.

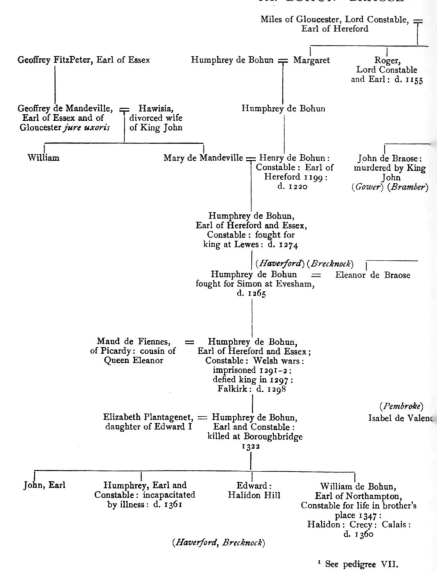

Miles of Gloucester, Lord Constable, = Earl of Hereford

Geoffrey FitzPeter, Earl of Essex

Humphrey de Bohun = Margaret

Roger,
Lord Constable
and Earl: d. 1155

Geoffrey de Mandeville, = Hawisia,
Earl of Essex and of    divorced wife
Gloucester *jure uxoris*    of King John

Humphrey de Bohun

William

Mary de Mandeville = Henry de Bohun:
Constable: Earl of
Hereford 1199:
d. 1220

John de Braose:
murdered by King
John
(*Gower*) (*Bramber*)

Humphrey de Bohun,
Earl of Hereford and Essex,
Constable: fought for
king at Lewes: d. 1274

(*Haverford*) (*Brecknock*)
Humphrey de Bohun    =    Eleanor de Braose
fought for Simon at Evesham,
d. 1265

Maud de Fiennes,    =    Humphrey de Bohun,
of Picardy: cousin of    Earl of Hereford and Essex;
Queen Eleanor    Constable: Welsh wars:
imprisoned 1291–2:
defied king in 1297:
Falkirk: d. 1298

(*Pembroke*)
Isabel de Valenc

Elizabeth Plantagenet, = Humphrey de Bohun,
daughter of Edward I    Earl and Constable:
killed at Boroughbridge
1322

John, Earl

Humphrey, Earl and
Constable: incapacitated
by illness: d. 1361

Edward:
Halidon Hill

William de Bohun,
Earl of Northampton,
Constable for life in brother's
place 1347:
Halidon: Crecy: Calais:
d. 1360

(*Haverford, Brecknock*)

[1] See pedigree VII.

MORRIS

# HASTINGS—MORTIMER

Mabel, daughter of Bernard de Neufmarché

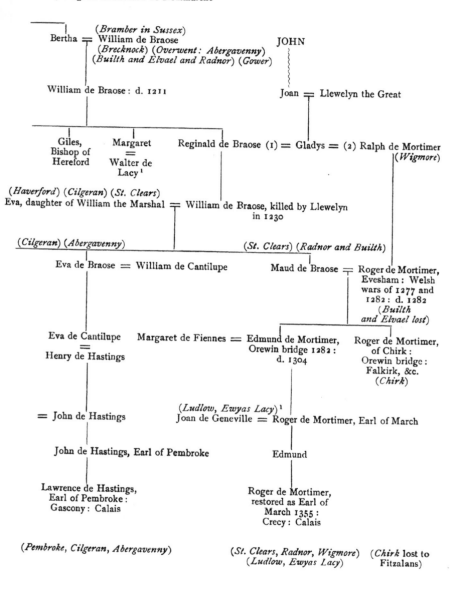

Bertha = *(Bramber in Sussex)*
William de Braose
*(Brecknock) (Overwent: Abergavenny)*
*(Builth and Elvael and Radnor) (Gower)*

JOHN

William de Braose: d. 1211

Joan = Llewelyn the Great

Giles, Bishop of Hereford

Margaret = Walter de Lacy [1]

Reginald de Braose (1) = Gladys = (2) Ralph de Mortimer
*(Wigmore)*

*(Haverford) (Cilgeran) (St. Clears)*
Eva, daughter of William the Marshal = William de Braose, killed by Llewelyn in 1230

*(Cilgeran) (Abergavenny)*
Eva de Braose = William de Cantilupe

*(St. Clears) (Radnor and Builth)*
Maud de Braose = Roger de Mortimer,
Evesham : Welsh wars of 1277 and 1282 : d. 1282
*(Builth and Elvael lost)*

Eva de Cantilupe = Henry de Hastings

Margaret de Fiennes = Edmund de Mortimer, Orewin bridge 1282 : d. 1304

Roger de Mortimer, of Chirk : Orewin bridge : Falkirk, &c. *(Chirk)*

= John de Hastings

*(Ludlow, Ewyas Lacy)* [1]
Joan de Geneville = Roger de Mortimer, Earl of March

John de Hastings, Earl of Pembroke

Edmund

Lawrence de Hastings, Earl of Pembroke : Gascony : Calais

Roger de Mortimer, restored as Earl of March 1355 : Crecy : Calais

*(Pembroke, Cilgeran, Abergavenny)*

*(St. Clears, Radnor, Wigmore)*
*(Ludlow, Ewyas Lacy)*

*(Chirk* lost to Fitzalans)

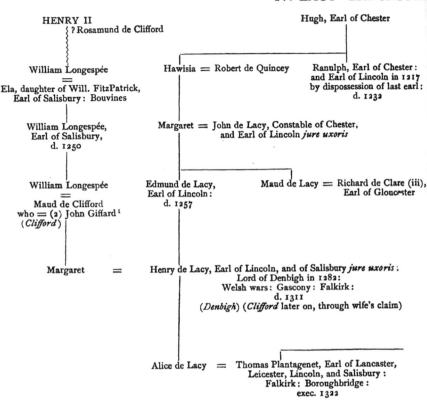

HENRY II
{ ? Rosamund de Clifford

Hugh, Earl of Chester

William Longespée
=
Ela, daughter of Will. FitzPatrick,
Earl of Salisbury : Bouvines

Hawisia = Robert de Quincey

Ranulph, Earl of Chester :
and Earl of Lincoln in 1217
by dispossession of last earl :
d. 1232

William Longespée,
Earl of Salisbury,
d. 1250

Margaret = John de Lacy, Constable of Chester,
and Earl of Lincoln *jure uxoris*

William Longespée
=
Maud de Clifford
who = (2) John Giffard [1]
(*Clifford*)

Edmund de Lacy,
Earl of Lincoln :
d. 1257

Maud de Lacy = Richard de Clare (iii),
Earl of Gloucester

Margaret      =

Henry de Lacy, Earl of Lincoln, and of Salisbury *jure uxoris* :
Lord of Denbigh in 1282 :
Welsh wars : Gascony : Falkirk :
d. 1311
(*Denbigh*) (*Clifford* later on, through wife's claim)

Alice de Lacy   =   Thomas Plantagenet, Earl of Lancaster,
Leicester, Lincoln, and Salisbury :
Falkirk : Boroughbridge :
exec. 1322

[1] See pedigree VI.

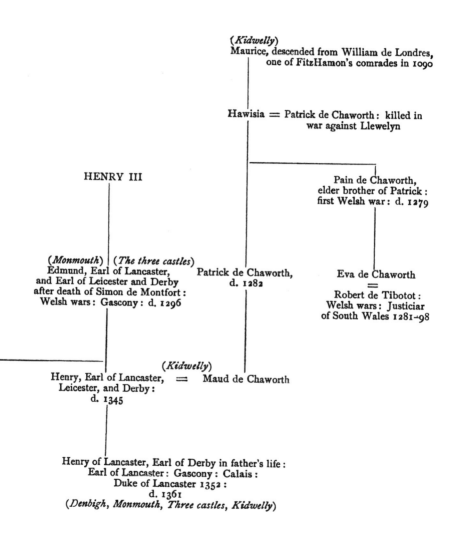

(*Kidwelly*)
Maurice, descended from William de Londres,
one of FitzHamon's comrades in 1090

Hawisia = Patrick de Chaworth: killed in
war against Llewelyn

HENRY III

Pain de Chaworth,
elder brother of Patrick:
first Welsh war: d. 1279

(*Monmouth*) | (*The three castles*)
Edmund, Earl of Lancaster,
and Earl of Leicester and Derby
after death of Simon de Montfort:
Welsh wars: Gascony: d. 1296

Patrick de Chaworth,
d. 1282

Eva de Chaworth
=
Robert de Tibotot:
Welsh wars: Justiciar
of South Wales 1281–98

(*Kidwelly*)
Henry, Earl of Lancaster, = Maud de Chaworth
Leicester, and Derby:
d. 1345

Henry of Lancaster, Earl of Derby in father's life:
Earl of Lancaster: Gascony: Calais:
Duke of Lancaster 1352:
d. 1361
(*Denbigh, Monmouth, Three castles, Kidwelly*)

# V. FITZALAN—WARENNE

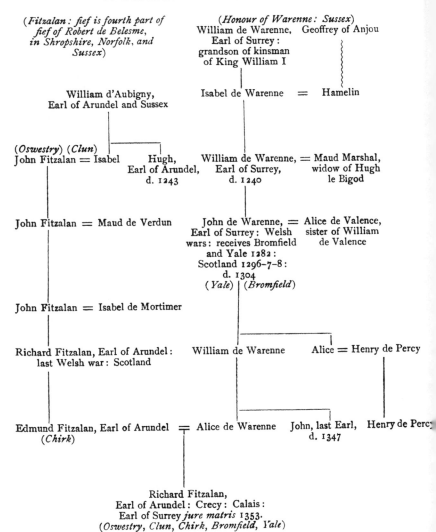

*(Fitzalan: fief is fourth part of fief of Robert de Belesme, in Shropshire, Norfolk, and Sussex)*

*(Honour of Warenne: Sussex)*
William de Warenne, Earl of Surrey: grandson of kinsman of King William I

Geoffrey of Anjou

William d'Aubigny, Earl of Arundel and Sussex

Isabel de Warenne  =  Hamelin

*(Oswestry) (Clun)*
John Fitzalan = Isabel

Hugh, Earl of Arundel, d. 1243

William de Warenne, = Maud Marshal, Earl of Surrey, widow of Hugh d. 1240 le Bigod

John Fitzalan = Maud de Verdun

John de Warenne, = Alice de Valence, Earl of Surrey: Welsh sister of William wars: receives Bromfield de Valence and Yale 1282: Scotland 1296–7–8: d. 1304
*(Yale) (Bromfield)*

John Fitzalan = Isabel de Mortimer

Richard Fitzalan, Earl of Arundel: last Welsh war: Scotland

William de Warenne

Alice = Henry de Percy

Edmund Fitzalan, Earl of Arundel = Alice de Warenne
*(Chirk)*

John, last Earl, d. 1347

Henry de Percy

Richard Fitzalan, Earl of Arundel: Crecy: Calais: Earl of Surrey *jure matris* 1353.
*(Oswestry, Clun, Chirk, Bromfield, Yale)*

# VI. BRAOSE—CLIFFORD

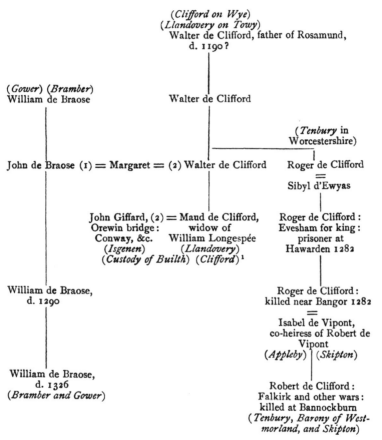

(*Clifford on Wye*)
(*Llandovery on Towy*)
Walter de Clifford, father of Rosamund,
d. 1190?

Walter de Clifford

(*Gower*) (*Bramber*)
William de Braose

(*Tenbury* in
Worcestershire)

John de Braose (1) = Margaret = (2) Walter de Clifford     Roger de Clifford
=
Sibyl d'Ewyas

John Giffard, (2) = Maud de Clifford,          Roger de Clifford :
Orewin bridge :     widow of                   Evesham for king :
Conway, &c.     William Longespée              prisoner at
(*Isgenen*)     (*Llandovery*)                 Hawarden 1282
(*Custody of Builth*) (*Clifford*)[1]

William de Braose,                             Roger de Clifford :
d. 1290                                        killed near Bangor 1282
=
Isabel de Vipont,
co-heiress of Robert de
Vipont
(*Appleby*) (*Skipton*)

William de Braose,                             Robert de Clifford :
d. 1326                                        Falkirk and other wars :
(*Bramber and Gower*)                          killed at Bannockburn
                                               (*Tenbury, Barony of West-
                                               morland, and Skipton*)

[1] But Clifford Castle reverts to Earl of Lincoln as heir to Maud de Clifford by
her first husband.

# VII. GENEVILLE—LACY—VERDUN

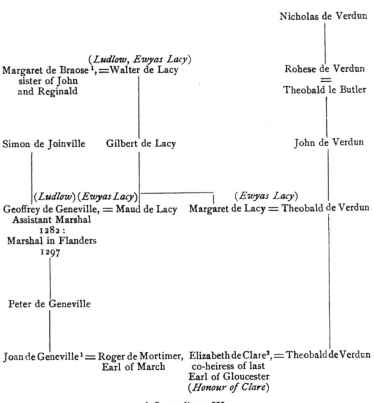

Nicholas de Verdun

(*Ludlow, Ewyas Lacy*)
Margaret de Braose [1], = Walter de Lacy
  sister of John
  and Reginald

Rohese de Verdun
=
Theobald le Butler

Simon de Joinville    Gilbert de Lacy

John de Verdun

(*Ludlow*) (*Ewyas Lacy*)
Geoffrey de Geneville, = Maud de Lacy  Margaret de Lacy = Theobald de Verdun
  Assistant Marshal                      (*Ewyas Lacy*)
      1282 :
  Marshal in Flanders
      1297

Peter de Geneville

Joan de Geneville [1] = Roger de Mortimer,  Elizabeth de Clare [2], = Theobald de Verdun
           Earl of March      co-heiress of last
                            Earl of Gloucester
                          (*Honour of Clare*)

[1] See pedigree III.
[2] See pedigree II.

# INDEX